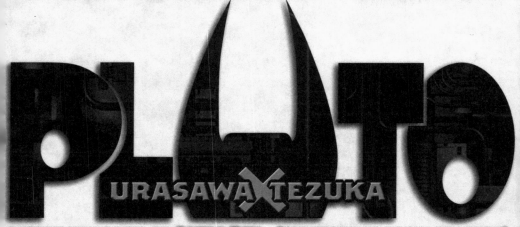

PLUTO

URASAWA X TEZUKA

**A NEW VISION BASED ON ASTRO BOY – 'THE GREATEST ROBOT ON EARTH'
BY NAOKI URASAWA AND OSAMU TEZUKA**

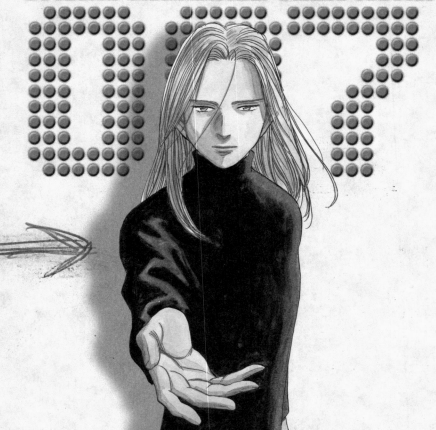

**CO-AUTHORED WITH TAKASHI NAGASAKI
SUPERVISED BY MACOTO TEZKA
WITH THE COOPERATION OF TEZUKA PRODUCTIONS**

Act 48 SIX BILLION PERSONALITIES

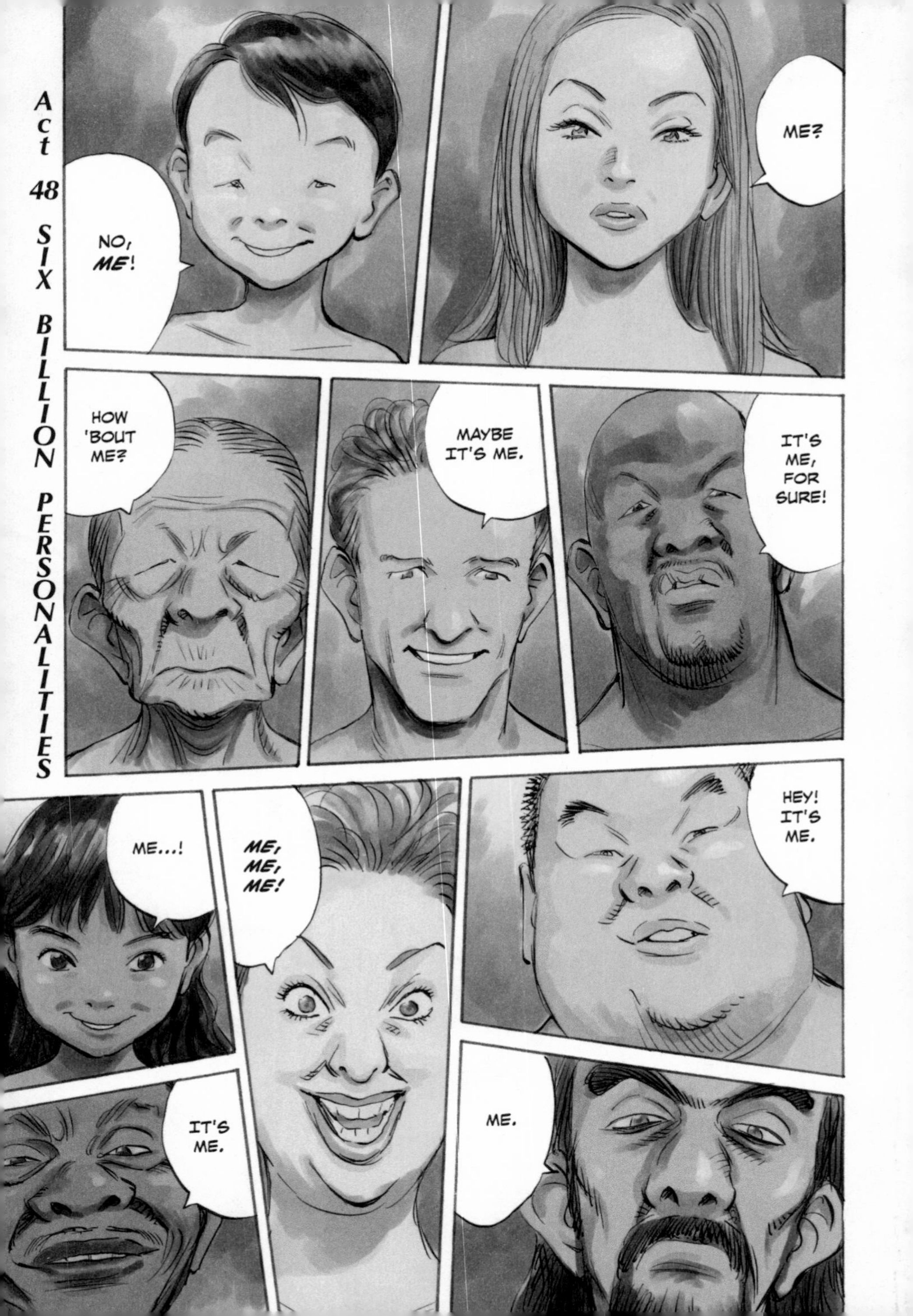
ME?
NO, ME!
IT'S ME, FOR SURE!
MAYBE IT'S ME.
HOW 'BOUT ME?
HEY! IT'S ME.
ME.
ME, ME, ME!
ME...!
IT'S ME.

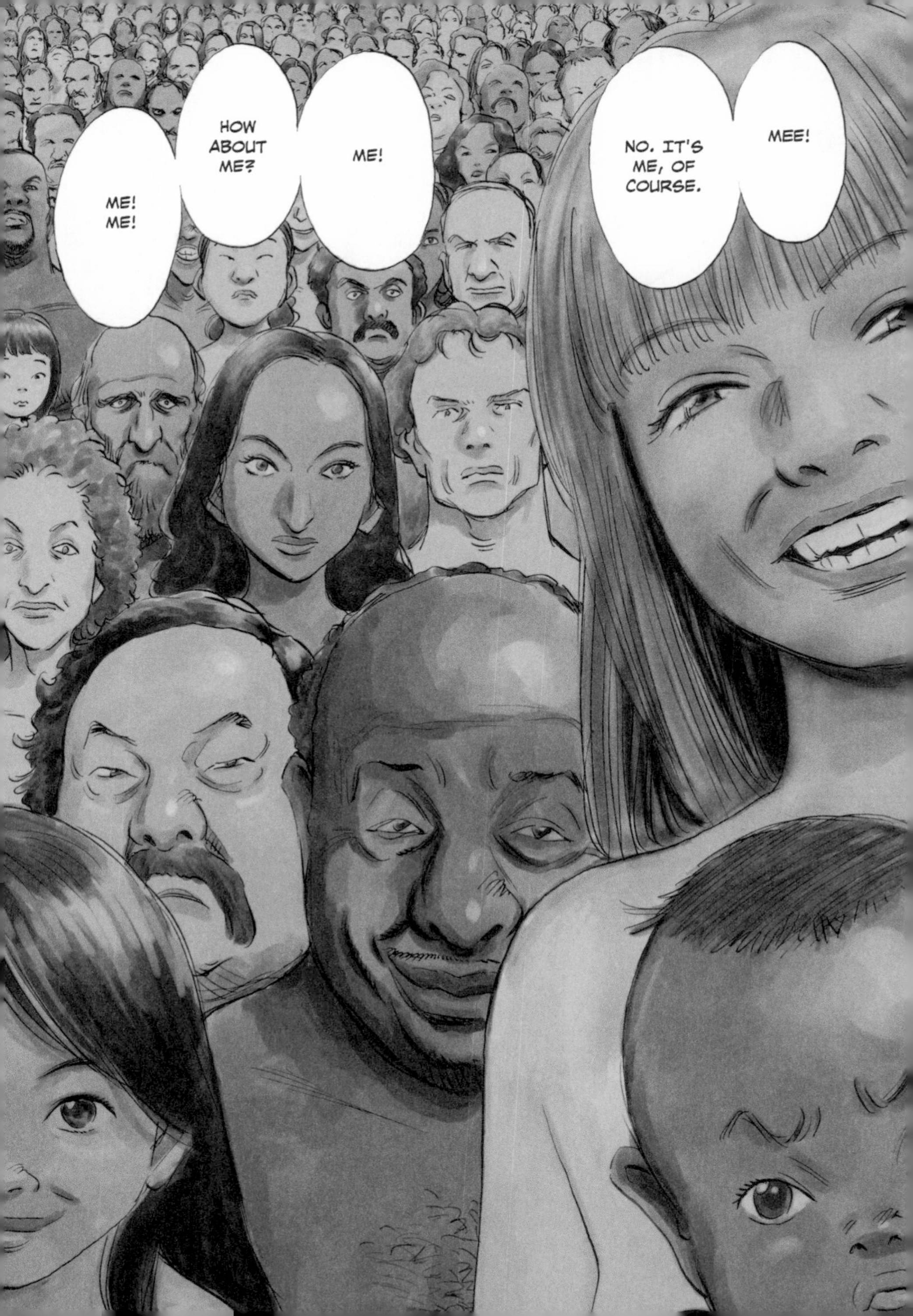
MEE!
NO. IT'S ME, OF COURSE.
ME!
HOW ABOUT ME?
ME! ME!

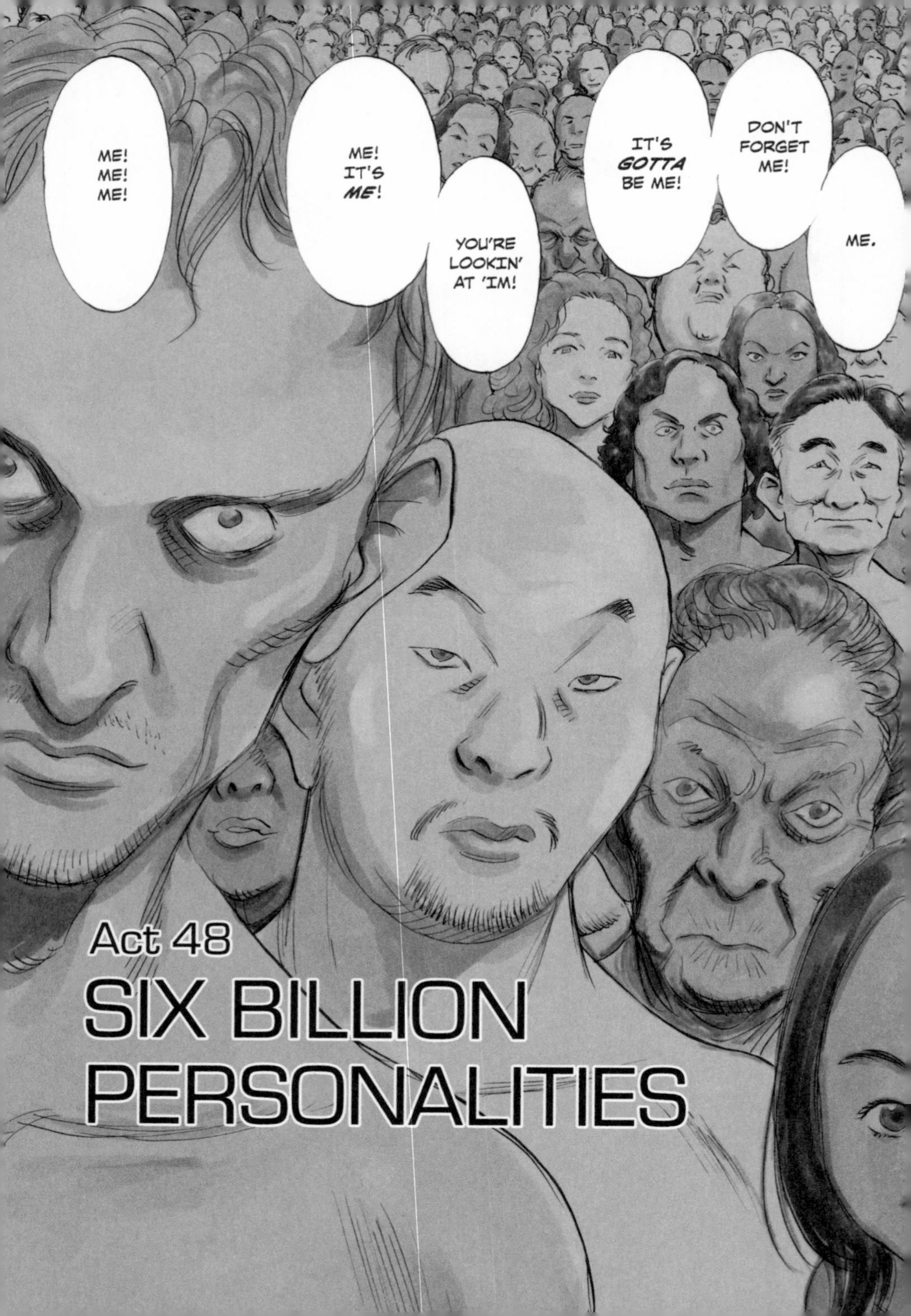
ME.
DON'T FORGET ME!
IT'S *GOTTA* BE ME!
YOU'RE LOOKIN' AT 'IM!
ME! IT'S *ME*!
ME! ME! ME!

Act 48

SIX BILLION PERSONALITIES

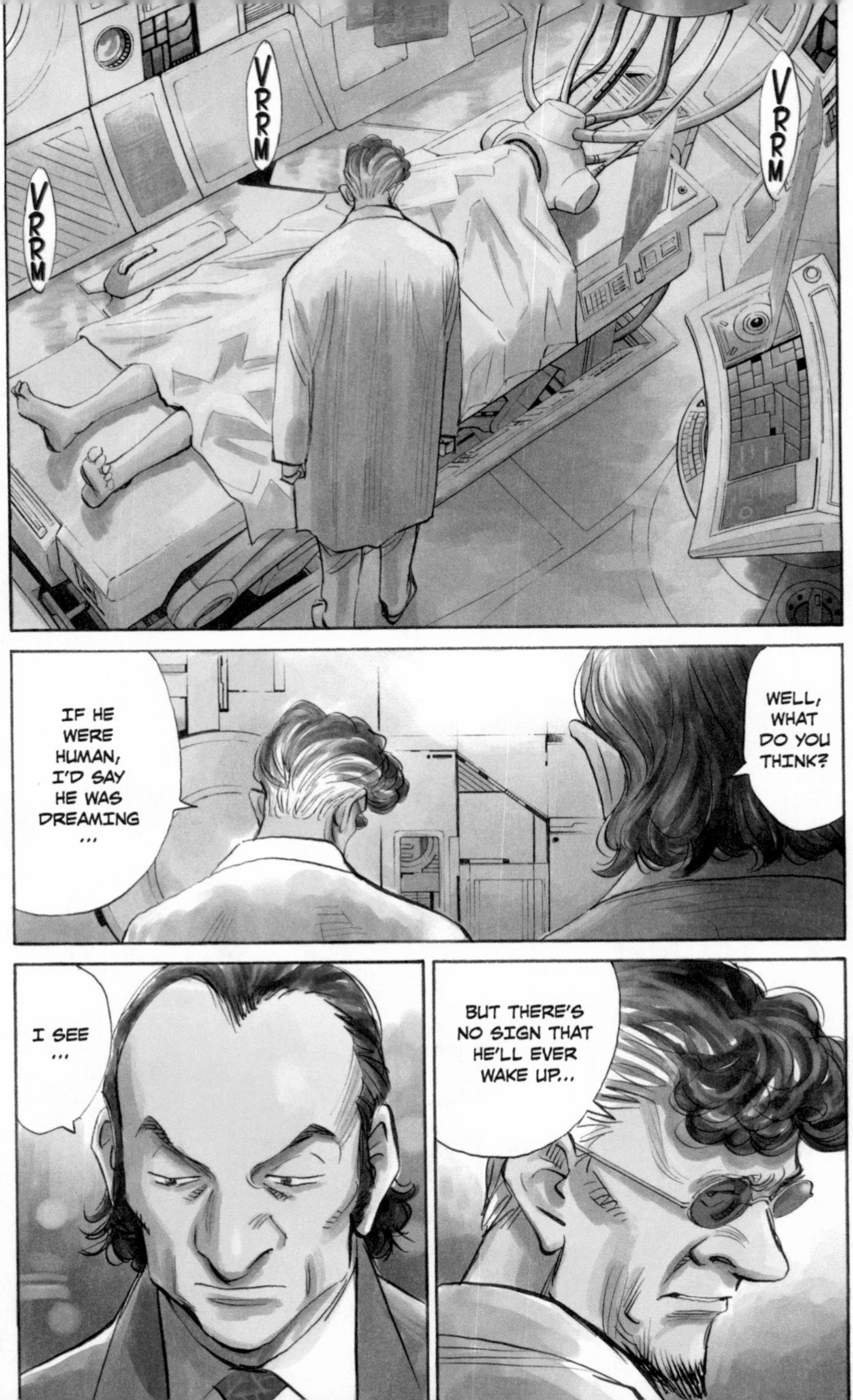
VRRM
VRRM
VRRM
WELL, WHAT DO YOU THINK?
IF HE WERE HUMAN, I'D SAY HE WAS DREAMING...
BUT THERE'S NO SIGN THAT HE'LL EVER WAKE UP...
I SEE...

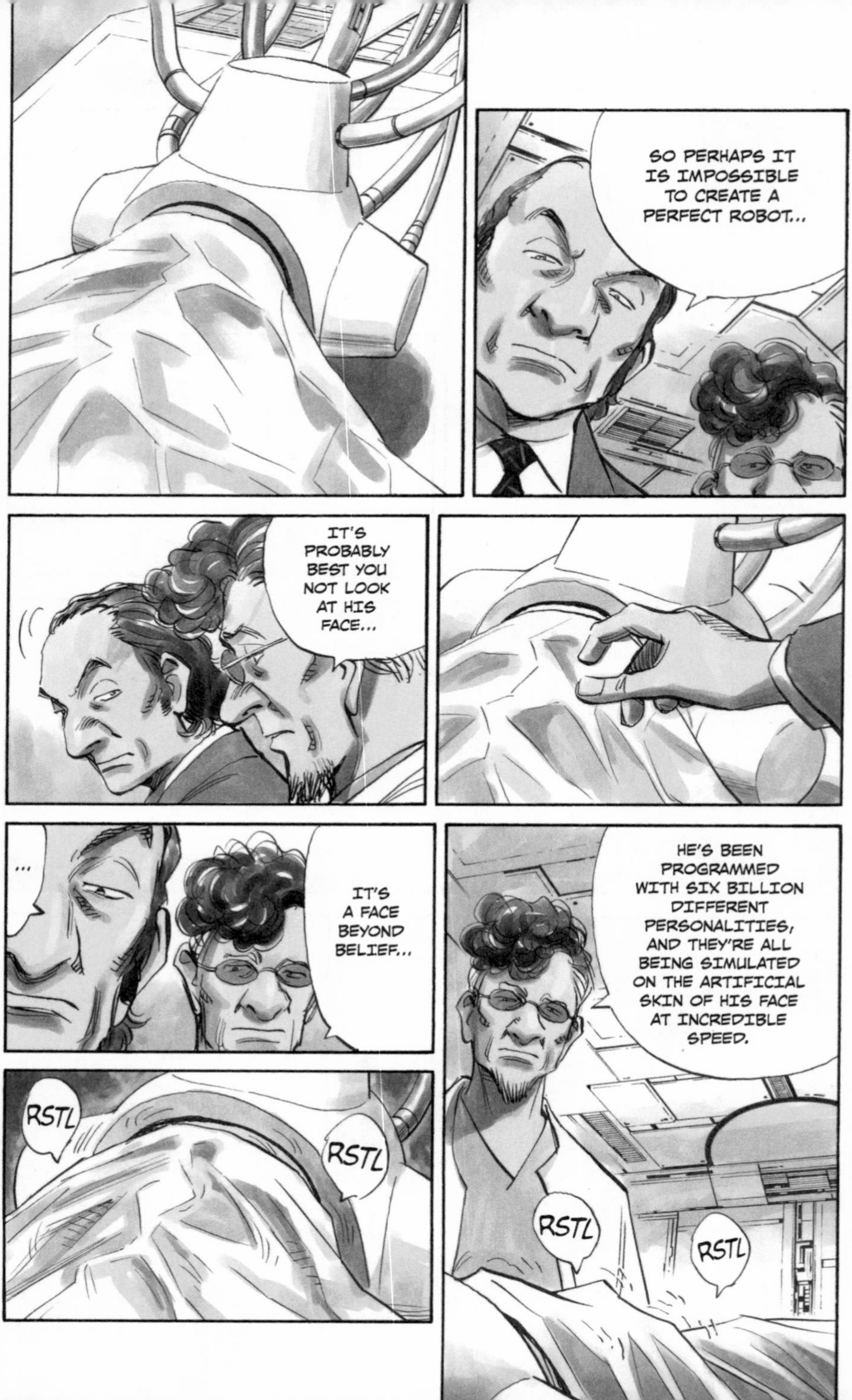
SO PERHAPS IT IS IMPOSSIBLE TO CREATE A PERFECT ROBOT...
IT'S PROBABLY BEST YOU NOT LOOK AT HIS FACE...
HE'S BEEN PROGRAMMED WITH SIX BILLION DIFFERENT PERSONALITIES, AND THEY'RE ALL BEING SIMULATED ON THE ARTIFICIAL SKIN OF HIS FACE AT INCREDIBLE SPEED.
RSTL
RSTL
IT'S A FACE BEYOND BELIEF...
...
RSTL
RSTL

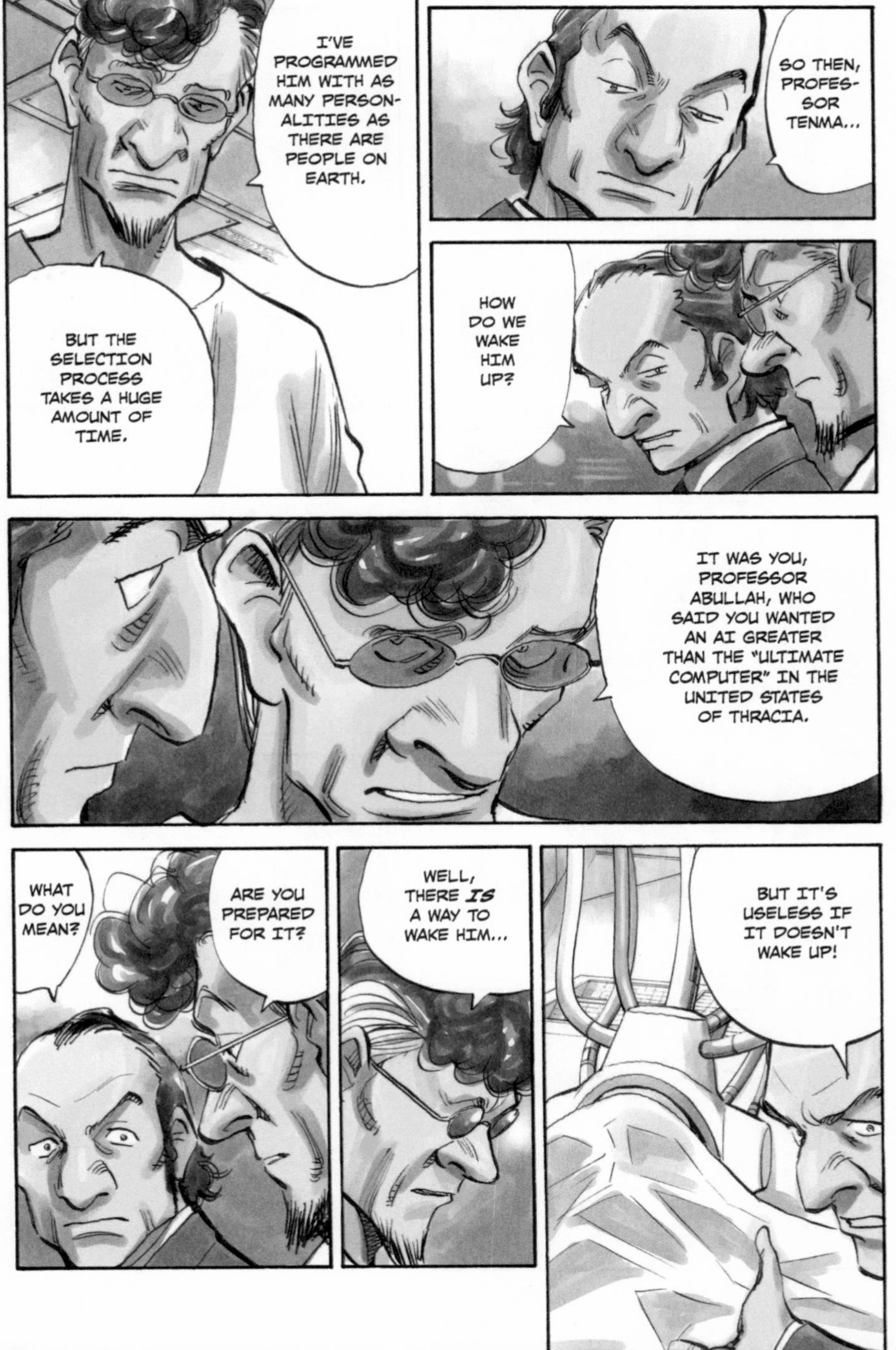
SO THEN, PROFESSOR TENMA...
HOW DO WE WAKE HIM UP?
I'VE PROGRAMMED HIM WITH AS MANY PERSONALITIES AS THERE ARE PEOPLE ON EARTH.
BUT THE SELECTION PROCESS TAKES A HUGE AMOUNT OF TIME.
IT WAS YOU, PROFESSOR ABULLAH, WHO SAID YOU WANTED AN AI GREATER THAN THE "ULTIMATE COMPUTER" IN THE UNITED STATES OF THRACIA.
BUT IT'S USELESS IF IT DOESN'T WAKE UP!
WELL, THERE *IS* A WAY TO WAKE HIM...
ARE YOU PREPARED FOR IT?
WHAT DO YOU MEAN?

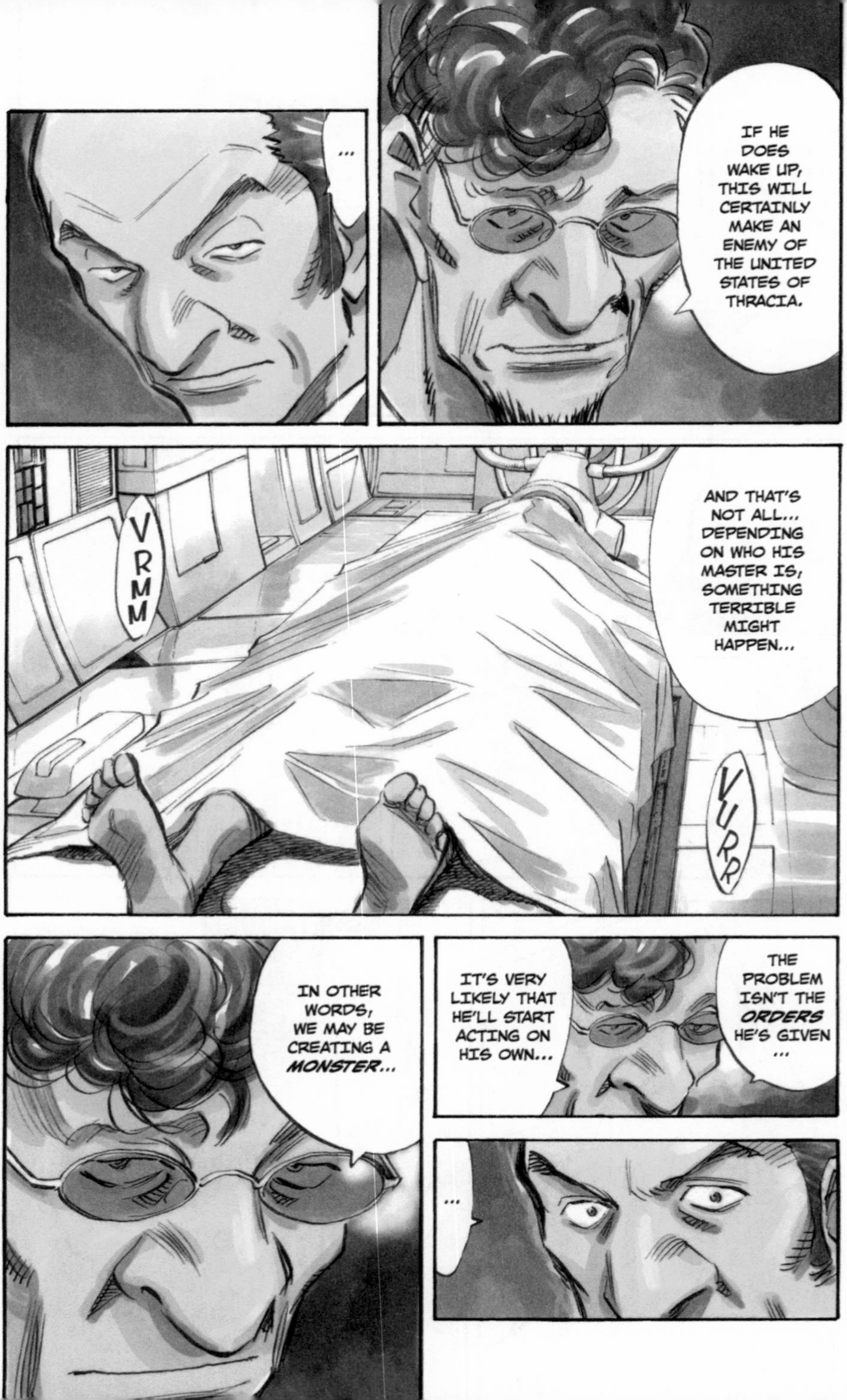
IF HE DOES WAKE UP, THIS WILL CERTAINLY MAKE AN ENEMY OF THE UNITED STATES OF THRACIA.
...
AND THAT'S NOT ALL... DEPENDING ON WHO HIS MASTER IS, SOMETHING TERRIBLE MIGHT HAPPEN...
VRMM
VURR
THE PROBLEM ISN'T THE *ORDERS* HE'S GIVEN ...
IT'S VERY LIKELY THAT HE'LL START ACTING ON HIS OWN...
...
IN OTHER WORDS, WE MAY BE CREATING A *MONSTER*...

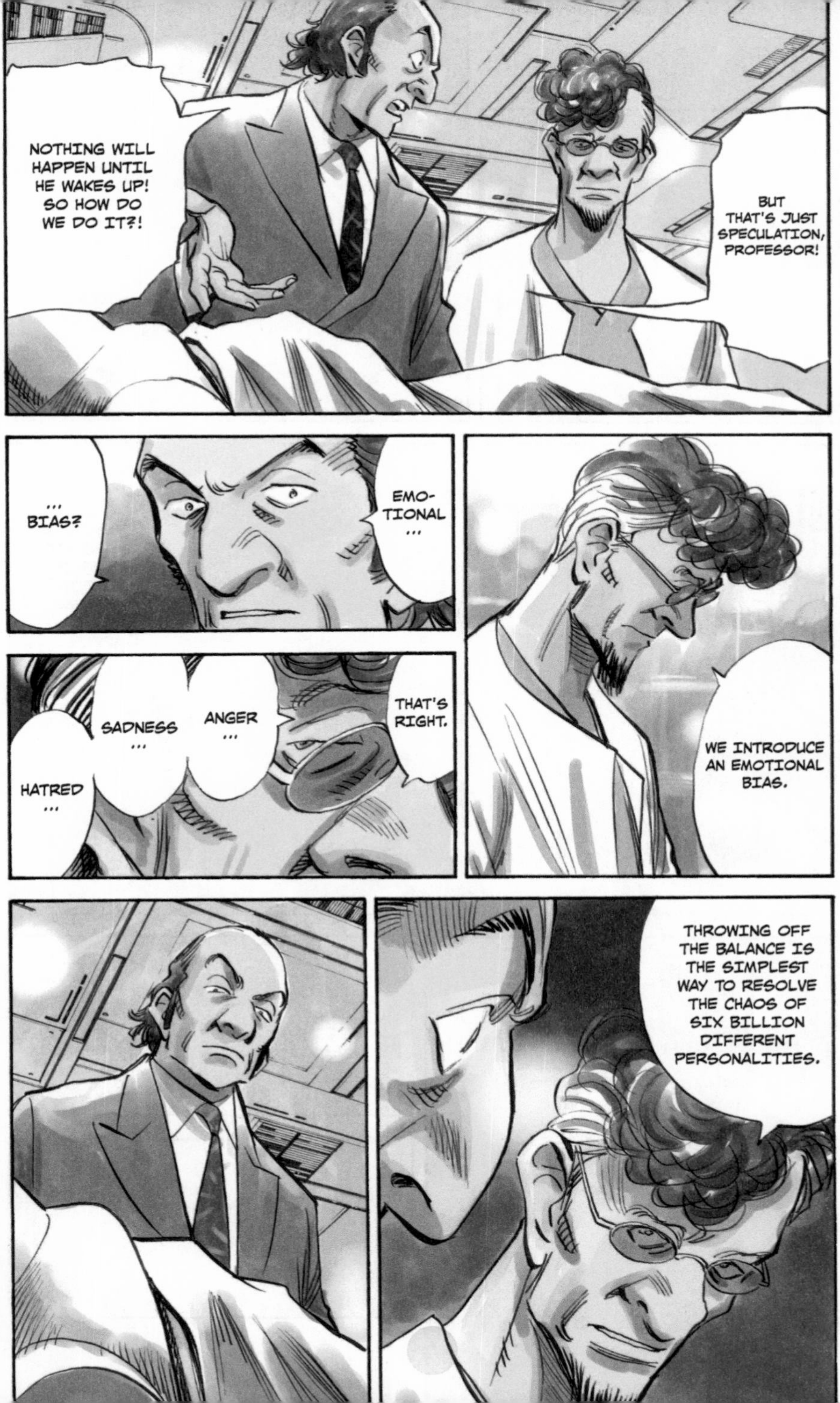
NOTHING WILL HAPPEN UNTIL HE WAKES UP! SO HOW DO WE DO IT?!
BUT THAT'S JUST SPECULATION, PROFESSOR!
WE INTRODUCE AN EMOTIONAL BIAS.
EMO-TIONAL ...
... BIAS?
THAT'S RIGHT.
ANGER ...
SADNESS ...
HATRED ...
THROWING OFF THE BALANCE IS THE SIMPLEST WAY TO RESOLVE THE CHAOS OF SIX BILLION DIFFERENT PERSONALITIES.

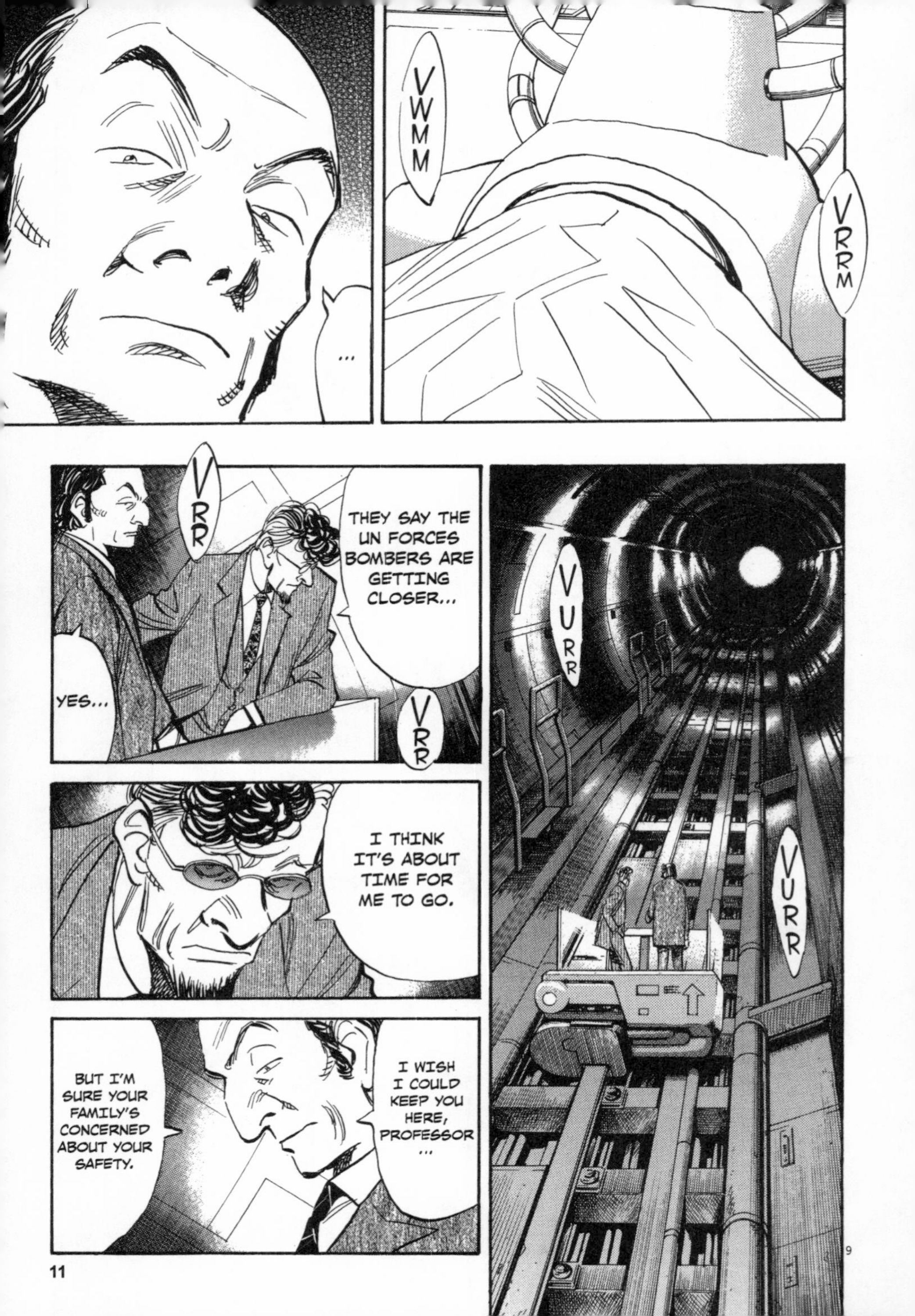
VWMM
VRRM
...
VURR
VURR
VRR
THEY SAY THE UN FORCES BOMBERS ARE GETTING CLOSER...
YES...
VRR
I THINK IT'S ABOUT TIME FOR ME TO GO.
I WISH I COULD KEEP YOU HERE, PROFESSOR...
BUT I'M SURE YOUR FAMILY'S CONCERNED ABOUT YOUR SAFETY.

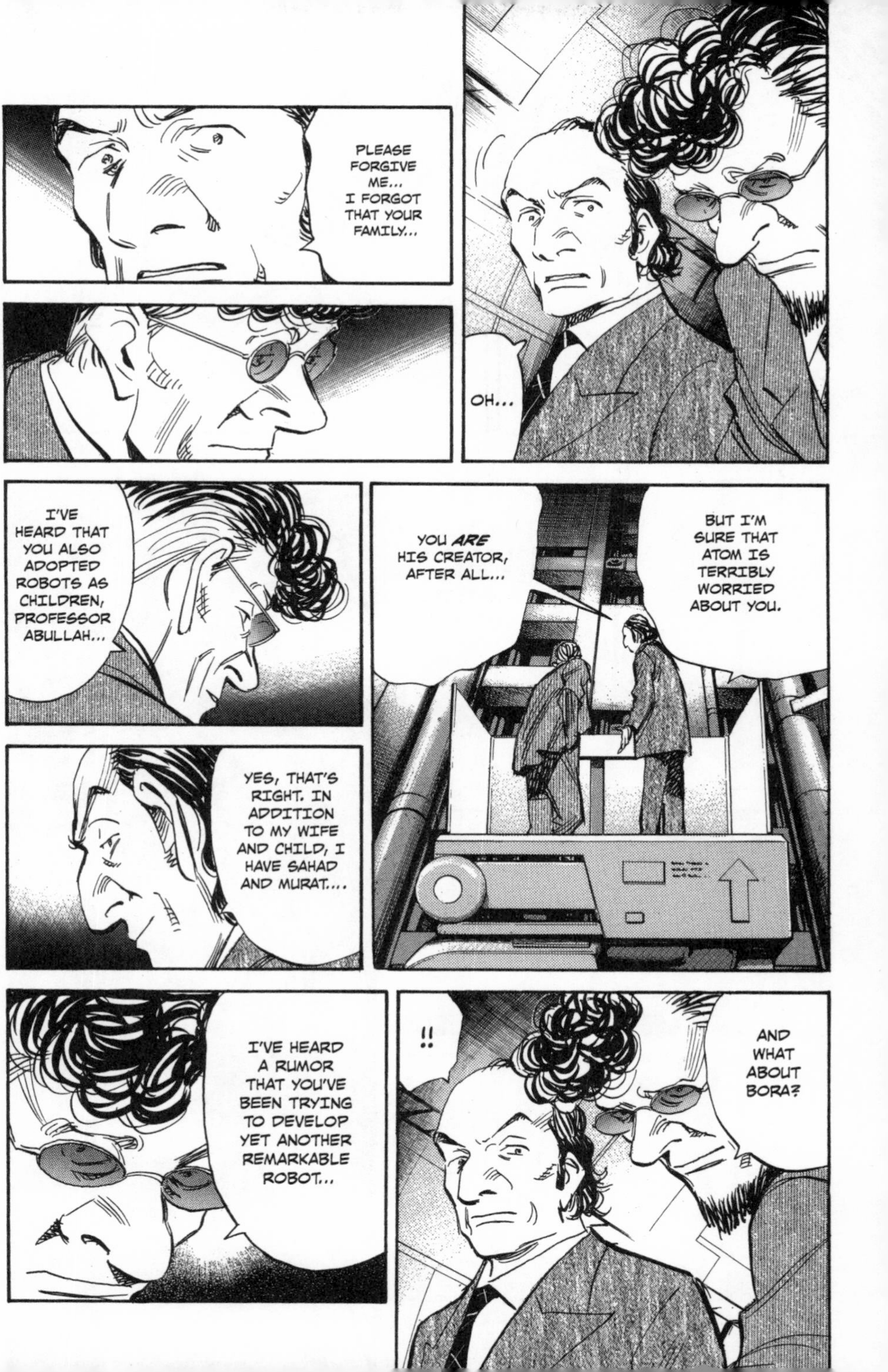
OH...
PLEASE FORGIVE ME... I FORGOT THAT YOUR FAMILY...
BUT I'M SURE THAT ATOM IS TERRIBLY WORRIED ABOUT YOU.
YOU ARE HIS CREATOR, AFTER ALL...
I'VE HEARD THAT YOU ALSO ADOPTED ROBOTS AS CHILDREN, PROFESSOR ABULLAH...
YES, THAT'S RIGHT. IN ADDITION TO MY WIFE AND CHILD, I HAVE SAHAD AND MURAT....
AND WHAT ABOUT BORA?
!!
I'VE HEARD A RUMOR THAT YOU'VE BEEN TRYING TO DEVELOP YET ANOTHER REMARKABLE ROBOT...

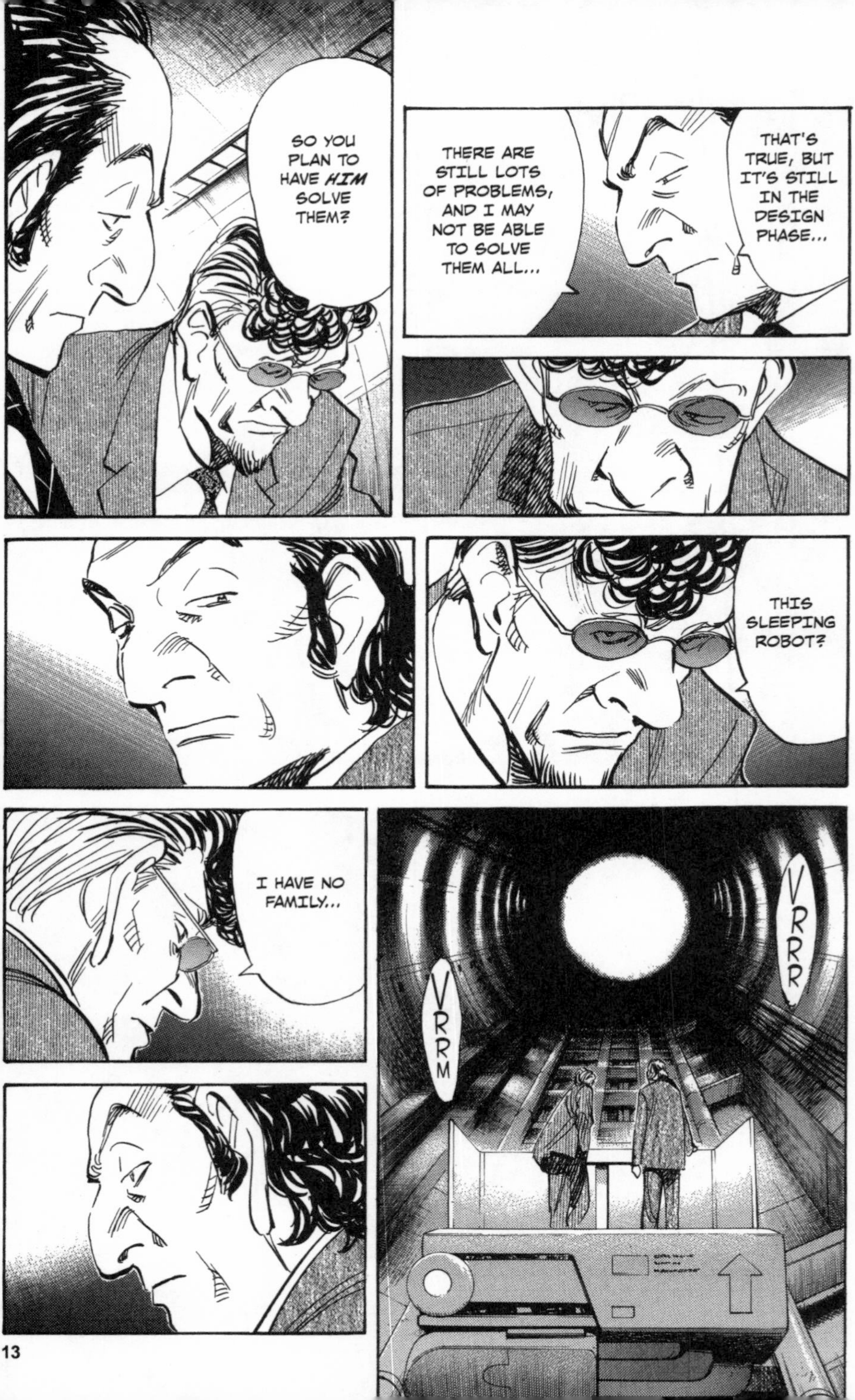
THAT'S TRUE, BUT IT'S STILL IN THE DESIGN PHASE...
THERE ARE STILL LOTS OF PROBLEMS, AND I MAY NOT BE ABLE TO SOLVE THEM ALL...
SO YOU PLAN TO HAVE *HIM* SOLVE THEM?
THIS SLEEPING ROBOT?
VRRR
VRRM
I HAVE NO FAMILY...

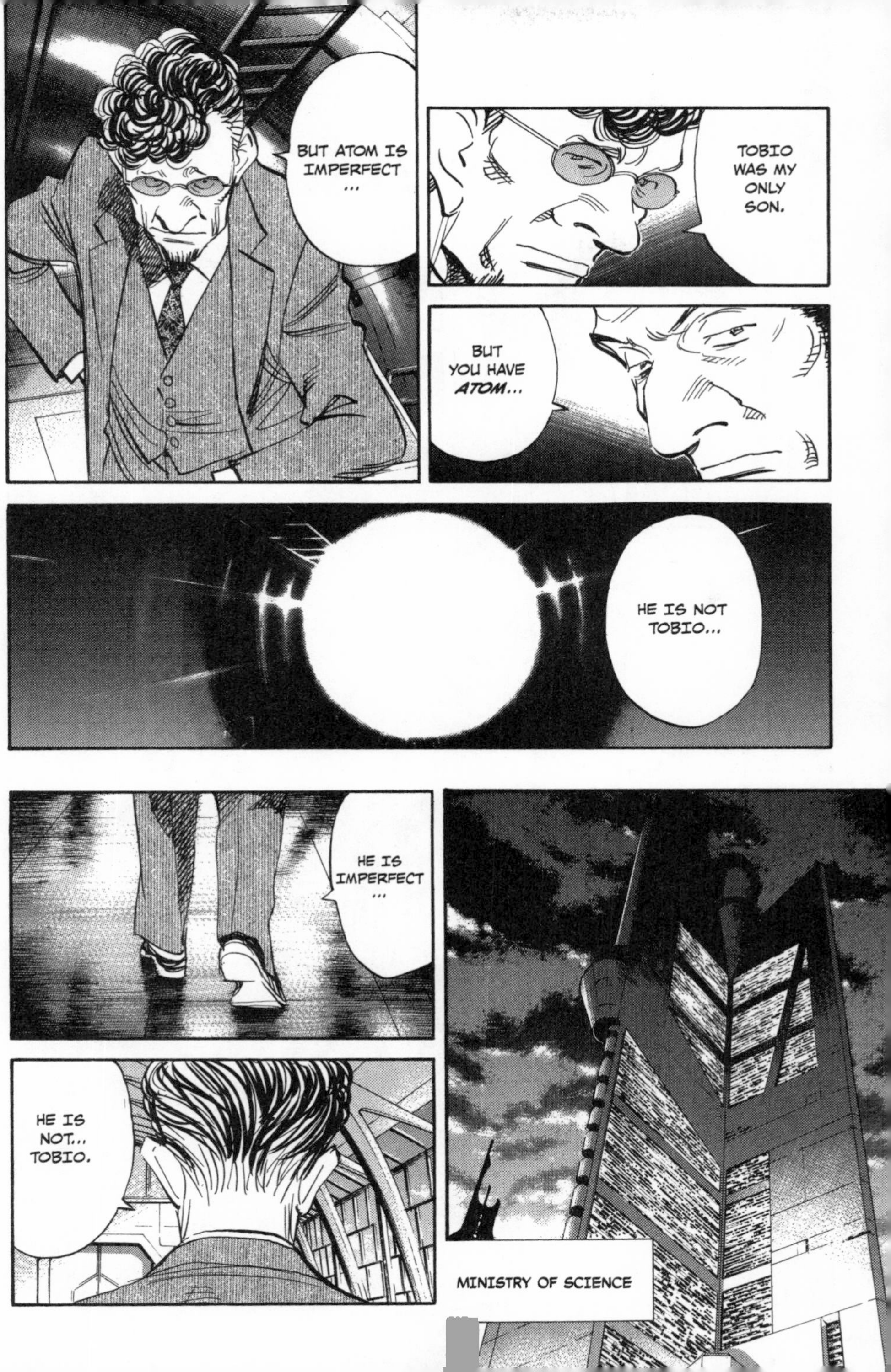
TOBIO WAS MY ONLY SON.
BUT YOU HAVE *ATOM*...
BUT ATOM IS IMPERFECT ...
HE IS NOT TOBIO...
MINISTRY OF SCIENCE
HE IS IMPERFECT ...
HE IS NOT... TOBIO.

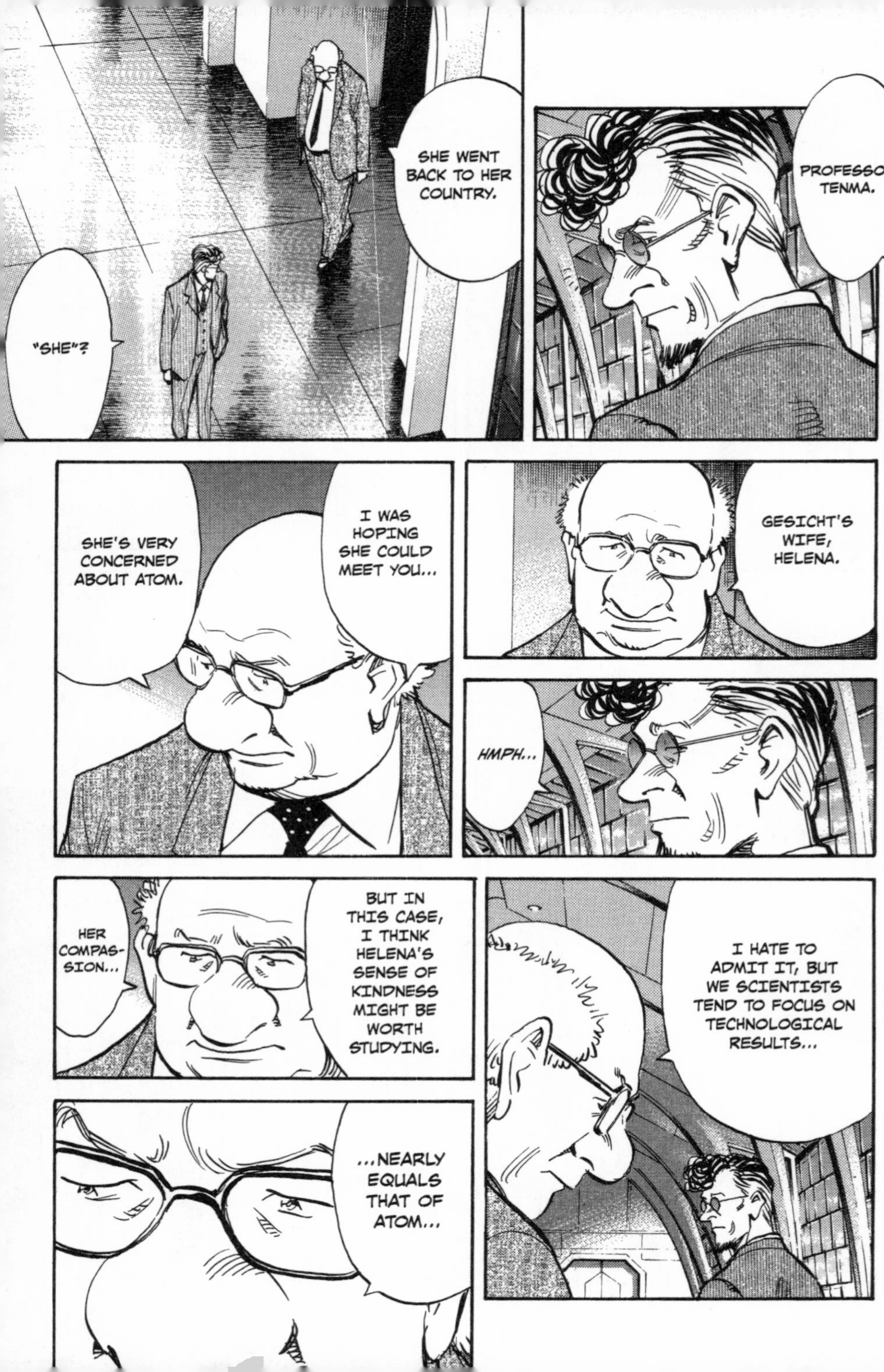
PROFESSOR TENMA.
SHE WENT BACK TO HER COUNTRY.
"SHE"?
GESICHT'S WIFE, HELENA.
HMPH...
I WAS HOPING SHE COULD MEET YOU...
SHE'S VERY CONCERNED ABOUT ATOM.
I HATE TO ADMIT IT, BUT WE SCIENTISTS TEND TO FOCUS ON TECHNOLOGICAL RESULTS...
BUT IN THIS CASE, I THINK HELENA'S SENSE OF KINDNESS MIGHT BE WORTH STUDYING.
HER COMPAS-SION...
...NEARLY EQUALS THAT OF ATOM...

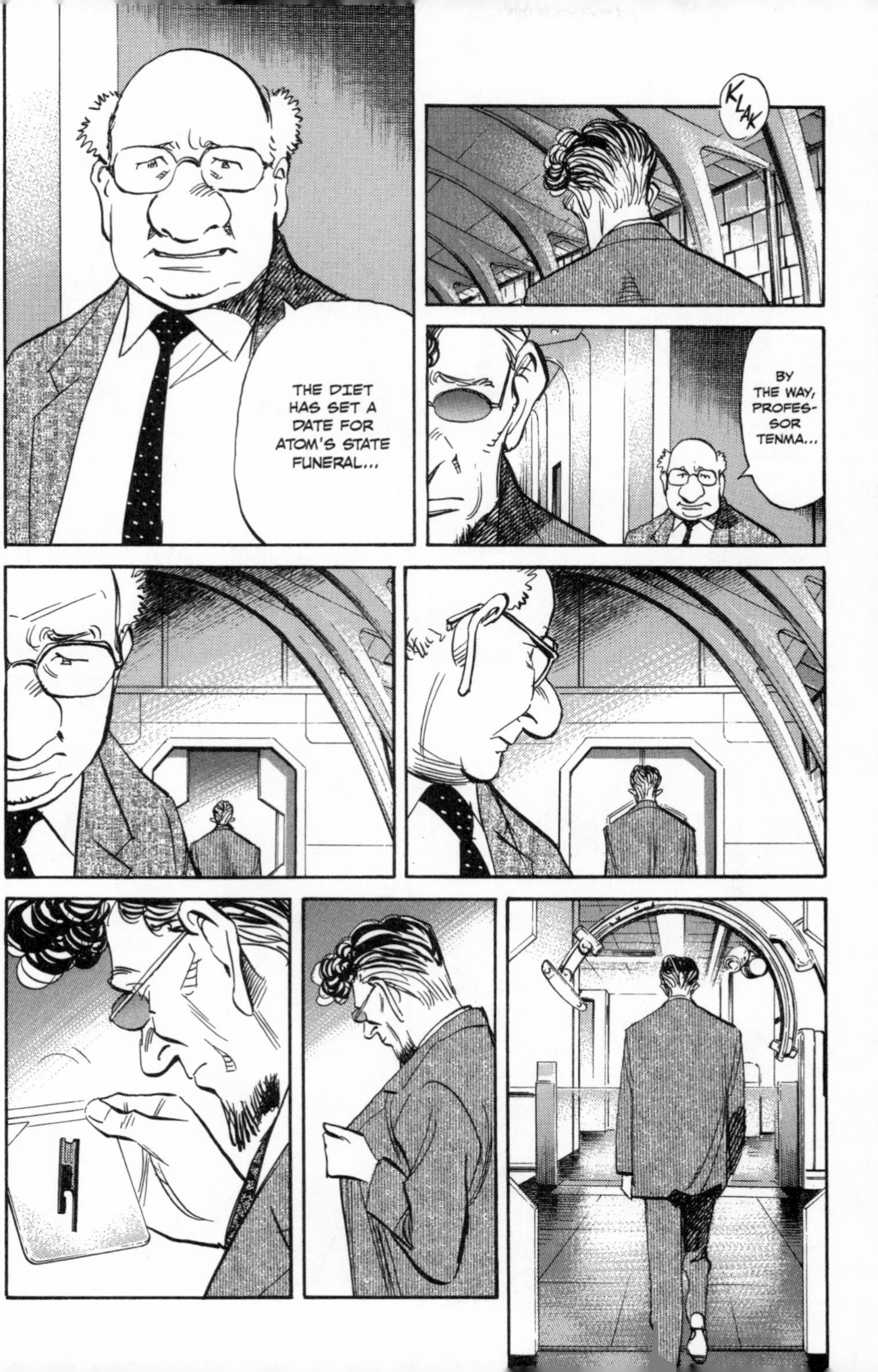
KLAK
BY THE WAY, PROFES-SOR TENMA...
THE DIET HAS SET A DATE FOR ATOM'S STATE FUNERAL...

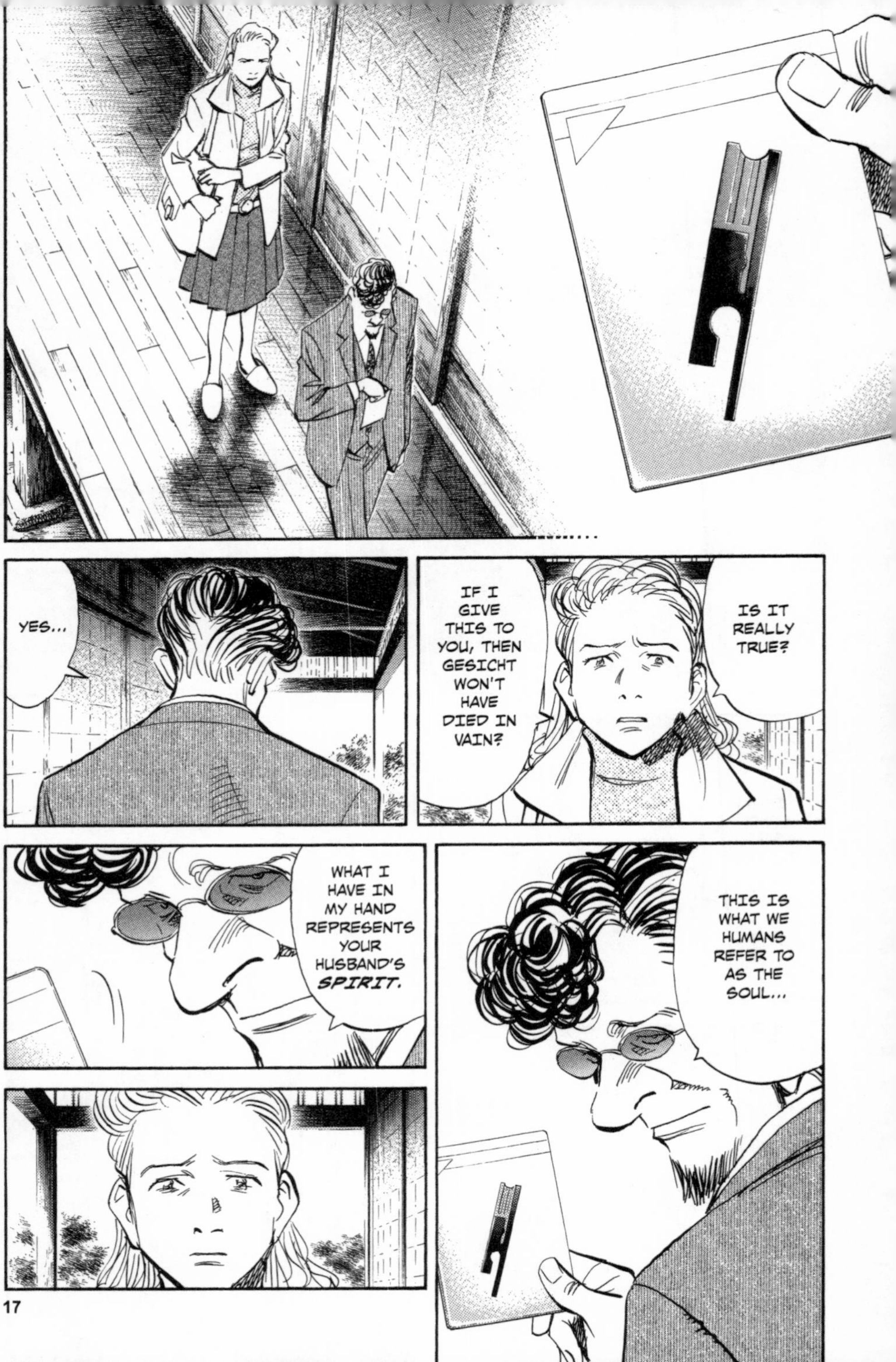
IS IT REALLY TRUE?
IF I GIVE THIS TO YOU, THEN GESICHT WON'T HAVE DIED IN VAIN?
YES...
THIS IS WHAT WE HUMANS REFER TO AS THE SOUL...
WHAT I HAVE IN MY HAND REPRESENTS YOUR HUSBAND'S *SPIRIT.*

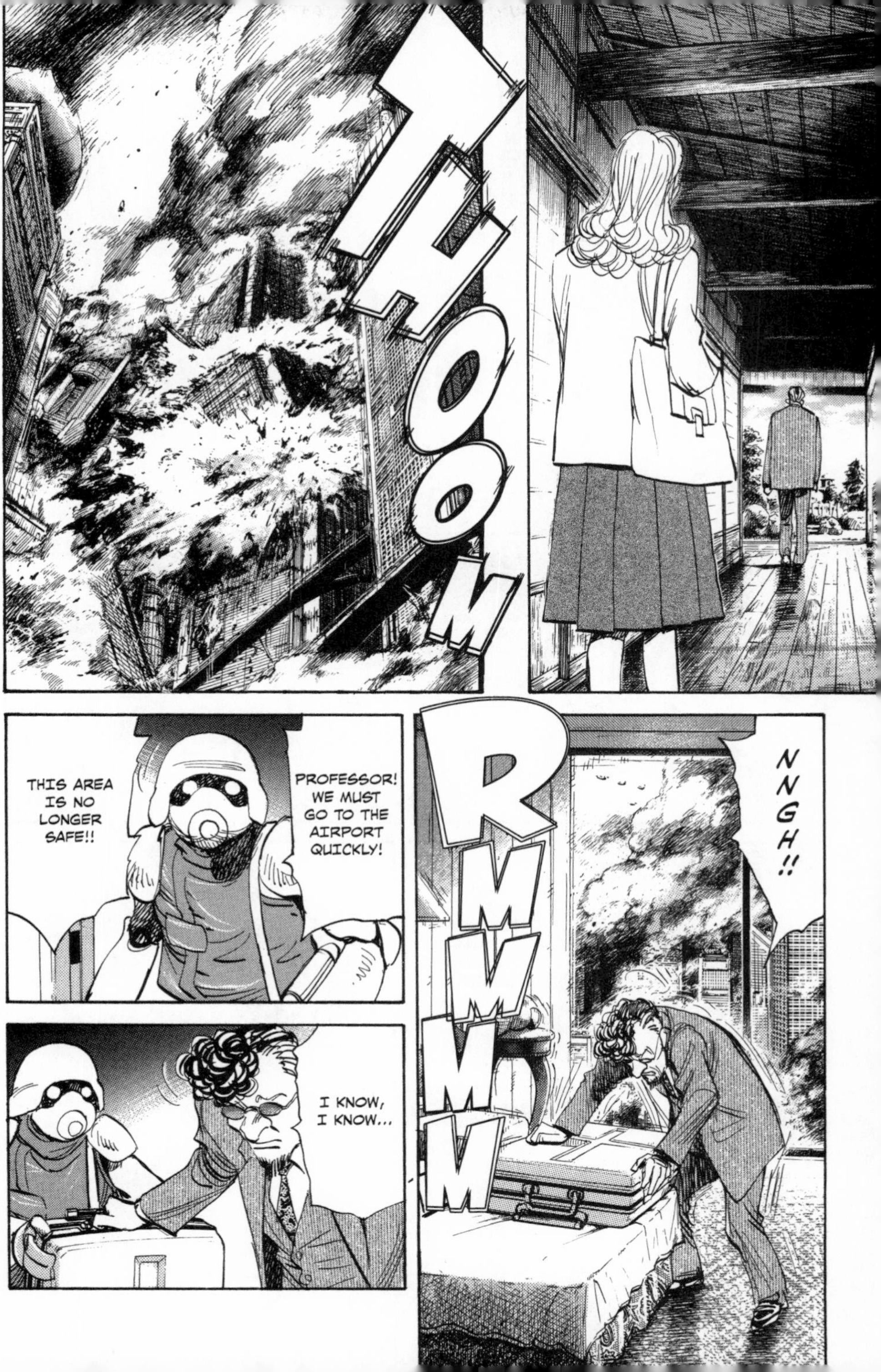
THOOOM
RMMMMM
NNGH!!
PROFESSOR! WE MUST GO TO THE AIRPORT QUICKLY!
THIS AREA IS NO LONGER SAFE!!
I KNOW, I KNOW...

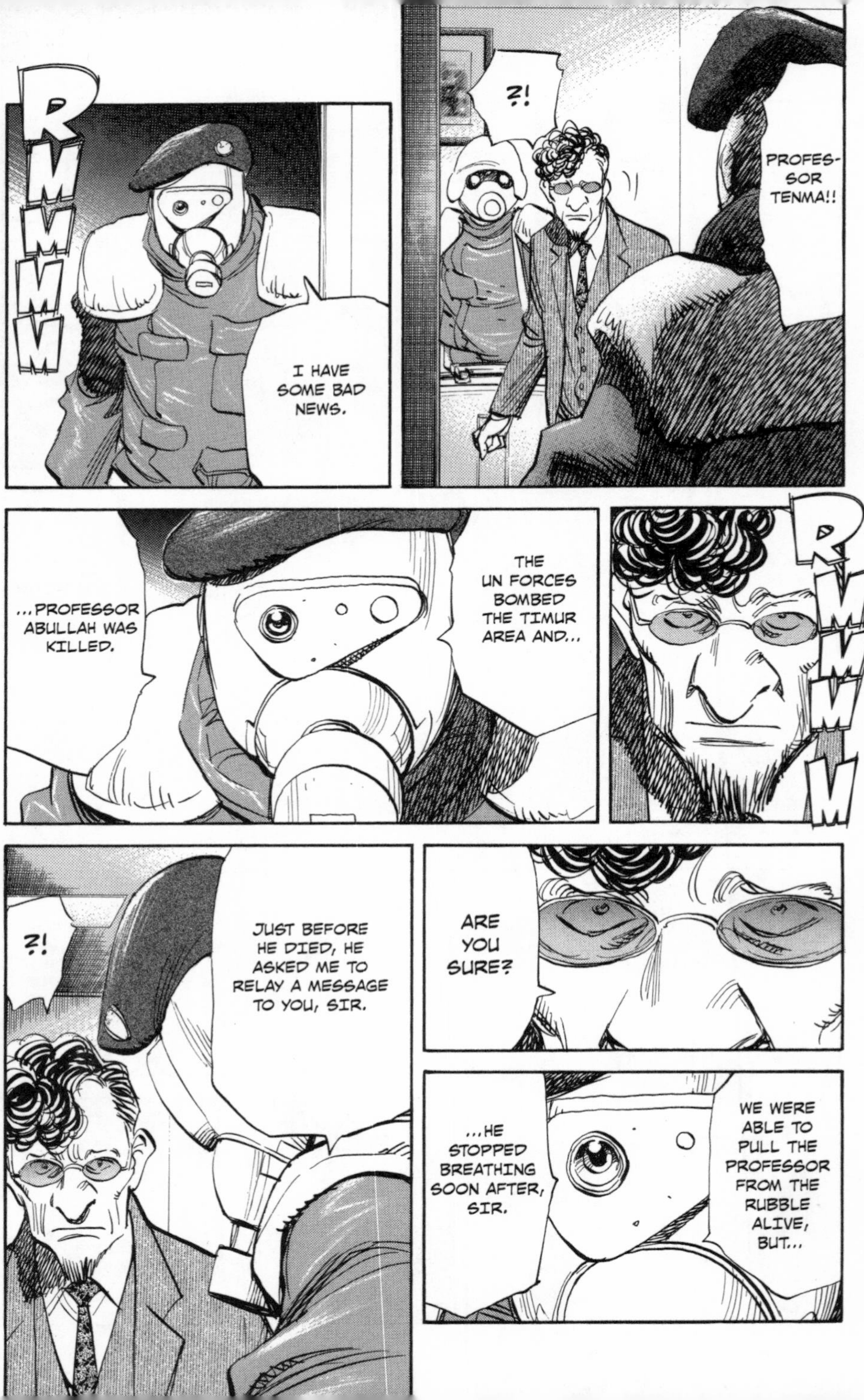
PROFES-SOR TENMA!!
?!
RMMMMM
I HAVE SOME BAD NEWS.
RMMMMM
THE UN FORCES BOMBED THE TIMUR AREA AND...
...PROFESSOR ABULLAH WAS KILLED.
ARE YOU SURE?
WE WERE ABLE TO PULL THE PROFESSOR FROM THE RUBBLE ALIVE, BUT...
...HE STOPPED BREATHING SOON AFTER, SIR.
JUST BEFORE HE DIED, HE ASKED ME TO RELAY A MESSAGE TO YOU, SIR.
?!

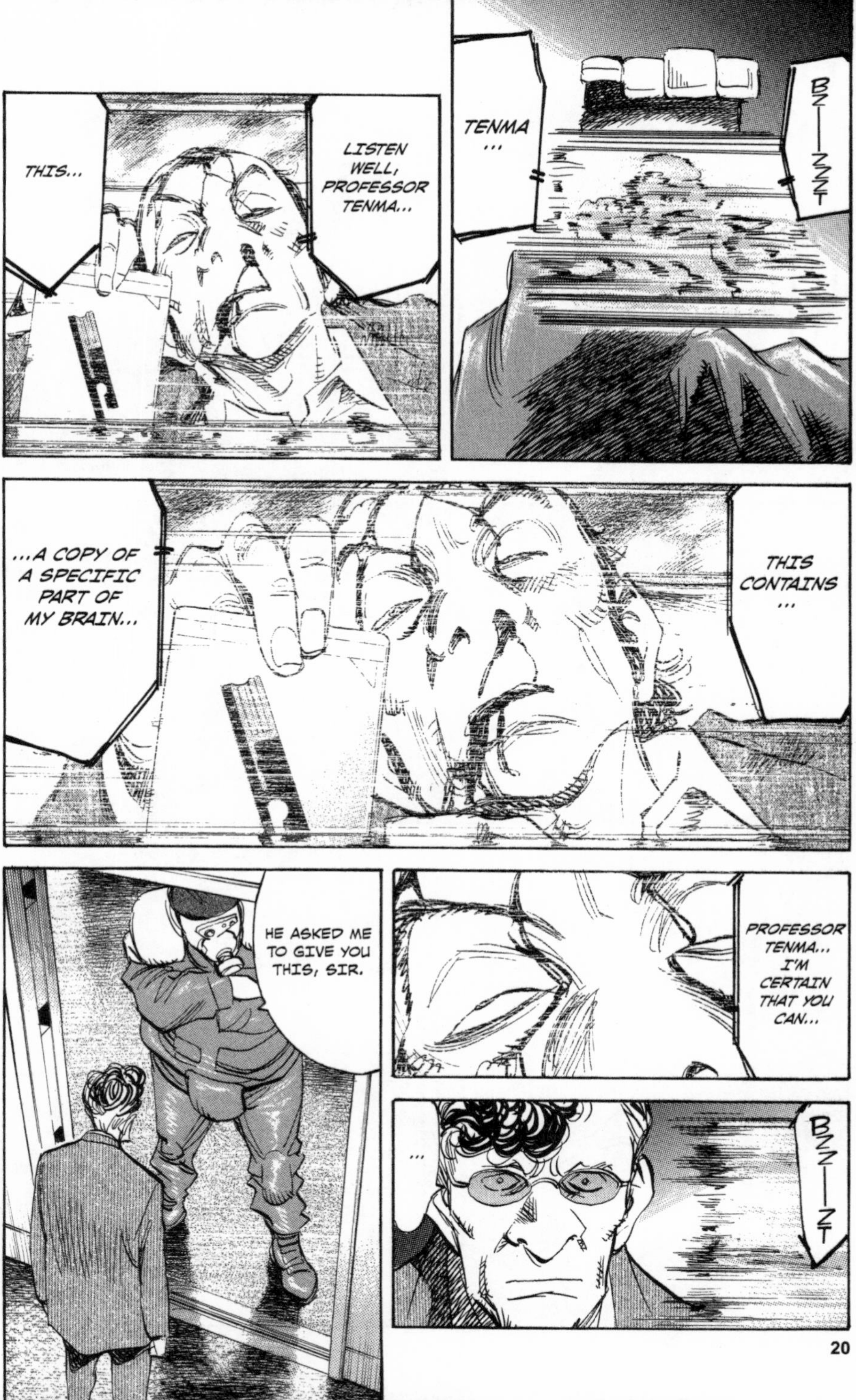
BZZ–ZZT
TENMA...
LISTEN WELL, PROFESSOR TENMA...
THIS...
THIS CONTAINS...
...A COPY OF A SPECIFIC PART OF MY BRAIN...
PROFESSOR TENMA... I'M CERTAIN THAT YOU CAN...
BZZ–ZT
...
HE ASKED ME TO GIVE YOU THIS, SIR.

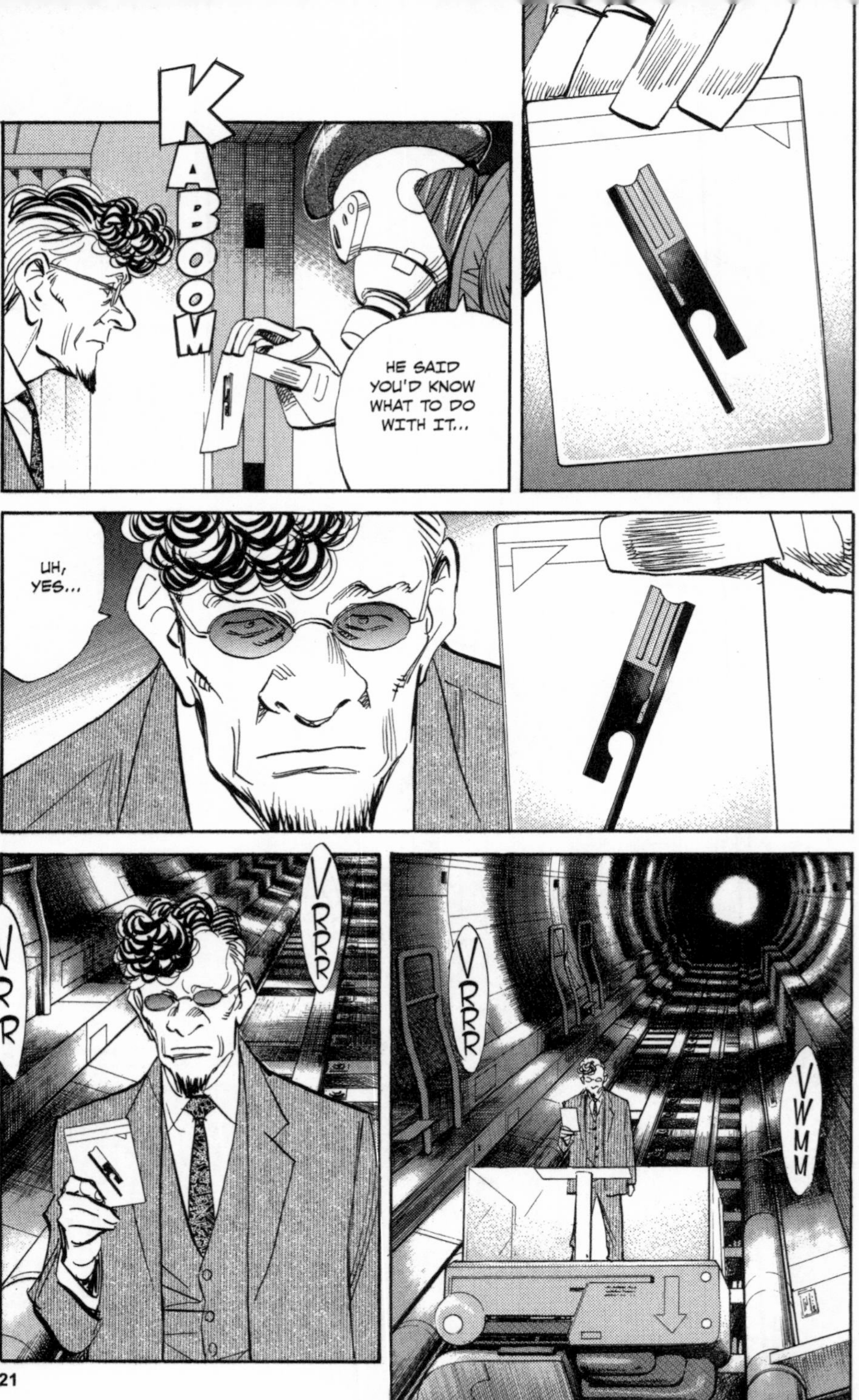
KABOOOM
HE SAID YOU'D KNOW WHAT TO DO WITH IT...
UH, YES...
VRRR
VWMM
VRRR
VRR

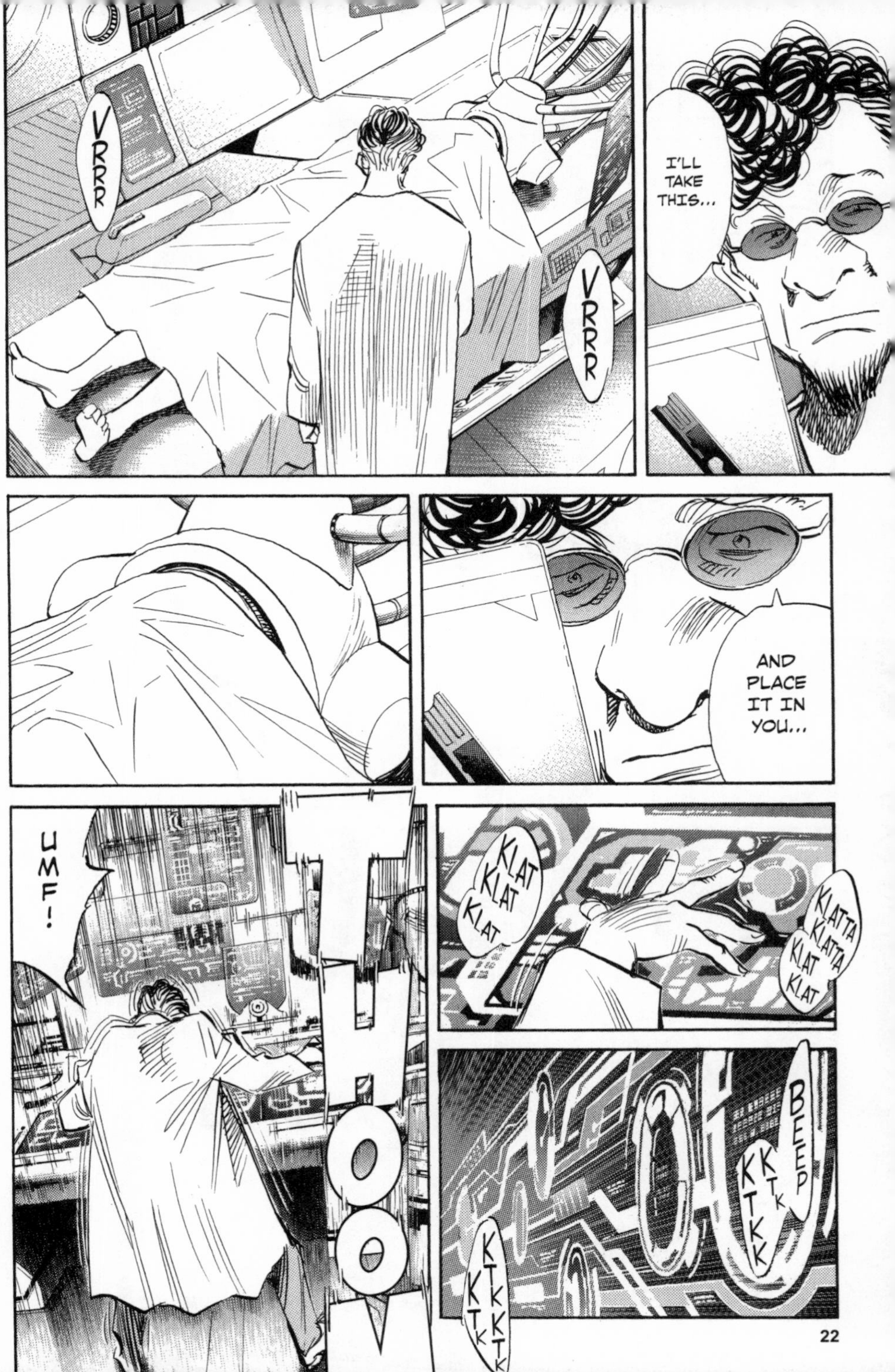
I'LL TAKE THIS...
VRRR
VRRR
AND PLACE IT IN YOU...
KLAT KLAT KLAT
KLATTA KLATTA KLAT KLAT
BEEP
KTKK KTk
KTKKTK KTk
UMF!
THOO

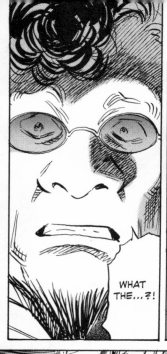

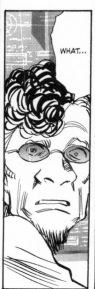

WHAT...

WHAT THE...?!

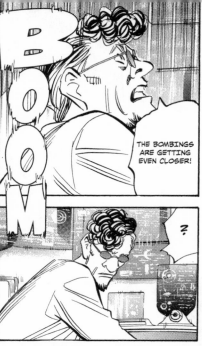

BOOM

THE BOMBINGS ARE GETTING EVEN CLOSER!

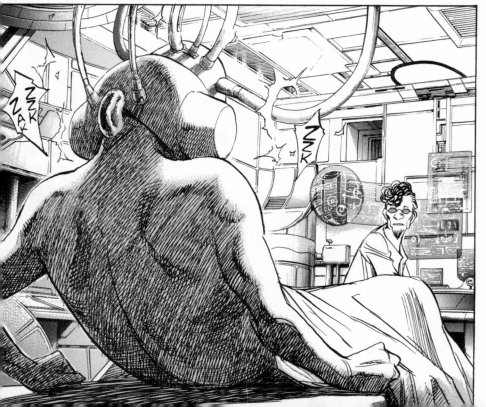

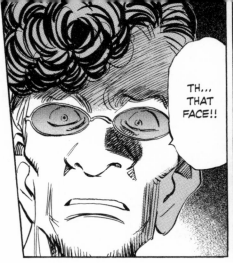

TH... THAT FACE!!

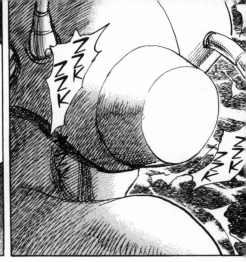

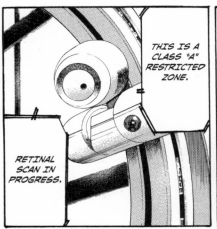

THIS IS A CLASS "A" RESTRICTED ZONE.

RETINAL SCAN IN PROGRESS.

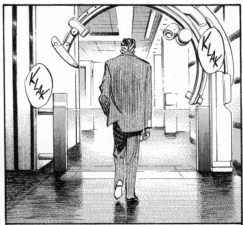

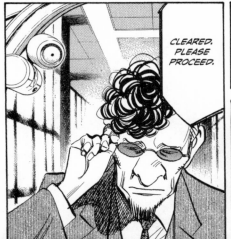

CLEARED. PLEASE PROCEED.

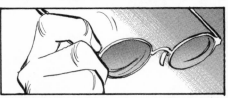

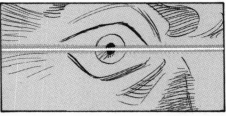

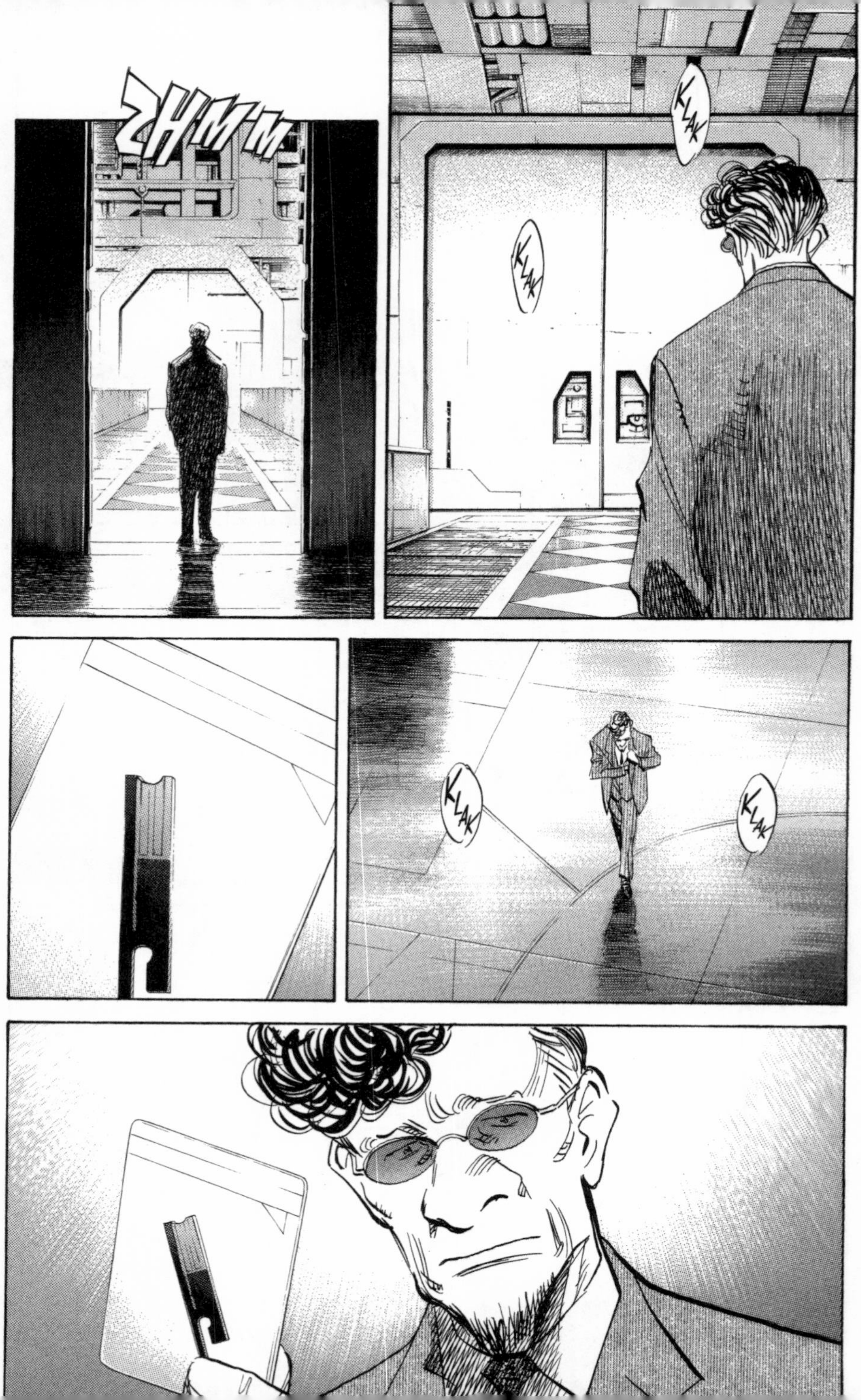
KLAK
KLAK
ZHMM
KLAK
KLAK

VRRM
VRRR
TO BRING YOU BACK TO LIFE, ATOM...
I'M WILLING TO BECOME A ***MONSTER***...
VRRR
VRRR

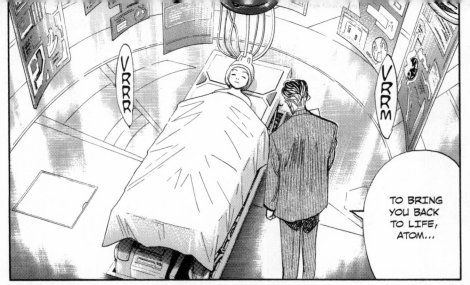

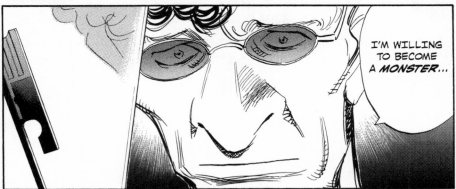

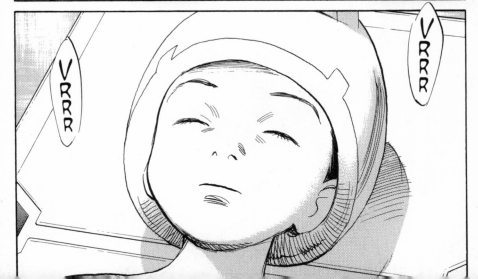

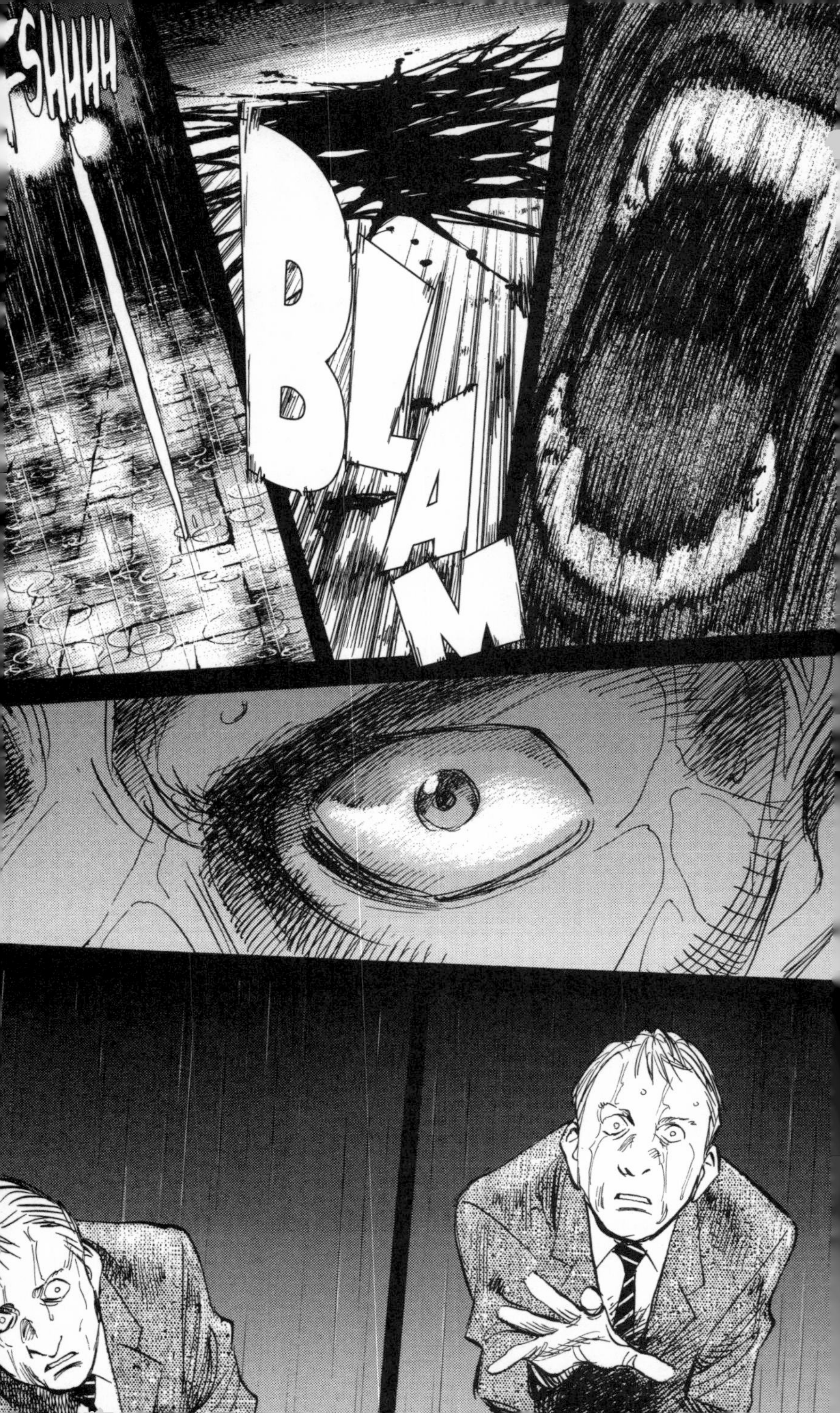
BLAM
SHHHH

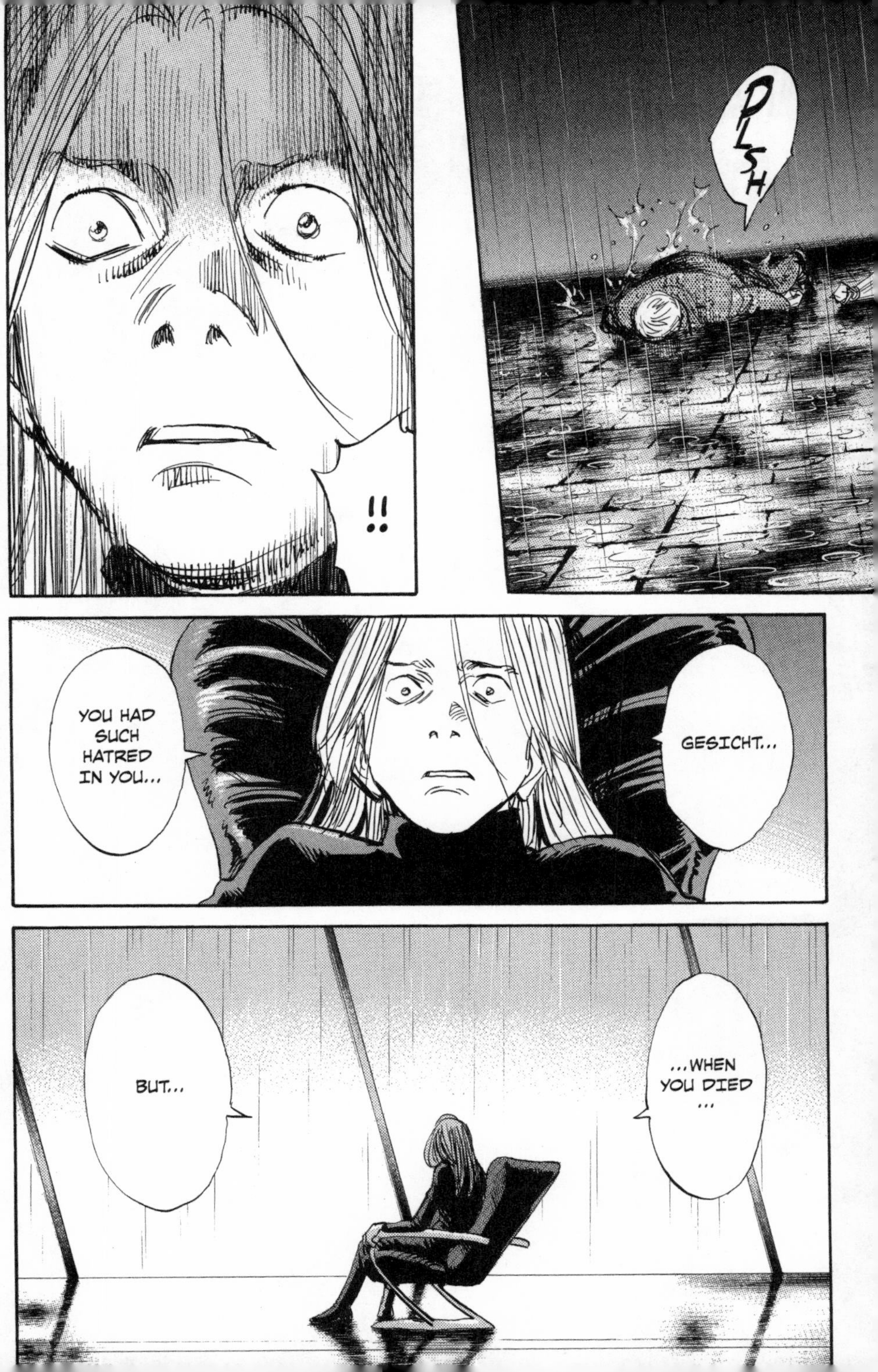
PLSH
!!
GESICHT...
YOU HAD SUCH HATRED IN YOU...
...WHEN YOU DIED ...
BUT...

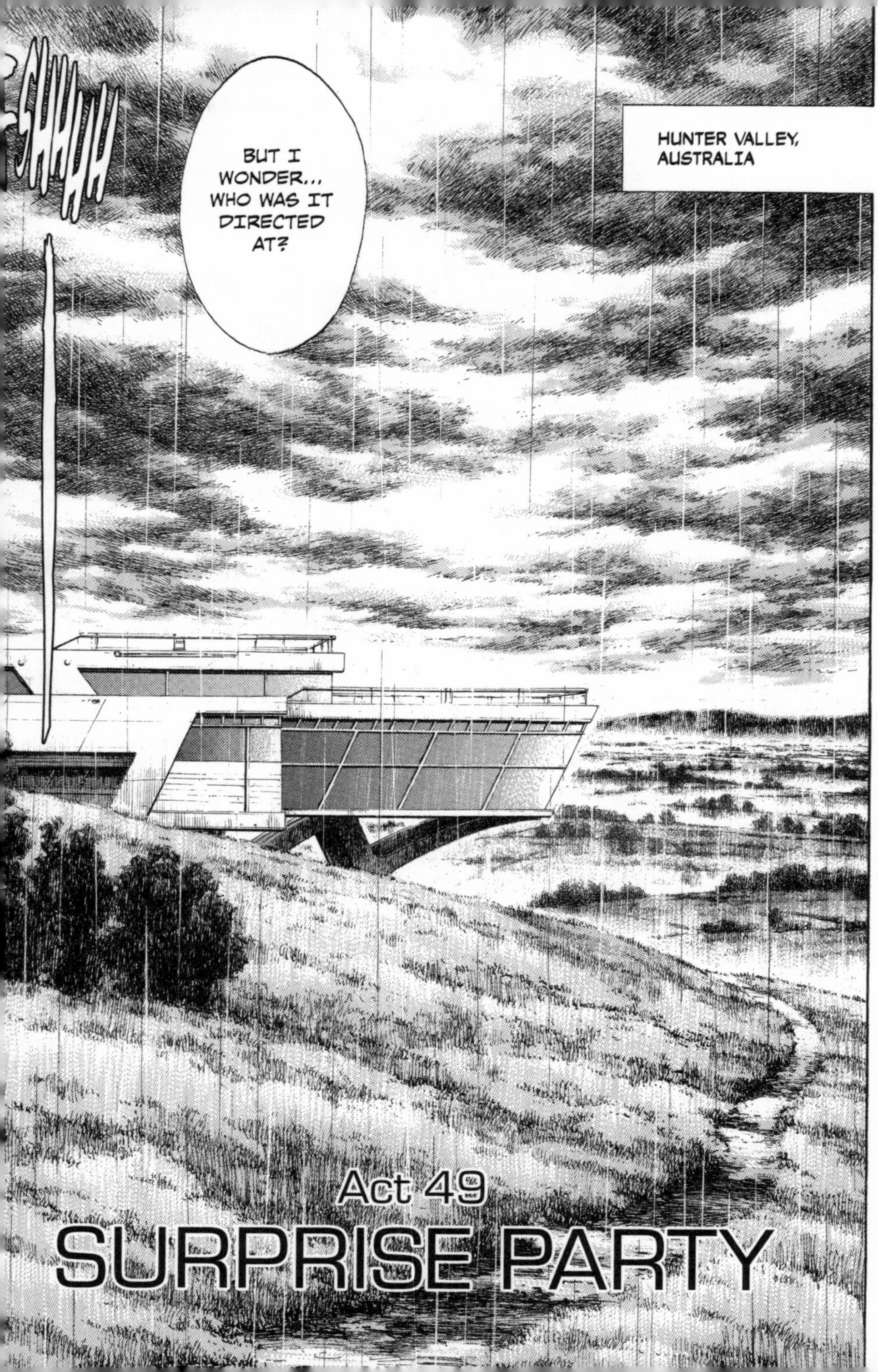
HUNTER VALLEY, AUSTRALIA
BUT I WONDER... WHO WAS IT DIRECTED AT?
SHHHH
Act 49
SURPRISE PARTY

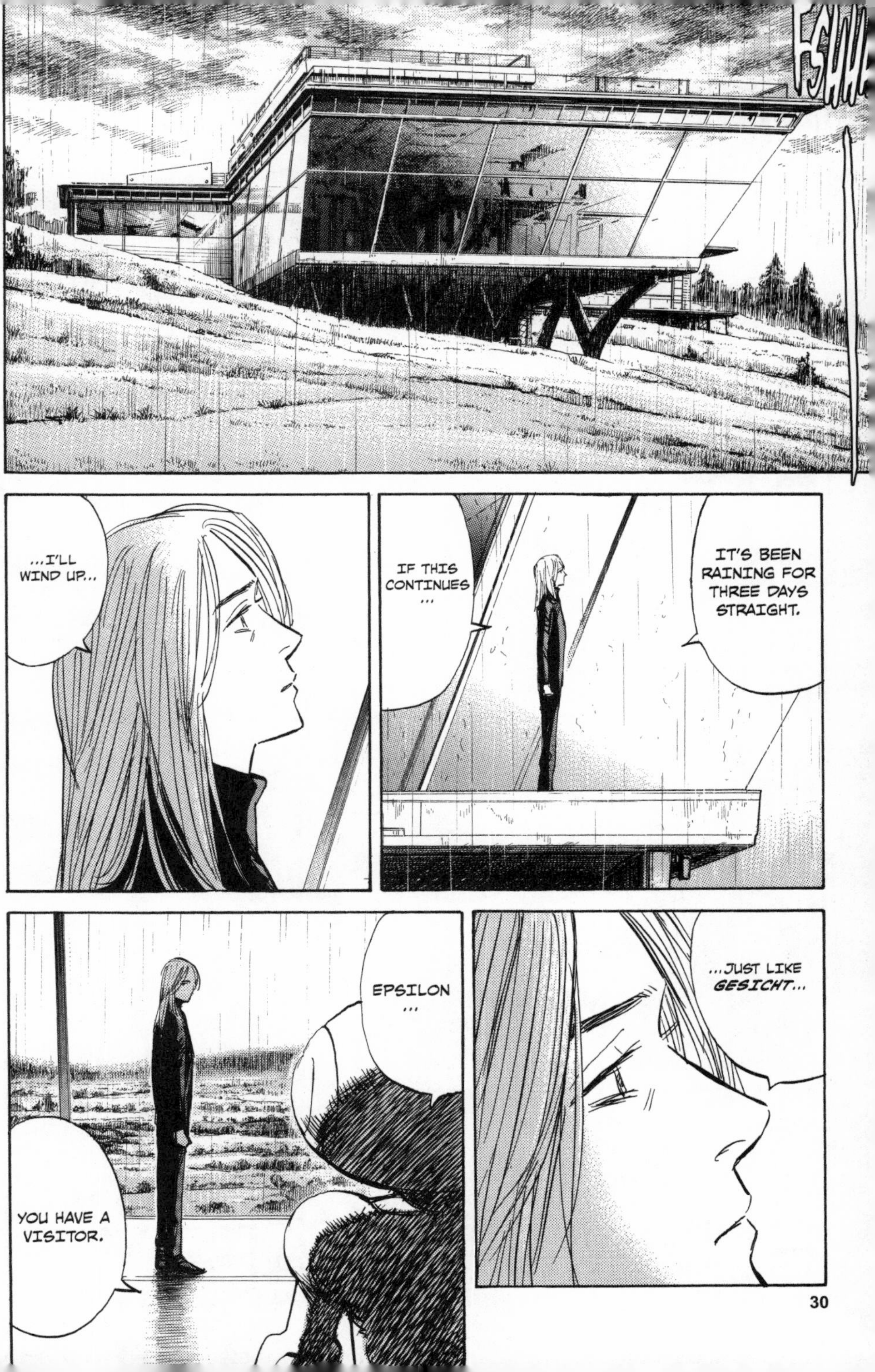
FSHH
IT'S BEEN RAINING FOR THREE DAYS STRAIGHT.
IF THIS CONTINUES ...
...I'LL WIND UP...
...JUST LIKE *GESICHT*...
EPSILON ...
YOU HAVE A VISITOR.

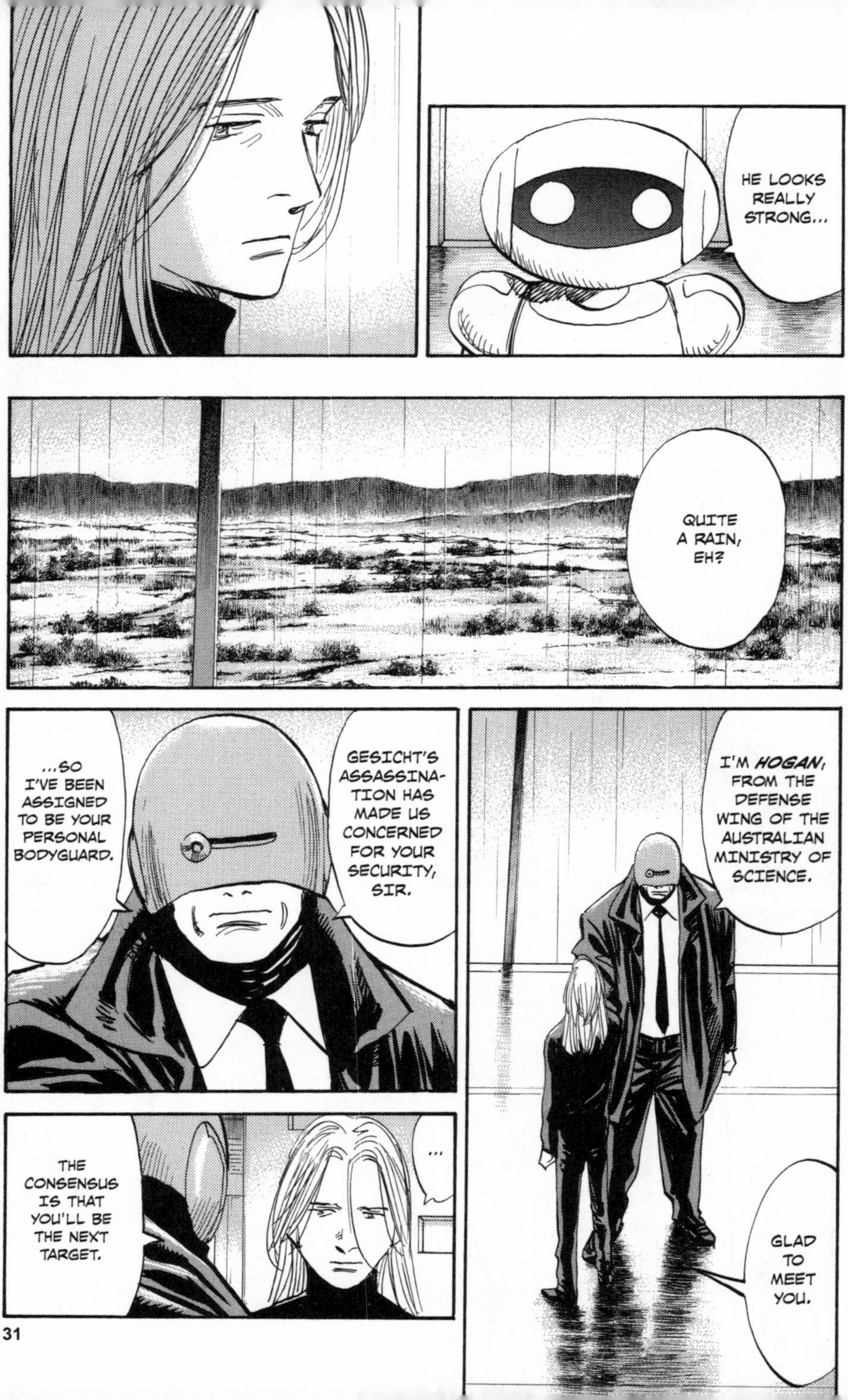
HE LOOKS REALLY STRONG...
QUITE A RAIN, EH?
I'M HOGAN, FROM THE DEFENSE WING OF THE AUSTRALIAN MINISTRY OF SCIENCE.
GLAD TO MEET YOU.
GESICHT'S ASSASSINATION HAS MADE US CONCERNED FOR YOUR SECURITY, SIR.
...SO I'VE BEEN ASSIGNED TO BE YOUR PERSONAL BODYGUARD.
...
THE CONSENSUS IS THAT YOU'LL BE THE NEXT TARGET.

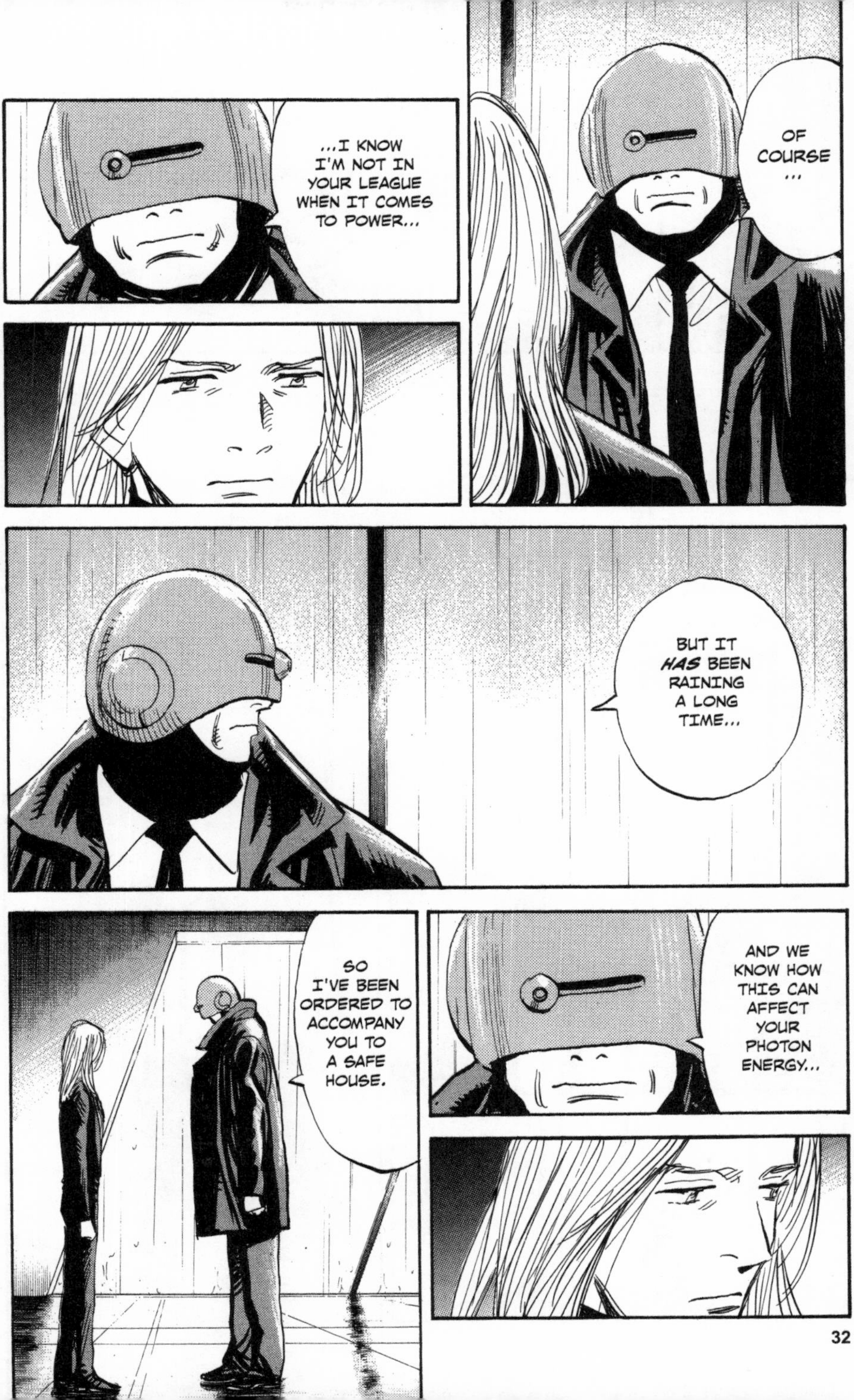
OF COURSE ...
...I KNOW I'M NOT IN YOUR LEAGUE WHEN IT COMES TO POWER...
BUT IT *HAS* BEEN RAINING A LONG TIME...
AND WE KNOW HOW THIS CAN AFFECT YOUR PHOTON ENERGY...
SO I'VE BEEN ORDERED TO ACCOMPANY YOU TO A SAFE HOUSE.

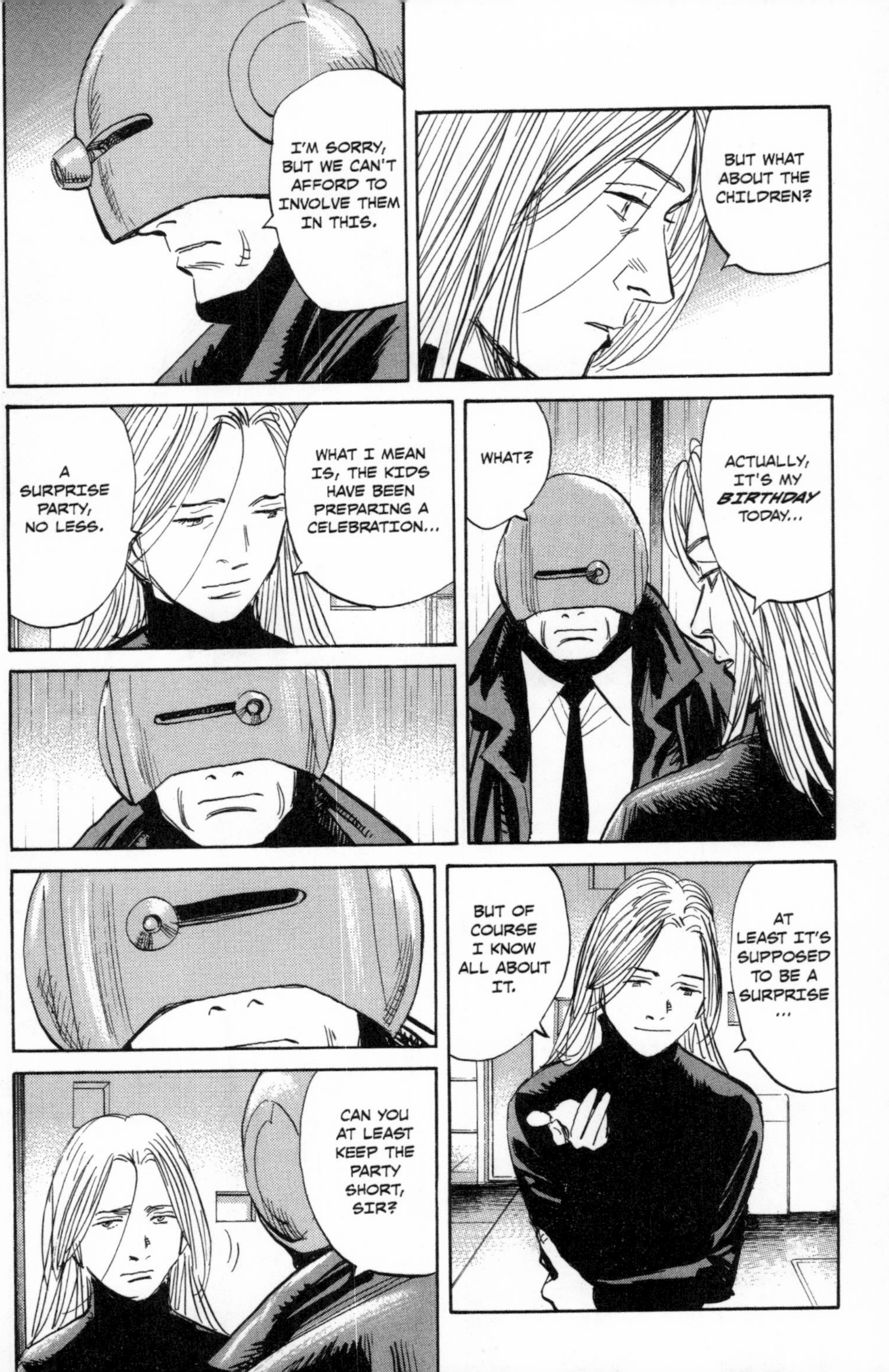
BUT WHAT ABOUT THE CHILDREN?
I'M SORRY, BUT WE CAN'T AFFORD TO INVOLVE THEM IN THIS.
ACTUALLY, IT'S MY *BIRTHDAY* TODAY...
WHAT?
WHAT I MEAN IS, THE KIDS HAVE BEEN PREPARING A CELEBRATION...
A SURPRISE PARTY, NO LESS.
AT LEAST IT'S SUPPOSED TO BE A SURPRISE...
BUT OF COURSE I KNOW ALL ABOUT IT.
CAN YOU AT LEAST KEEP THE PARTY SHORT, SIR?

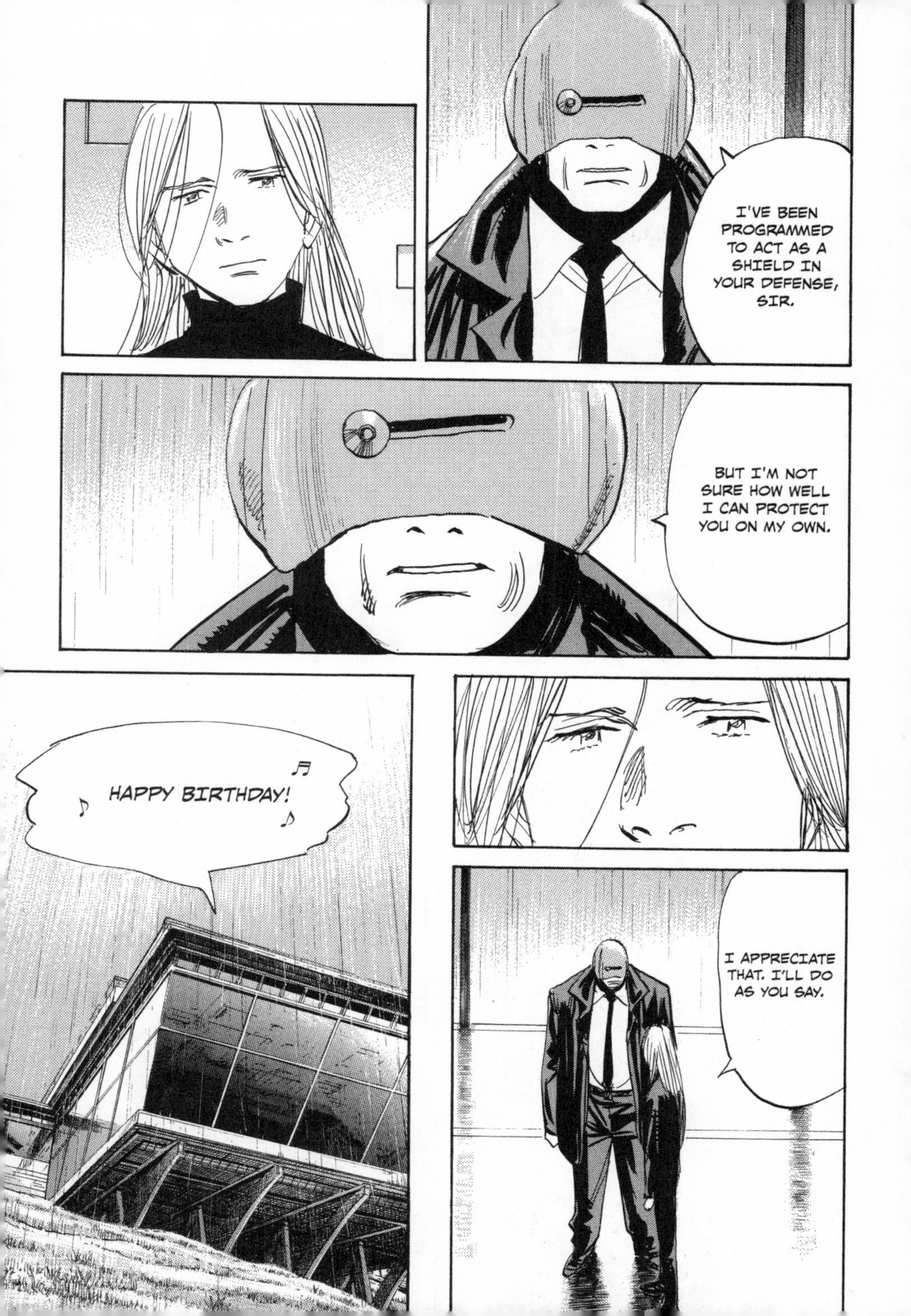
I'VE BEEN PROGRAMMED TO ACT AS A SHIELD IN YOUR DEFENSE, SIR.
BUT I'M NOT SURE HOW WELL I CAN PROTECT YOU ON MY OWN.
I APPRECIATE THAT. I'LL DO AS YOU SAY.
HAPPY BIRTHDAY!

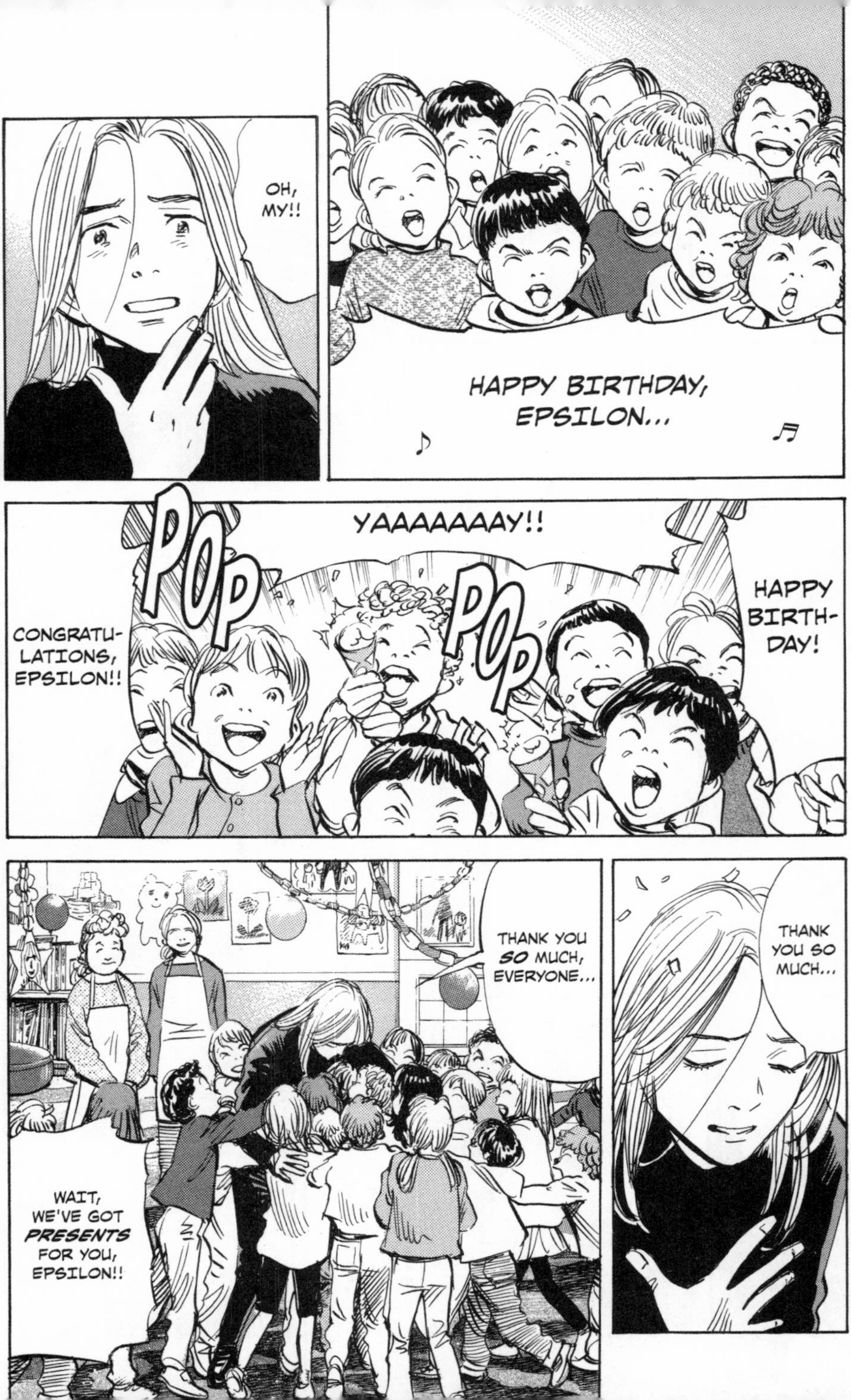
HAPPY BIRTHDAY, EPSILON...
OH, MY!!
HAPPY BIRTH-DAY!
YAAAAAAAY!!
POP
POP
CONGRATU-LATIONS, EPSILON!!
THANK YOU SO MUCH...
THANK YOU *SO* MUCH, EVERYONE...
WAIT, WE'VE GOT ***PRESENTS*** FOR YOU, EPSILON!!

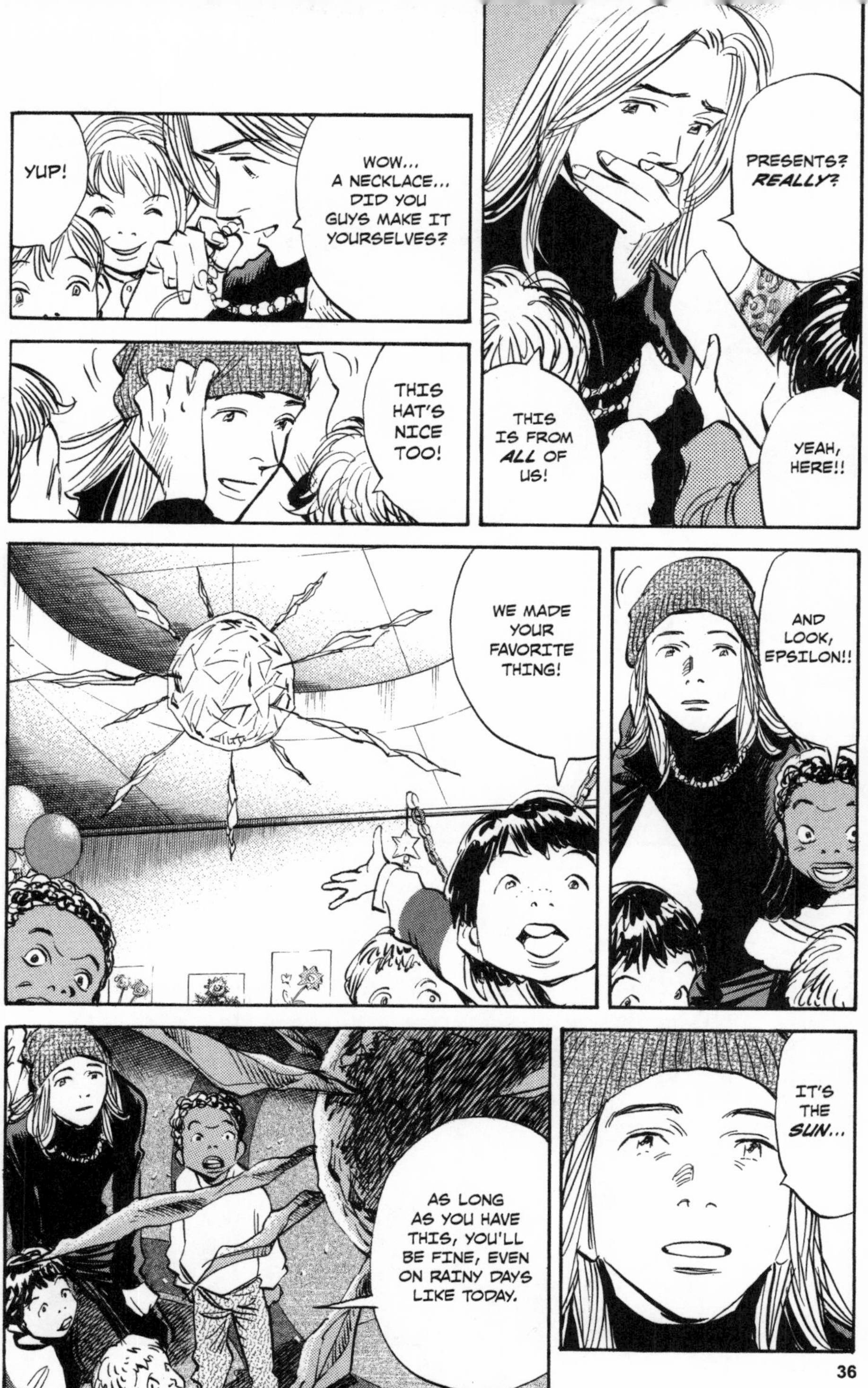
PRESENTS? *REALLY?*
YEAH, HERE!!
THIS IS FROM *ALL* OF US!
WOW... A NECKLACE... DID YOU GUYS MAKE IT YOURSELVES?
YUP!
THIS HAT'S NICE TOO!
AND LOOK, EPSILON!!
WE MADE YOUR FAVORITE THING!
IT'S THE *SUN*...
AS LONG AS YOU HAVE THIS, YOU'LL BE FINE, EVEN ON RAINY DAYS LIKE TODAY.

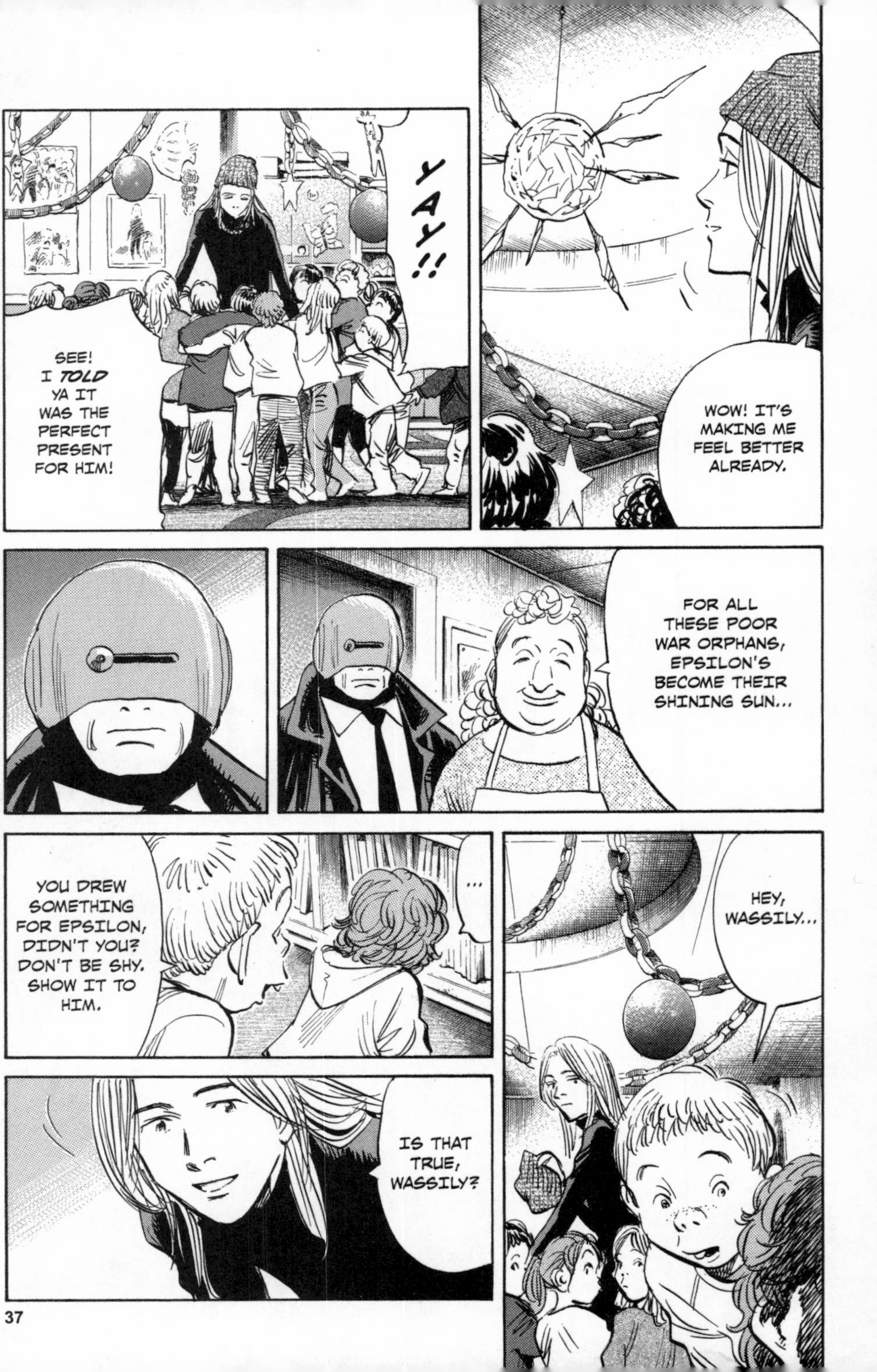
WOW! IT'S MAKING ME FEEL BETTER ALREADY.
YAY!!
SEE! I TOLD YA IT WAS THE PERFECT PRESENT FOR HIM!
FOR ALL THESE POOR WAR ORPHANS, EPSILON'S BECOME THEIR SHINING SUN...
HEY, WASSILY...
...
YOU DREW SOMETHING FOR EPSILON, DIDN'T YOU? DON'T BE SHY. SHOW IT TO HIM.
IS THAT TRUE, WASSILY?

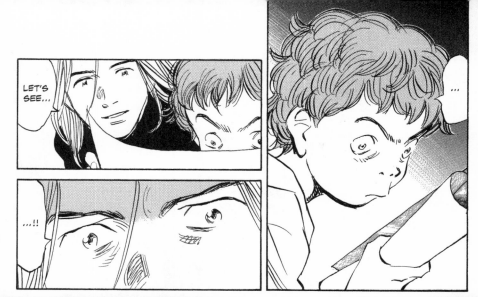

LET'S
SEE...

...

...!!

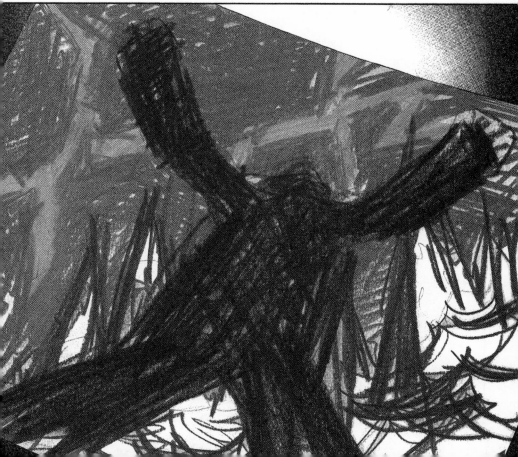

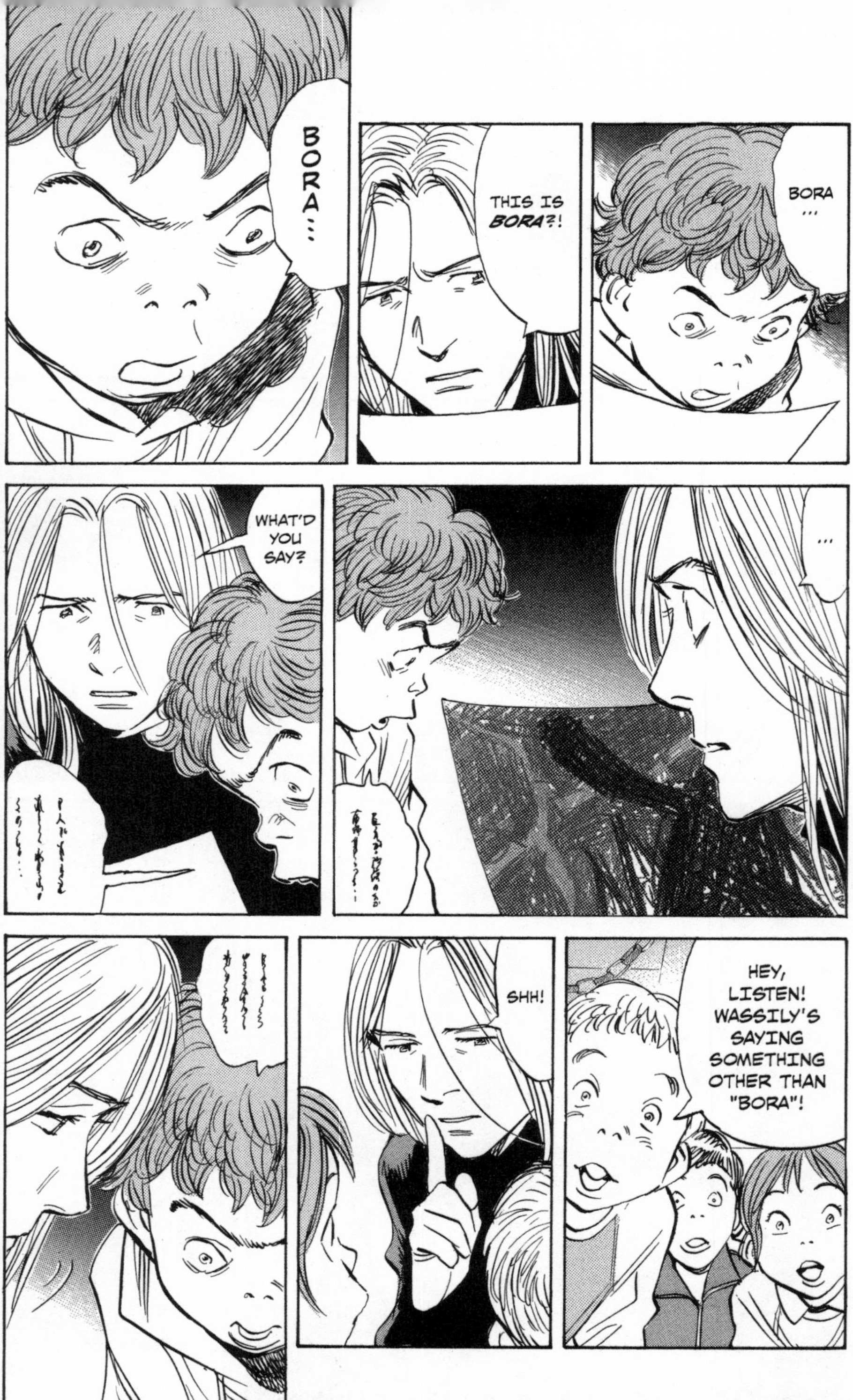
BORA ...
THIS IS BORA?!
BORA...
...
WHAT'D YOU SAY?
HEY, LISTEN! WASSILY'S SAYING SOMETHING OTHER THAN "BORA"!
SHH!

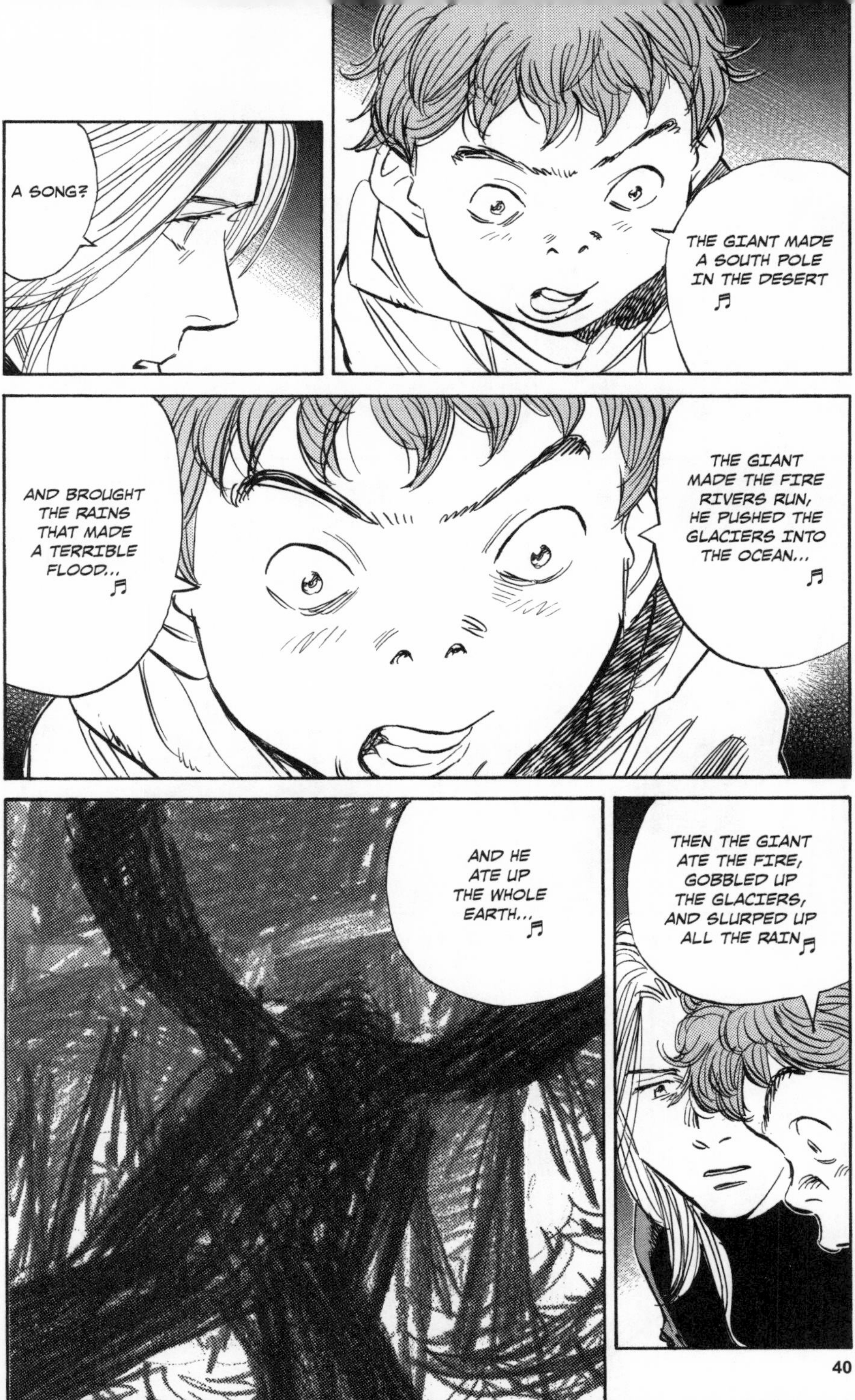
THE GIANT MADE A SOUTH POLE IN THE DESERT ♬
A SONG?
THE GIANT MADE THE FIRE RIVERS RUN, HE PUSHED THE GLACIERS INTO THE OCEAN... ♬
AND BROUGHT THE RAINS THAT MADE A TERRIBLE FLOOD... ♬
THEN THE GIANT ATE THE FIRE, GOBBLED UP THE GLACIERS, AND SLURPED UP ALL THE RAIN ♬
AND HE ATE UP THE WHOLE EARTH... ♬

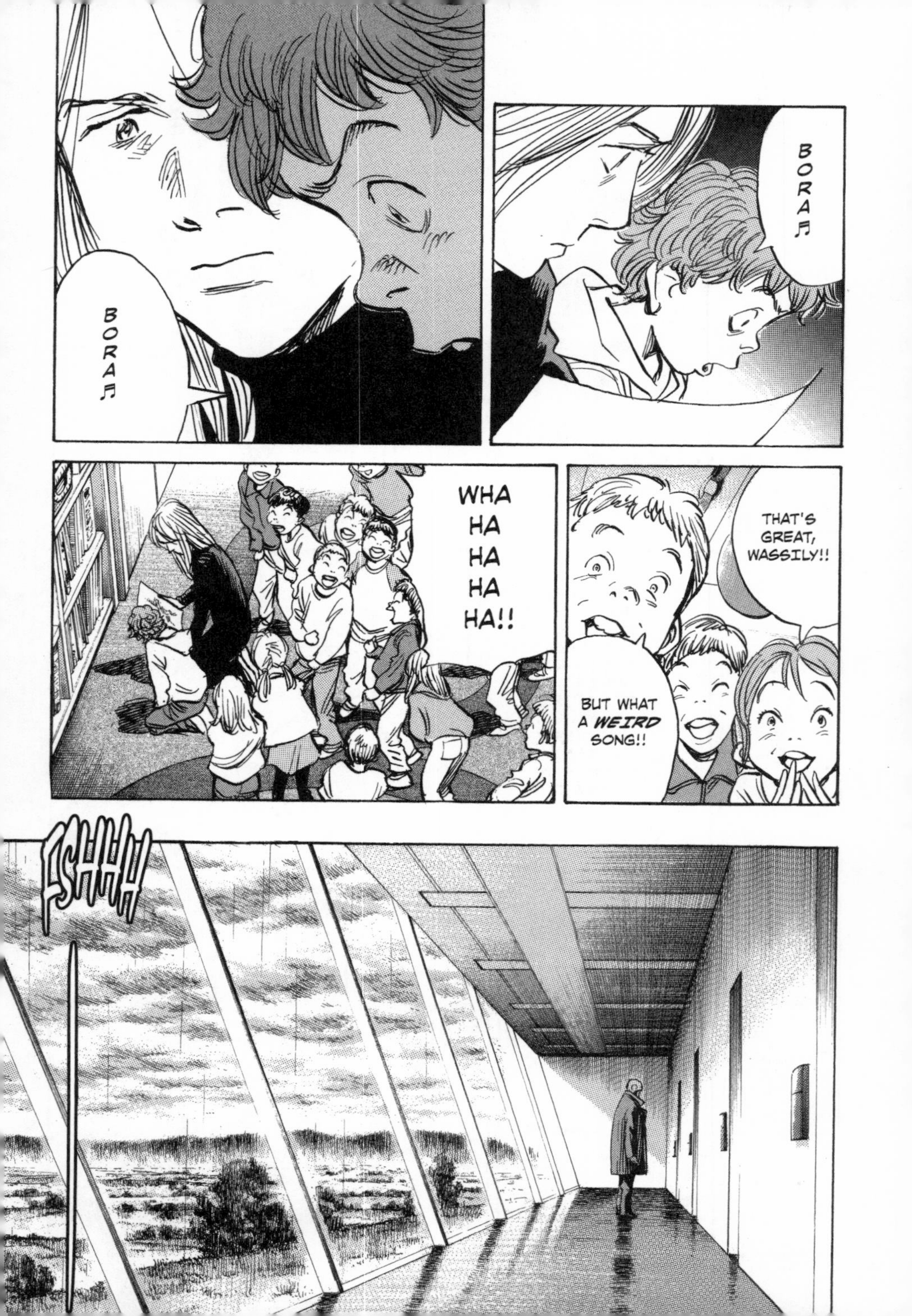
BORA♬
BORA♬
THAT'S GREAT, WASSILY!!
BUT WHAT A WEIRD SONG!!
WHA HA HA HA HA!!
FSHHH

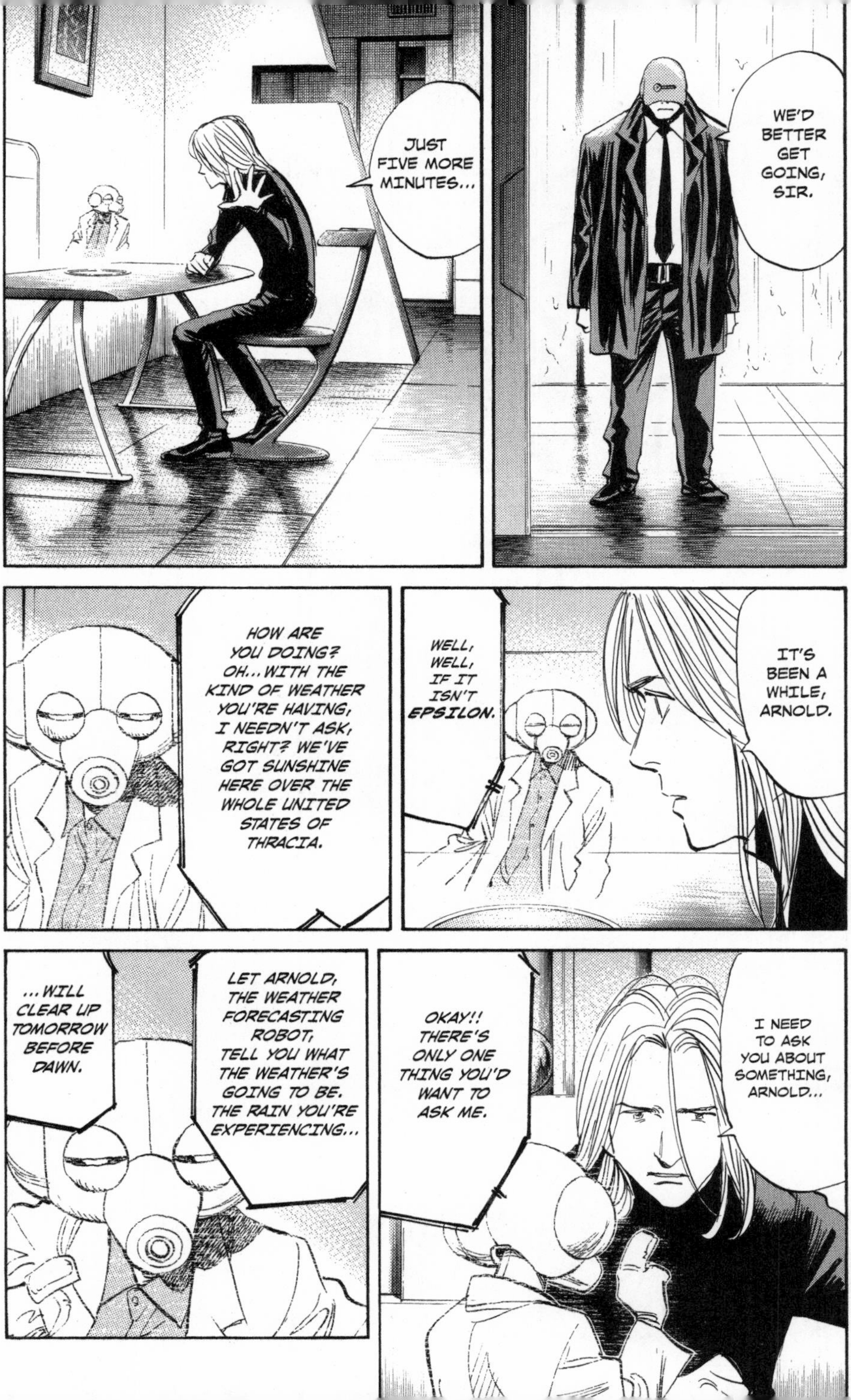
WE'D BETTER GET GOING, SIR.
JUST FIVE MORE MINUTES...
IT'S BEEN A WHILE, ARNOLD.
WELL, WELL, IF IT ISN'T EPSILON.
HOW ARE YOU DOING? OH...WITH THE KIND OF WEATHER YOU'RE HAVING, I NEEDN'T ASK, RIGHT? WE'VE GOT SUNSHINE HERE OVER THE WHOLE UNITED STATES OF THRACIA.
I NEED TO ASK YOU ABOUT SOMETHING, ARNOLD...
OKAY!! THERE'S ONLY ONE THING YOU'D WANT TO ASK ME.
LET ARNOLD, THE WEATHER FORECASTING ROBOT, TELL YOU WHAT THE WEATHER'S GOING TO BE. THE RAIN YOU'RE EXPERIENCING...
...WILL CLEAR UP TOMORROW BEFORE DAWN.

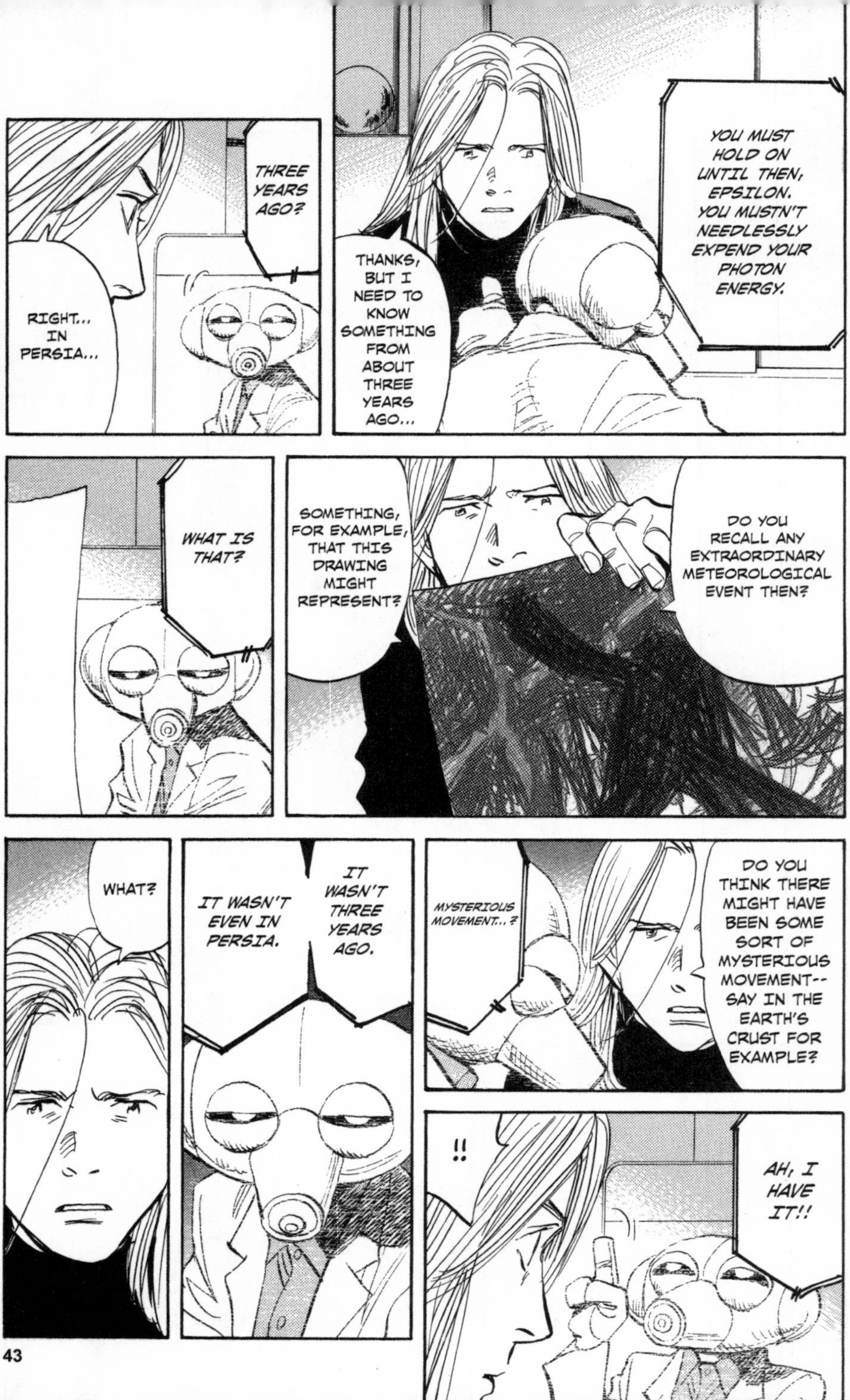
YOU MUST HOLD ON UNTIL THEN, EPSILON. YOU MUSTN'T NEEDLESSLY EXPEND YOUR PHOTON ENERGY.
THANKS, BUT I NEED TO KNOW SOMETHING FROM ABOUT THREE YEARS AGO...
THREE YEARS AGO?
RIGHT... IN PERSIA...
DO YOU RECALL ANY EXTRAORDINARY METEOROLOGICAL EVENT THEN?
SOMETHING, FOR EXAMPLE, THAT THIS DRAWING MIGHT REPRESENT?
WHAT IS THAT?
DO YOU THINK THERE MIGHT HAVE BEEN SOME SORT OF MYSTERIOUS MOVEMENT-- SAY IN THE EARTH'S CRUST FOR EXAMPLE?
MYSTERIOUS MOVEMENT...?
AH, I HAVE IT!!
!!
IT WASN'T THREE YEARS AGO.
IT WASN'T EVEN IN PERSIA.
WHAT?

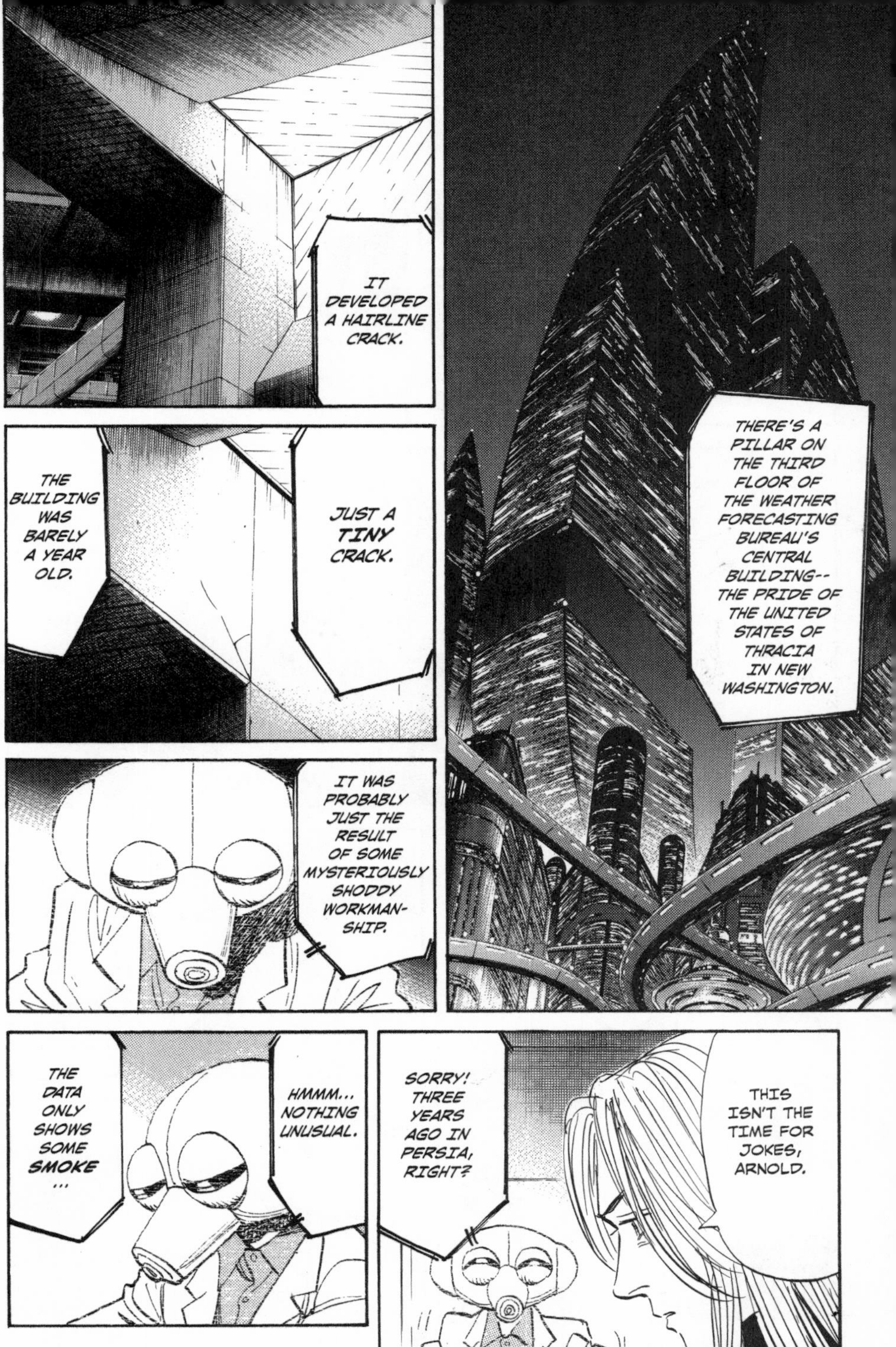
THERE'S A PILLAR ON THE THIRD FLOOR OF THE WEATHER FORECASTING BUREAU'S CENTRAL BUILDING-- THE PRIDE OF THE UNITED STATES OF THRACIA IN NEW WASHINGTON.
IT DEVELOPED A HAIRLINE CRACK.
JUST A TINY CRACK.
THE BUILDING WAS BARELY A YEAR OLD.
IT WAS PROBABLY JUST THE RESULT OF SOME MYSTERIOUSLY SHODDY WORKMAN-SHIP.
THIS ISN'T THE TIME FOR JOKES, ARNOLD.
SORRY! THREE YEARS AGO IN PERSIA, RIGHT?
HMMM... NOTHING UNUSUAL.
THE DATA ONLY SHOWS SOME SMOKE...

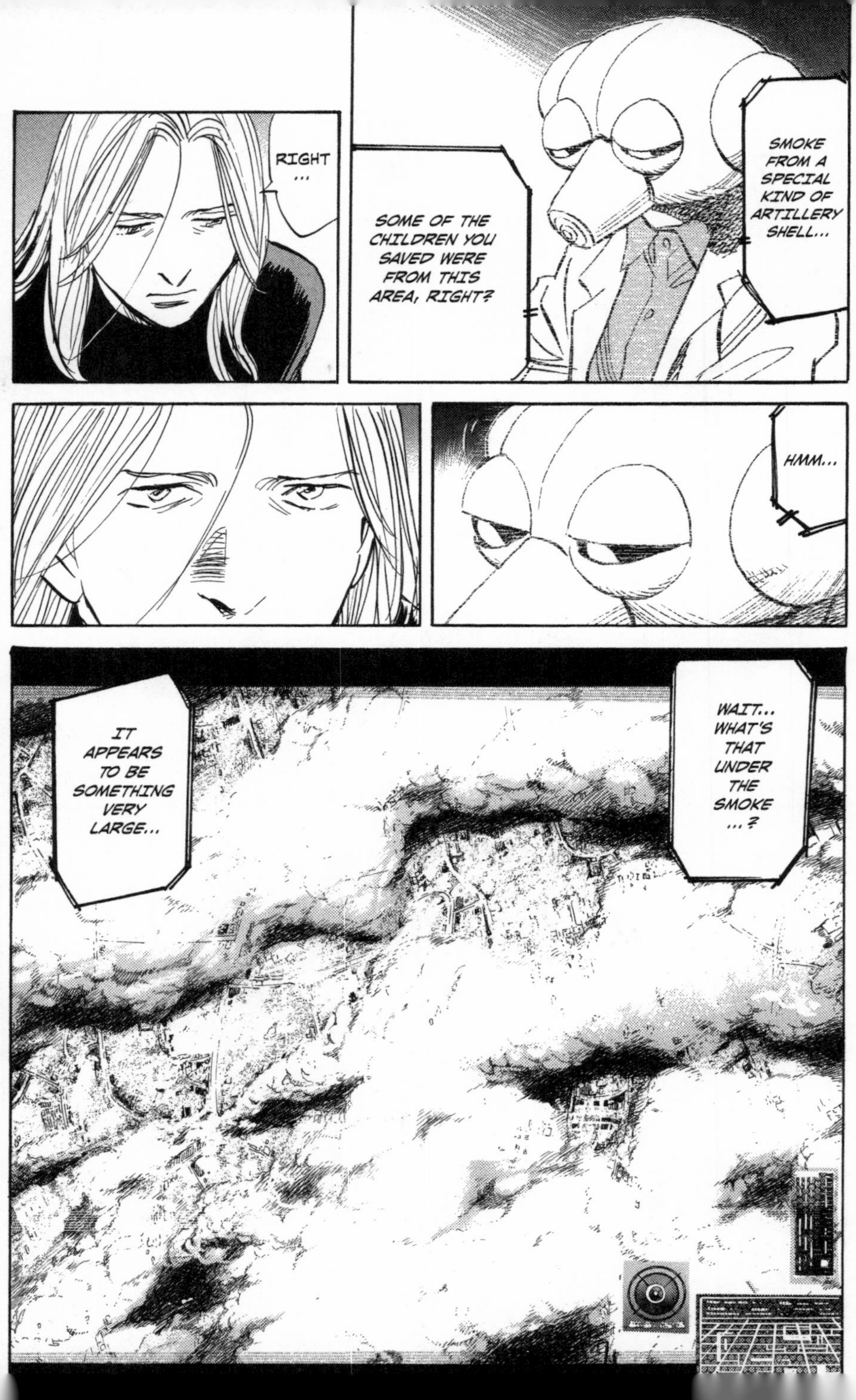
SMOKE FROM A SPECIAL KIND OF ARTILLERY SHELL...
SOME OF THE CHILDREN YOU SAVED WERE FROM THIS AREA, RIGHT?
RIGHT ...
HMM...
WAIT... WHAT'S THAT UNDER THE SMOKE ...?
IT APPEARS TO BE SOMETHING VERY LARGE...

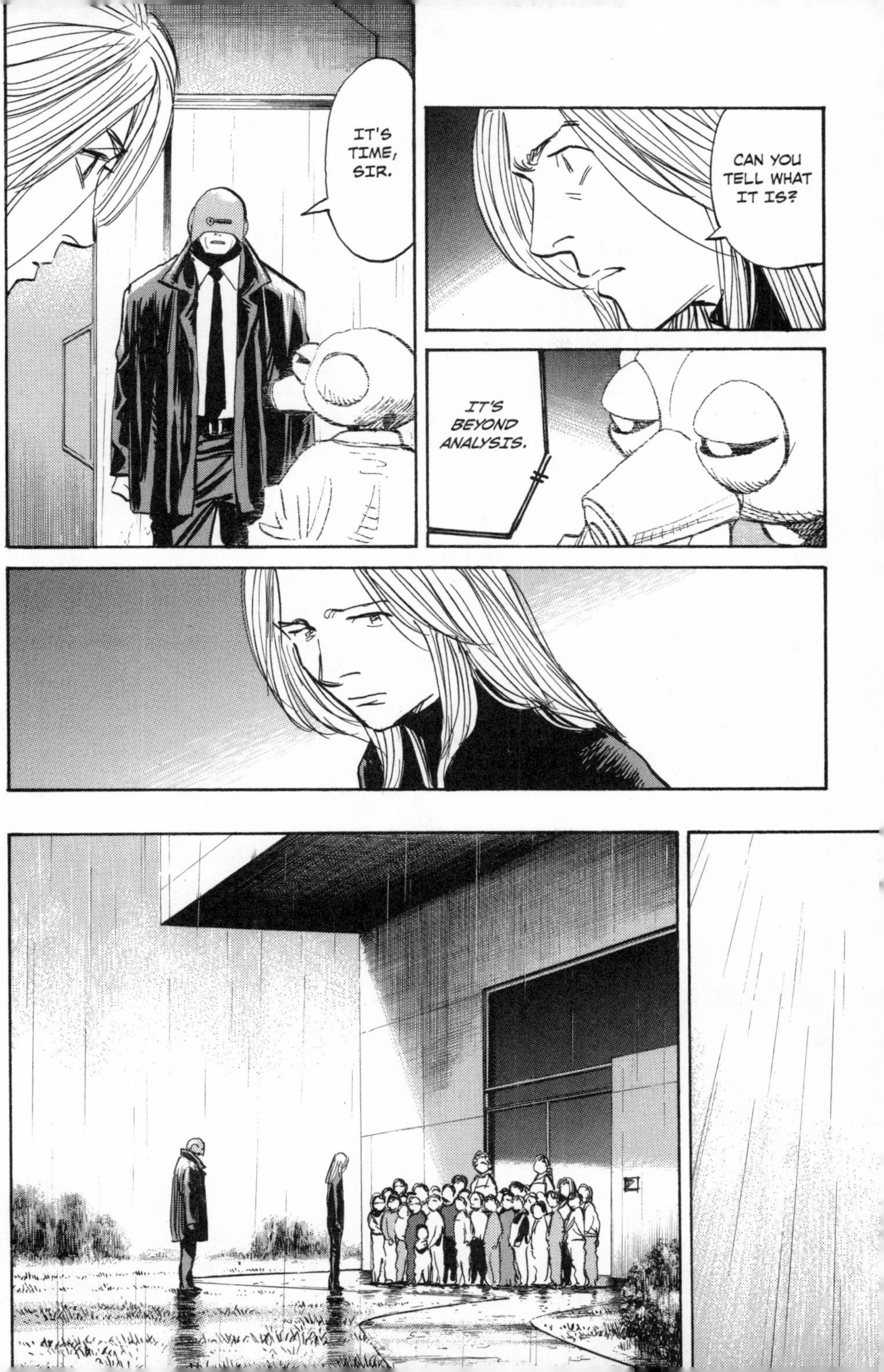
CAN YOU TELL WHAT IT IS?
IT'S BEYOND ANALYSIS.
IT'S TIME, SIR.

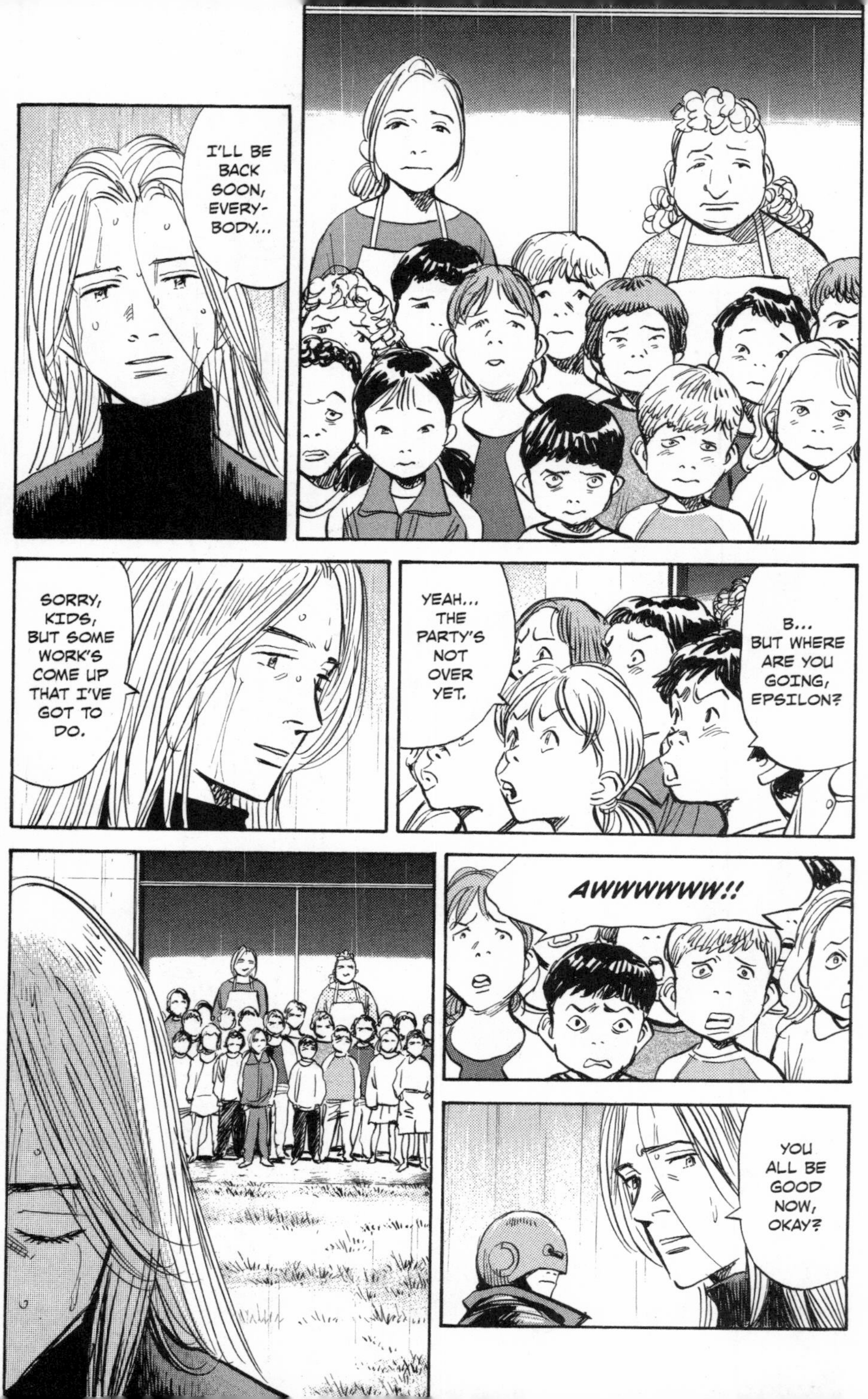
I'LL BE BACK SOON, EVERY-BODY...
B... BUT WHERE ARE YOU GOING, EPSILON?
YEAH... THE PARTY'S NOT OVER YET.
SORRY, KIDS, BUT SOME WORK'S COME UP THAT I'VE GOT TO DO.
AWWWWWW!!
YOU ALL BE GOOD NOW, OKAY?

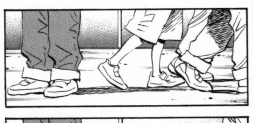

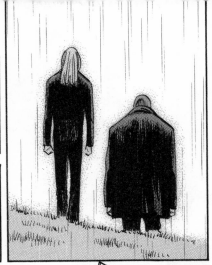

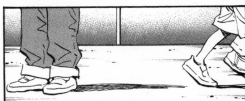

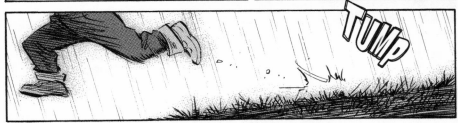

TUMP

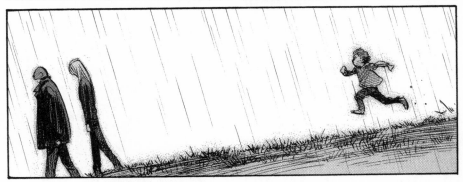

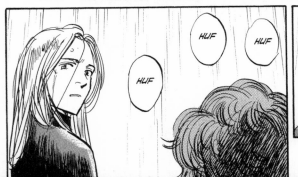

HUF

HUF

HUF

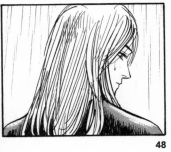

48

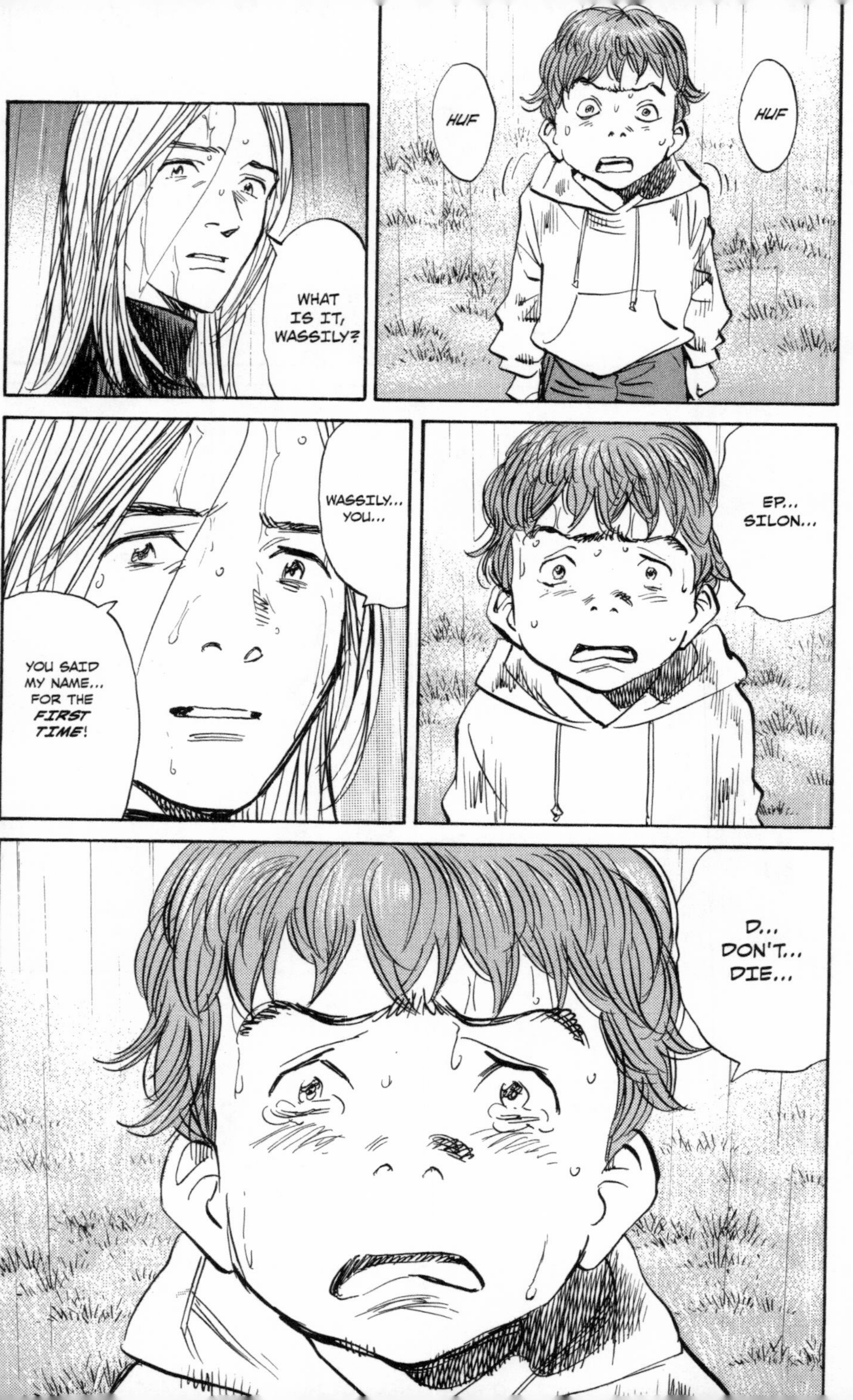
HUF
HUF
WHAT IS IT, WASSILY?
EP... SILON...
WASSILY... YOU...
YOU SAID MY NAME... FOR THE *FIRST TIME*!
D... DON'T... DIE...

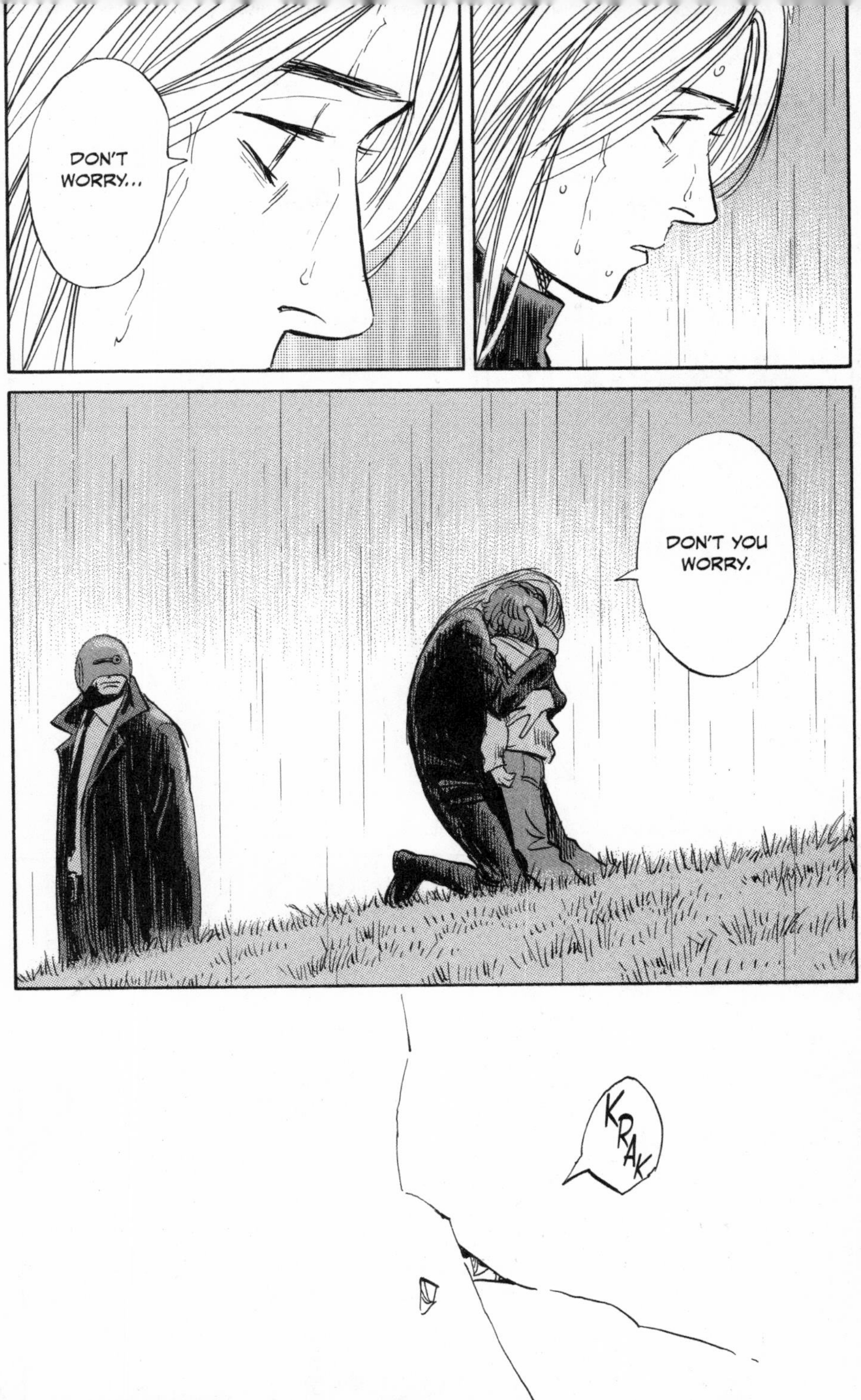
DON'T WORRY...
DON'T YOU WORRY.
KRAK

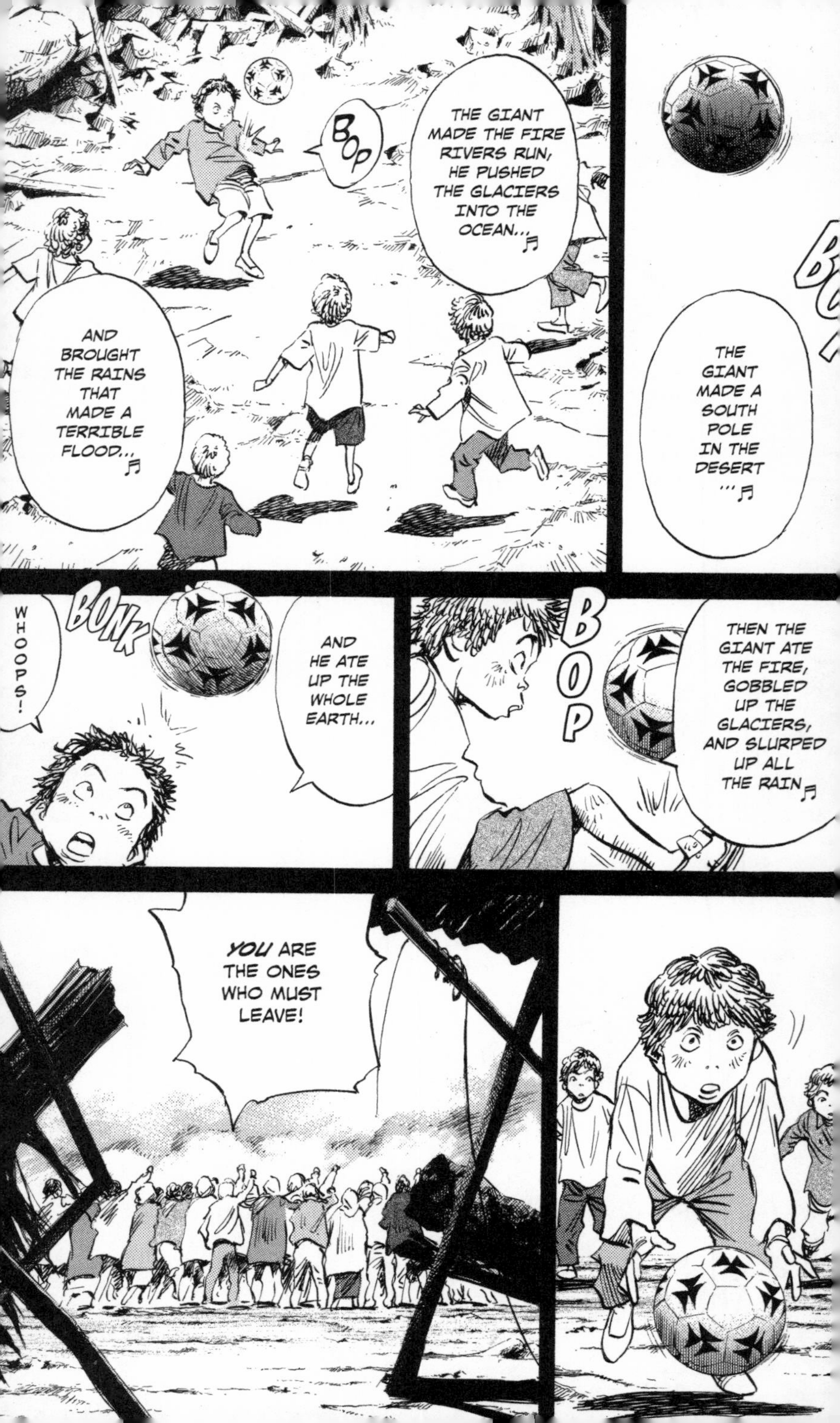
THE GIANT MADE A SOUTH POLE IN THE DESERT…♬
THE GIANT MADE THE FIRE RIVERS RUN, HE PUSHED THE GLACIERS INTO THE OCEAN…♬
BOP
AND BROUGHT THE RAINS THAT MADE A TERRIBLE FLOOD…♬
THEN THE GIANT ATE THE FIRE, GOBBLED UP THE GLACIERS, AND SLURPED UP ALL THE RAIN♬
BOP
BOP
AND HE ATE UP THE WHOLE EARTH…
BONK
WHOOPS!
YOU ARE THE ONES WHO MUST LEAVE!

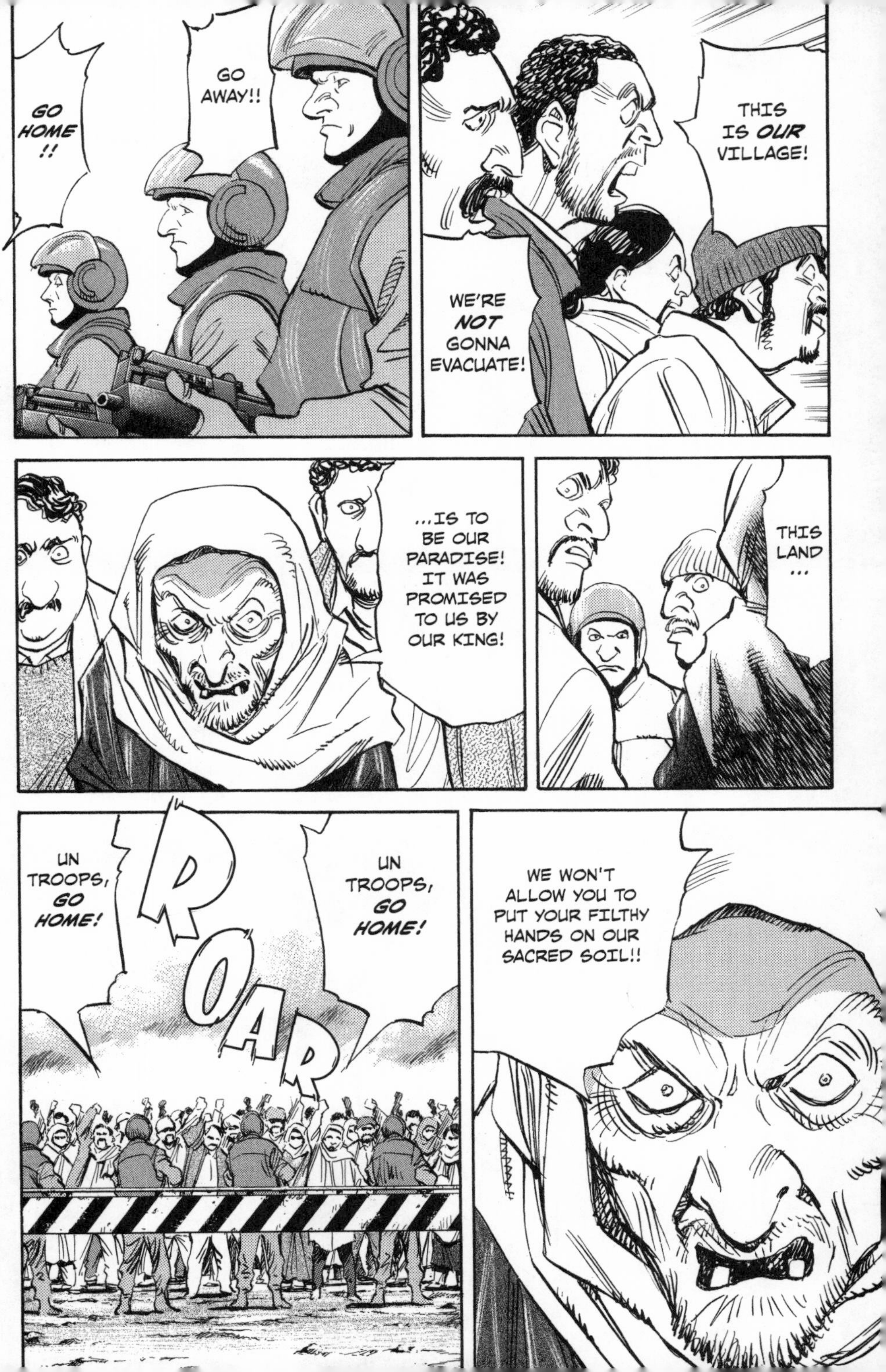
THIS IS OUR VILLAGE!
WE'RE NOT GONNA EVACUATE!
GO AWAY!!
GO HOME!!
THIS LAND ...
...IS TO BE OUR PARADISE! IT WAS PROMISED TO US BY OUR KING!
WE WON'T ALLOW YOU TO PUT YOUR FILTHY HANDS ON OUR SACRED SOIL!!
UN TROOPS, GO HOME!
ROAR
UN TROOPS, GO HOME!

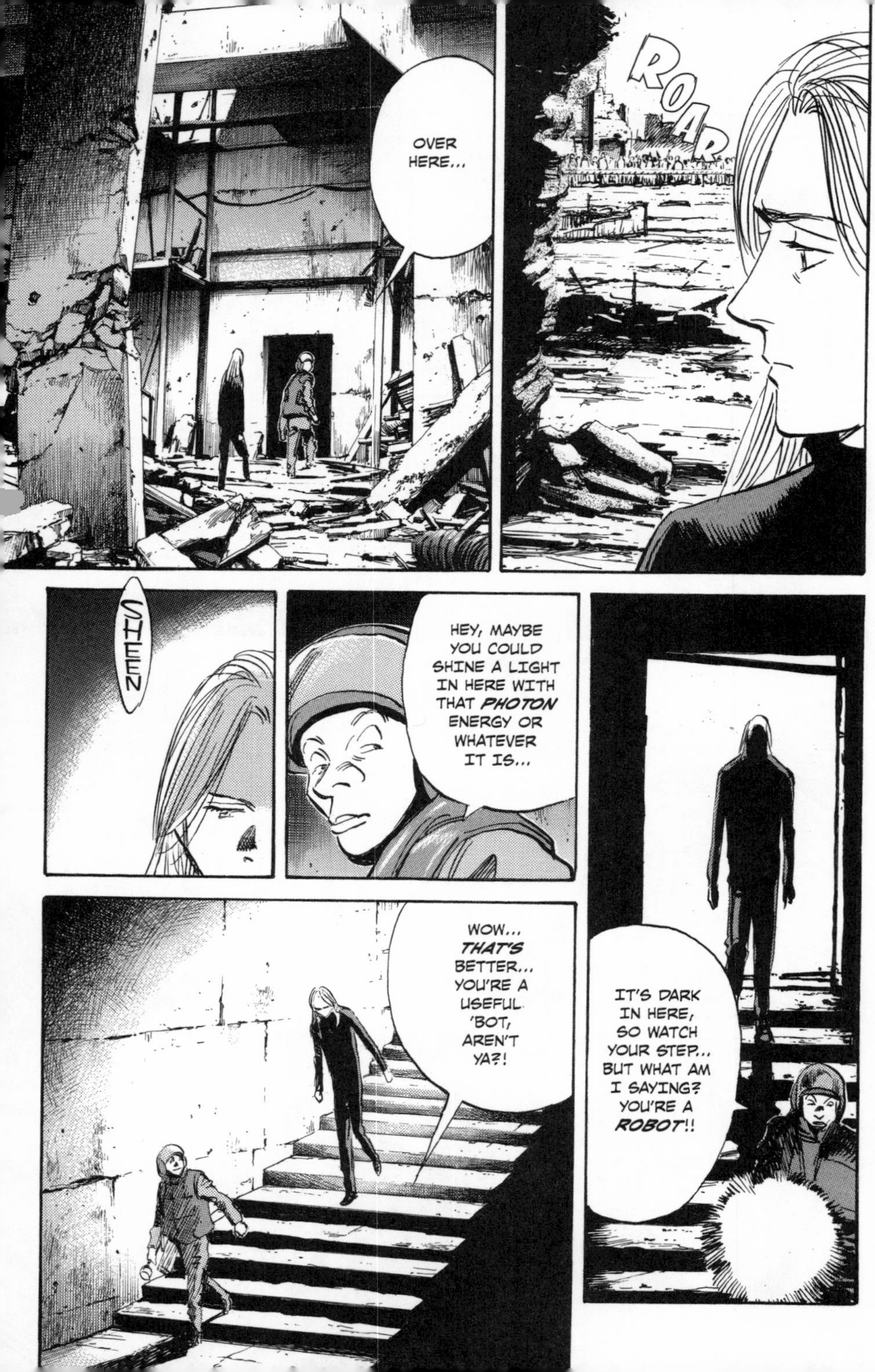
ROAR
OVER HERE...
IT'S DARK IN HERE, SO WATCH YOUR STEP... BUT WHAT AM I SAYING? YOU'RE A *ROBOT*!!
HEY, MAYBE YOU COULD SHINE A LIGHT IN HERE WITH THAT *PHOTON* ENERGY OR WHATEVER IT IS...
SHEEN
WOW... *THAT'S* BETTER... YOU'RE A USEFUL 'BOT, AREN'T YA?!

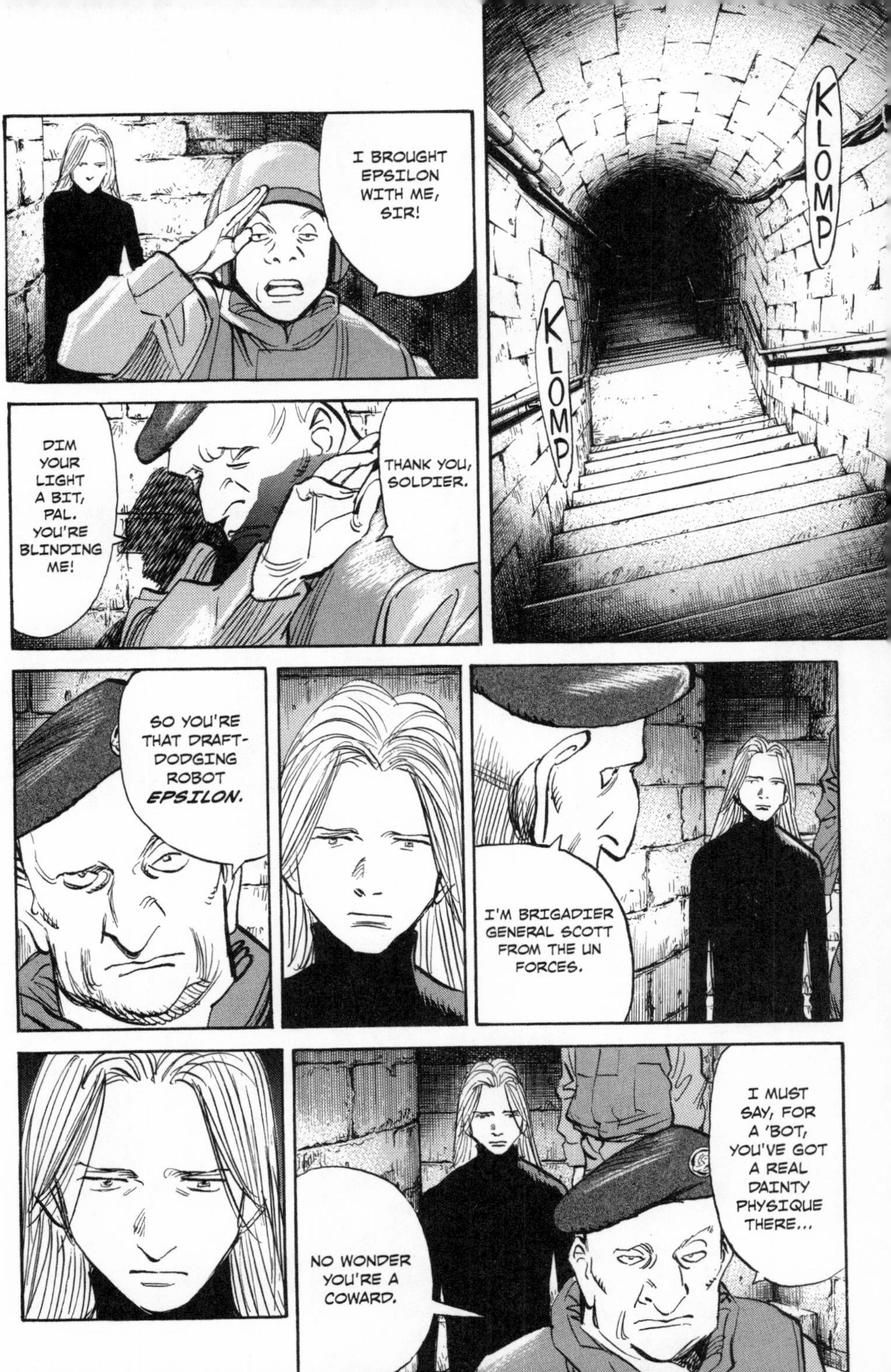
KLOMP
KLOMP
I BROUGHT EPSILON WITH ME, SIR!
THANK YOU, SOLDIER.
DIM YOUR LIGHT A BIT, PAL. YOU'RE BLINDING ME!
I'M BRIGADIER GENERAL SCOTT FROM THE UN FORCES.
SO YOU'RE THAT DRAFT-DODGING ROBOT ***EPSILON***.
I MUST SAY, FOR A 'BOT, YOU'VE GOT A REAL DAINTY PHYSIQUE THERE...
NO WONDER YOU'RE A COWARD.

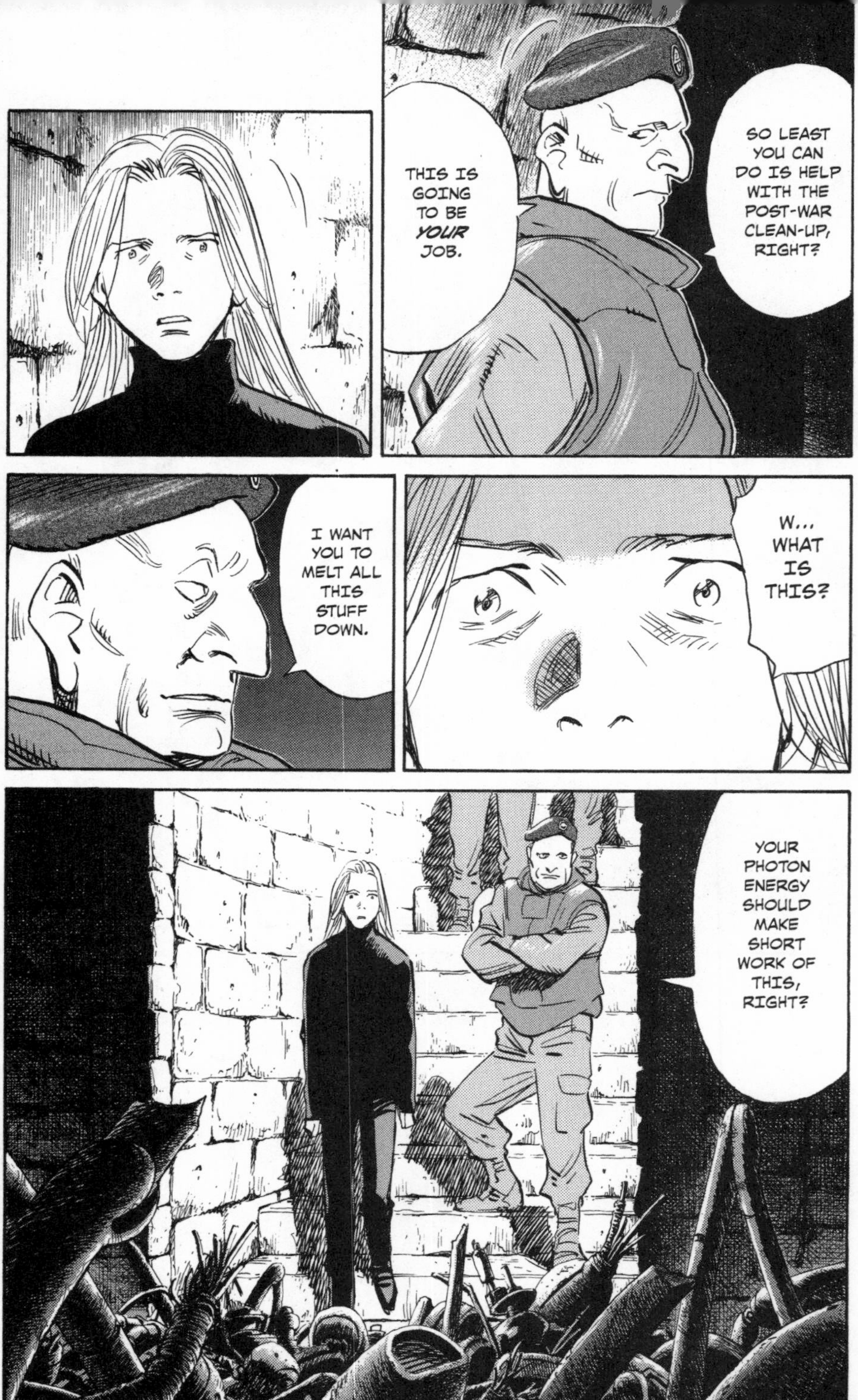
SO LEAST YOU CAN DO IS HELP WITH THE POST-WAR CLEAN-UP, RIGHT?
THIS IS GOING TO BE *YOUR* JOB.
W... WHAT IS THIS?
I WANT YOU TO MELT ALL THIS STUFF DOWN.
YOUR PHOTON ENERGY SHOULD MAKE SHORT WORK OF THIS, RIGHT?

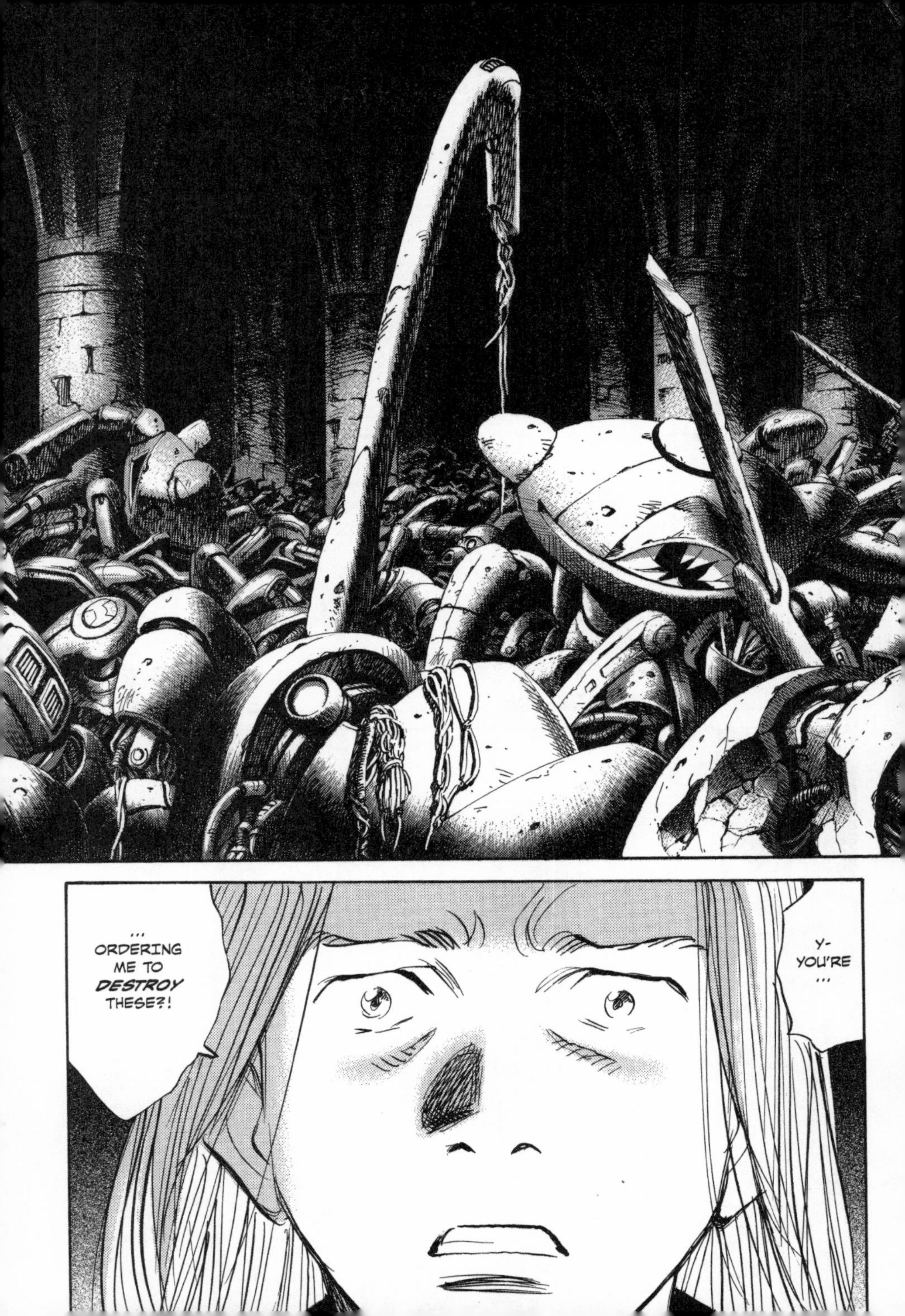
Y- YOU'RE ...
... ORDERING ME TO DESTROY THESE?!

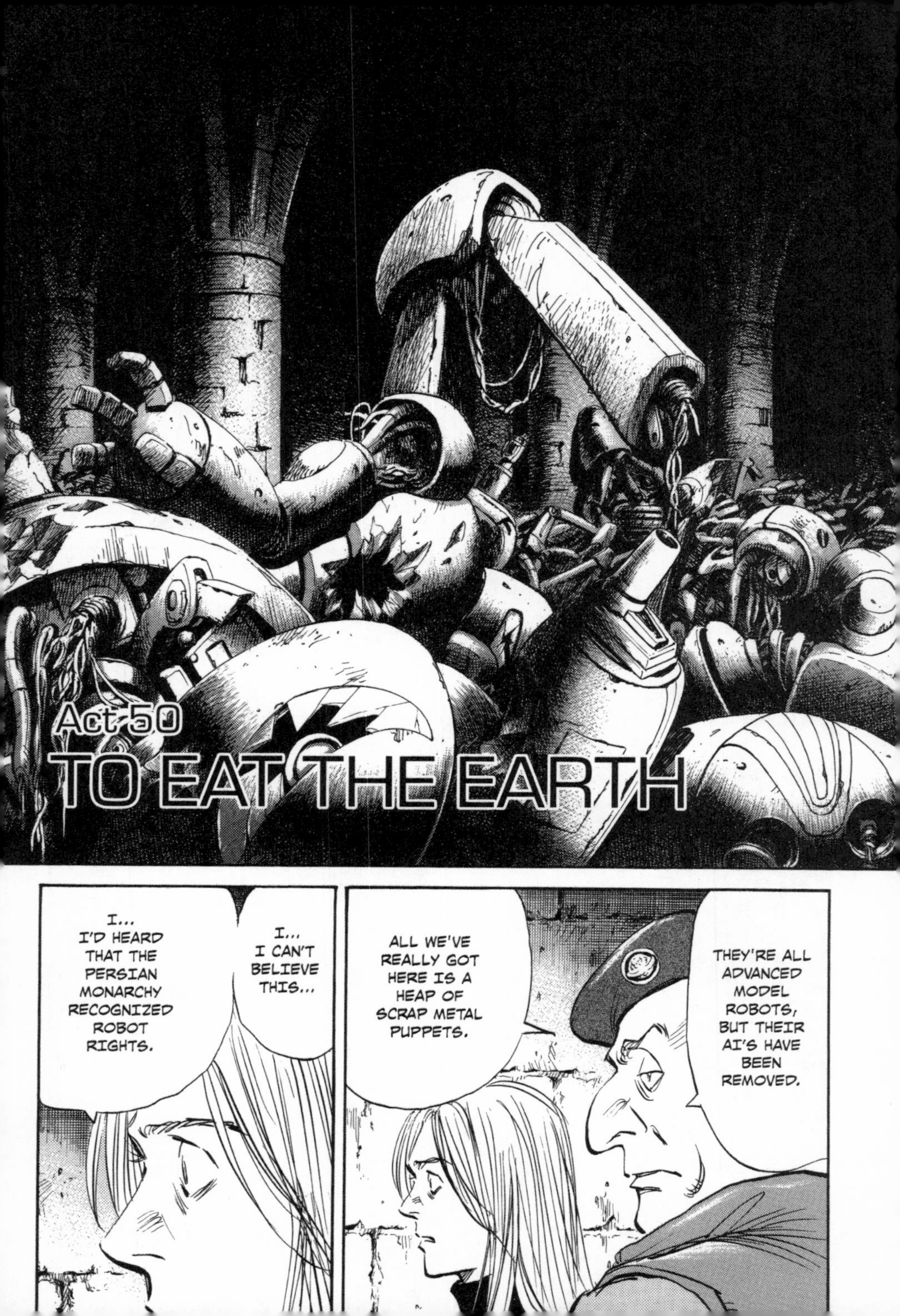
Act 50
TO EAT THE EARTH
THEY'RE ALL ADVANCED MODEL ROBOTS, BUT THEIR AI'S HAVE BEEN REMOVED.
ALL WE'VE REALLY GOT HERE IS A HEAP OF SCRAP METAL PUPPETS.
I... I CAN'T BELIEVE THIS...
I... I'D HEARD THAT THE PERSIAN MONARCHY RECOGNIZED ROBOT RIGHTS.

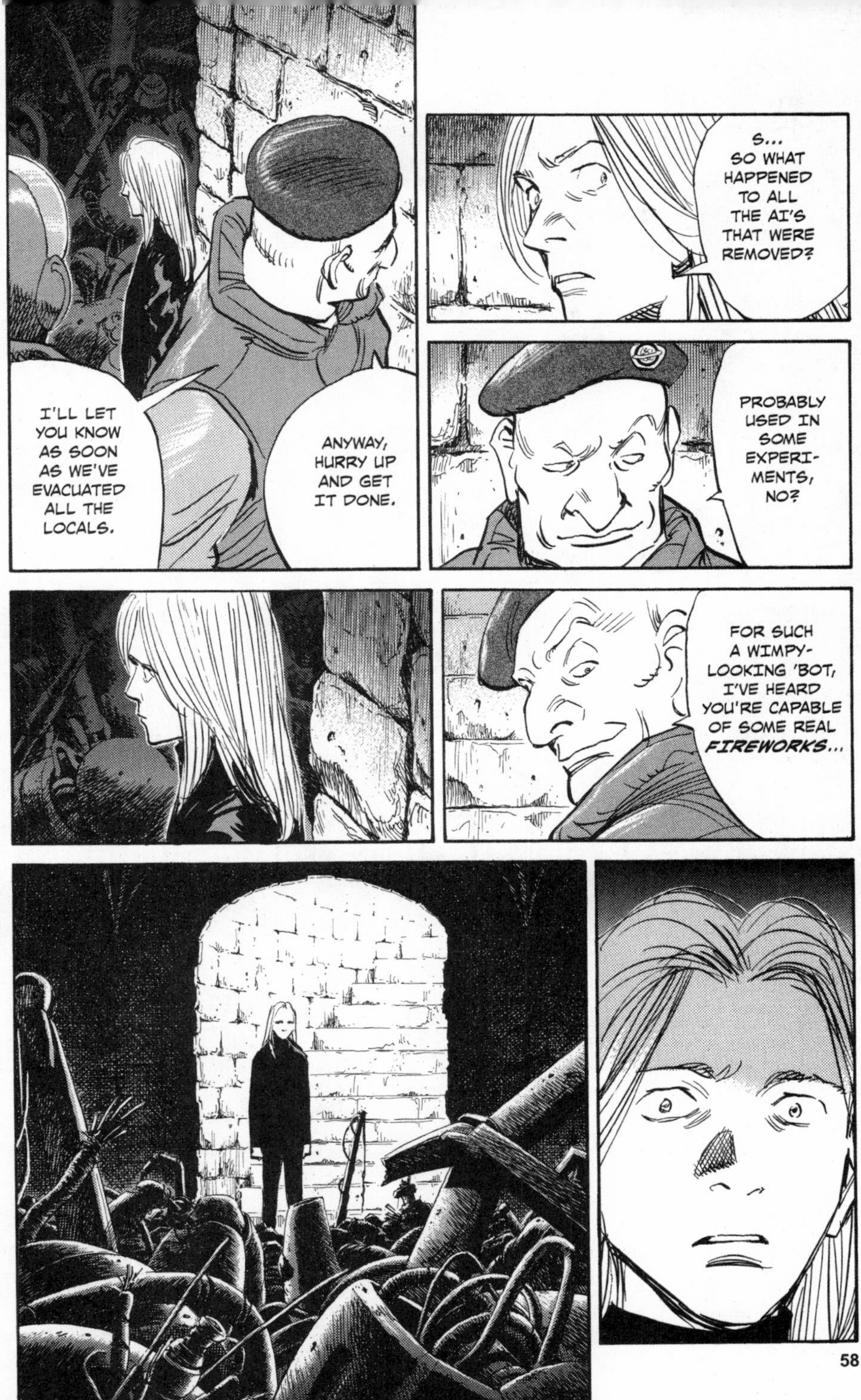
S... SO WHAT HAPPENED TO ALL THE AI'S THAT WERE REMOVED?
PROBABLY USED IN SOME EXPERI-MENTS, NO?
ANYWAY, HURRY UP AND GET IT DONE.
I'LL LET YOU KNOW AS SOON AS WE'VE EVACUATED ALL THE LOCALS.
FOR SUCH A WIMPY-LOOKING 'BOT, I'VE HEARD YOU'RE CAPABLE OF SOME REAL FIREWORKS...

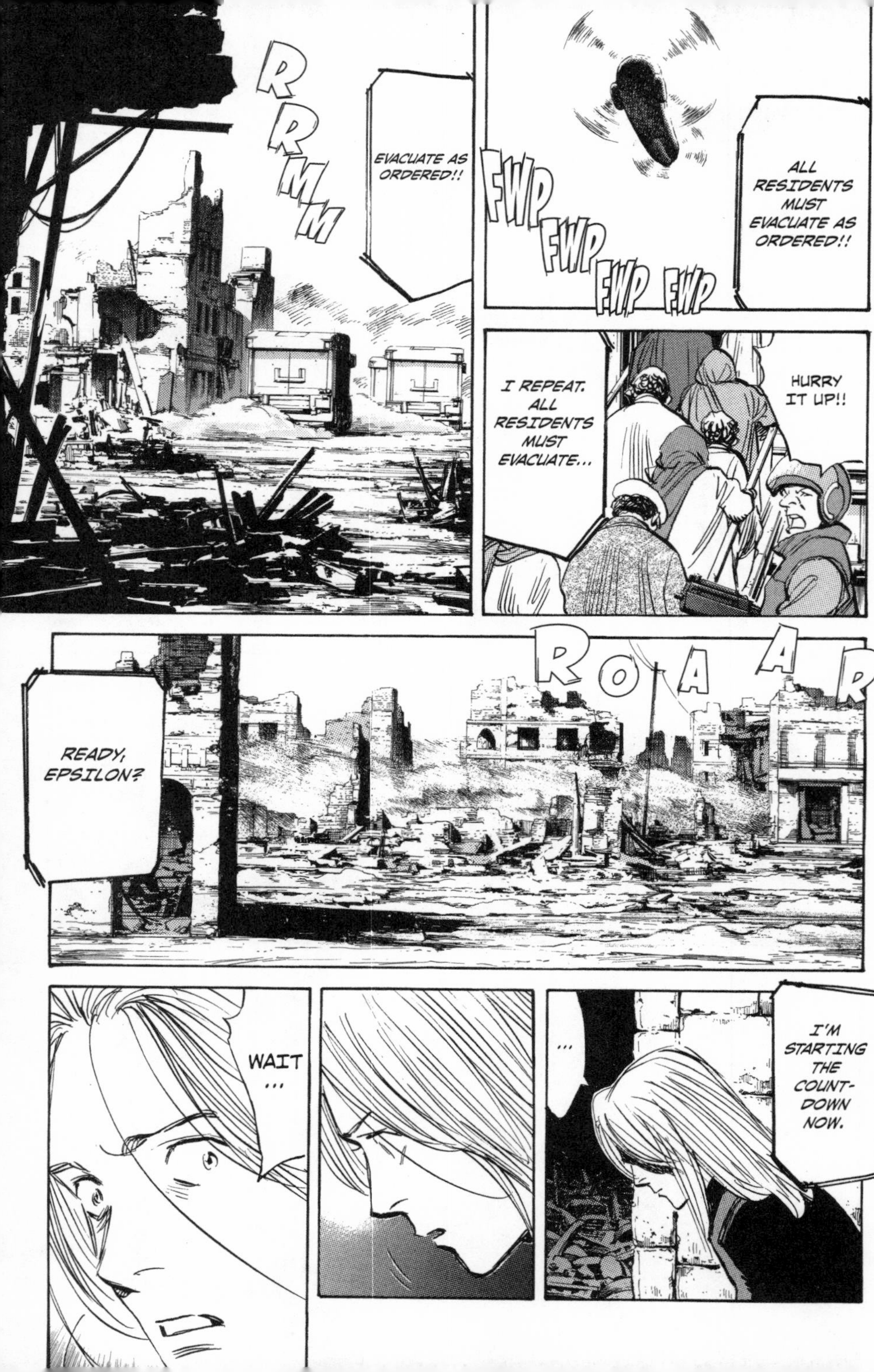

ALL RESIDENTS MUST EVACUATE AS ORDERED!!
FWP FWP FWP FWP
HURRY IT UP!!
I REPEAT. ALL RESIDENTS MUST EVACUATE...
RRMM
EVACUATE AS ORDERED!!
ROAAR
READY, EPSILON?
I'M STARTING THE COUNT-DOWN NOW.
...
WAIT ...

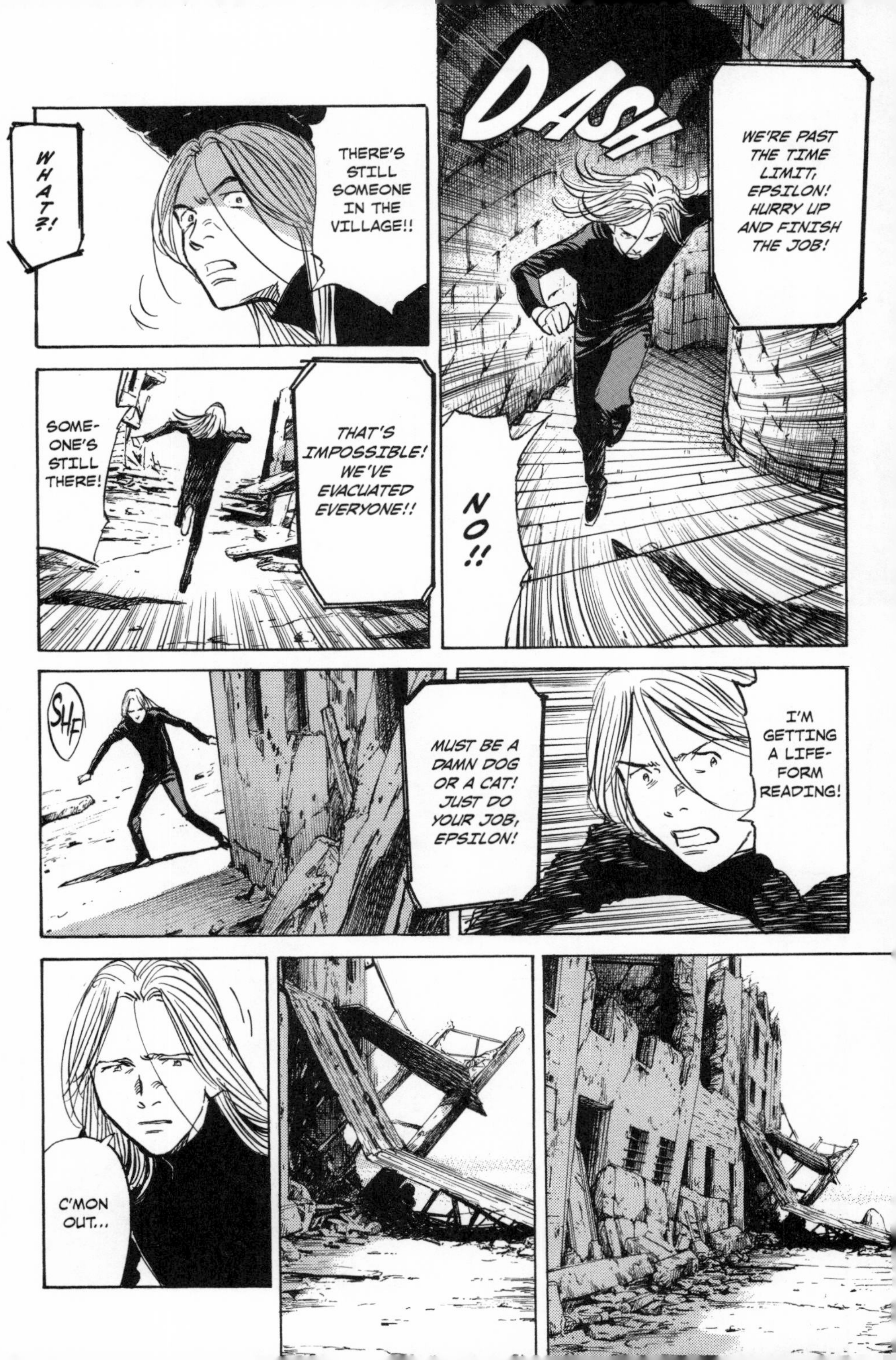
WE'RE PAST THE TIME LIMIT, EPSILON! HURRY UP AND FINISH THE JOB!
DASH
NO!!
THERE'S STILL SOMEONE IN THE VILLAGE!!
WHAT?!
THAT'S IMPOSSIBLE! WE'VE EVACUATED EVERYONE!!
SOME-ONE'S STILL THERE!
I'M GETTING A LIFE-FORM READING!
MUST BE A DAMN DOG OR A CAT! JUST DO YOUR JOB, EPSILON!
SHF
C'MON OUT...

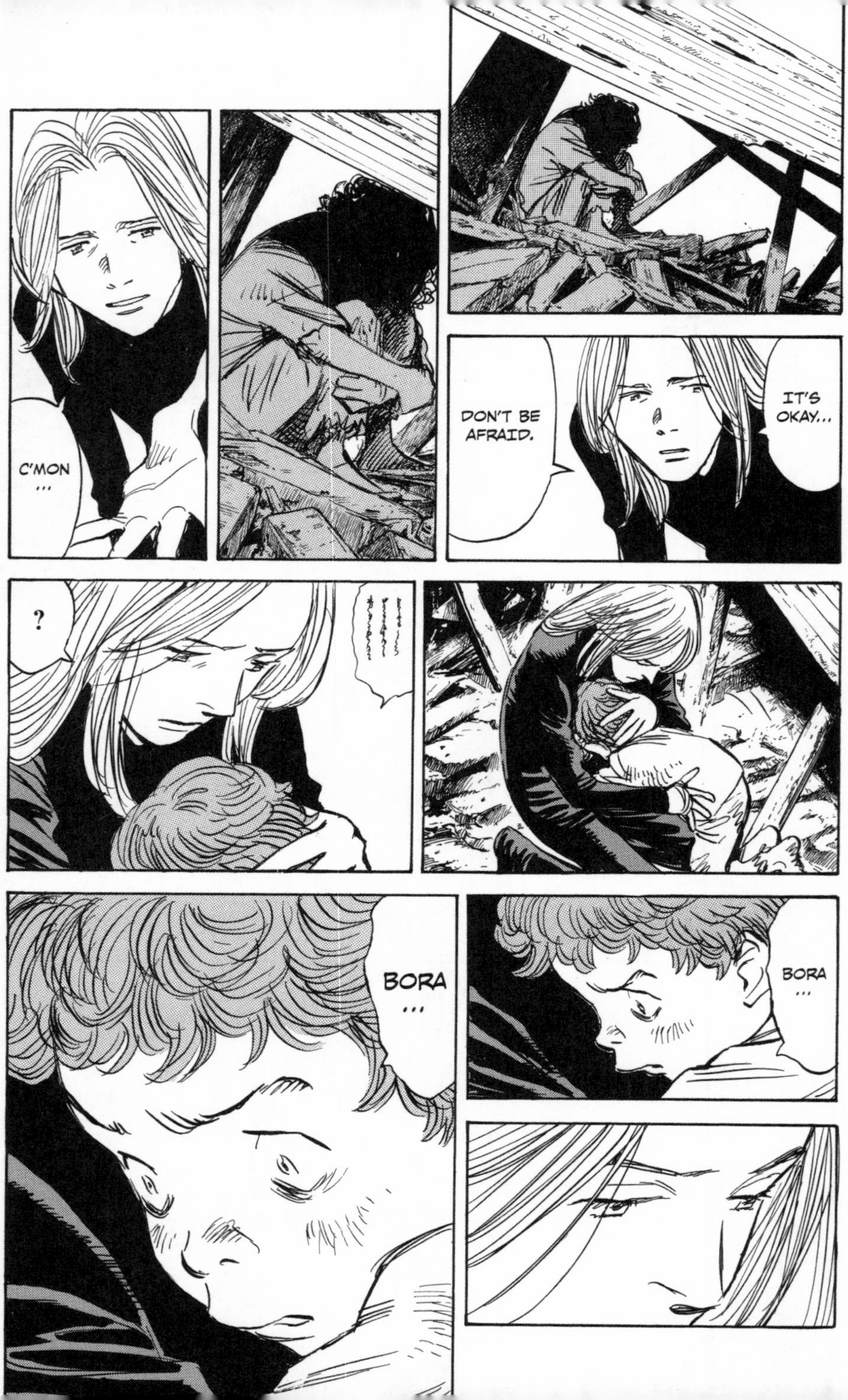
IT'S OKAY...
DON'T BE AFRAID.
C'MON ...
?
BORA ...
BORA ...

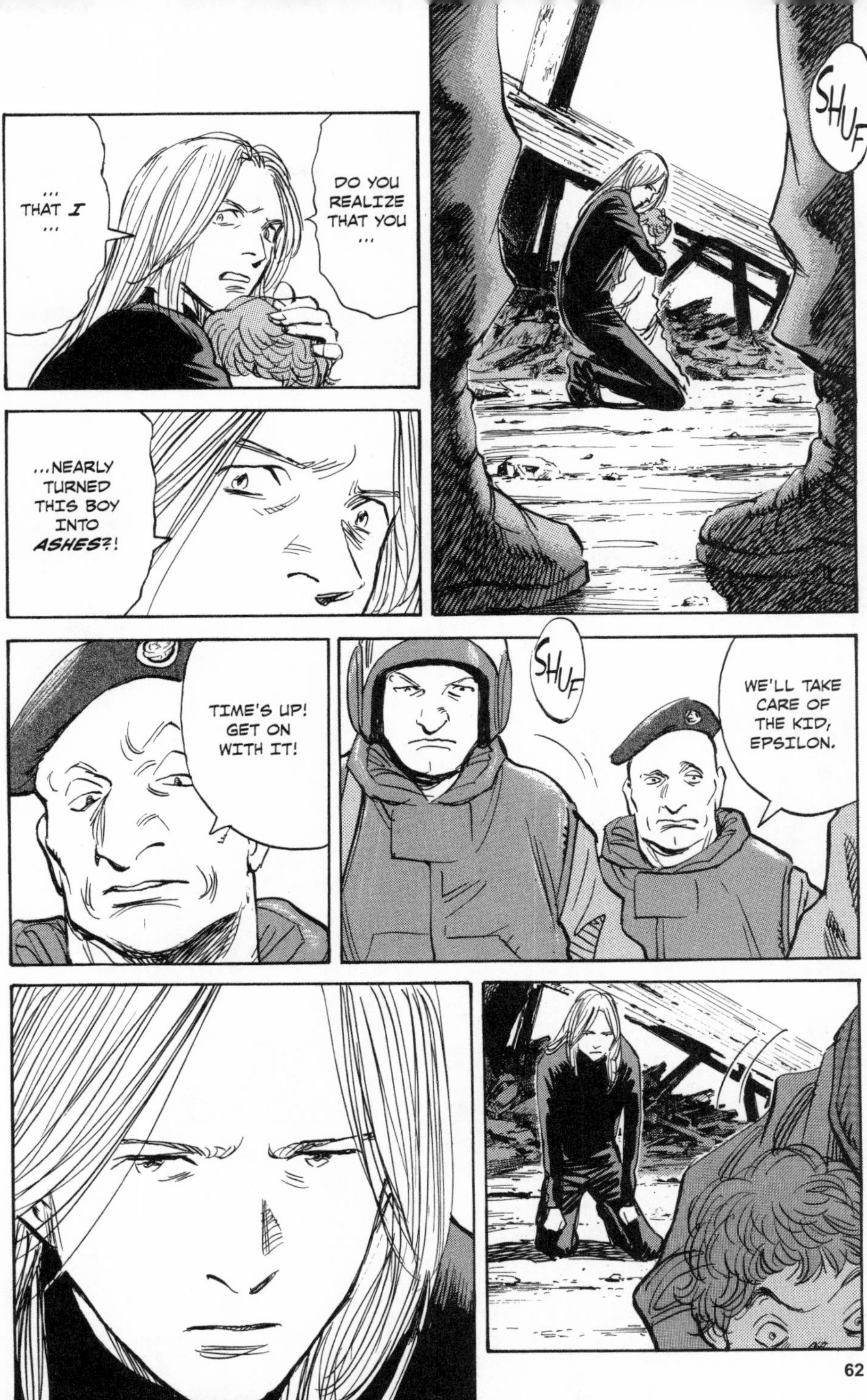
SHUF
DO YOU REALIZE THAT YOU ...
... THAT I ...
...NEARLY TURNED THIS BOY INTO ASHES?!
WE'LL TAKE CARE OF THE KID, EPSILON.
SHUF
TIME'S UP! GET ON WITH IT!

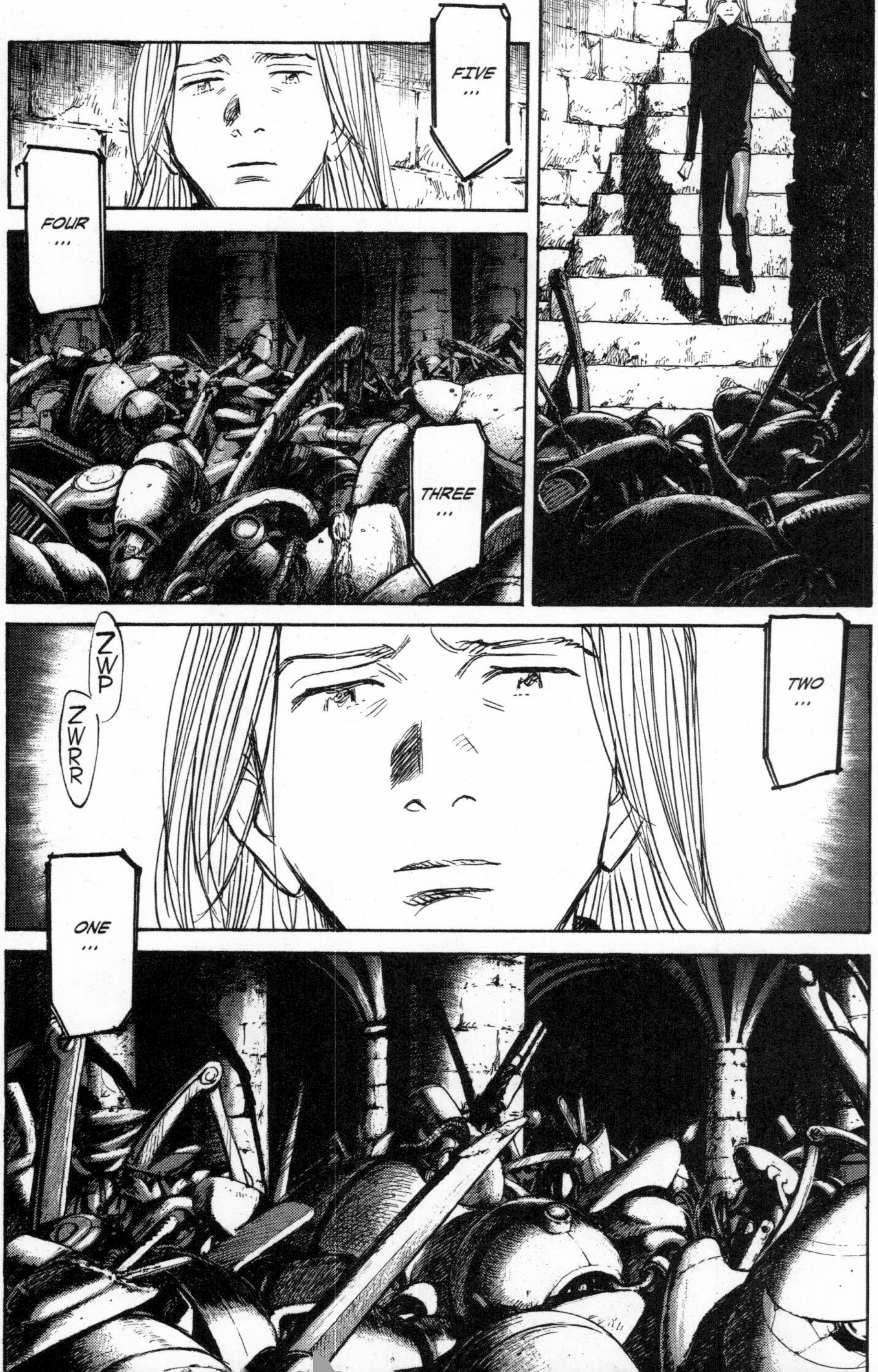
FIVE ...
FOUR ...
THREE ...
TWO ...
ZWP
ZWRR
ONE ...

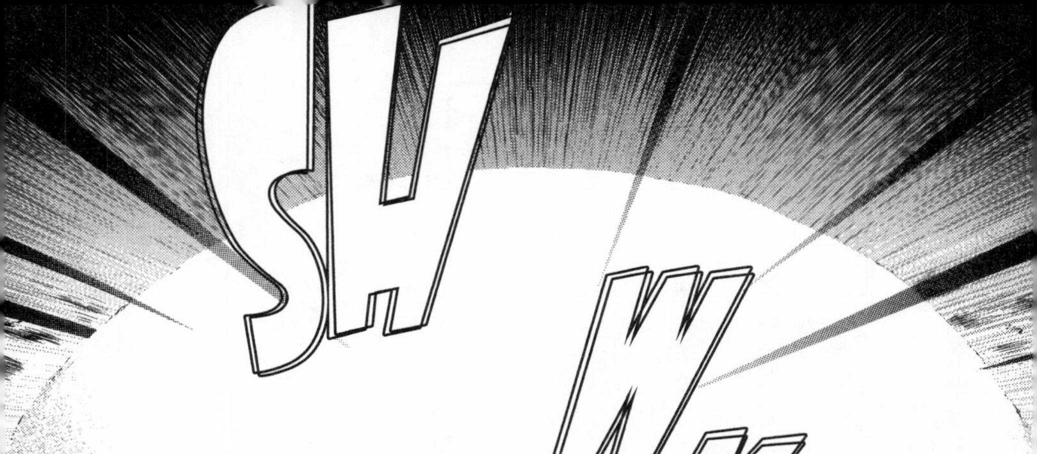
SHWM
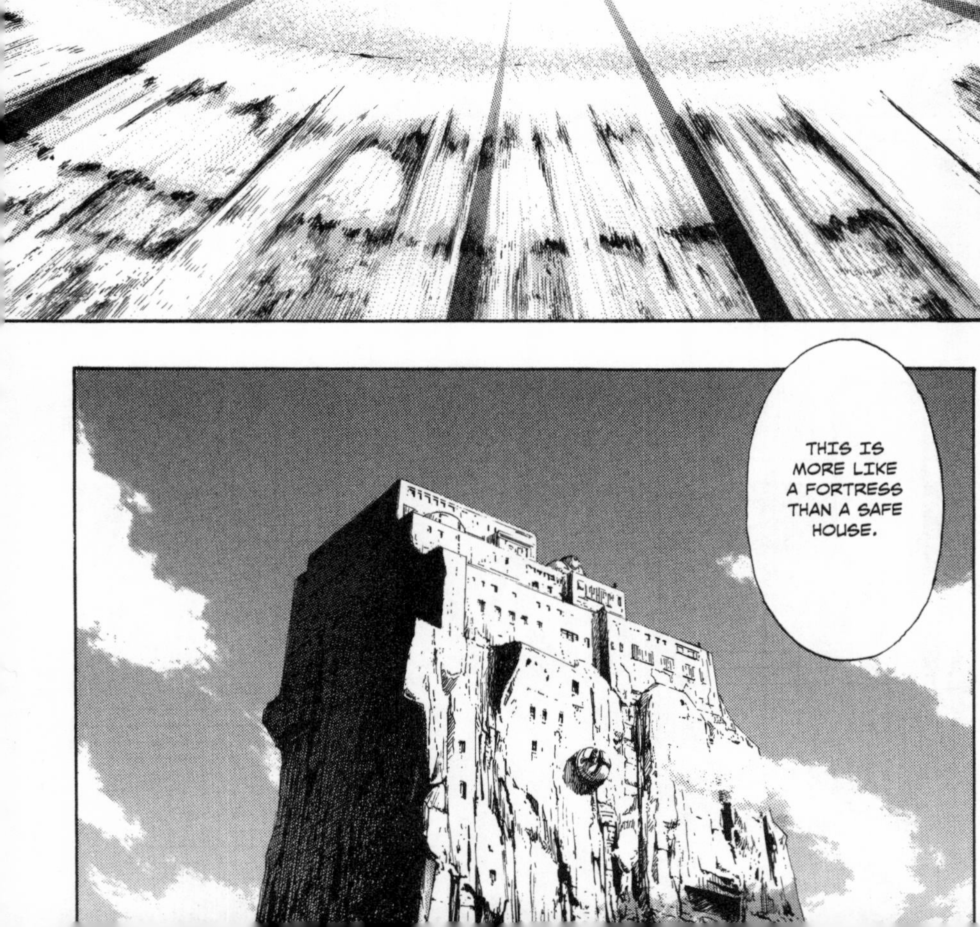
THIS IS MORE LIKE A FORTRESS THAN A SAFE HOUSE.

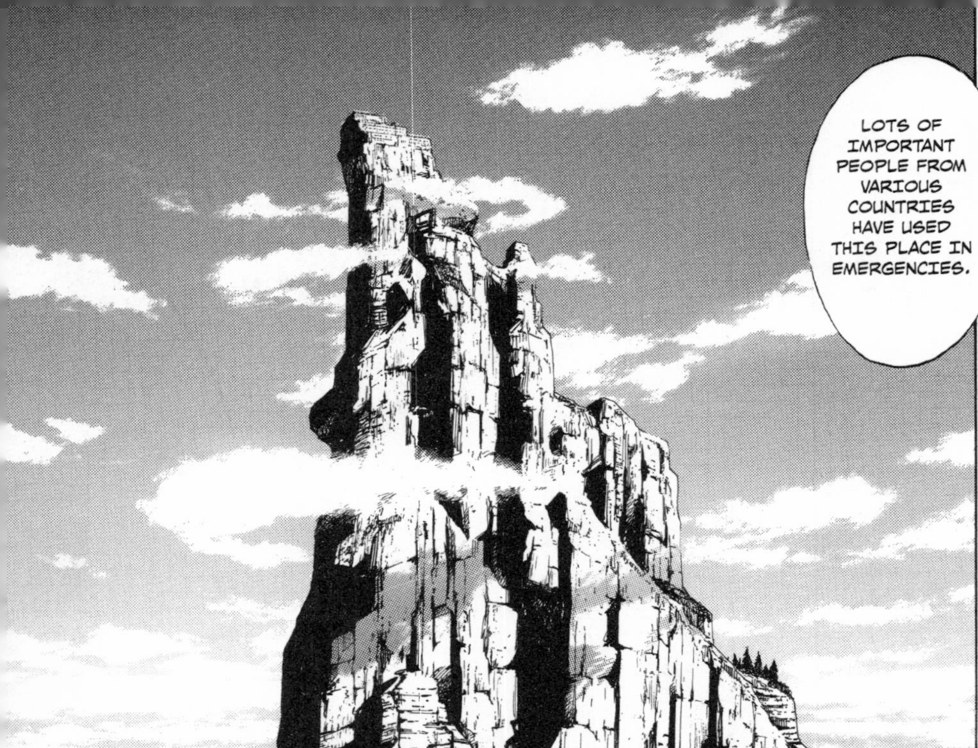
LOTS OF IMPORTANT PEOPLE FROM VARIOUS COUNTRIES HAVE USED THIS PLACE IN EMERGENCIES.

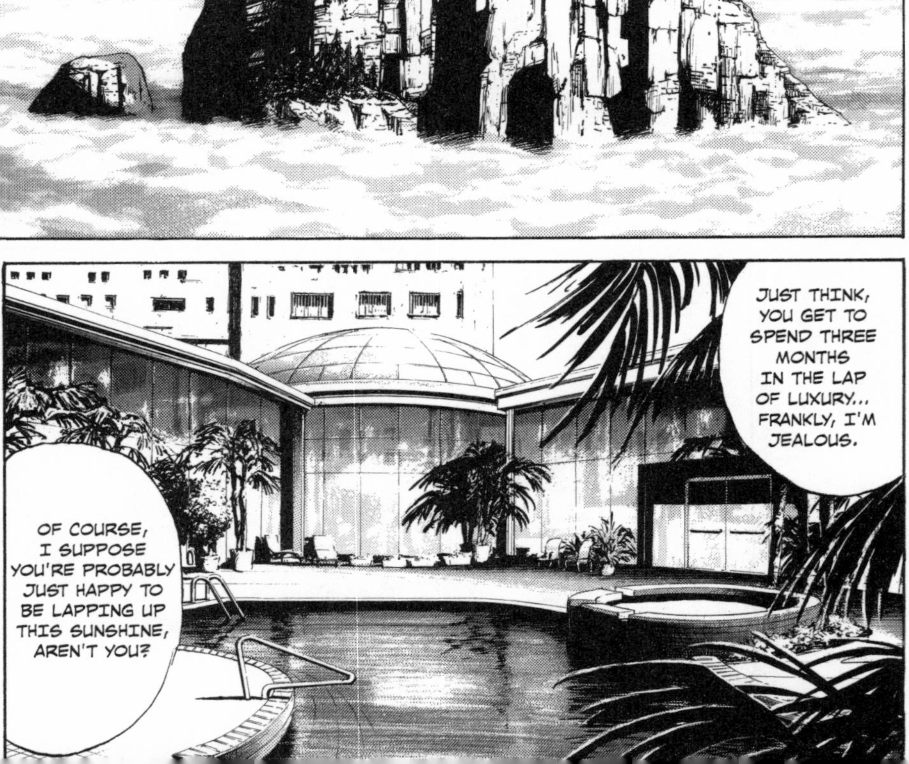
JUST THINK, YOU GET TO SPEND THREE MONTHS IN THE LAP OF LUXURY... FRANKLY, I'M JEALOUS.
OF COURSE, I SUPPOSE YOU'RE PROBABLY JUST HAPPY TO BE LAPPING UP THIS SUNSHINE, AREN'T YOU?

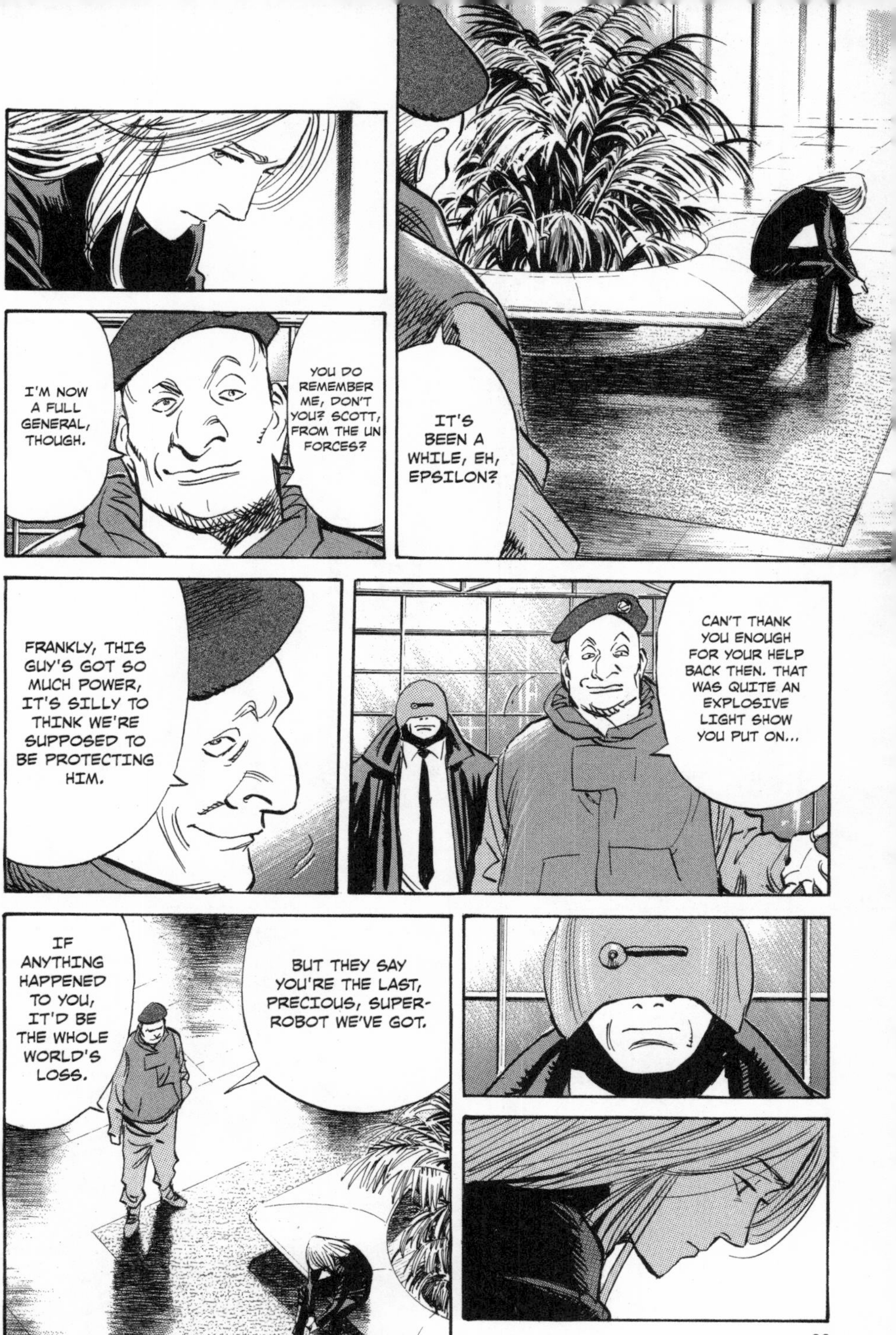
IT'S BEEN A WHILE, EH, EPSILON?
YOU DO REMEMBER ME, DON'T YOU? SCOTT, FROM THE UN FORCES?
I'M NOW A FULL GENERAL, THOUGH.
CAN'T THANK YOU ENOUGH FOR YOUR HELP BACK THEN. THAT WAS QUITE AN EXPLOSIVE LIGHT SHOW YOU PUT ON...
FRANKLY, THIS GUY'S GOT SO MUCH POWER, IT'S SILLY TO THINK WE'RE SUPPOSED TO BE PROTECTING HIM.
BUT THEY SAY YOU'RE THE LAST, PRECIOUS, SUPER-ROBOT WE'VE GOT.
IF ANYTHING HAPPENED TO YOU, IT'D BE THE WHOLE WORLD'S LOSS.

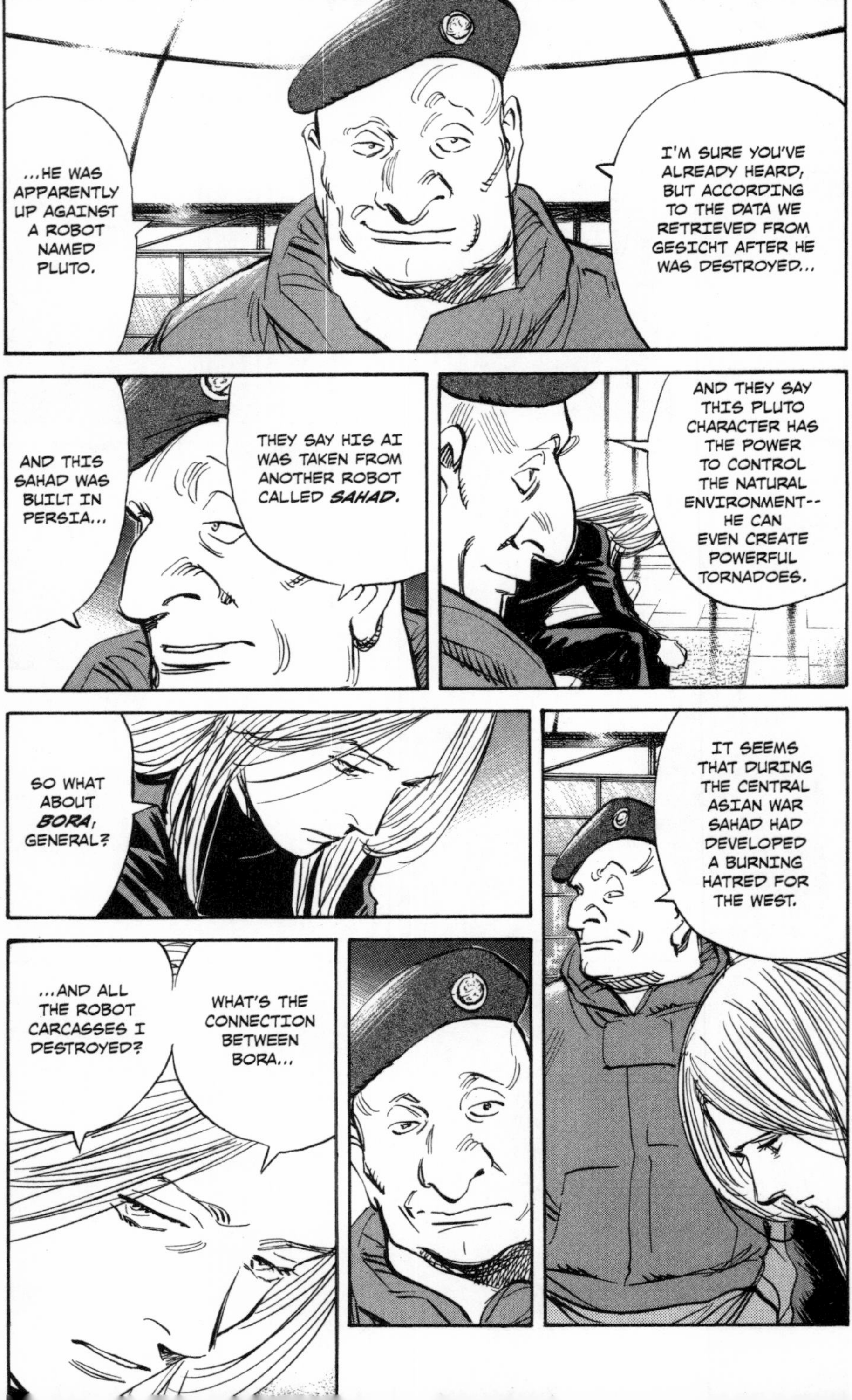
I'M SURE YOU'VE ALREADY HEARD, BUT ACCORDING TO THE DATA WE RETRIEVED FROM GESICHT AFTER HE WAS DESTROYED...
...HE WAS APPARENTLY UP AGAINST A ROBOT NAMED PLUTO.
AND THEY SAY THIS PLUTO CHARACTER HAS THE POWER TO CONTROL THE NATURAL ENVIRONMENT-- HE CAN EVEN CREATE POWERFUL TORNADOES.
THEY SAY HIS AI WAS TAKEN FROM ANOTHER ROBOT CALLED *SAHAD*.
AND THIS SAHAD WAS BUILT IN PERSIA...
IT SEEMS THAT DURING THE CENTRAL ASIAN WAR SAHAD HAD DEVELOPED A BURNING HATRED FOR THE WEST.
SO WHAT ABOUT *BORA*, GENERAL?
WHAT'S THE CONNECTION BETWEEN BORA...
...AND ALL THE ROBOT CARCASSES I DESTROYED?

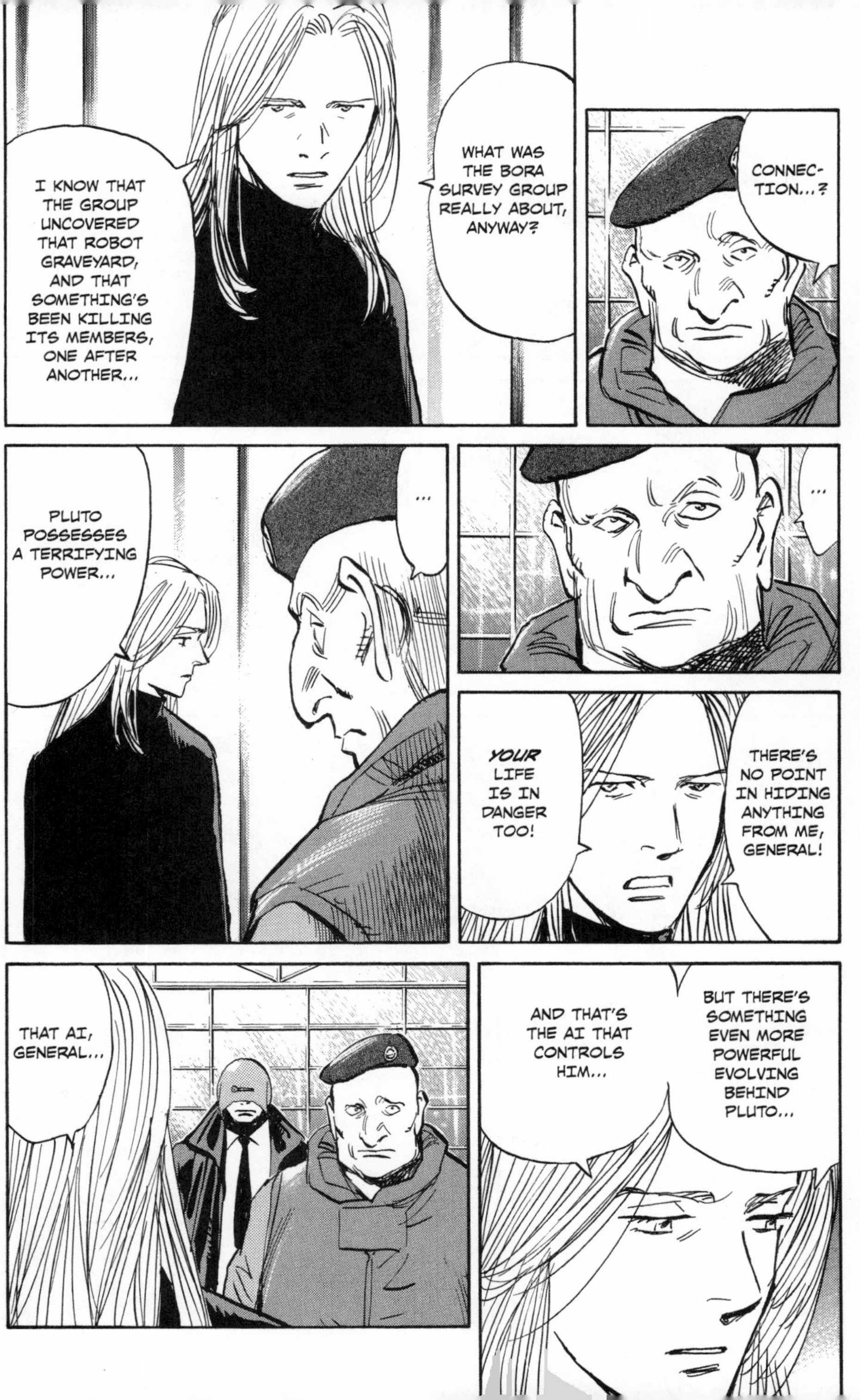
CONNEC-TION...?
WHAT WAS THE BORA SURVEY GROUP REALLY ABOUT, ANYWAY?
I KNOW THAT THE GROUP UNCOVERED THAT ROBOT GRAVEYARD, AND THAT SOMETHING'S BEEN KILLING ITS MEMBERS, ONE AFTER ANOTHER...
...
THERE'S NO POINT IN HIDING ANYTHING FROM ME, GENERAL!
YOUR LIFE IS IN DANGER TOO!
...
PLUTO POSSESSES A TERRIFYING POWER...
BUT THERE'S SOMETHING EVEN MORE POWERFUL EVOLVING BEHIND PLUTO...
AND THAT'S THE AI THAT CONTROLS HIM...
THAT AI, GENERAL...

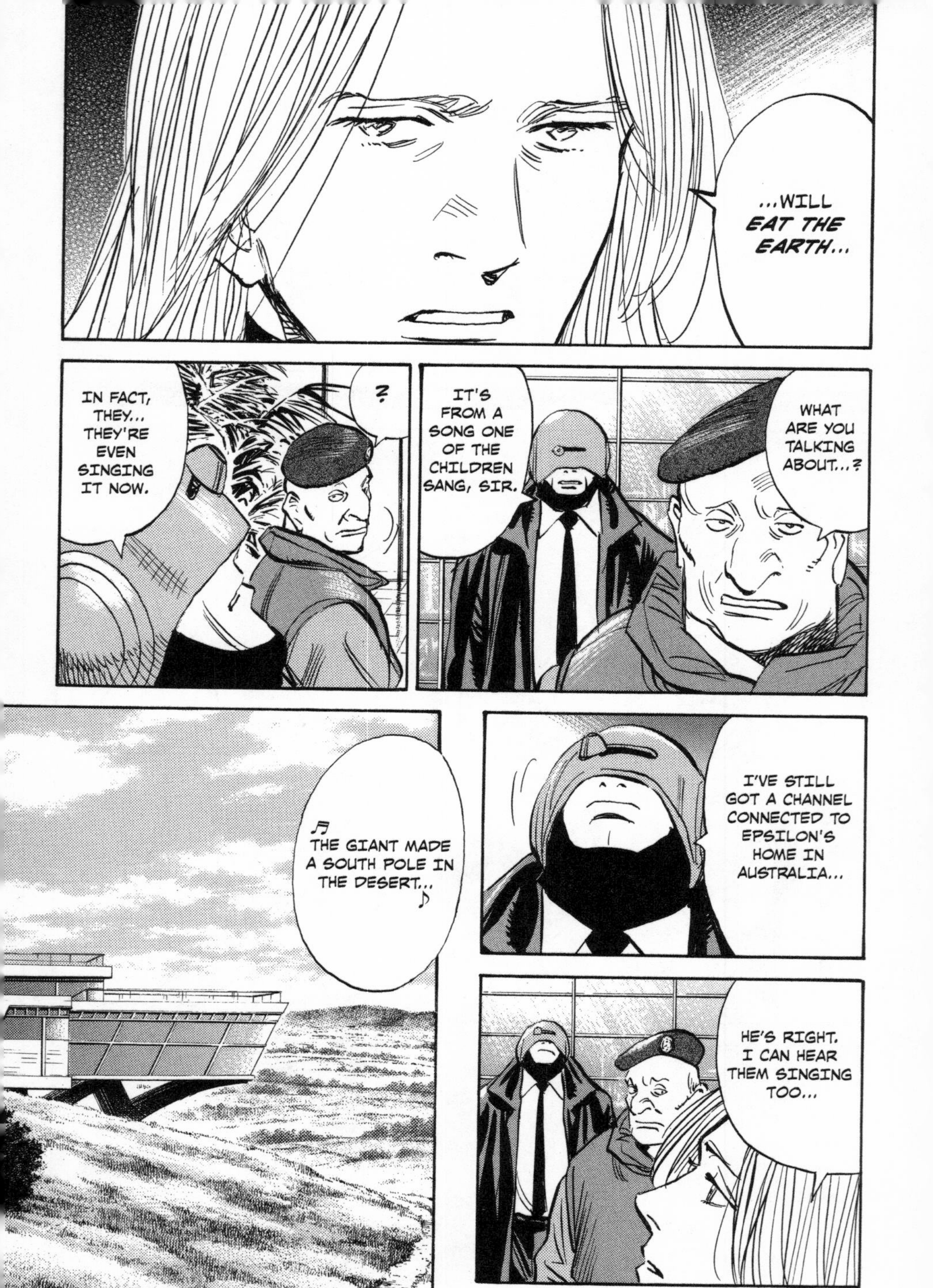
...WILL EAT THE EARTH...
WHAT ARE YOU TALKING ABOUT...?
IT'S FROM A SONG ONE OF THE CHILDREN SANG, SIR.
?
IN FACT, THEY... THEY'RE EVEN SINGING IT NOW.
I'VE STILL GOT A CHANNEL CONNECTED TO EPSILON'S HOME IN AUSTRALIA...
HE'S RIGHT. I CAN HEAR THEM SINGING TOO...
♬ THE GIANT MADE A SOUTH POLE IN THE DESERT... ♪

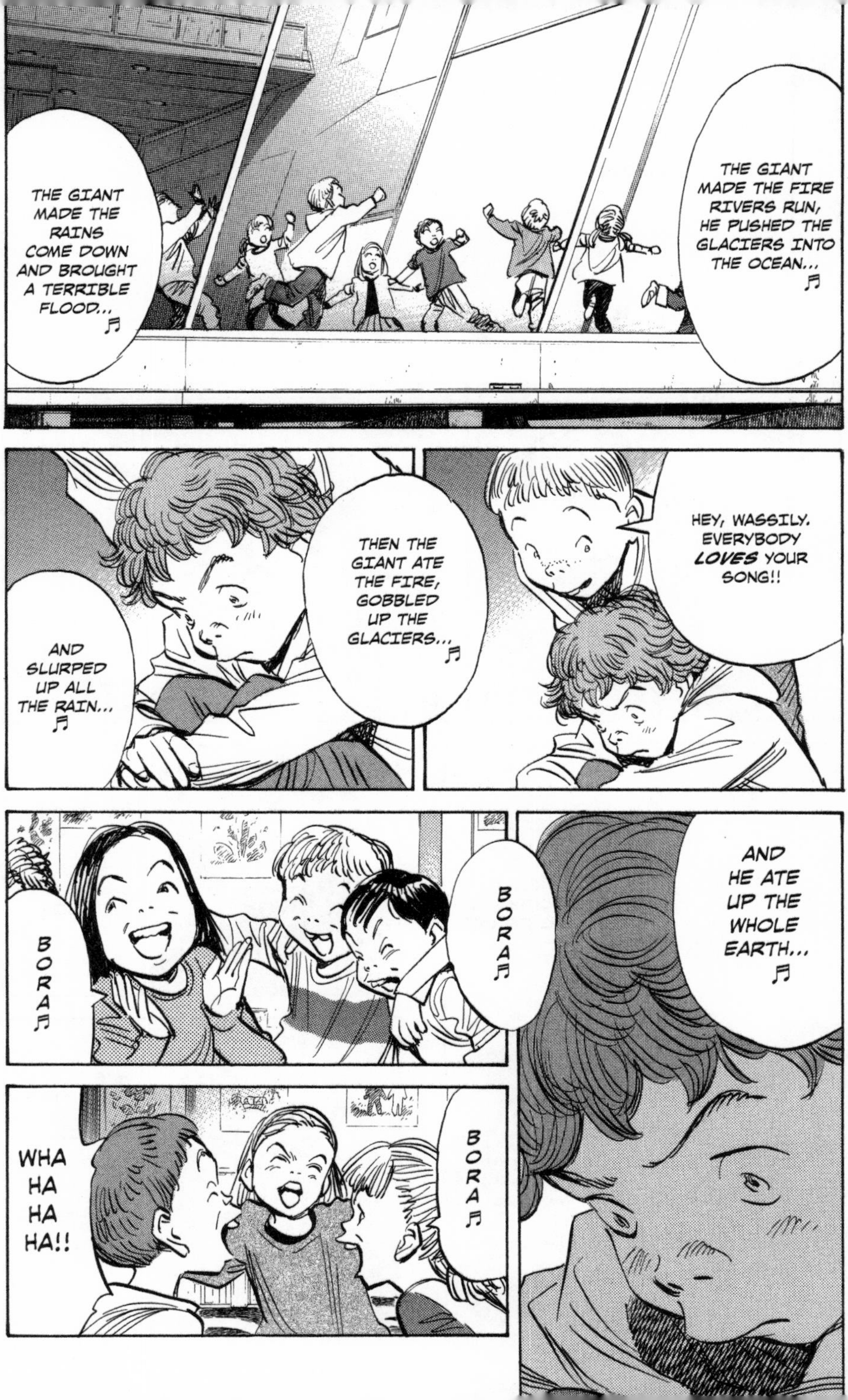
THE GIANT MADE THE FIRE RIVERS RUN, HE PUSHED THE GLACIERS INTO THE OCEAN... ♬
THE GIANT MADE THE RAINS COME DOWN AND BROUGHT A TERRIBLE FLOOD... ♬
HEY, WASSILY. EVERYBODY *LOVES* YOUR SONG!!
THEN THE GIANT ATE THE FIRE, GOBBLED UP THE GLACIERS... ♬
AND SLURPED UP ALL THE RAIN... ♬
AND HE ATE UP THE WHOLE EARTH... ♬
BORA♬
BORA♬
BORA♬
WHA HA HA HA!!

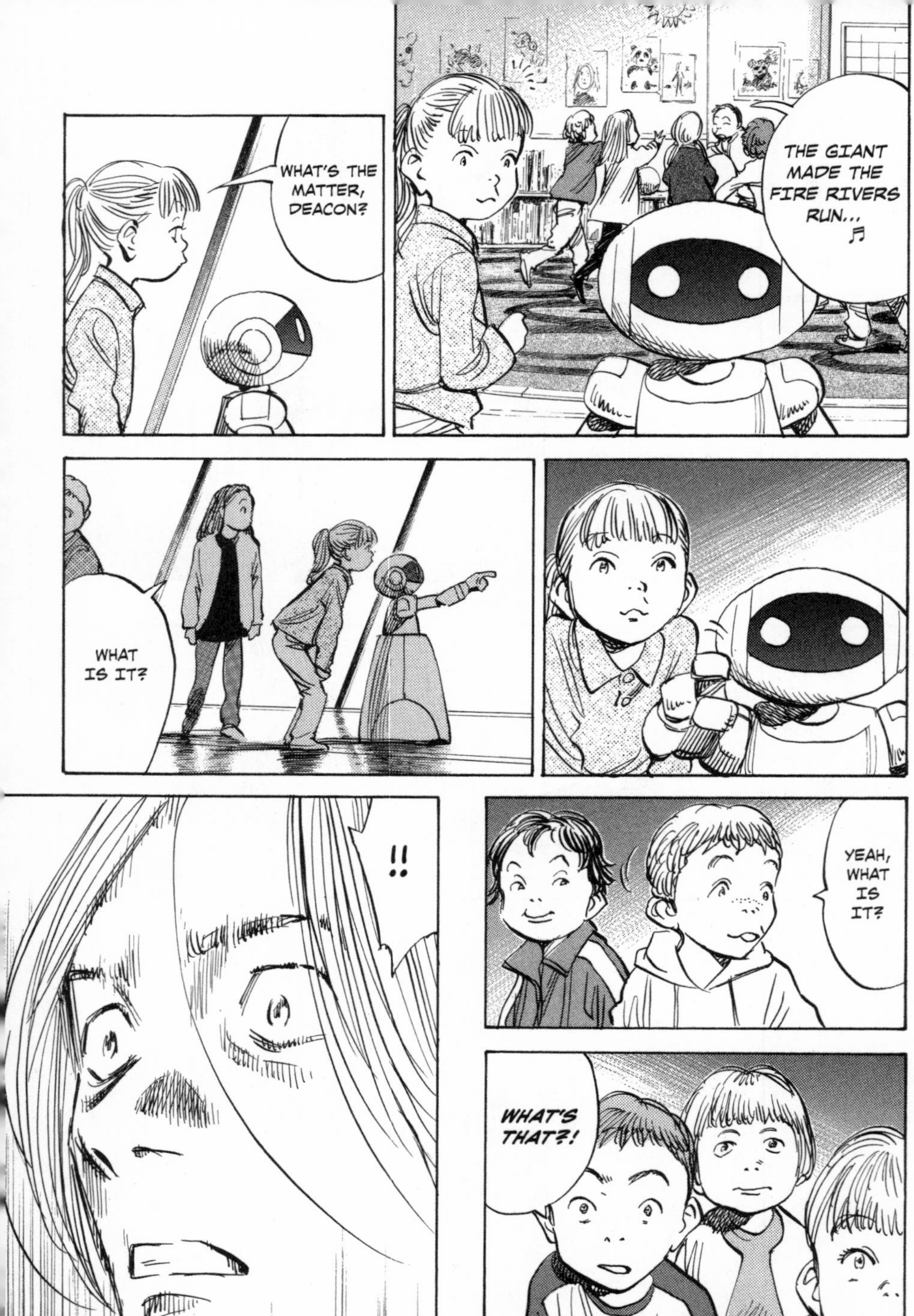
THE GIANT MADE THE FIRE RIVERS RUN... ♬
WHAT'S THE MATTER, DEACON?
WHAT IS IT?
YEAH, WHAT IS IT?
WHAT'S THAT?!
!!

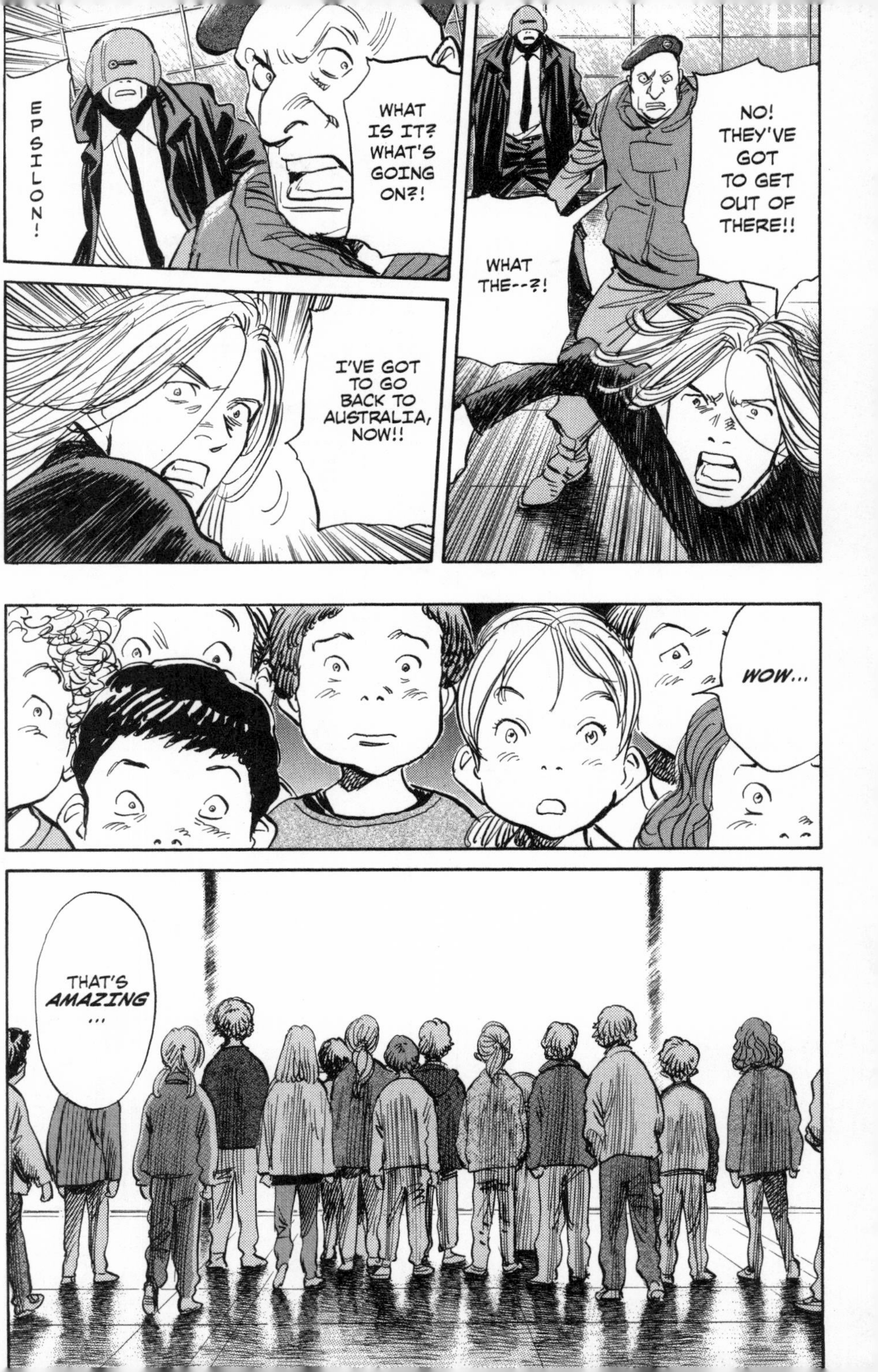
NO! THEY'VE GOT TO GET OUT OF THERE!!
WHAT THE--?!
WHAT IS IT? WHAT'S GOING ON?!
EPSILON!
I'VE GOT TO GO BACK TO AUSTRALIA, NOW!!
WOW...
THAT'S *AMAZING* ...

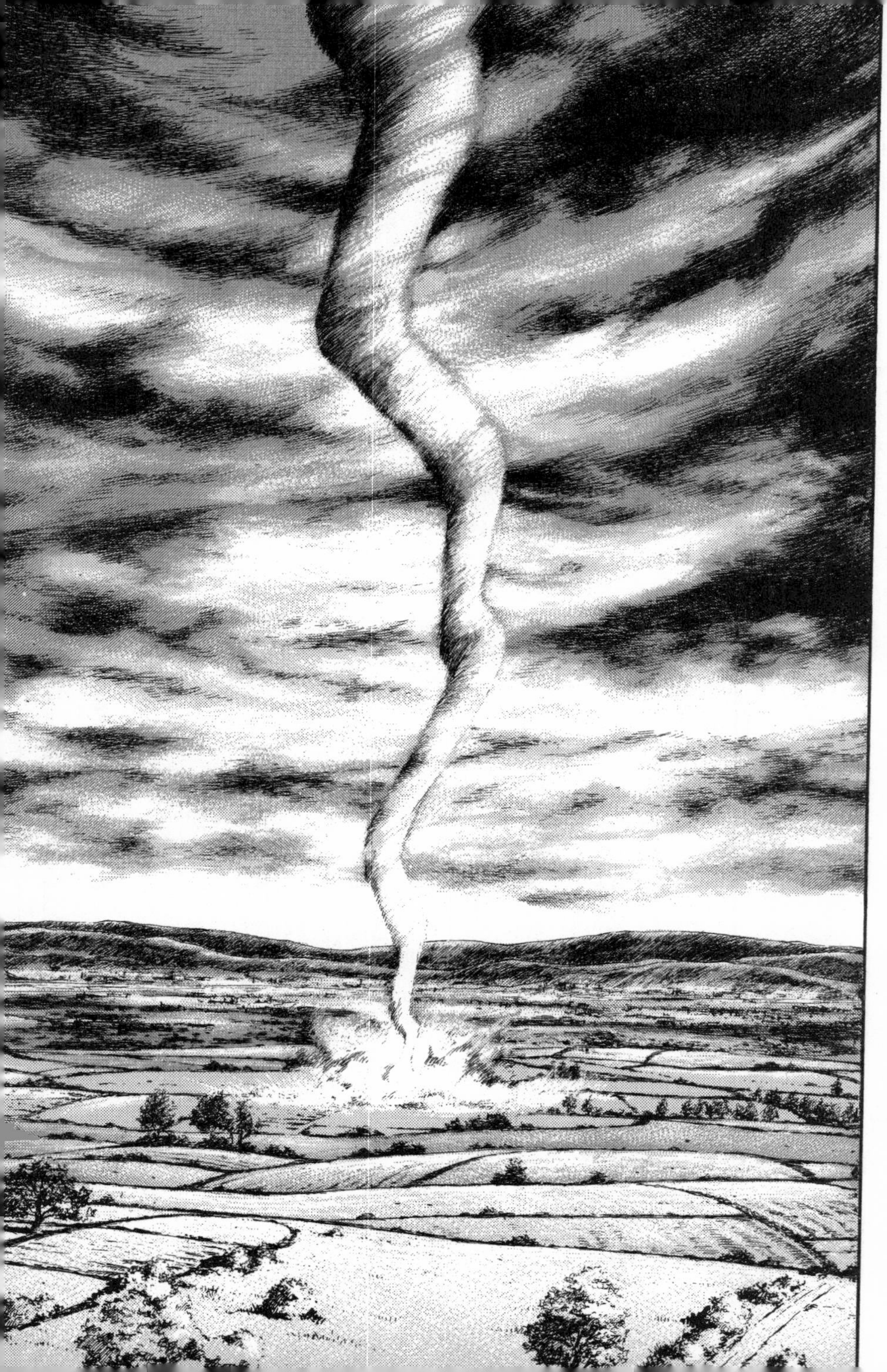

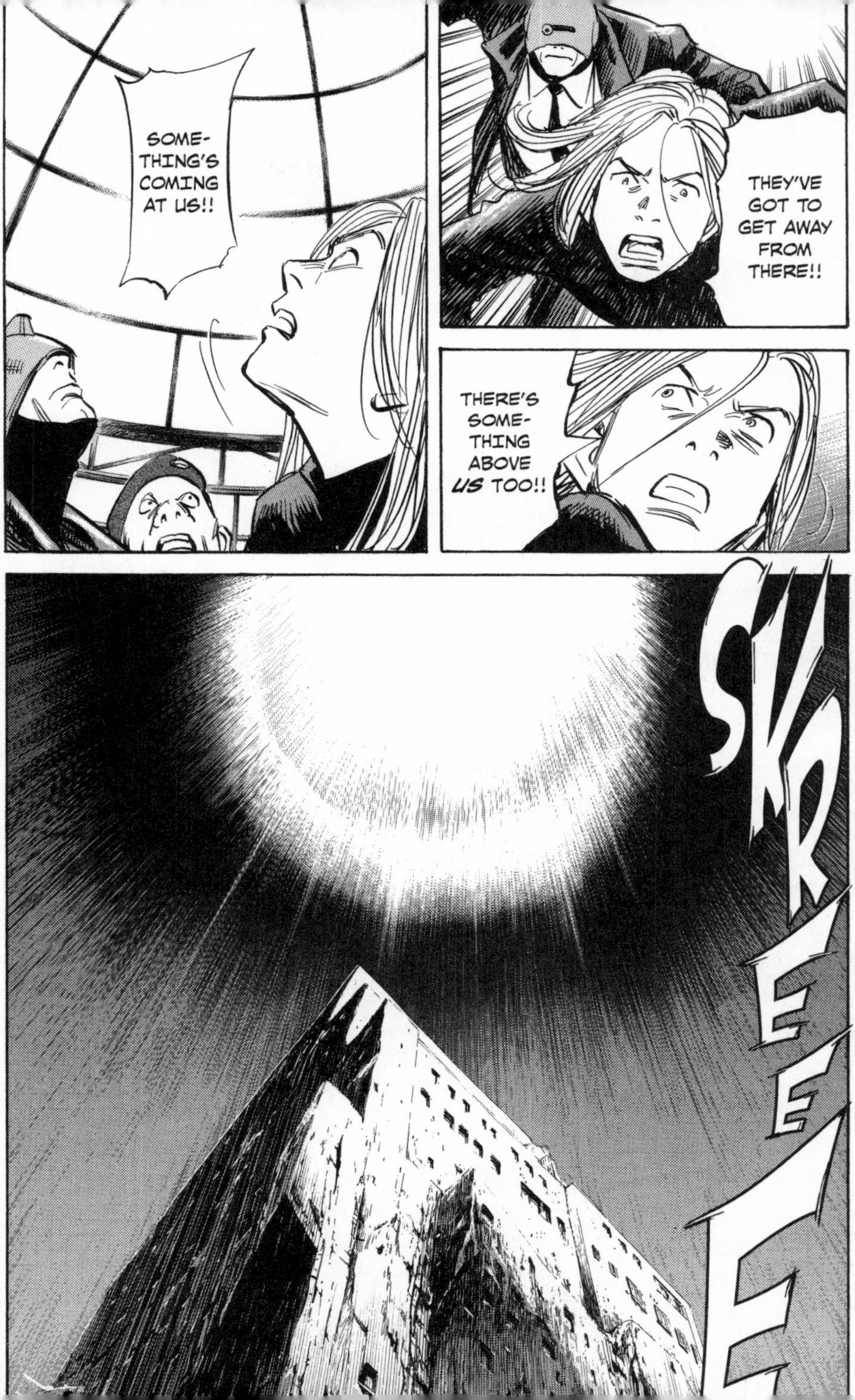
THEY'VE GOT TO GET AWAY FROM THERE!!
THERE'S SOMETHING ABOVE *US* TOO!!
SOME-THING'S COMING AT US!!
SKREEEE

Act 51 TWO SUNS

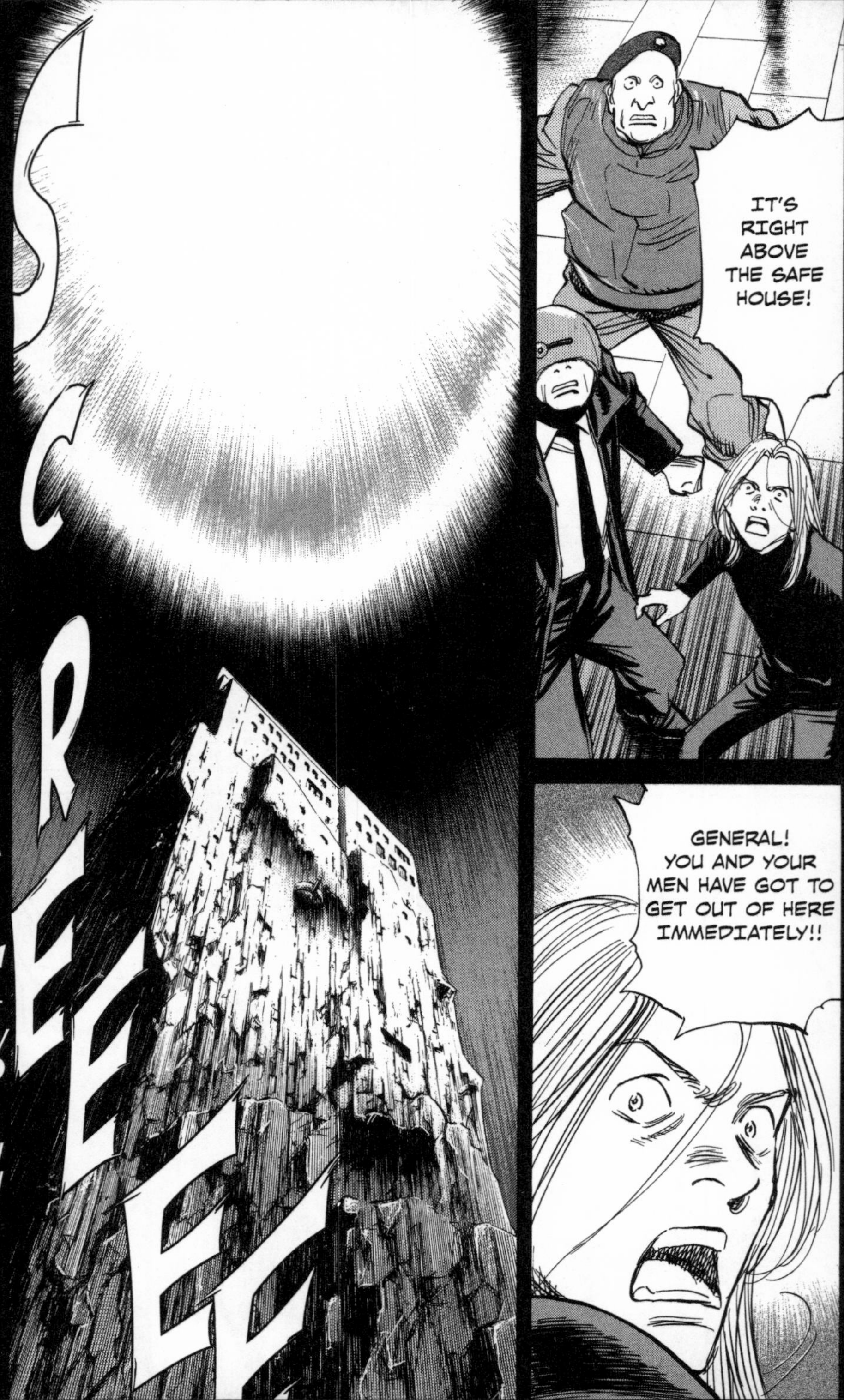

IT'S RIGHT ABOVE THE SAFE HOUSE!
GENERAL! YOU AND YOUR MEN HAVE GOT TO GET OUT OF HERE IMMEDIATELY!!
SCREEEE

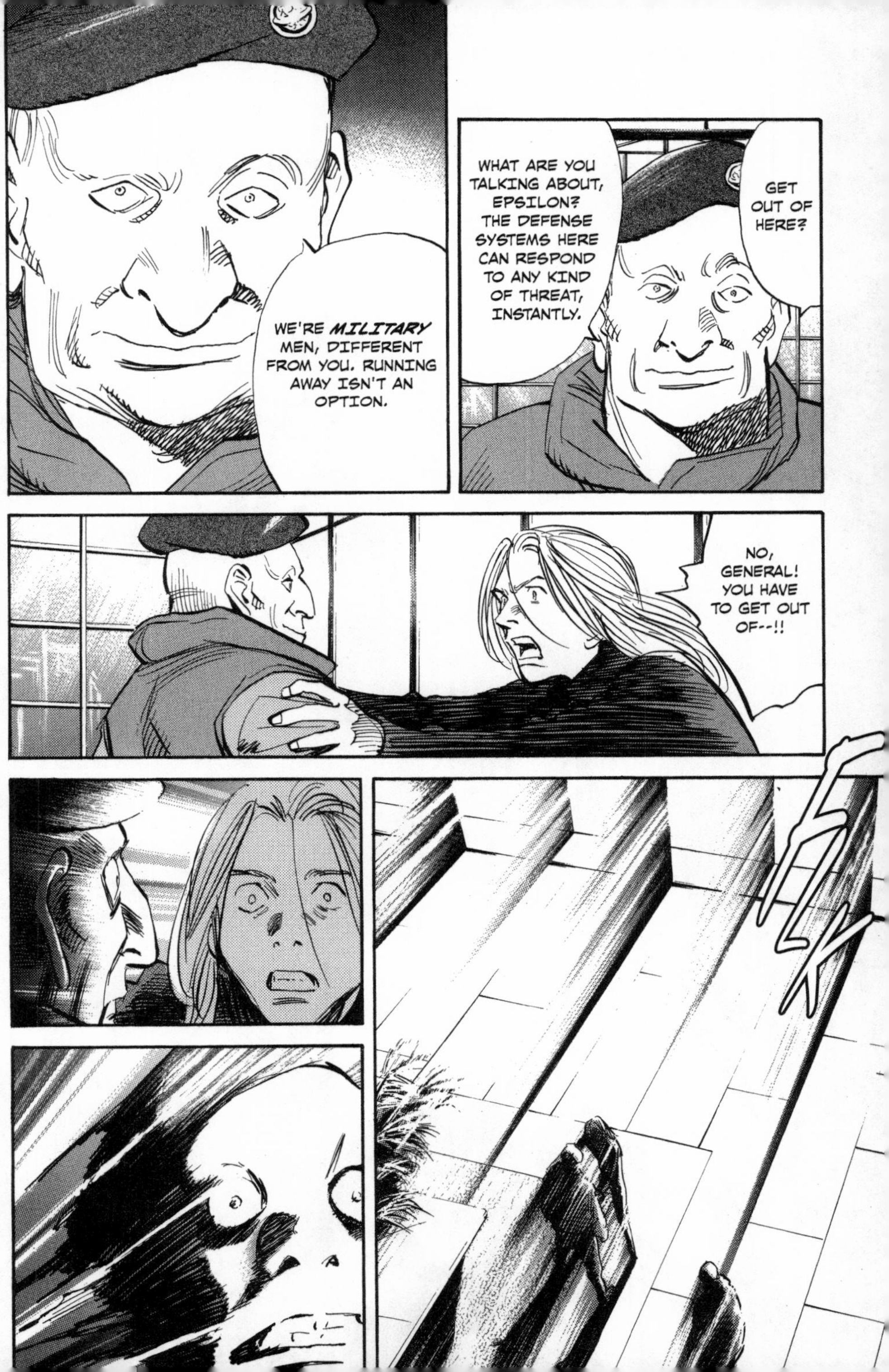
GET OUT OF HERE?
WHAT ARE YOU TALKING ABOUT, EPSILON? THE DEFENSE SYSTEMS HERE CAN RESPOND TO ANY KIND OF THREAT, INSTANTLY.
WE'RE *MILITARY* MEN, DIFFERENT FROM YOU. RUNNING AWAY ISN'T AN OPTION.
NO, GENERAL! YOU HAVE TO GET OUT OF--!!

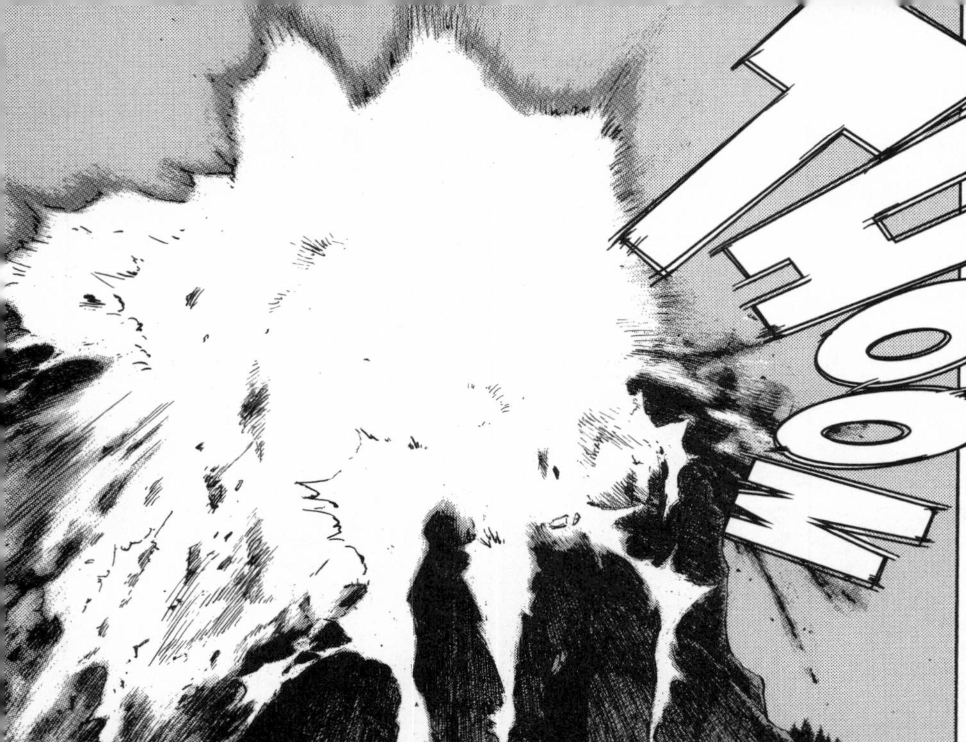
WHOOM
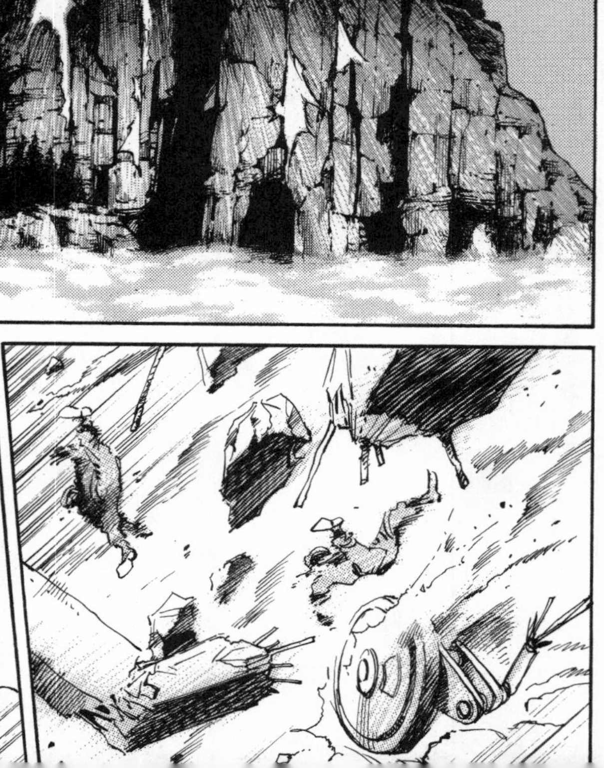
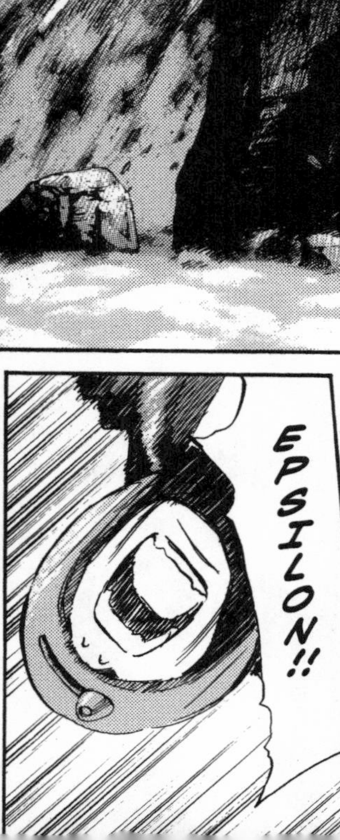
EPSILON!!

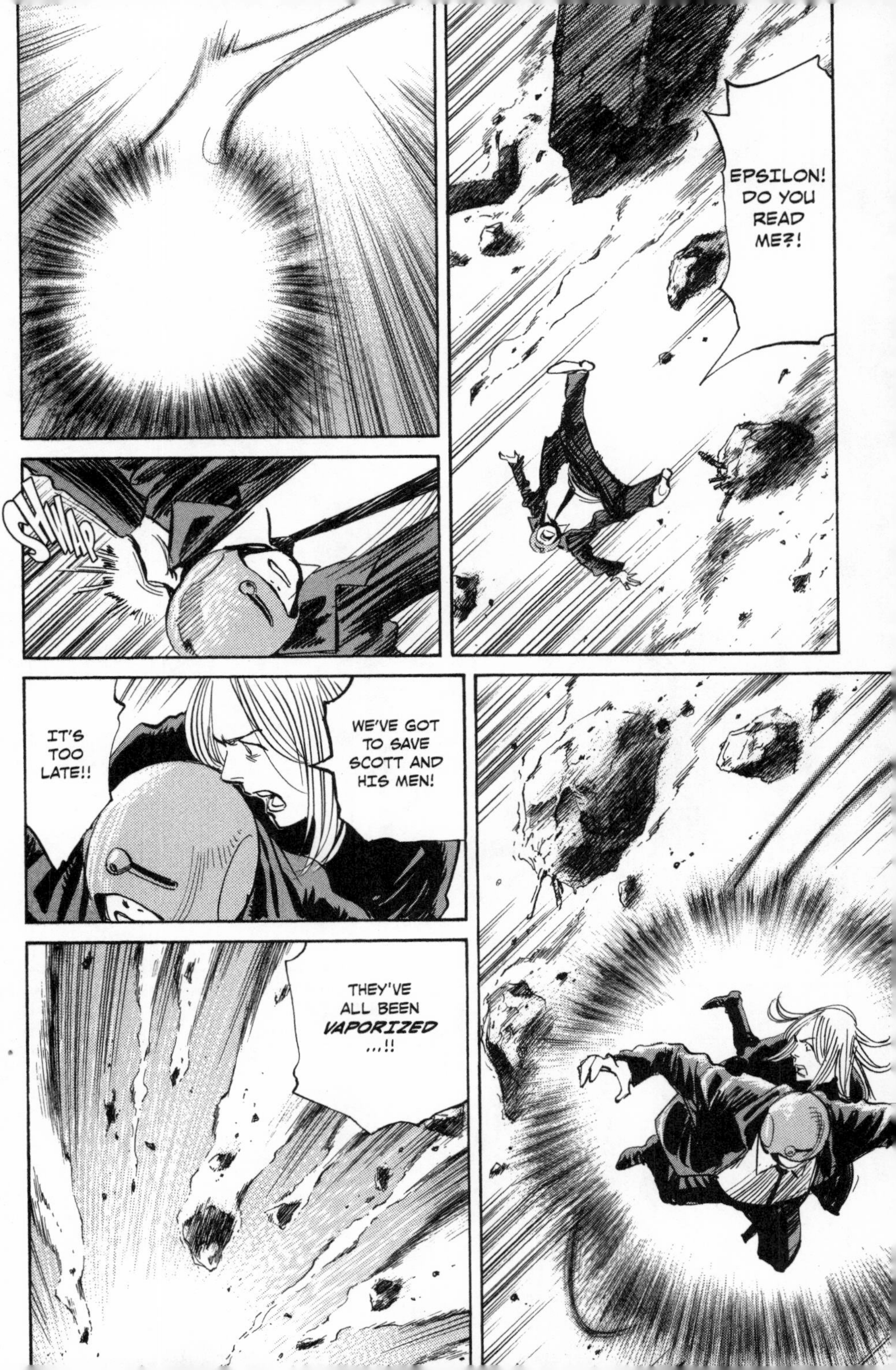
EPSILON! DO YOU READ ME?!
SHWAP
WE'VE GOT TO SAVE SCOTT AND HIS MEN!
IT'S TOO LATE!!
THEY'VE ALL BEEN *VAPORIZED* ...!!

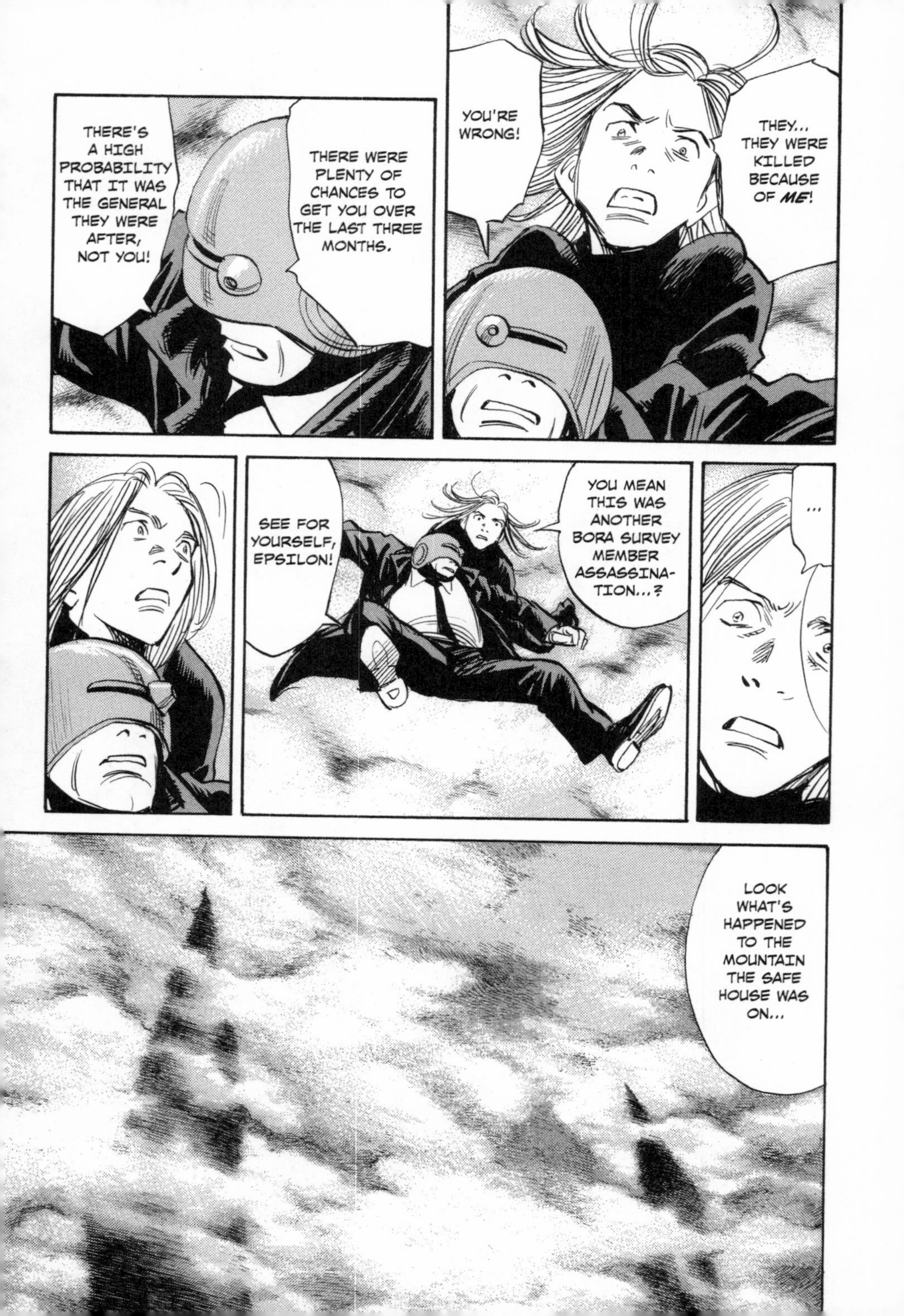
THEY... THEY WERE KILLED BECAUSE OF *ME*!
YOU'RE WRONG!
THERE WERE PLENTY OF CHANCES TO GET YOU OVER THE LAST THREE MONTHS.
THERE'S A HIGH PROBABILITY THAT IT WAS THE GENERAL THEY WERE AFTER, NOT YOU!
...
YOU MEAN THIS WAS ANOTHER BORA SURVEY MEMBER ASSASSINATION...?
SEE FOR YOURSELF, EPSILON!
LOOK WHAT'S HAPPENED TO THE MOUNTAIN THE SAFE HOUSE WAS ON...

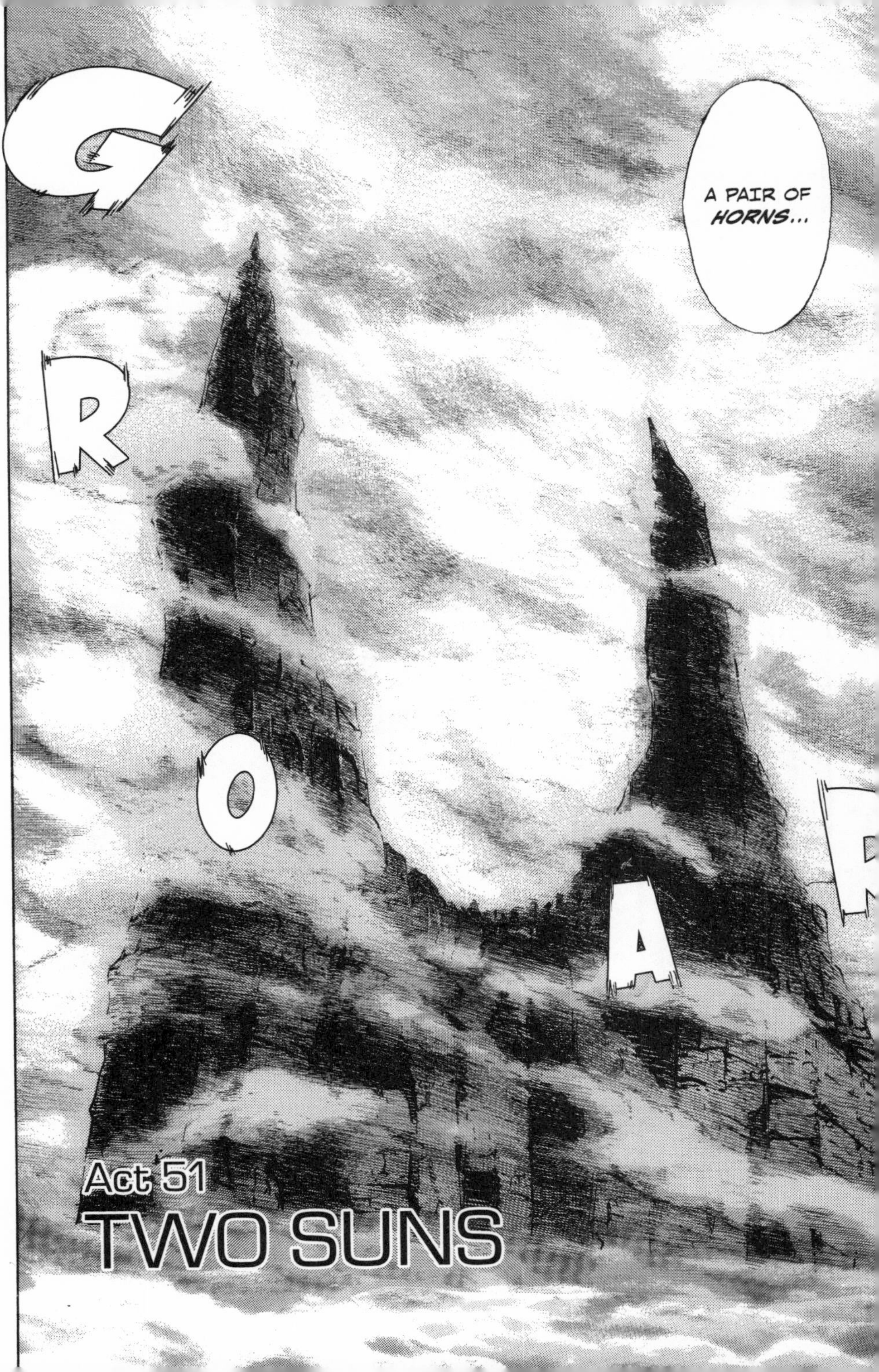
A PAIR OF *HORNS*...
GROAR

Act 51
TWO SUNS

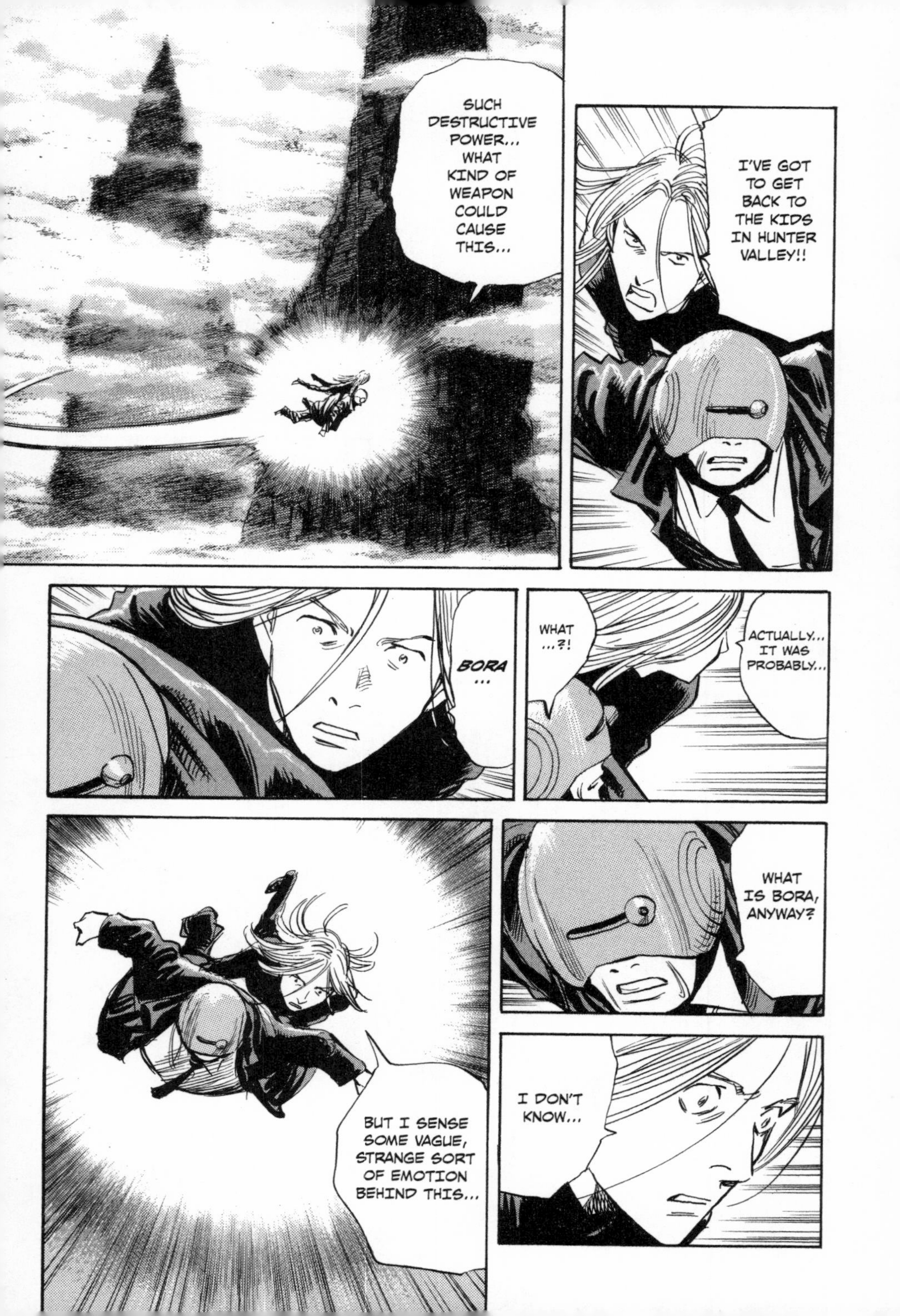
I'VE GOT TO GET BACK TO THE KIDS IN HUNTER VALLEY!!
SUCH DESTRUCTIVE POWER... WHAT KIND OF WEAPON COULD CAUSE THIS...
ACTUALLY... IT WAS PROBABLY...
WHAT ...?!
BORA ...
WHAT IS BORA, ANYWAY?
I DON'T KNOW...
BUT I SENSE SOME VAGUE, STRANGE SORT OF EMOTION BEHIND THIS...

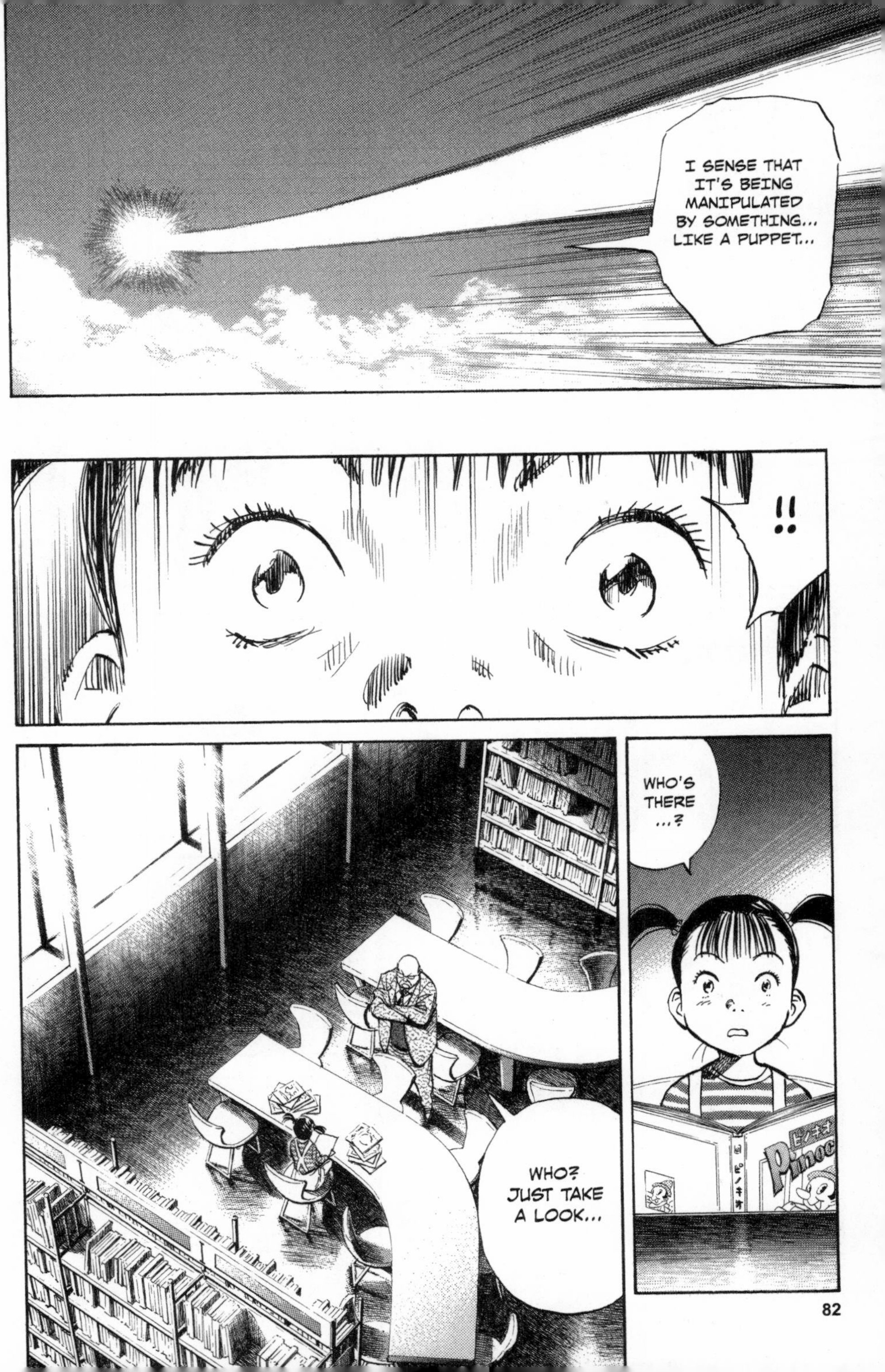
I SENSE THAT IT'S BEING MANIPULATED BY SOMETHING... LIKE A PUPPET...
!!
WHO'S THERE ...?
WHO? JUST TAKE A LOOK...

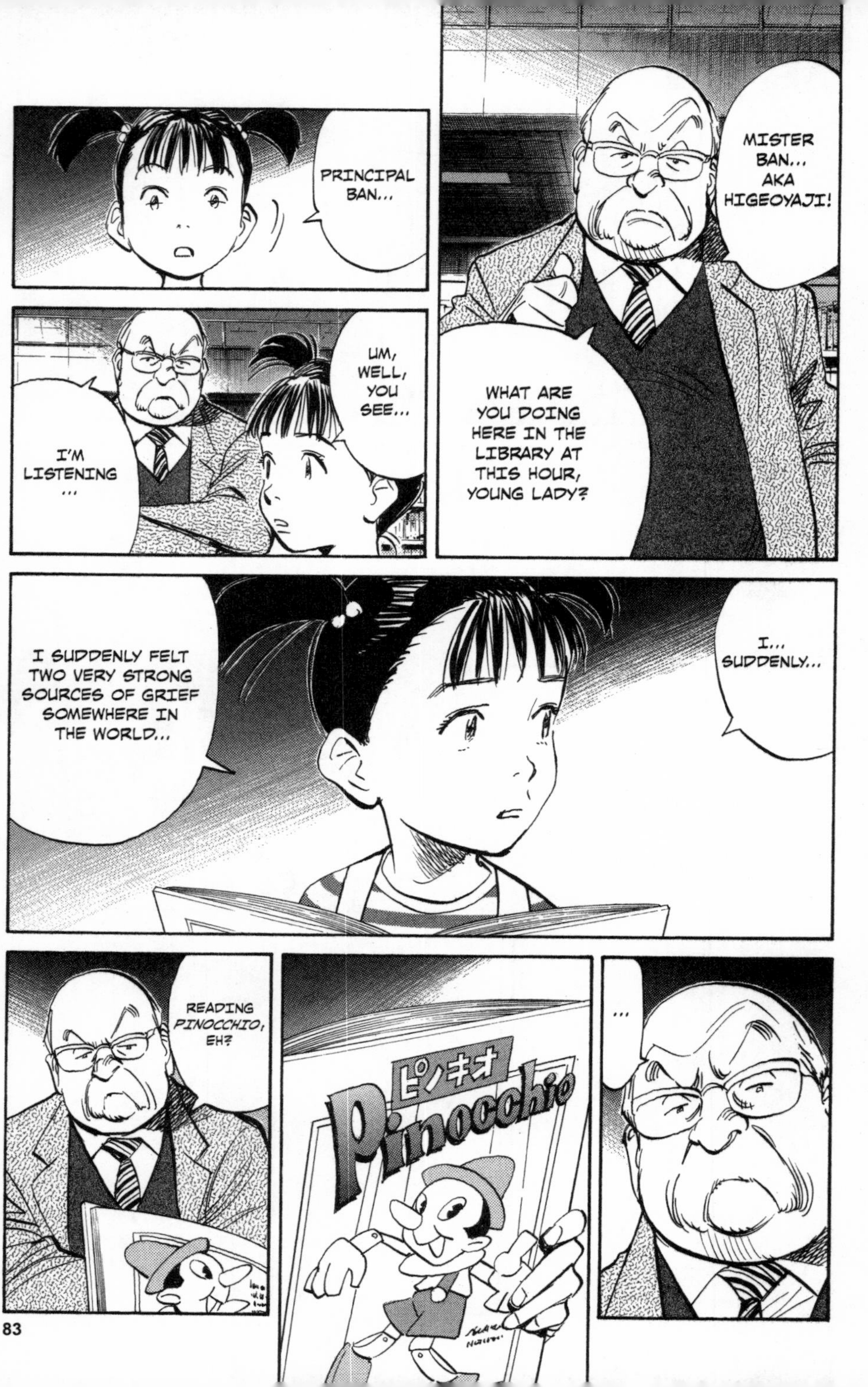

MISTER BAN... AKA HIGEOYAJI!
WHAT ARE YOU DOING HERE IN THE LIBRARY AT THIS HOUR, YOUNG LADY?
PRINCIPAL BAN...
UM, WELL, YOU SEE...
I'M LISTENING...
I... SUDDENLY...
I SUDDENLY FELT TWO VERY STRONG SOURCES OF GRIEF SOMEWHERE IN THE WORLD...
...
ピノキオ
Pinocchio
READING *PINOCCHIO*, EH?

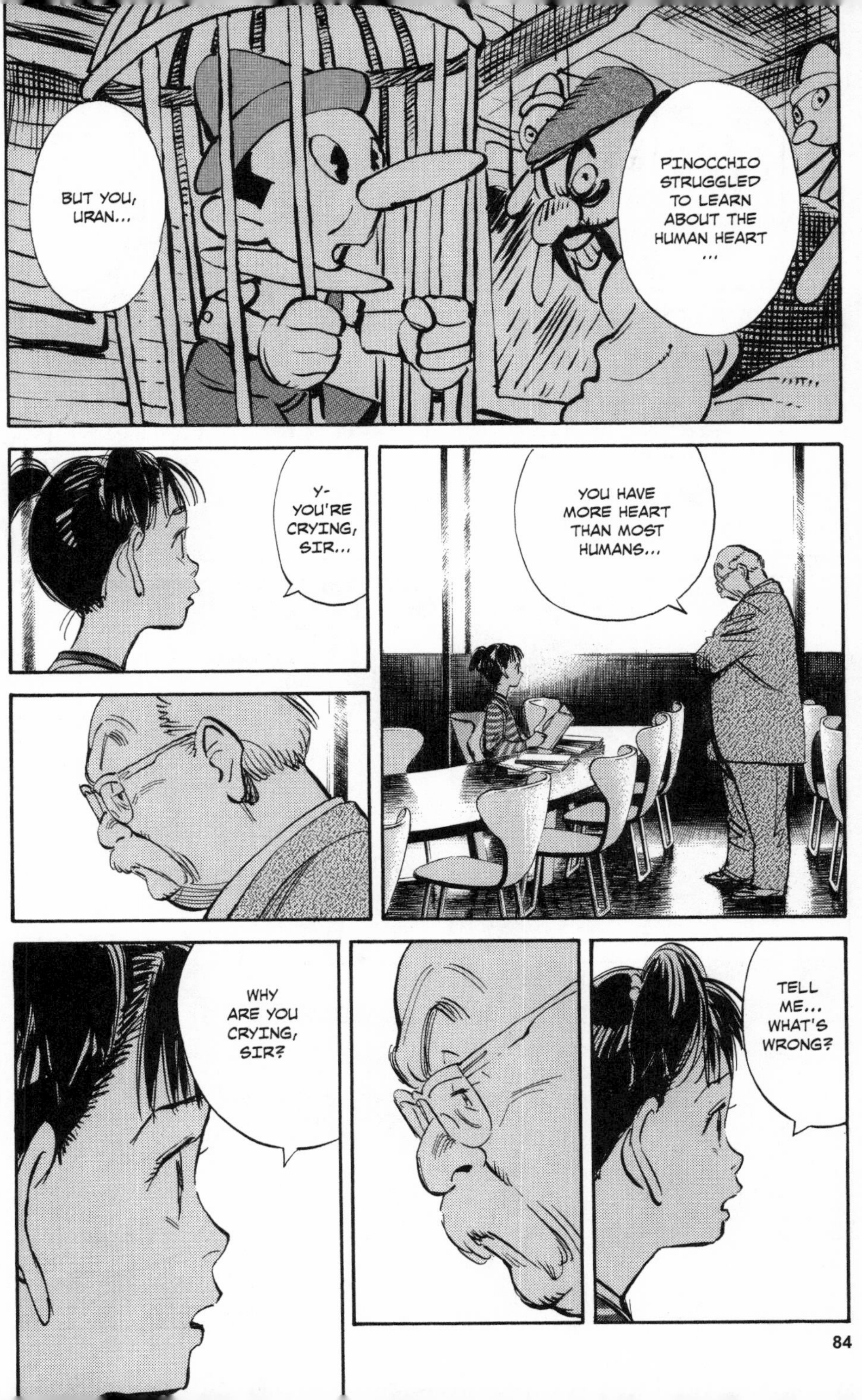
PINOCCHIO STRUGGLED TO LEARN ABOUT THE HUMAN HEART ...
BUT YOU, URAN...
YOU HAVE MORE HEART THAN MOST HUMANS...
Y- YOU'RE CRYING, SIR...
TELL ME... WHAT'S WRONG?
WHY ARE YOU CRYING, SIR?

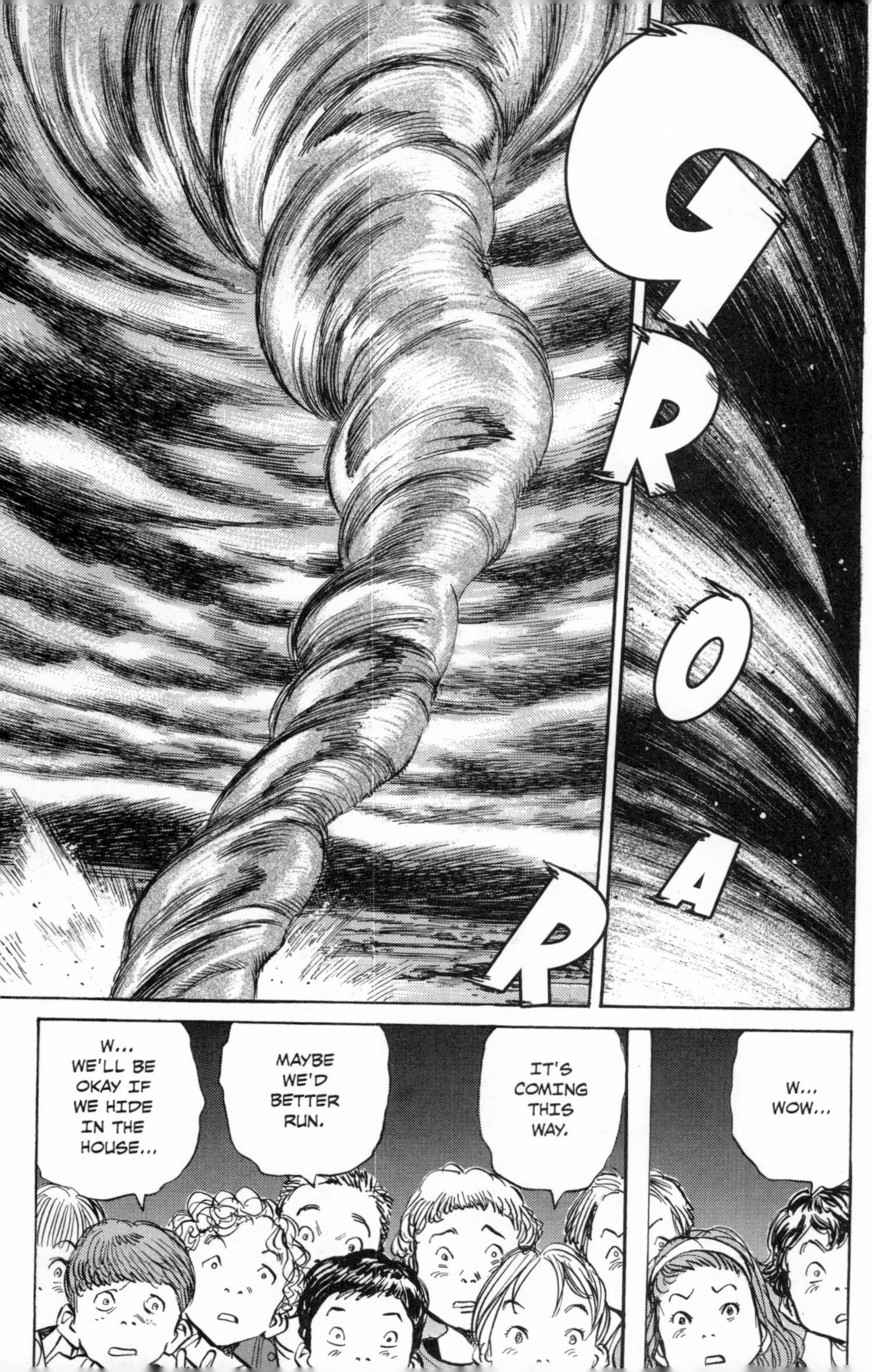
GROAR
W... WOW...
IT'S COMING THIS WAY.
MAYBE WE'D BETTER RUN.
W... WE'LL BE OKAY IF WE HIDE IN THE HOUSE...

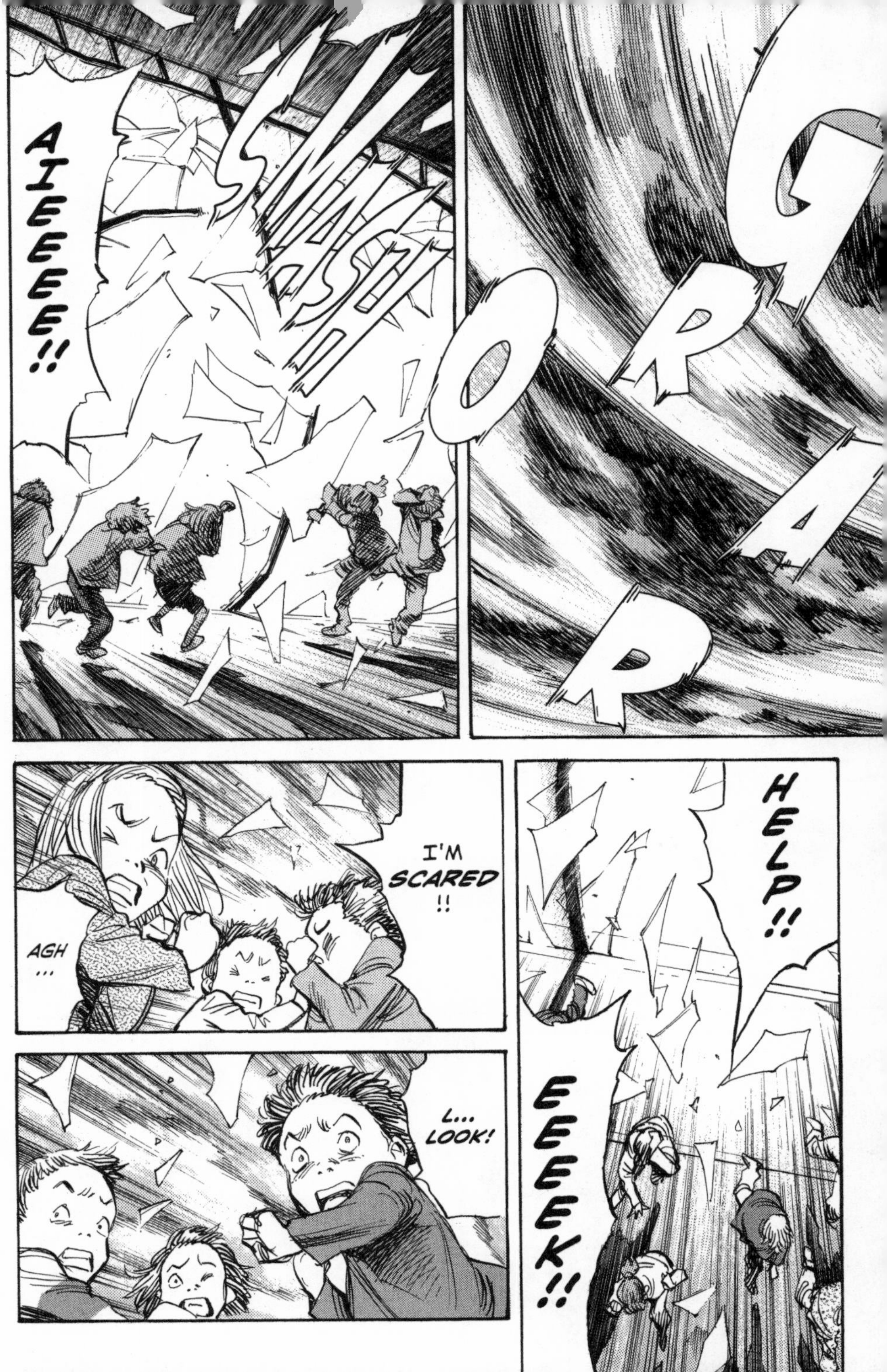
GROAR
SMASH
AIEEEEE!!
HELP!!
EEEEEK!!
I'M SCARED !!
AGH ...
L... LOOK!

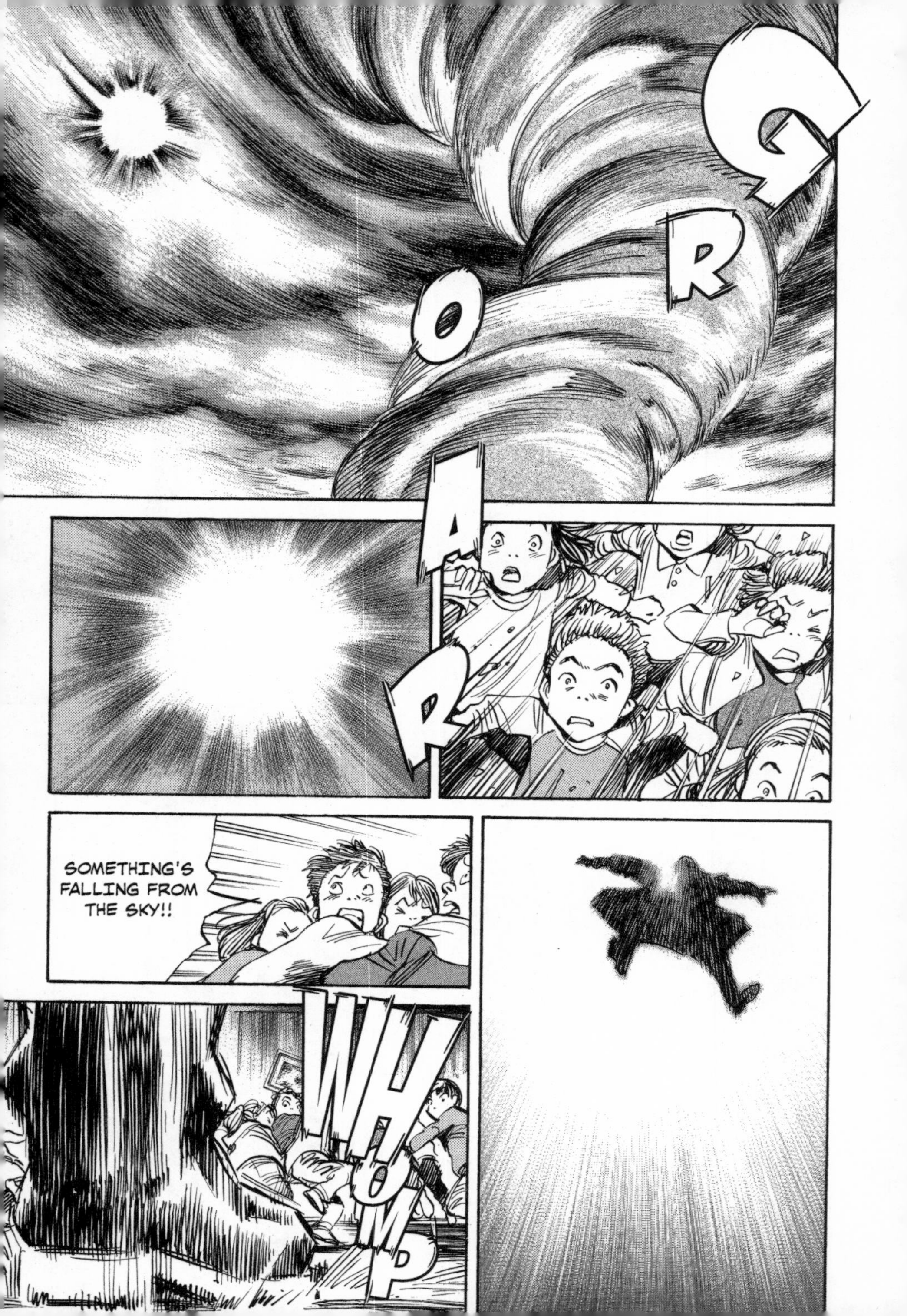
GROAR
SOMETHING'S FALLING FROM THE SKY!!
WHUMP

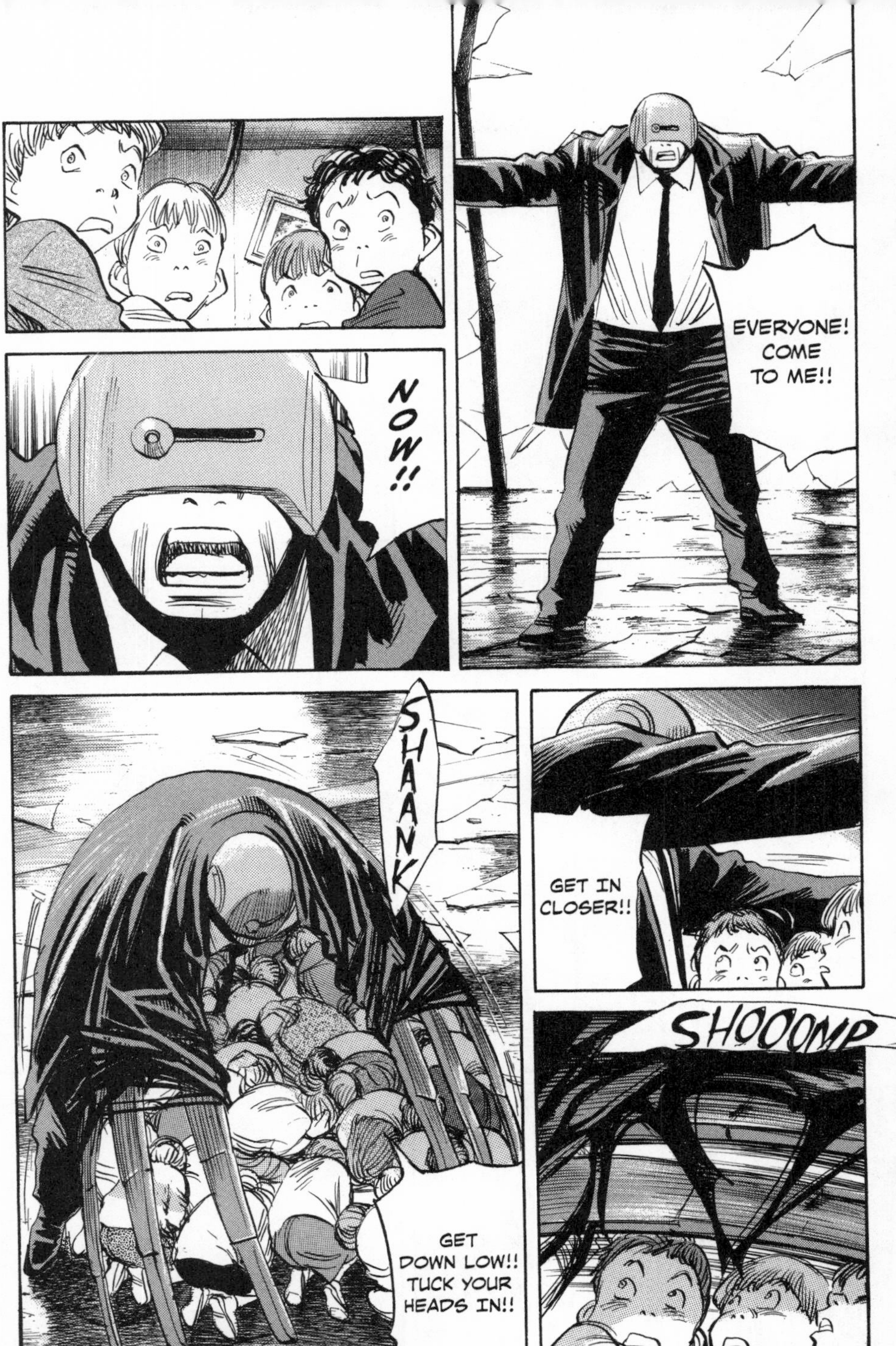
EVERYONE! COME TO ME!!
NOW!!
GET IN CLOSER!!
SHOOOMP
SHAANK
GET DOWN LOW!! TUCK YOUR HEADS IN!!

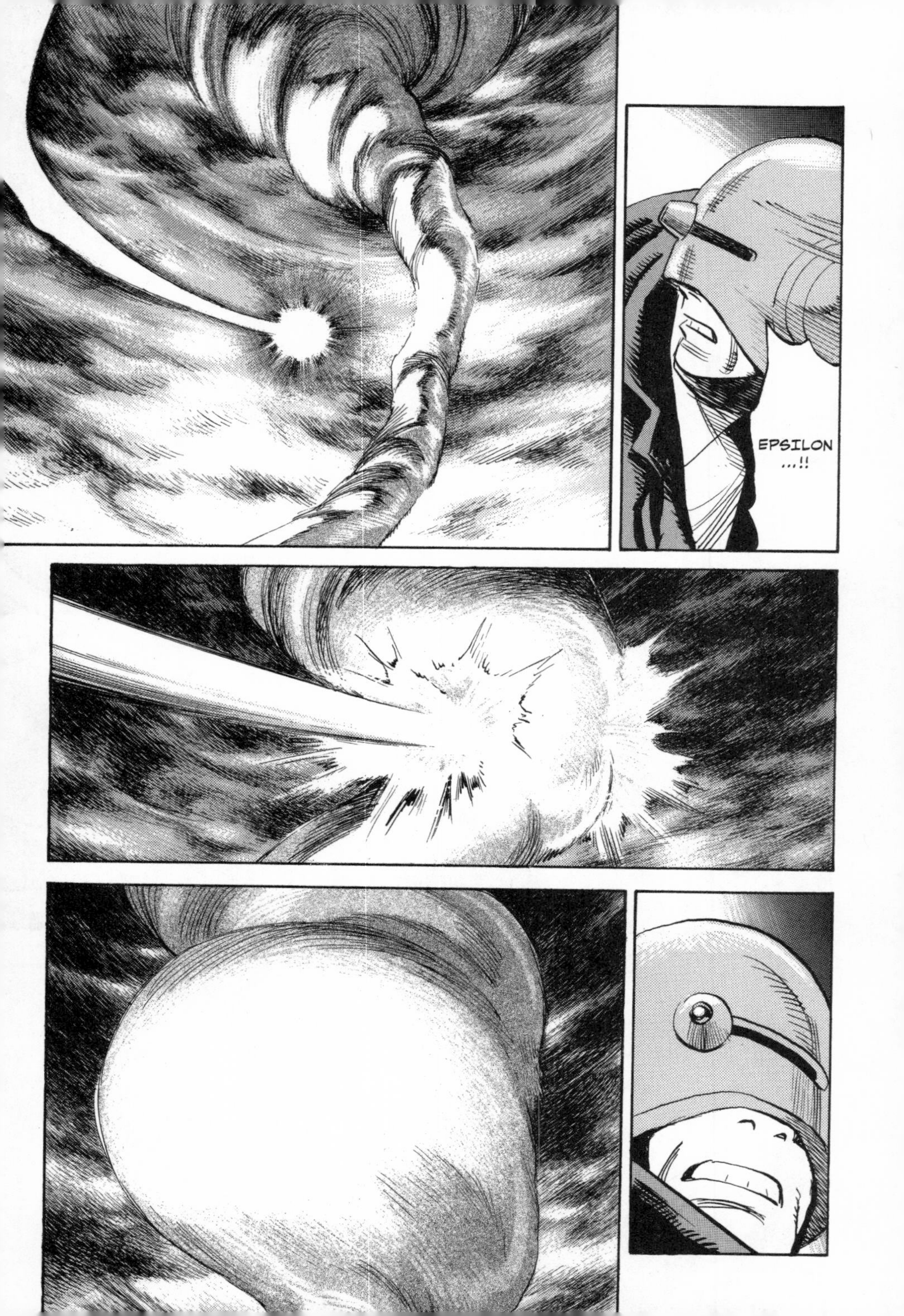
EPSILON
...!!

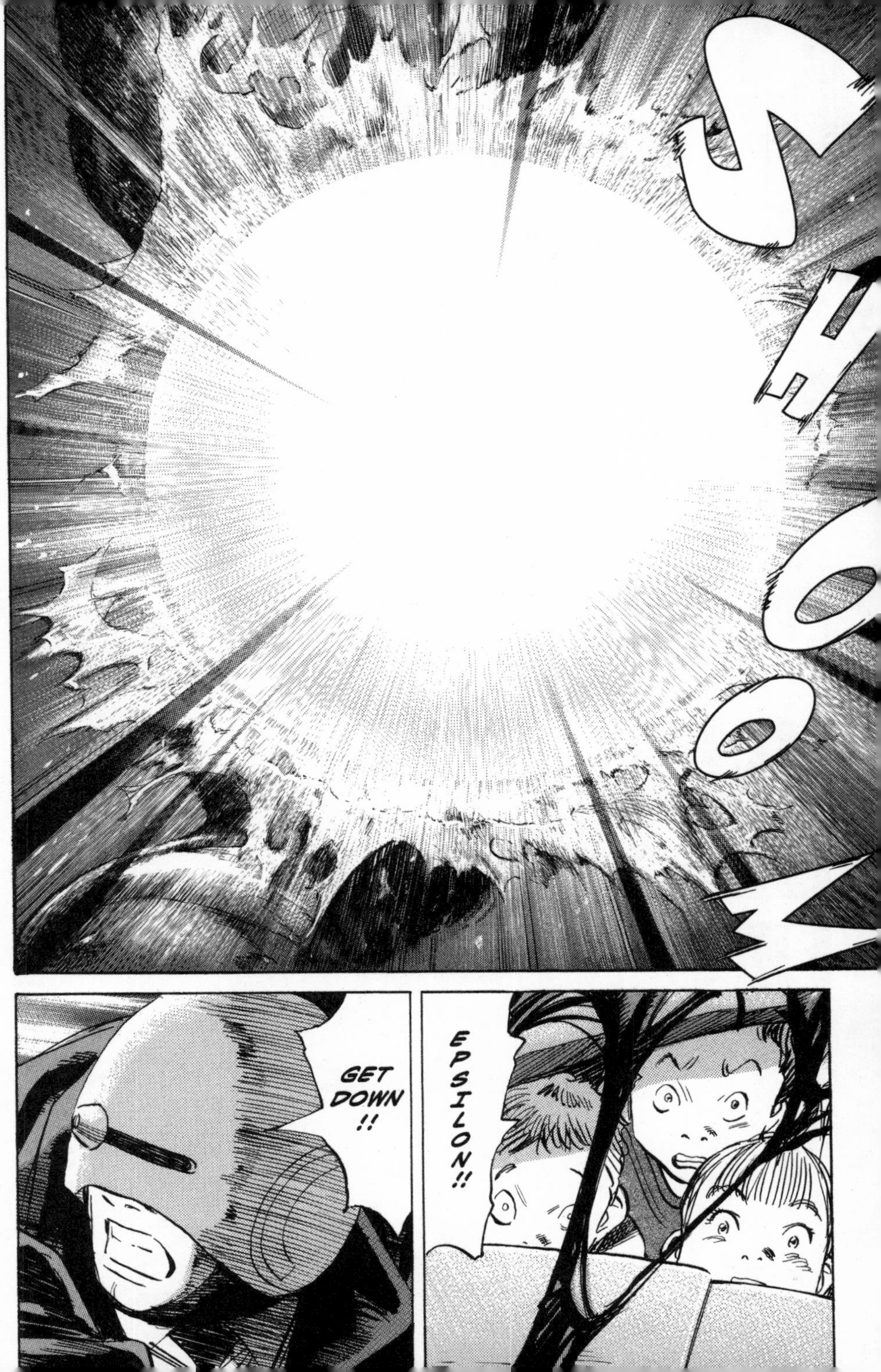
SHOOM
EPSILON!!
GET DOWN!!

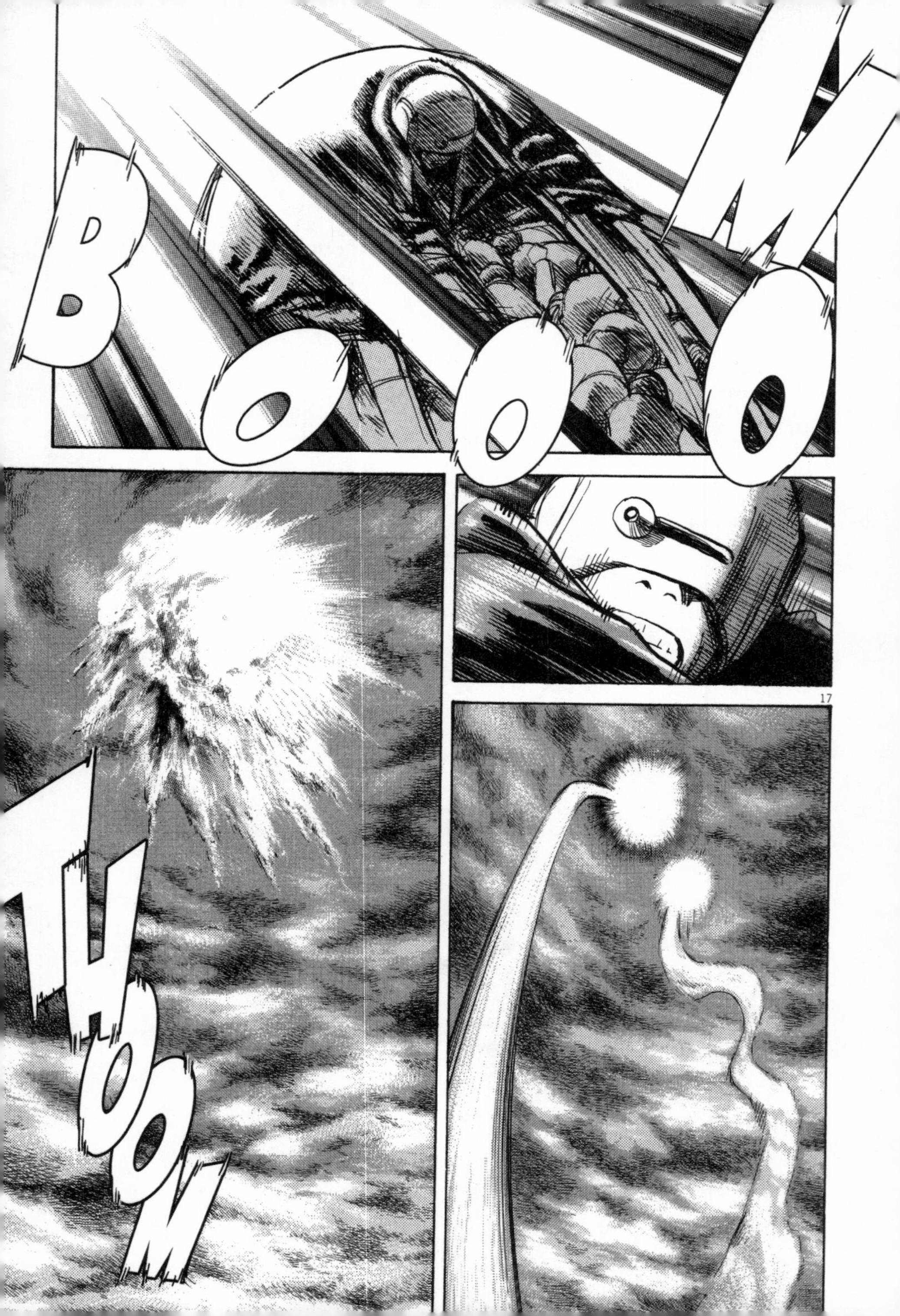
BOOOM
THOOM

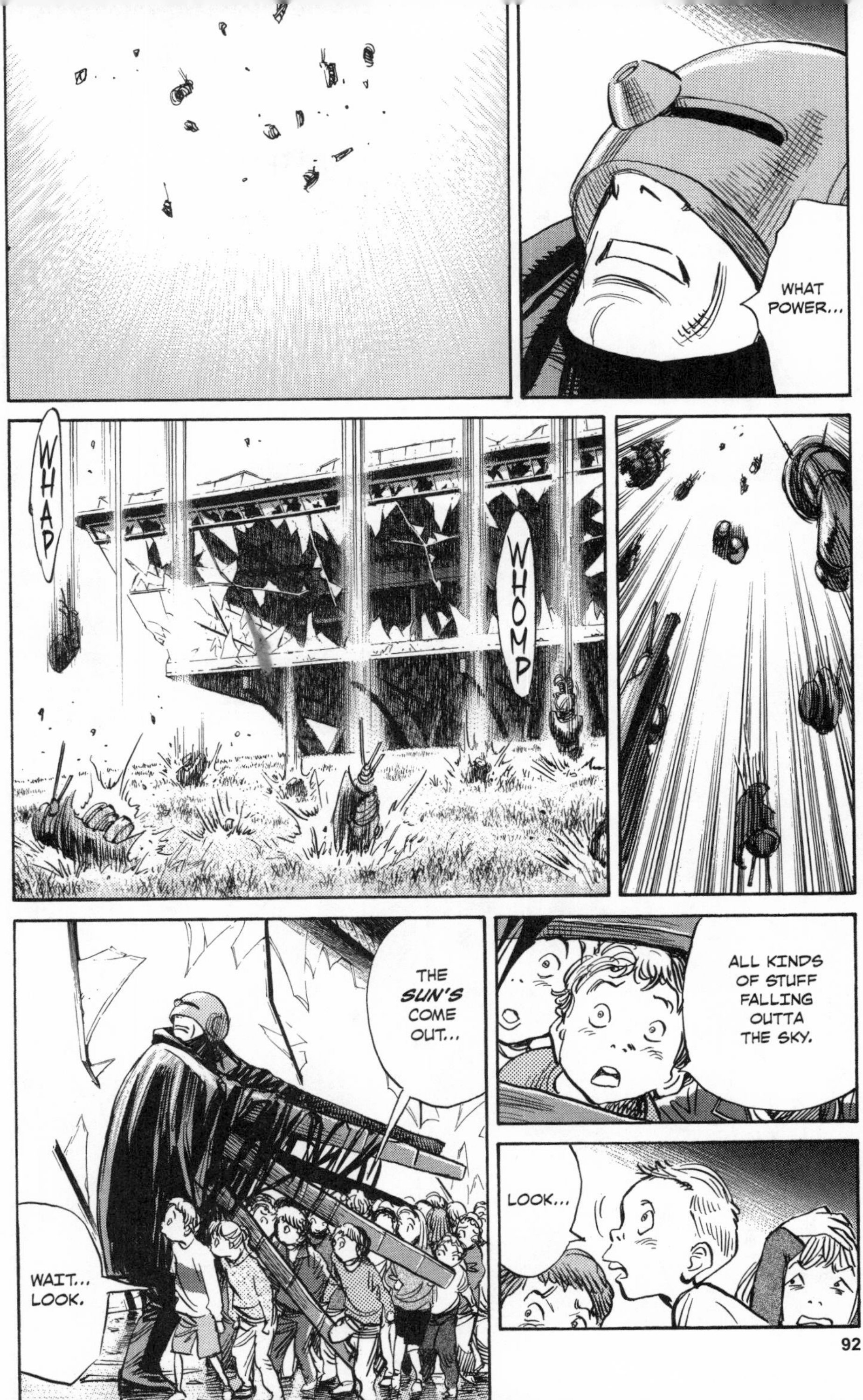
WHAT POWER...
WHOMP
WHAP
ALL KINDS OF STUFF FALLING OUTTA THE SKY.
LOOK...
THE SUN'S COME OUT...
WAIT... LOOK.

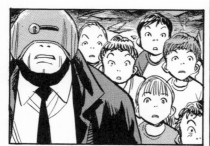
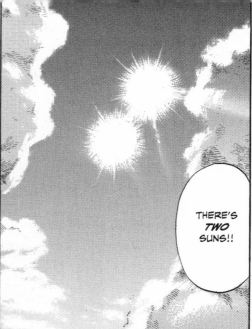

THERE'S *TWO* SUNS!!

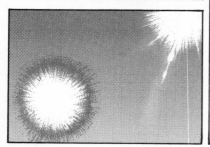
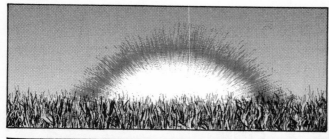
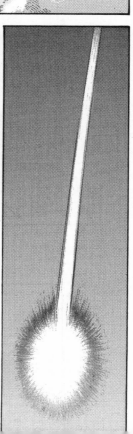
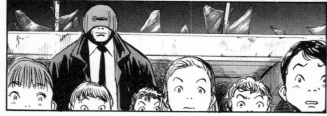
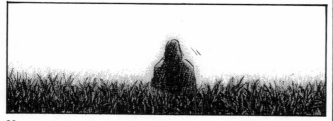

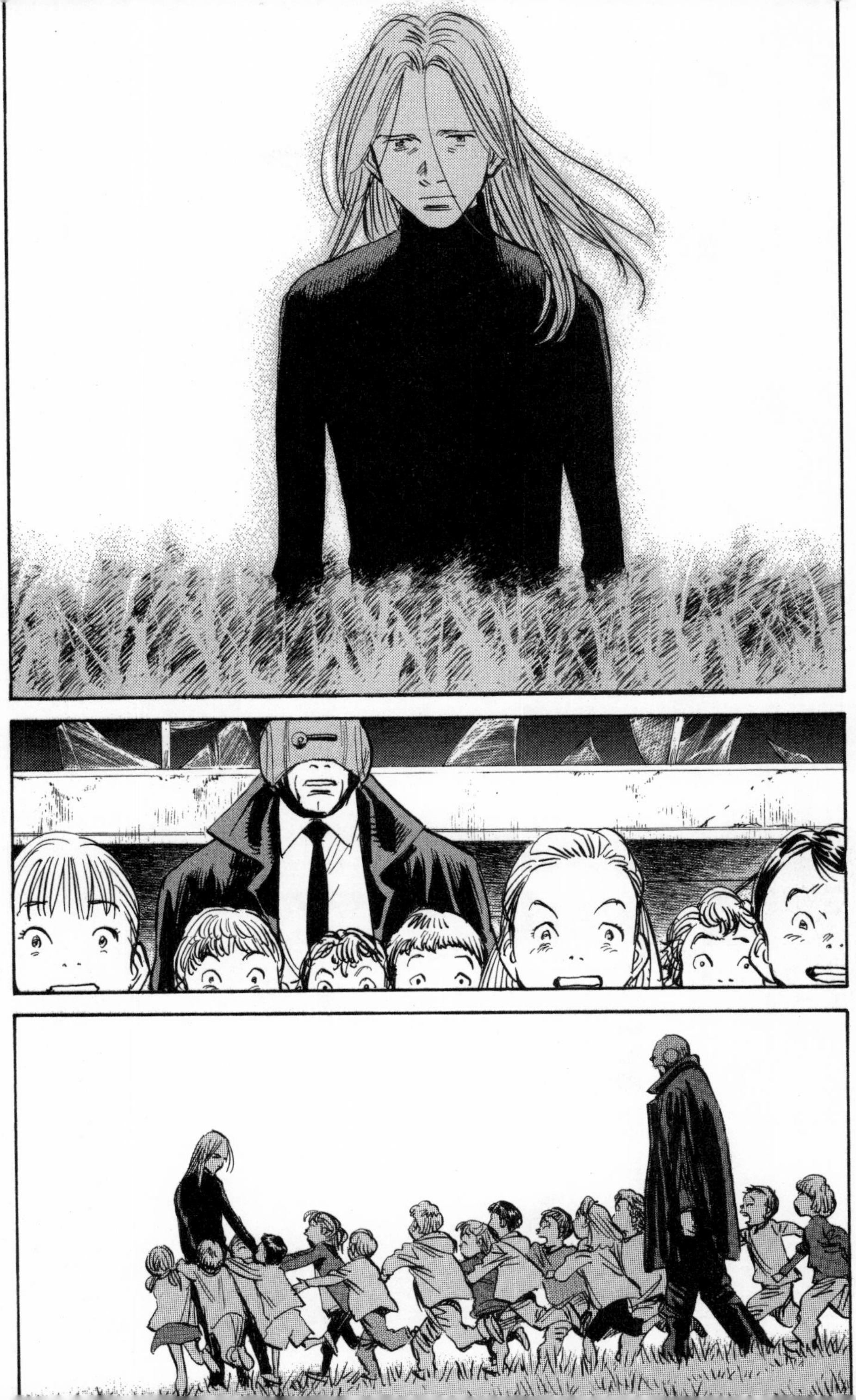

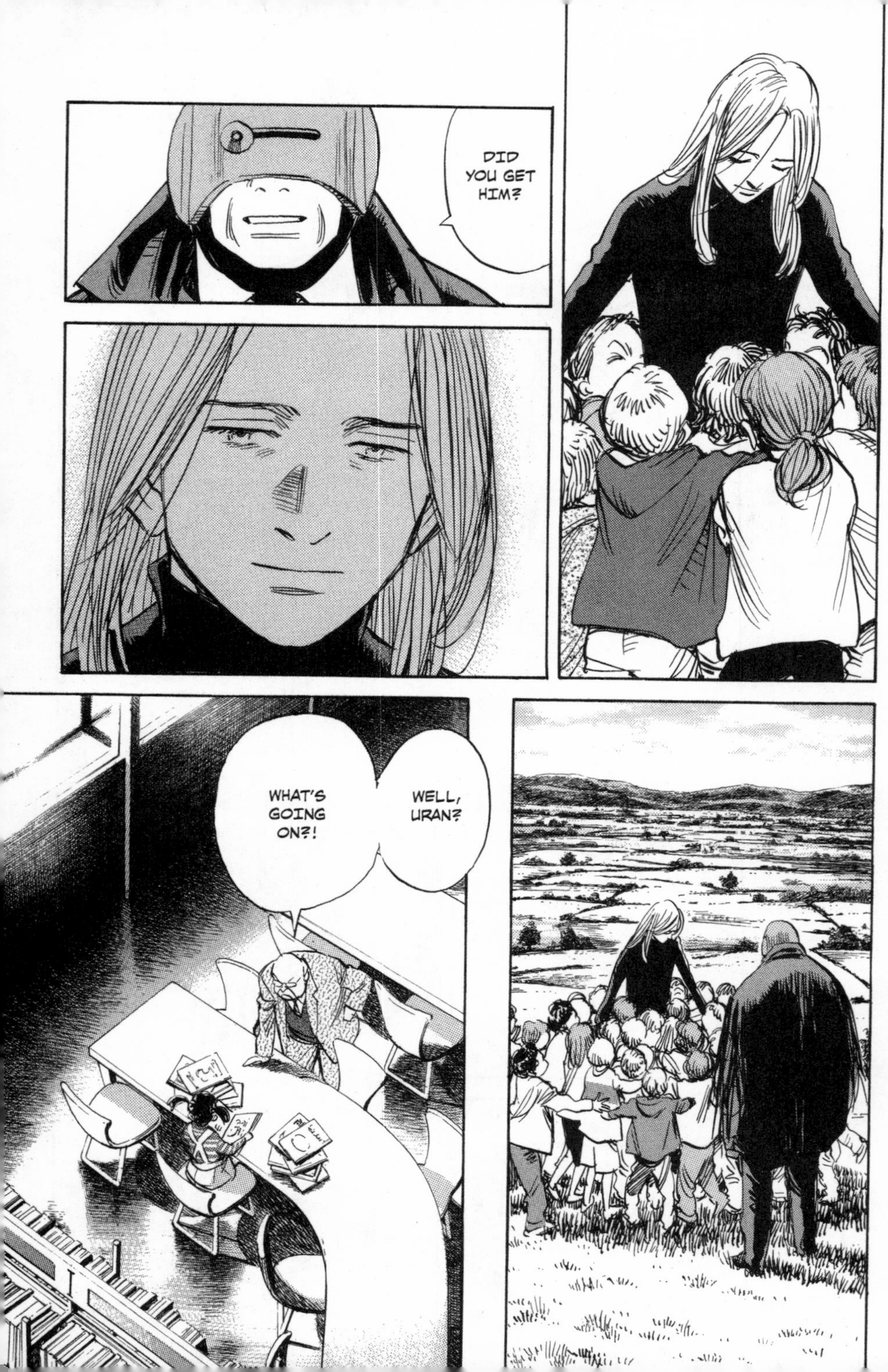
DID YOU GET HIM?
WELL, URAN?
WHAT'S GOING ON?!

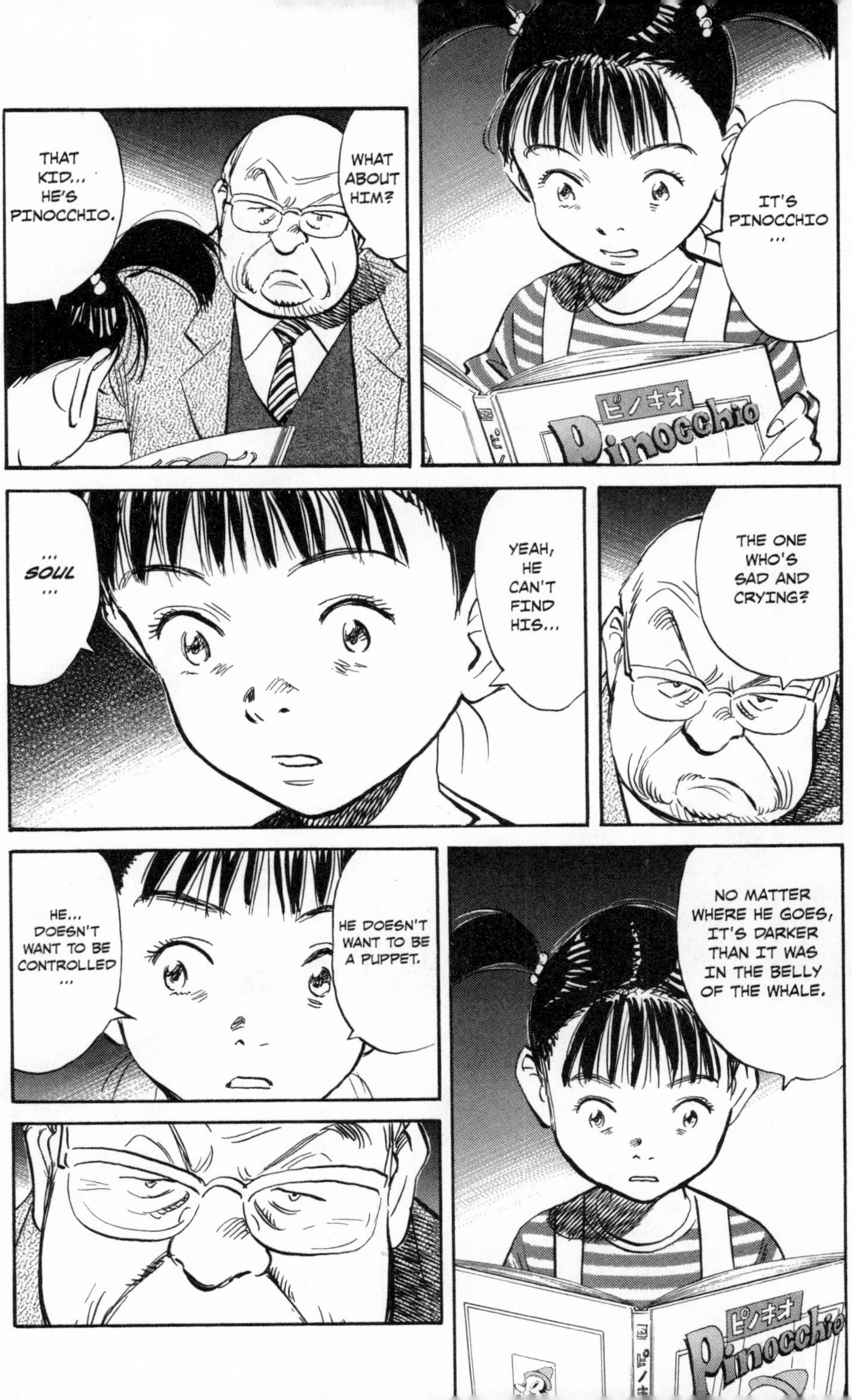
IT'S PINOCCHIO ...
ピノキオ
Pinocchio
WHAT ABOUT HIM?
THAT KID... HE'S PINOCCHIO.
THE ONE WHO'S SAD AND CRYING?
YEAH, HE CAN'T FIND HIS...
... SOUL ...
NO MATTER WHERE HE GOES, IT'S DARKER THAN IT WAS IN THE BELLY OF THE WHALE.
ピノキオ
Pinocchio
HE DOESN'T WANT TO BE A PUPPET.
HE... DOESN'T WANT TO BE CONTROLLED ...

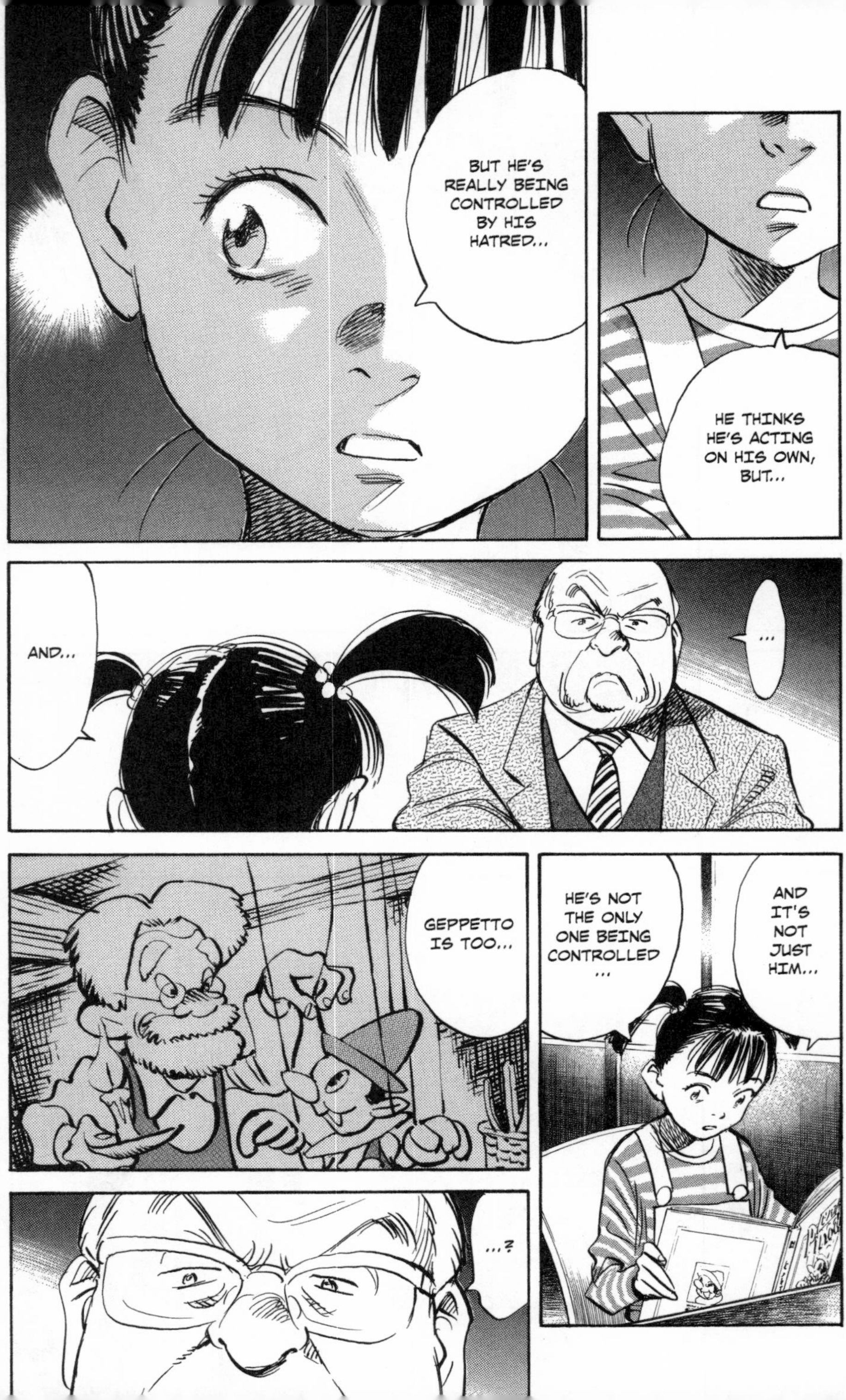
HE THINKS HE'S ACTING ON HIS OWN, BUT...
BUT HE'S REALLY BEING CONTROLLED BY HIS HATRED...
...
AND...
AND IT'S NOT JUST HIM...
HE'S NOT THE ONLY ONE BEING CONTROLLED ...
GEPPETTO IS TOO...
...?

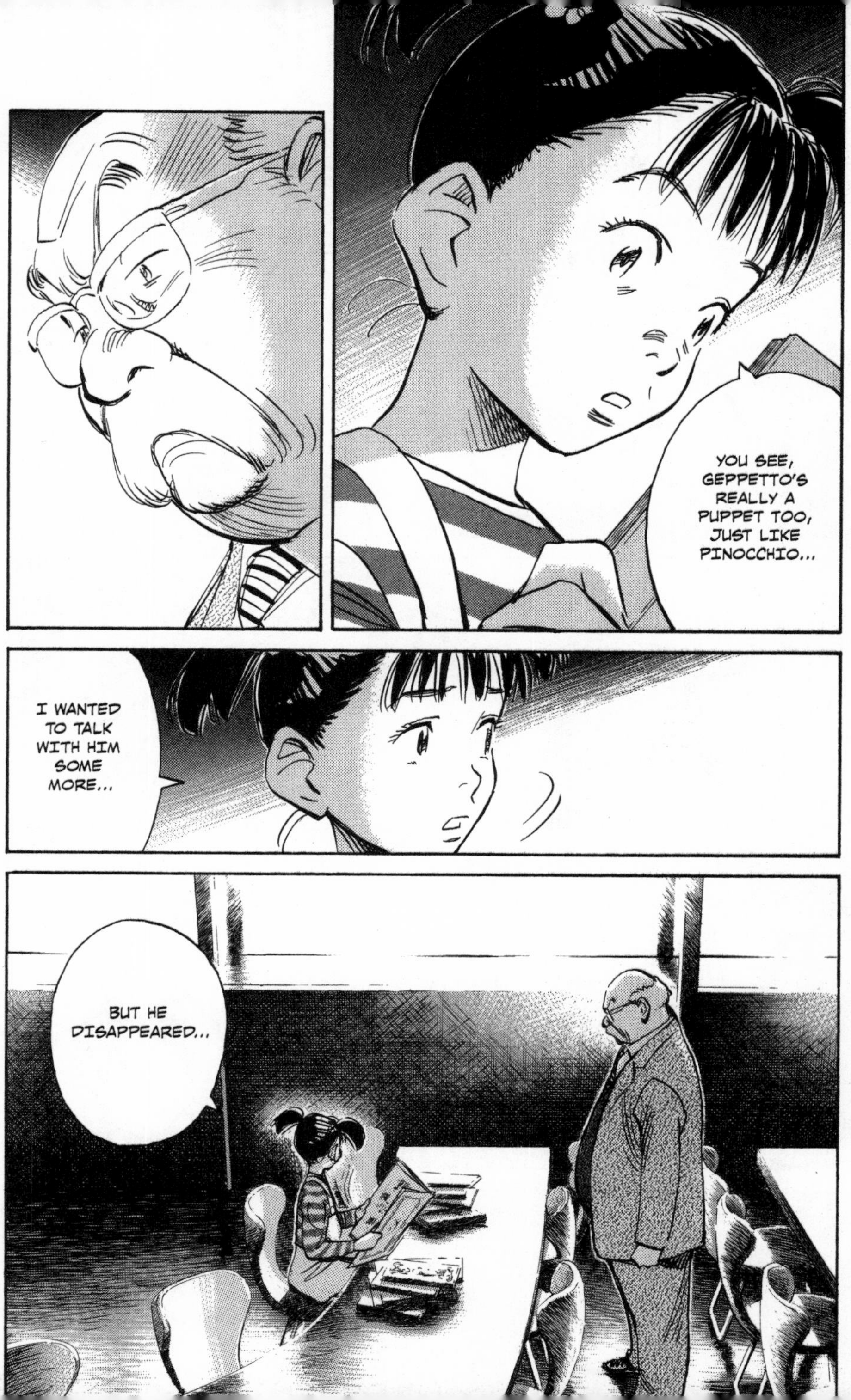
YOU SEE, GEPPETTO'S REALLY A PUPPET TOO, JUST LIKE PINOCCHIO...
I WANTED TO TALK WITH HIM SOME MORE...
BUT HE DISAPPEARED...

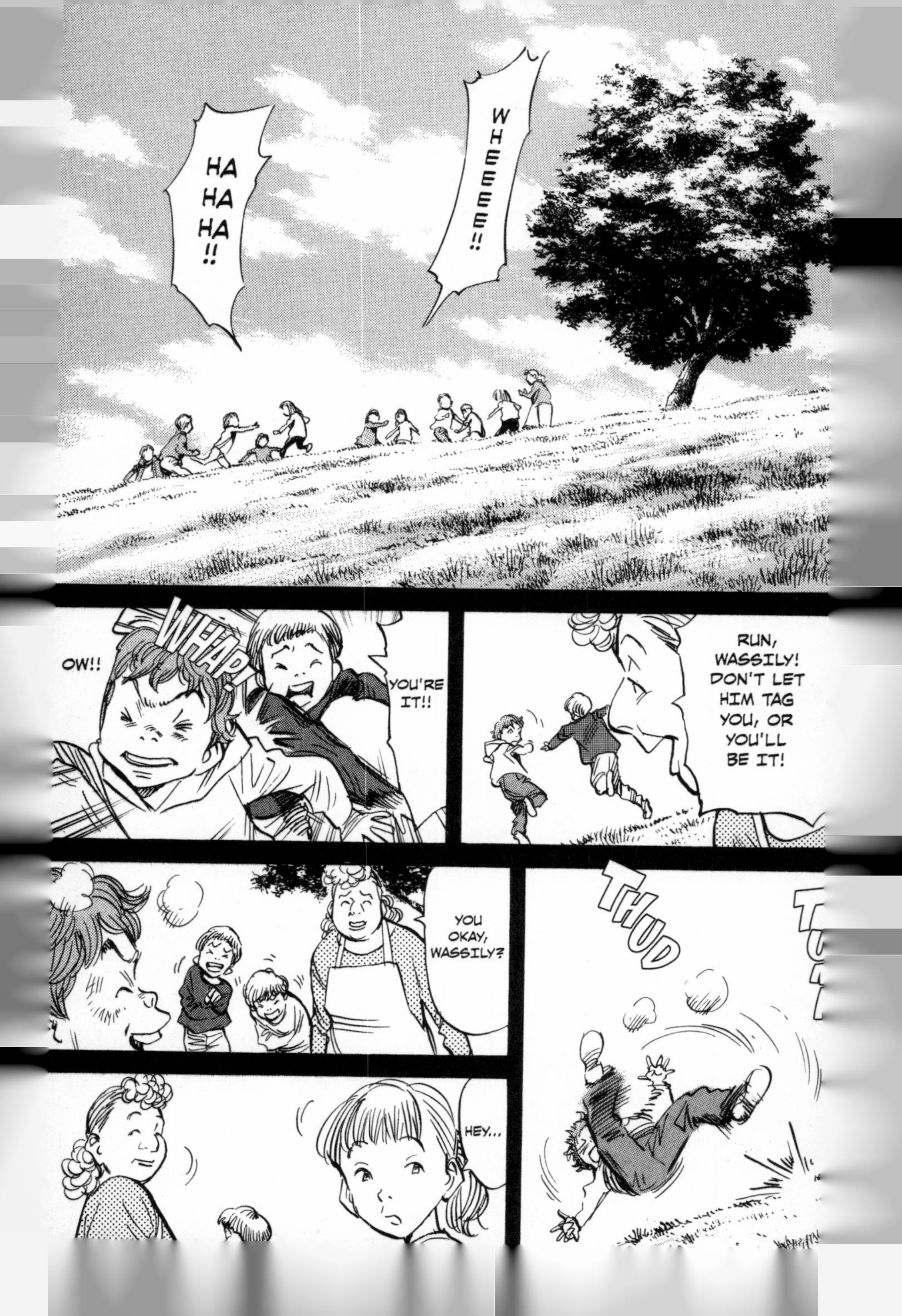
WHEEEEE!!
HA HA HA!!
RUN, WASSILY! DON'T LET HIM TAG YOU, OR YOU'LL BE IT!
WHAP
YOU'RE IT!!
OW!!
THUD
YOU OKAY, WASSILY?
HEY...

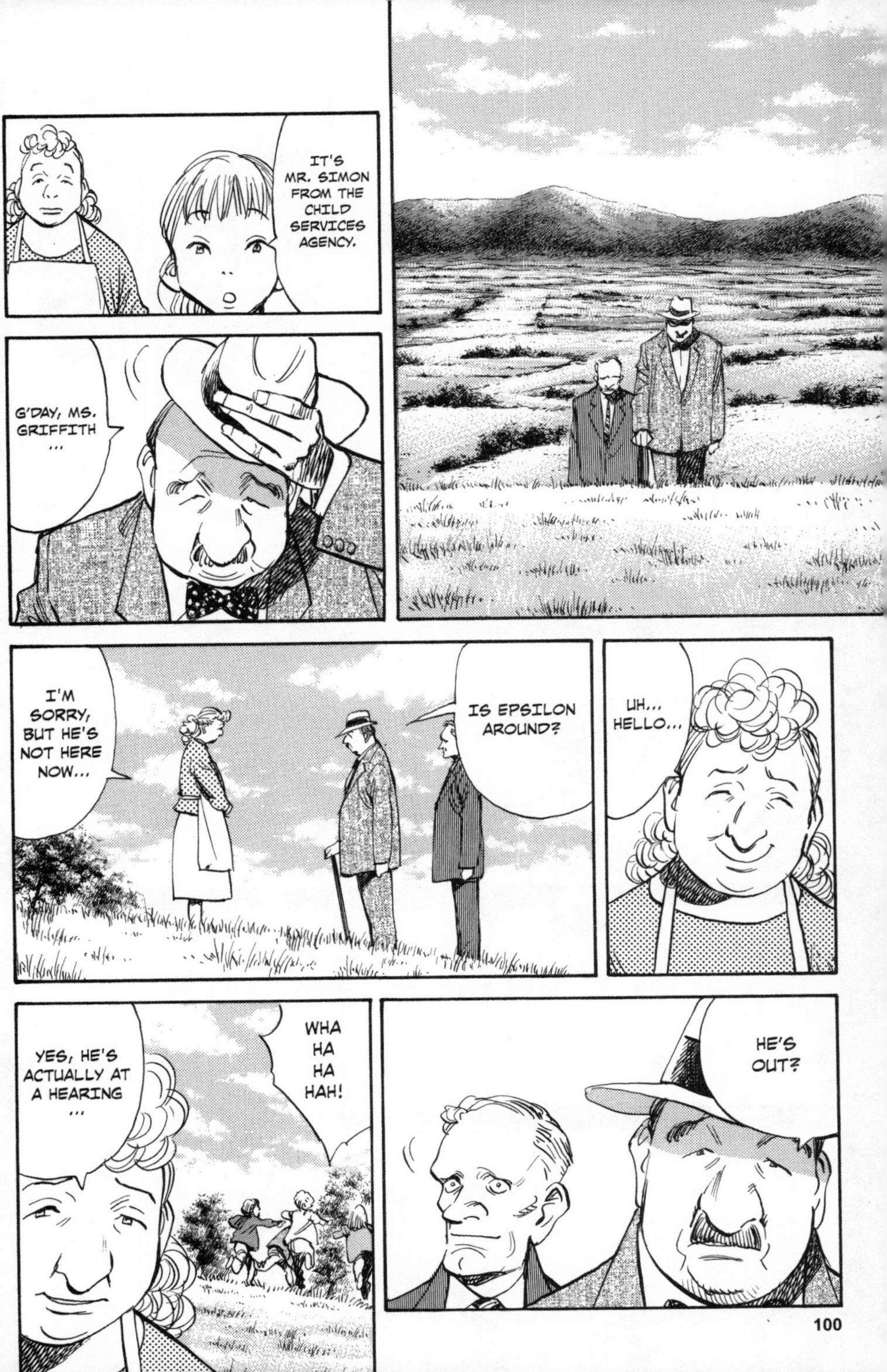
IT'S MR. SIMON FROM THE CHILD SERVICES AGENCY.
G'DAY, MS. GRIFFITH ...
UH... HELLO...
IS EPSILON AROUND?
I'M SORRY, BUT HE'S NOT HERE NOW...
HE'S OUT?
WHA HA HA HAH!
YES, HE'S ACTUALLY AT A HEARING ...

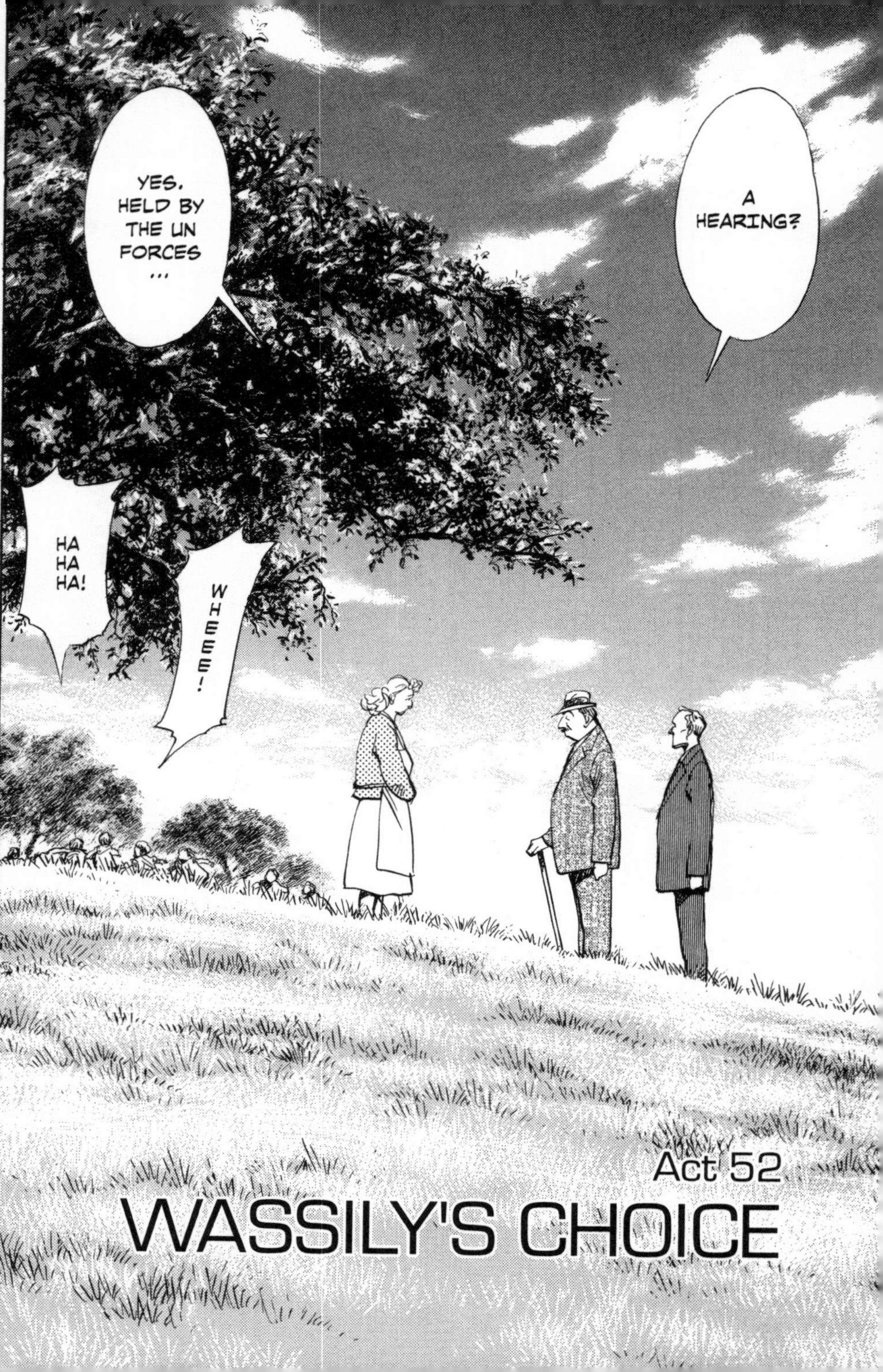
A HEARING?
YES. HELD BY THE UN FORCES ...
WHEEEE!
HA HA HA!
Act 52
WASSILY'S CHOICE

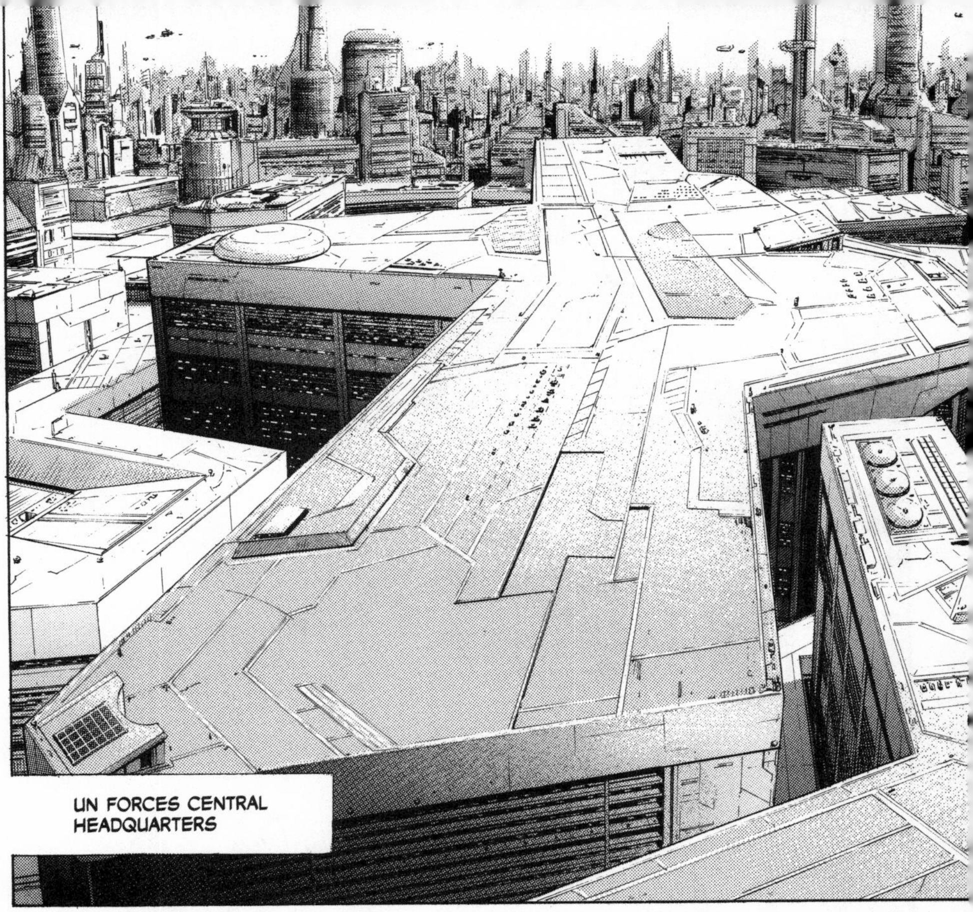
UN FORCES CENTRAL HEADQUARTERS
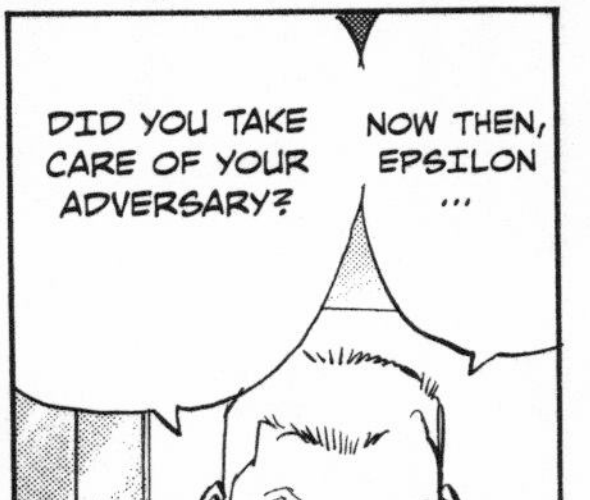
NOW THEN, EPSILON ...
DID YOU TAKE CARE OF YOUR ADVERSARY?
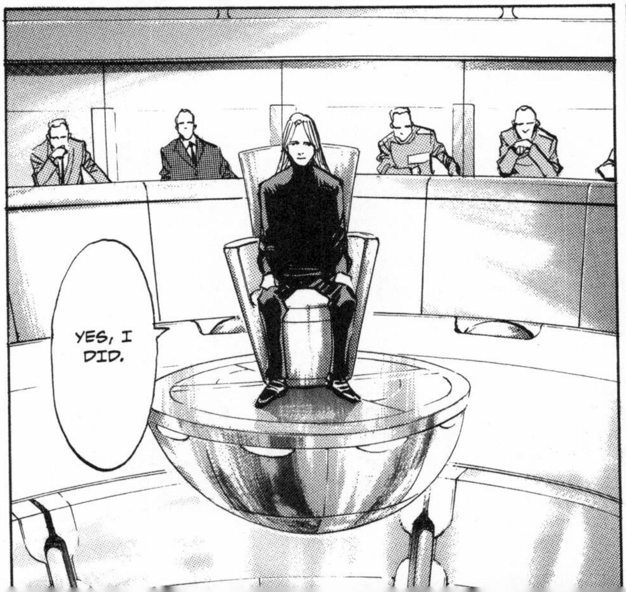
YES, I DID.

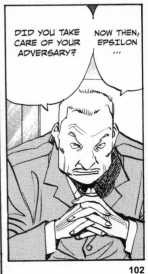

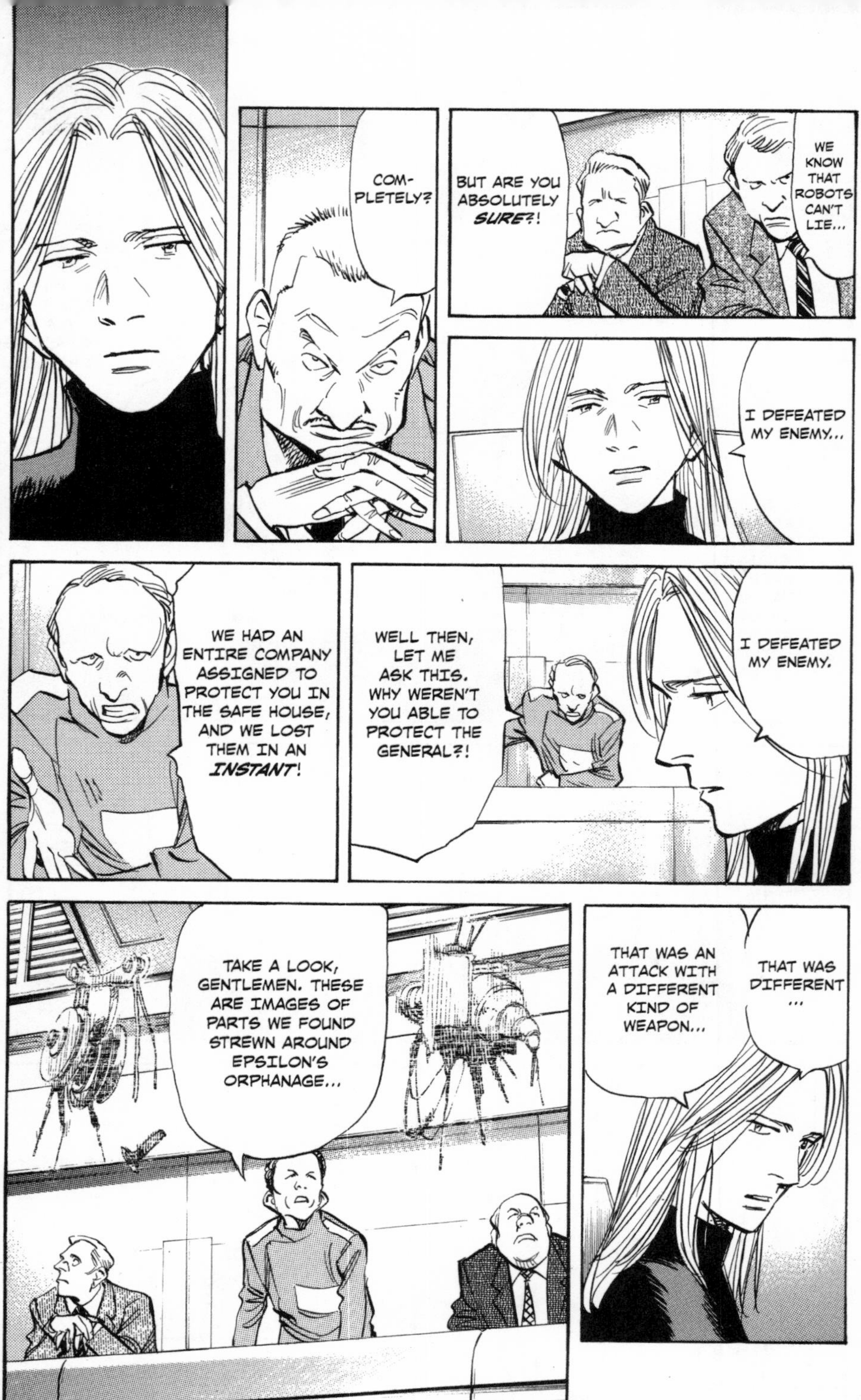
WE KNOW THAT ROBOTS CAN'T LIE...
BUT ARE YOU ABSOLUTELY SURE?!
I DEFEATED MY ENEMY...
COM-PLETELY?
I DEFEATED MY ENEMY.
WELL THEN, LET ME ASK THIS. WHY WEREN'T YOU ABLE TO PROTECT THE GENERAL?!
WE HAD AN ENTIRE COMPANY ASSIGNED TO PROTECT YOU IN THE SAFE HOUSE, AND WE LOST THEM IN AN INSTANT!
THAT WAS DIFFERENT...
THAT WAS AN ATTACK WITH A DIFFERENT KIND OF WEAPON...
TAKE A LOOK, GENTLEMEN. THESE ARE IMAGES OF PARTS WE FOUND STREWN AROUND EPSILON'S ORPHANAGE...

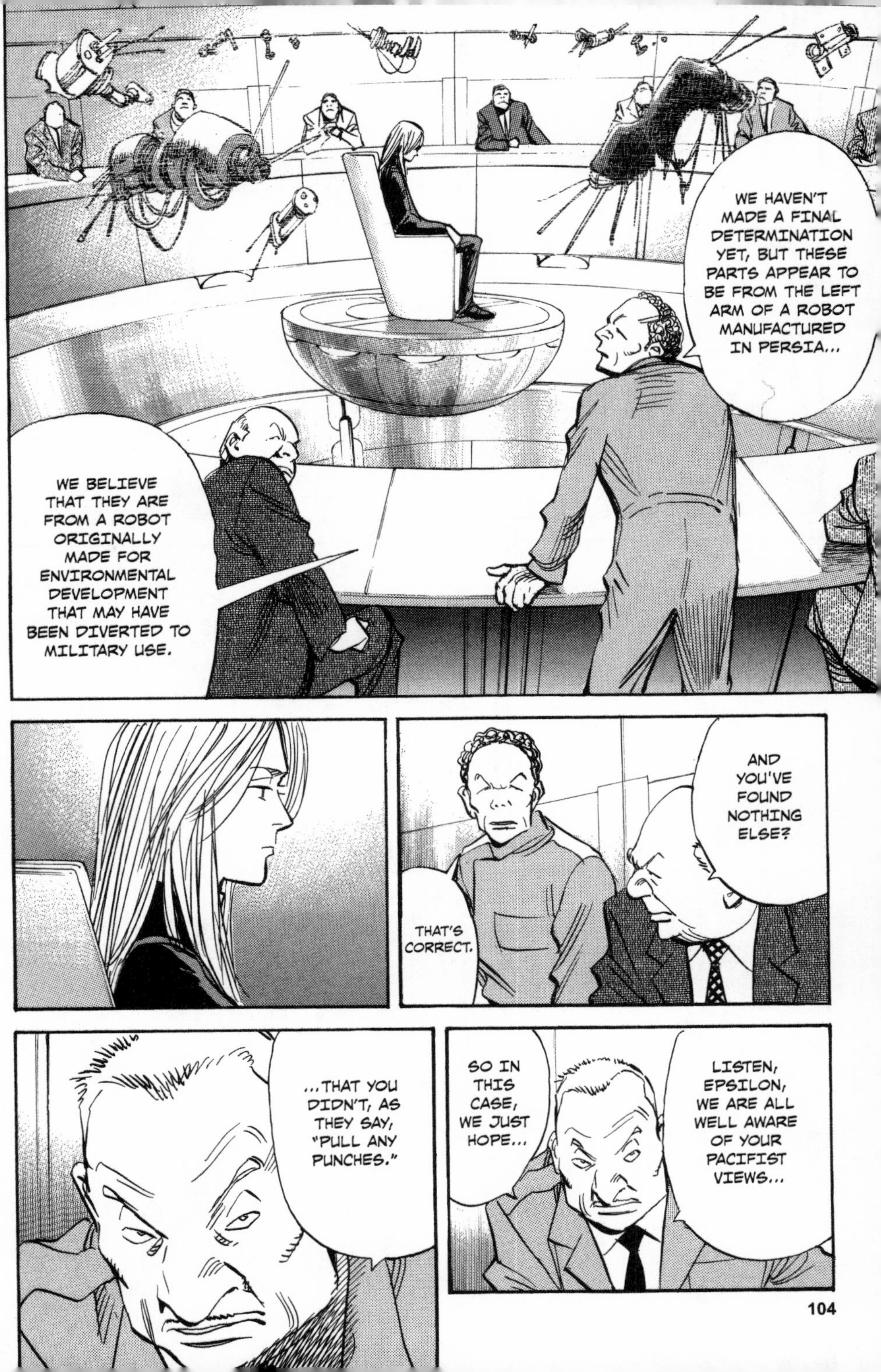
WE HAVEN'T MADE A FINAL DETERMINATION YET, BUT THESE PARTS APPEAR TO BE FROM THE LEFT ARM OF A ROBOT MANUFACTURED IN PERSIA...
WE BELIEVE THAT THEY ARE FROM A ROBOT ORIGINALLY MADE FOR ENVIRONMENTAL DEVELOPMENT THAT MAY HAVE BEEN DIVERTED TO MILITARY USE.
AND YOU'VE FOUND NOTHING ELSE?
THAT'S CORRECT.
LISTEN, EPSILON, WE ARE ALL WELL AWARE OF YOUR PACIFIST VIEWS...
SO IN THIS CASE, WE JUST HOPE...
...THAT YOU DIDN'T, AS THEY SAY, "PULL ANY PUNCHES."

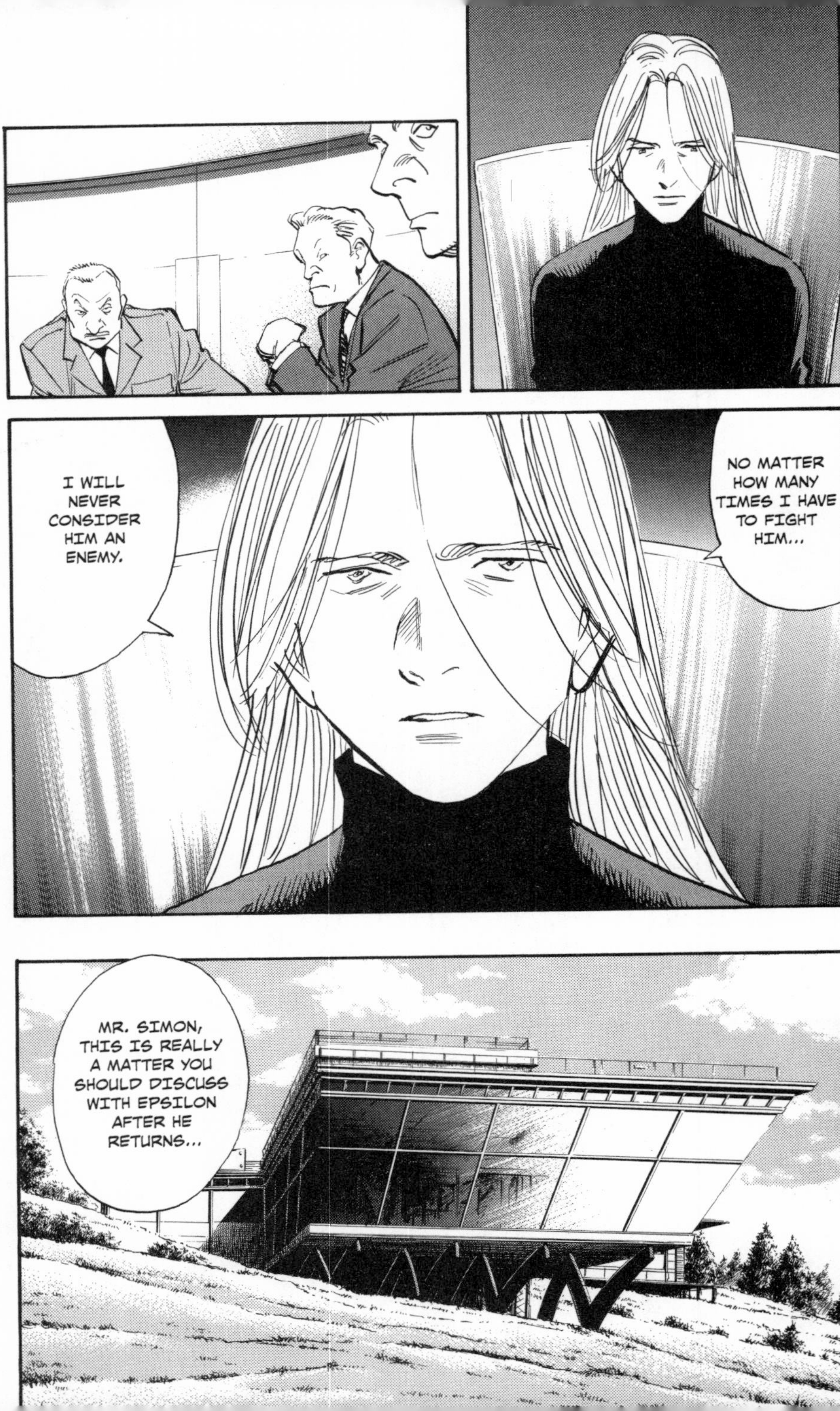
NO MATTER HOW MANY TIMES I HAVE TO FIGHT HIM...
I WILL NEVER CONSIDER HIM AN ENEMY.
MR. SIMON, THIS IS REALLY A MATTER YOU SHOULD DISCUSS WITH EPSILON AFTER HE RETURNS...

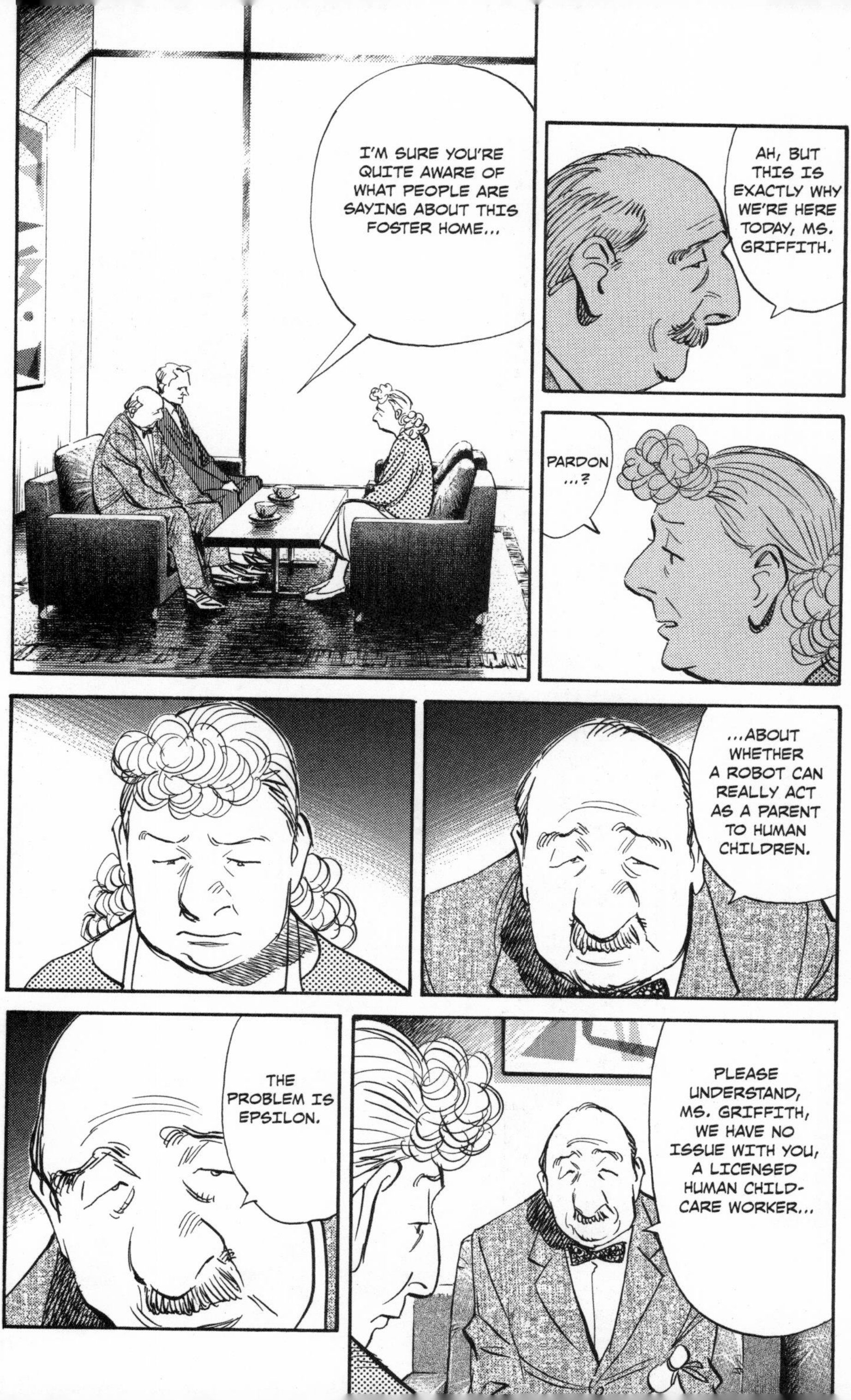
AH, BUT THIS IS EXACTLY WHY WE'RE HERE TODAY, MS. GRIFFITH.
PARDON ...?
I'M SURE YOU'RE QUITE AWARE OF WHAT PEOPLE ARE SAYING ABOUT THIS FOSTER HOME...
...ABOUT WHETHER A ROBOT CAN REALLY ACT AS A PARENT TO HUMAN CHILDREN.
PLEASE UNDERSTAND, MS. GRIFFITH, WE HAVE NO ISSUE WITH YOU, A LICENSED HUMAN CHILD-CARE WORKER...
THE PROBLEM IS EPSILON.

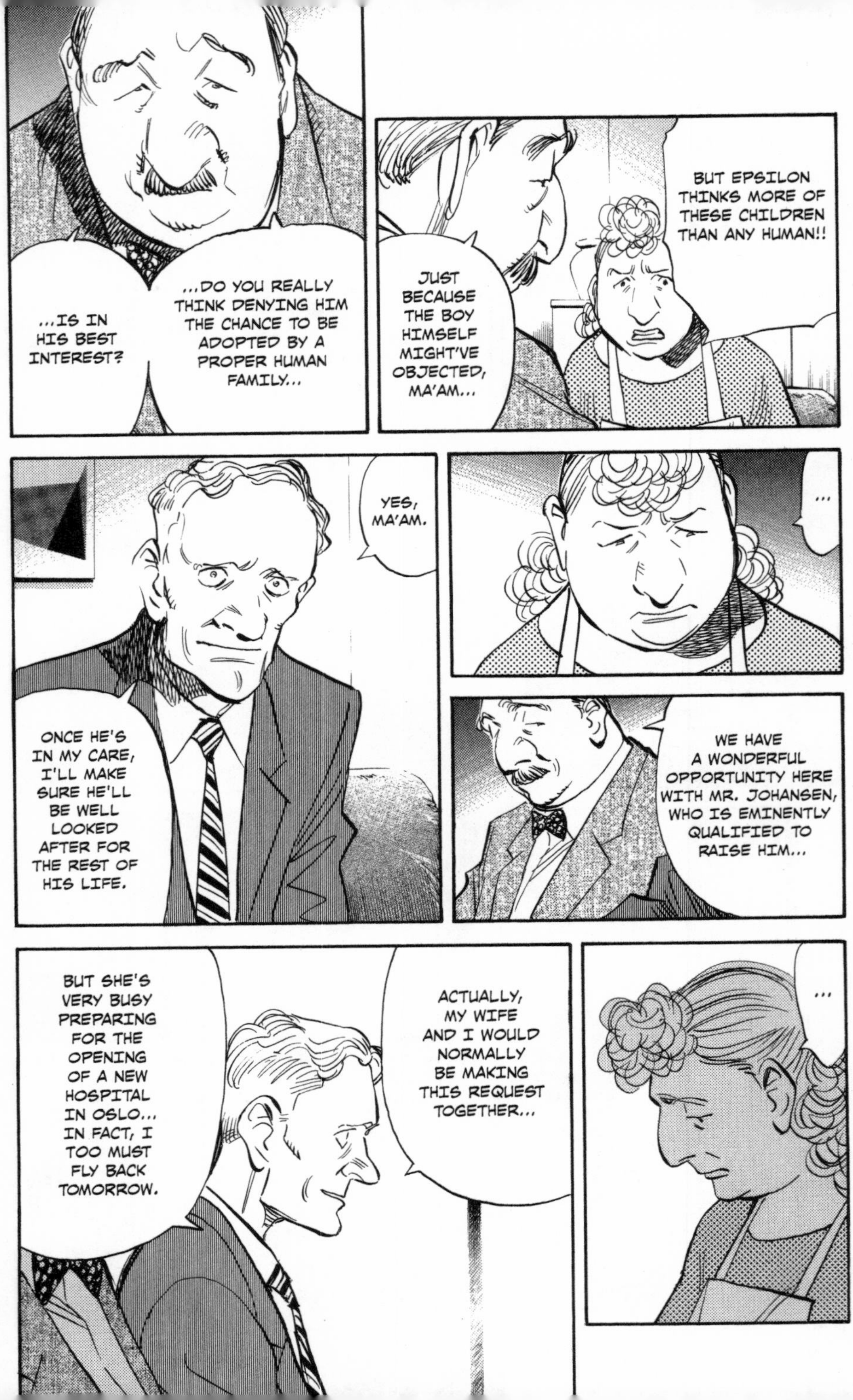
BUT EPSILON THINKS MORE OF THESE CHILDREN THAN ANY HUMAN!!
JUST BECAUSE THE BOY HIMSELF MIGHT'VE OBJECTED, MA'AM...
...DO YOU REALLY THINK DENYING HIM THE CHANCE TO BE ADOPTED BY A PROPER HUMAN FAMILY...
...IS IN HIS BEST INTEREST?
...
WE HAVE A WONDERFUL OPPORTUNITY HERE WITH MR. JOHANSEN, WHO IS EMINENTLY QUALIFIED TO RAISE HIM...
YES, MA'AM.
ONCE HE'S IN MY CARE, I'LL MAKE SURE HE'LL BE WELL LOOKED AFTER FOR THE REST OF HIS LIFE.
...
ACTUALLY, MY WIFE AND I WOULD NORMALLY BE MAKING THIS REQUEST TOGETHER...
BUT SHE'S VERY BUSY PREPARING FOR THE OPENING OF A NEW HOSPITAL IN OSLO... IN FACT, I TOO MUST FLY BACK TOMORROW.

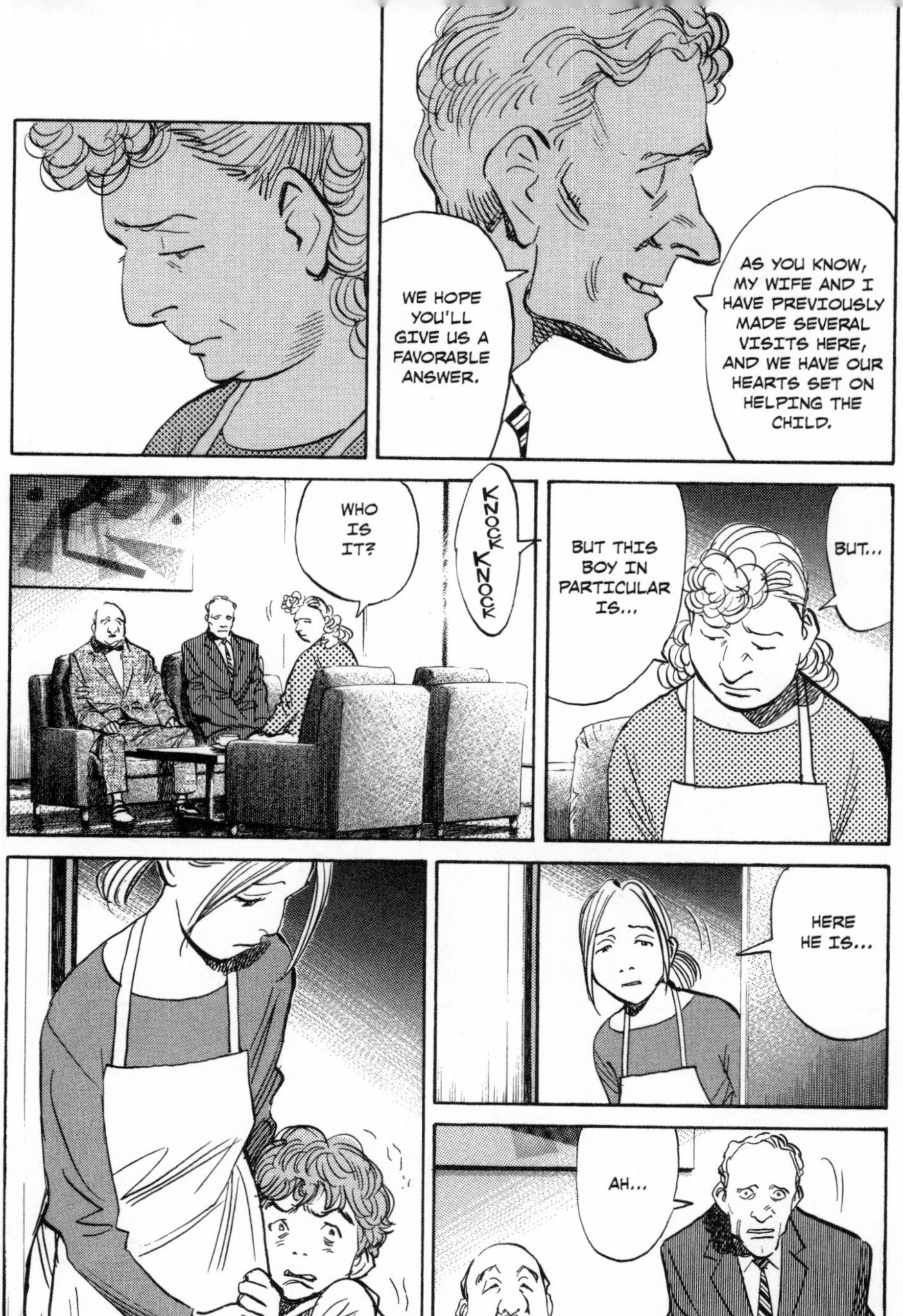
AS YOU KNOW, MY WIFE AND I HAVE PREVIOUSLY MADE SEVERAL VISITS HERE, AND WE HAVE OUR HEARTS SET ON HELPING THE CHILD.
WE HOPE YOU'LL GIVE US A FAVORABLE ANSWER.
BUT...
BUT THIS BOY IN PARTICULAR IS...
KNOCK KNOCK
WHO IS IT?
HERE HE IS...
AH...

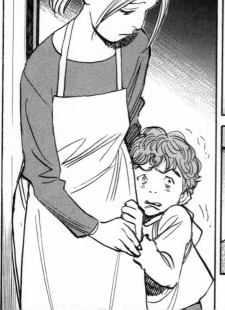

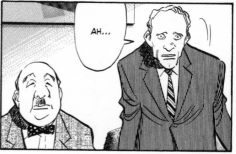

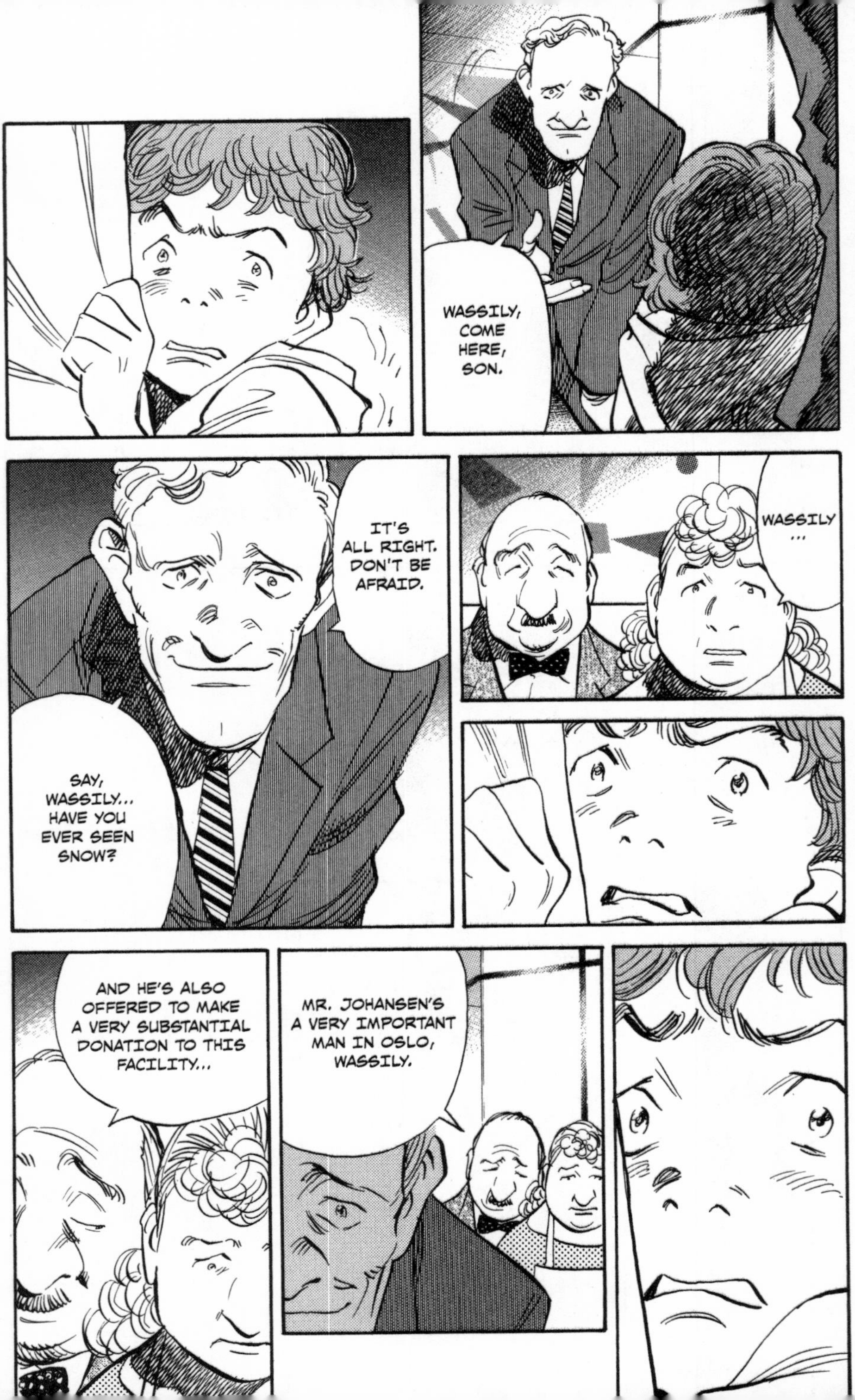
WASSILY, COME HERE, SON.
WASSILY ...
IT'S ALL RIGHT. DON'T BE AFRAID.
SAY, WASSILY... HAVE YOU EVER SEEN SNOW?
MR. JOHANSEN'S A VERY IMPORTANT MAN IN OSLO, WASSILY.
AND HE'S ALSO OFFERED TO MAKE A VERY SUBSTANTIAL DONATION TO THIS FACILITY...

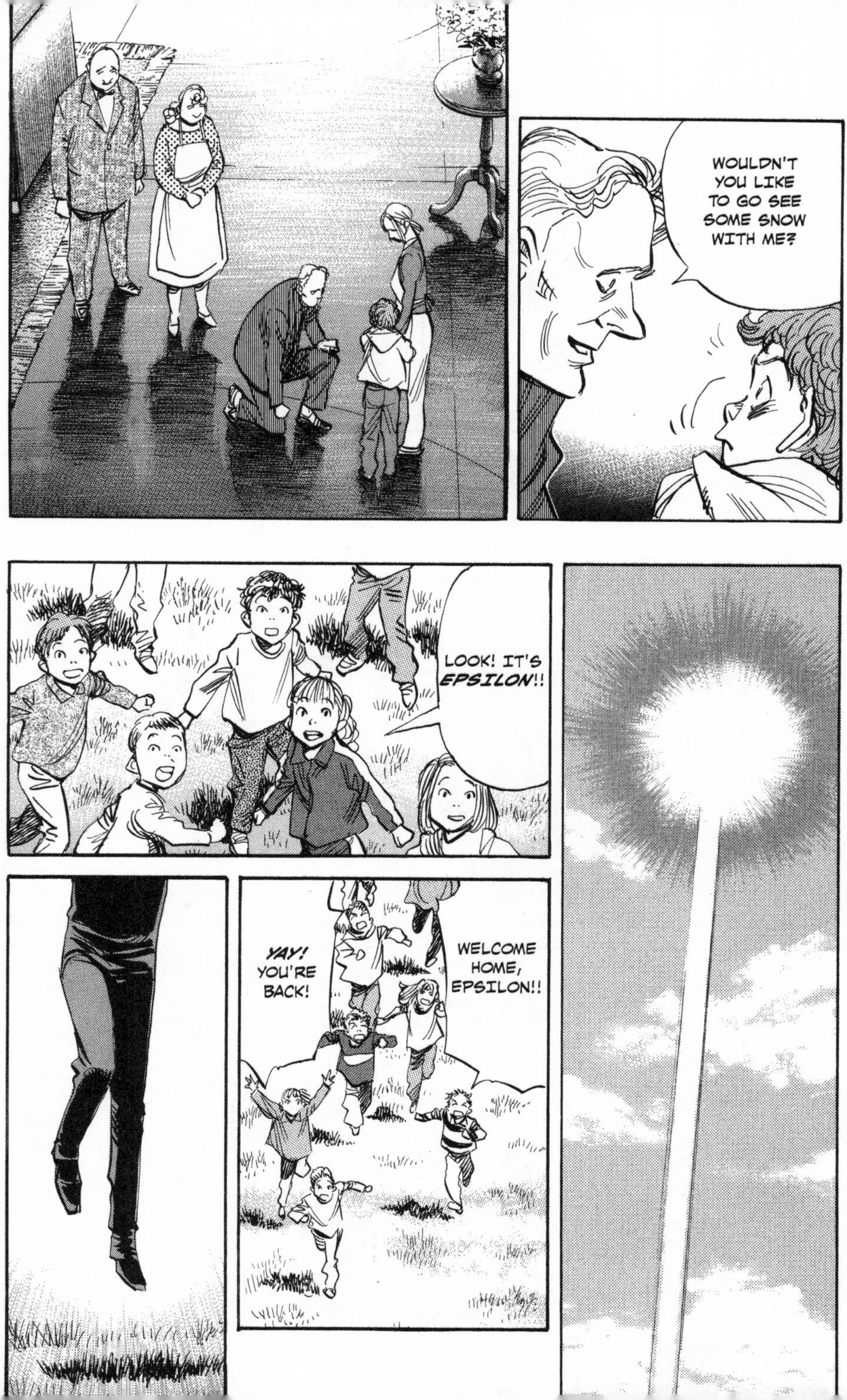
WOULDN'T YOU LIKE TO GO SEE SOME SNOW WITH ME?
LOOK! IT'S *EPSILON*!!
WELCOME HOME, EPSILON!!
YAY! YOU'RE BACK!

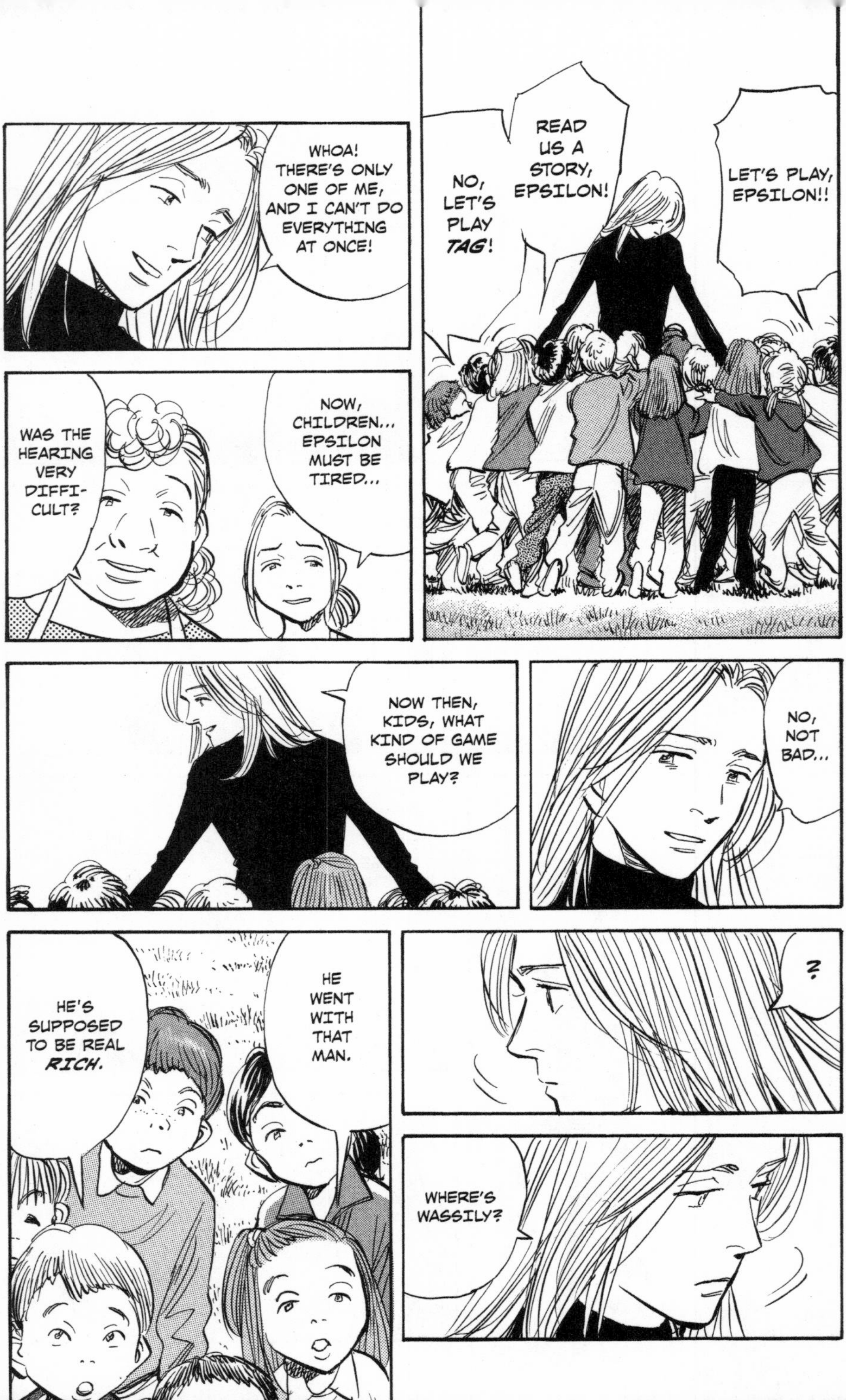
LET'S PLAY, EPSILON!!
READ US A STORY, EPSILON!
NO, LET'S PLAY TAG!
WHOA! THERE'S ONLY ONE OF ME, AND I CAN'T DO EVERYTHING AT ONCE!
NOW, CHILDREN... EPSILON MUST BE TIRED...
WAS THE HEARING VERY DIFFI-CULT?
NO, NOT BAD...
NOW THEN, KIDS, WHAT KIND OF GAME SHOULD WE PLAY?
?
WHERE'S WASSILY?
HE WENT WITH THAT MAN.
HE'S SUPPOSED TO BE REAL RICH.

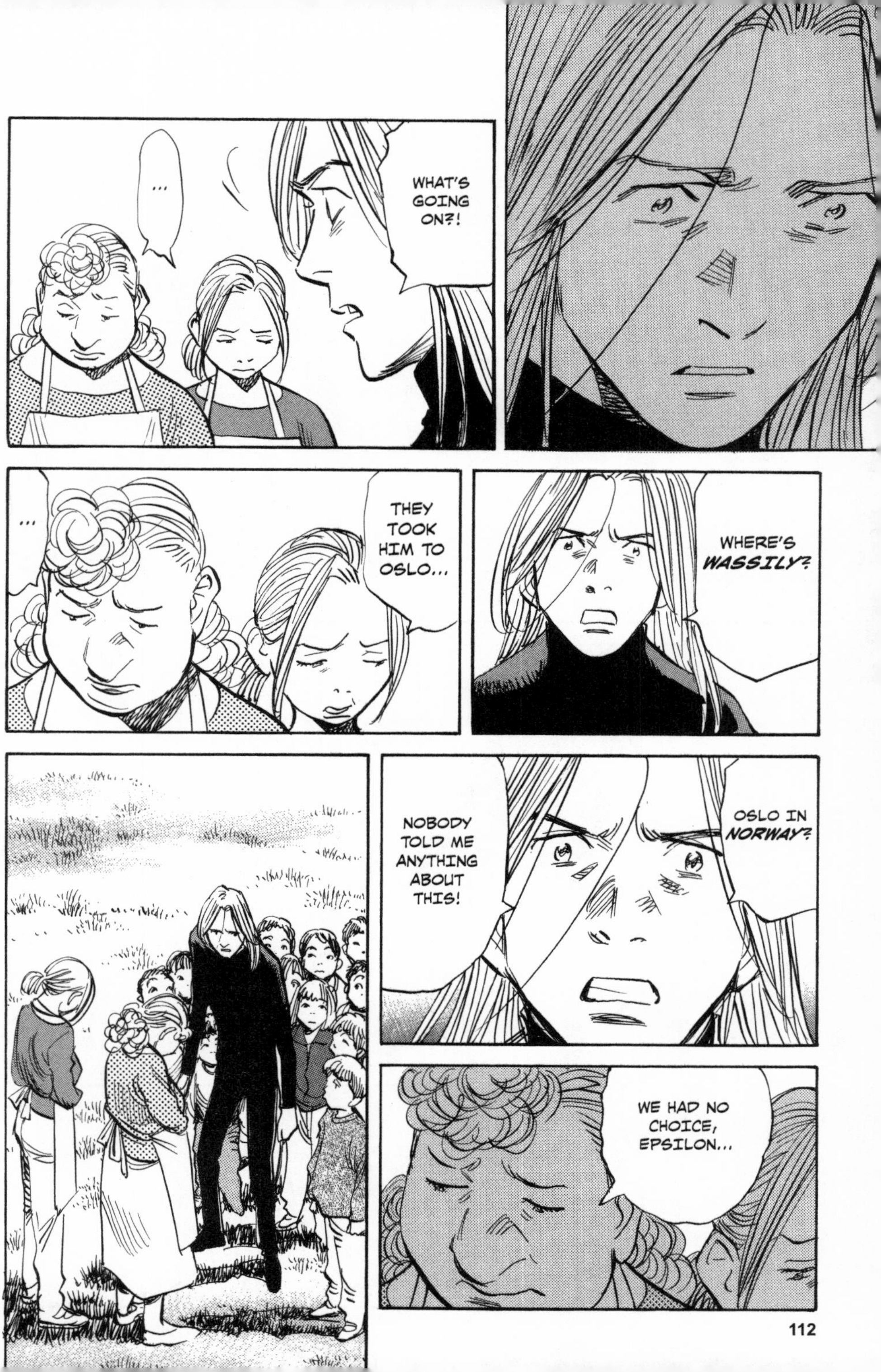
WHAT'S GOING ON?!
...
WHERE'S *WASSILY?*
THEY TOOK HIM TO OSLO...
...
OSLO IN *NORWAY?*
NOBODY TOLD ME ANYTHING ABOUT THIS!
WE HAD NO CHOICE, EPSILON...

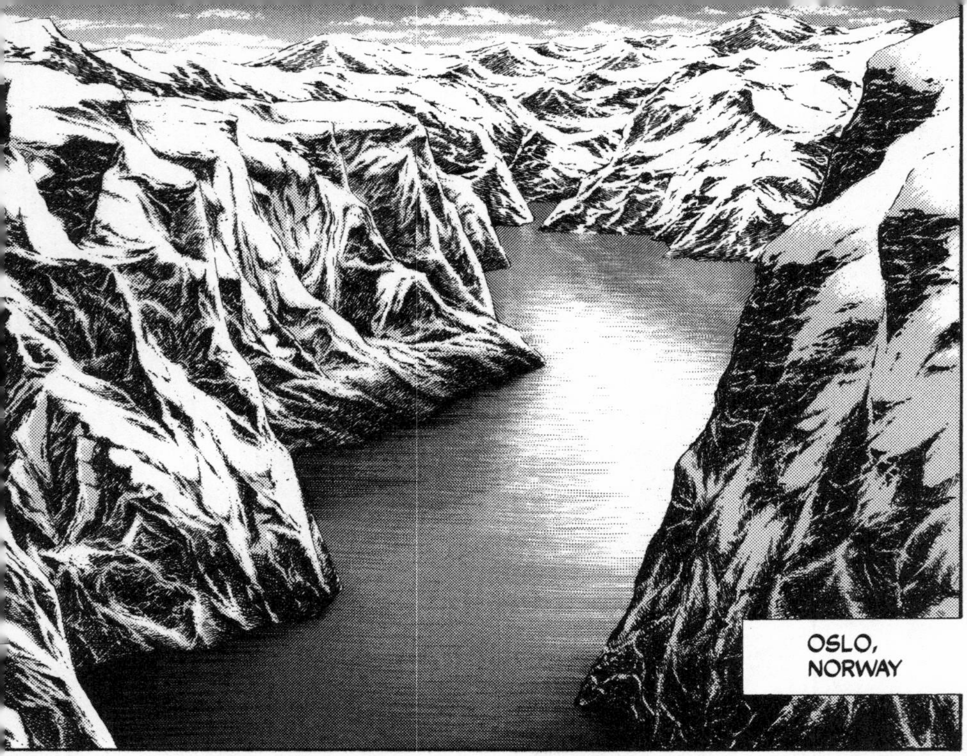
OSLO, NORWAY

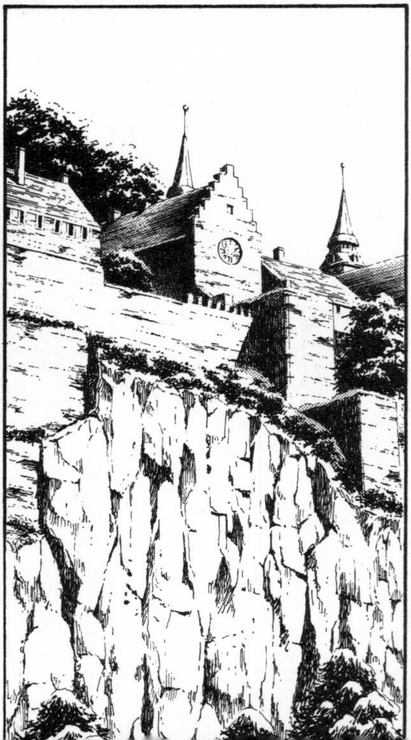

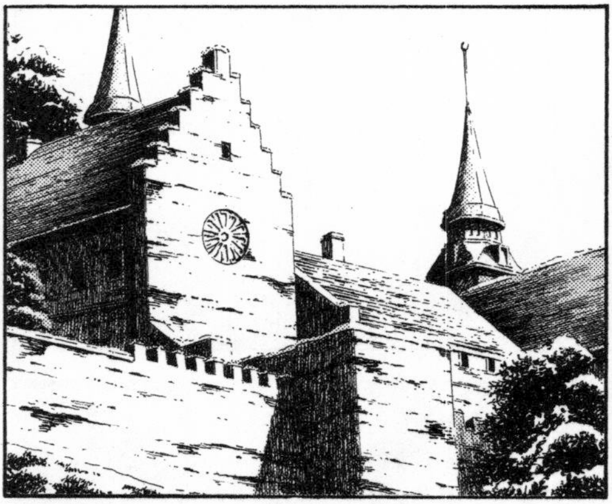

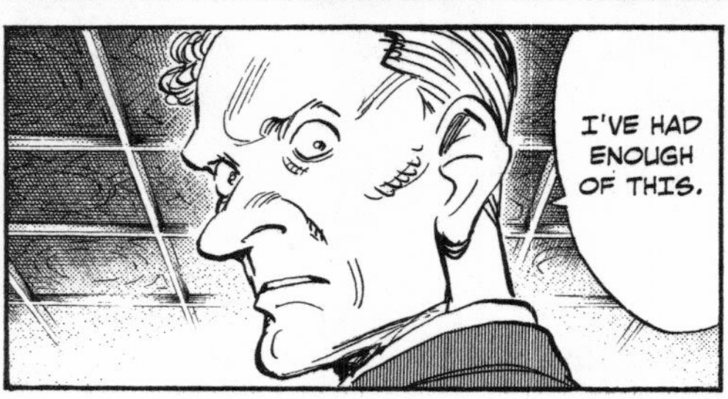
I'VE HAD ENOUGH OF THIS.

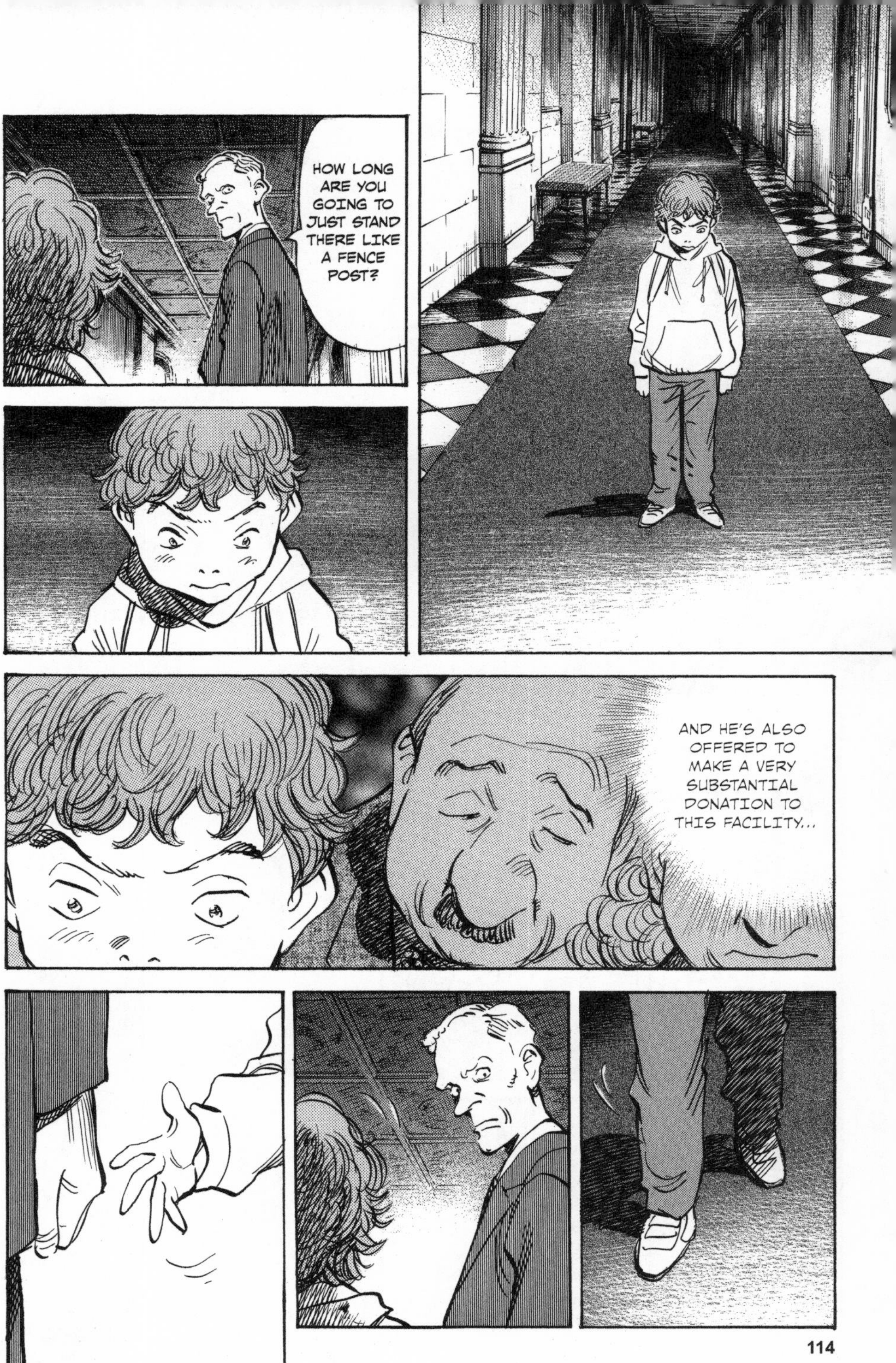
HOW LONG ARE YOU GOING TO JUST STAND THERE LIKE A FENCE POST?
AND HE'S ALSO OFFERED TO MAKE A VERY SUBSTANTIAL DONATION TO THIS FACILITY...

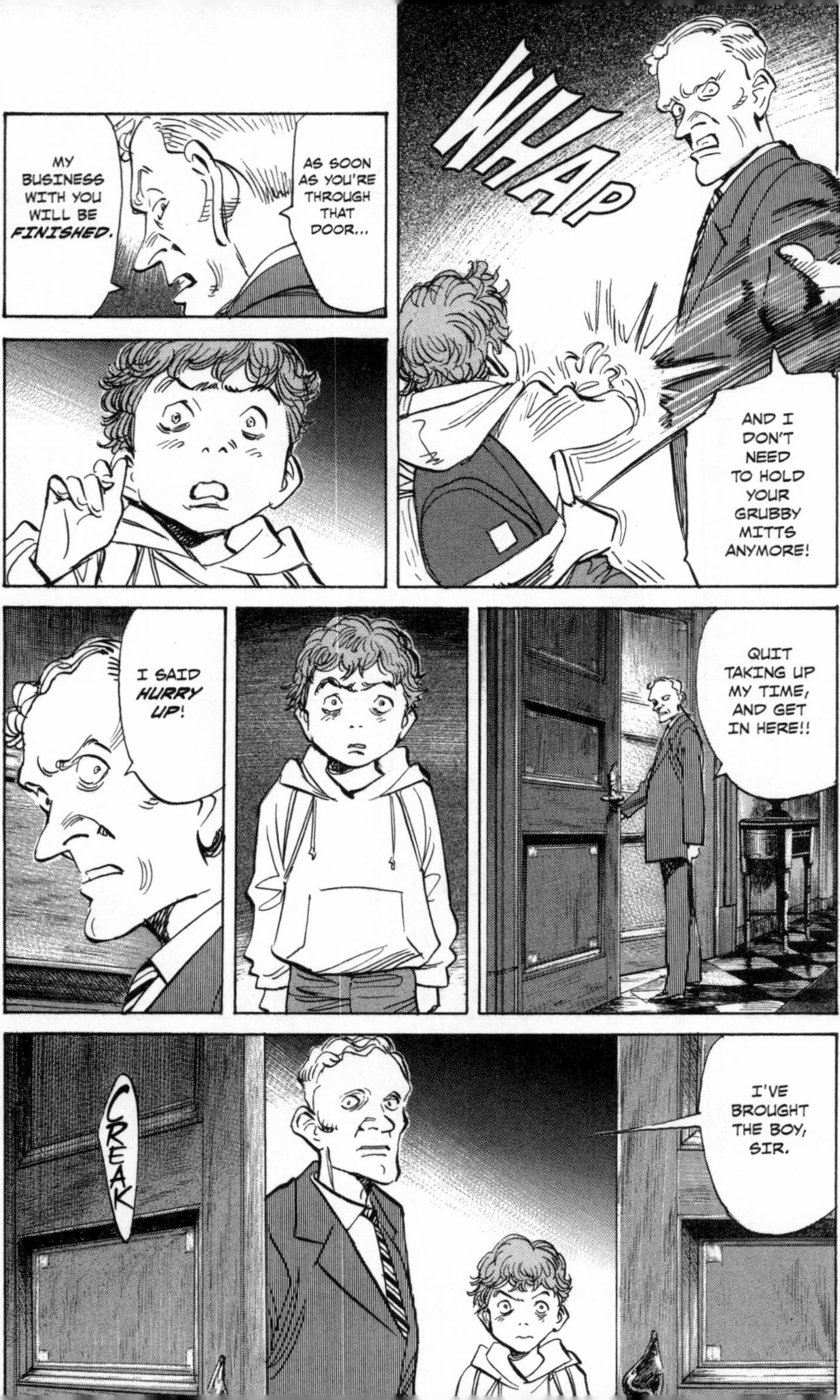
WHAP
AND I DON'T NEED TO HOLD YOUR GRUBBY MITTS ANYMORE!
AS SOON AS YOU'RE THROUGH THAT DOOR...
MY BUSINESS WITH YOU WILL BE ***FINISHED***.
QUIT TAKING UP MY TIME, AND GET IN HERE!!
I SAID ***HURRY UP***!
I'VE BROUGHT THE BOY, SIR.
CREAK

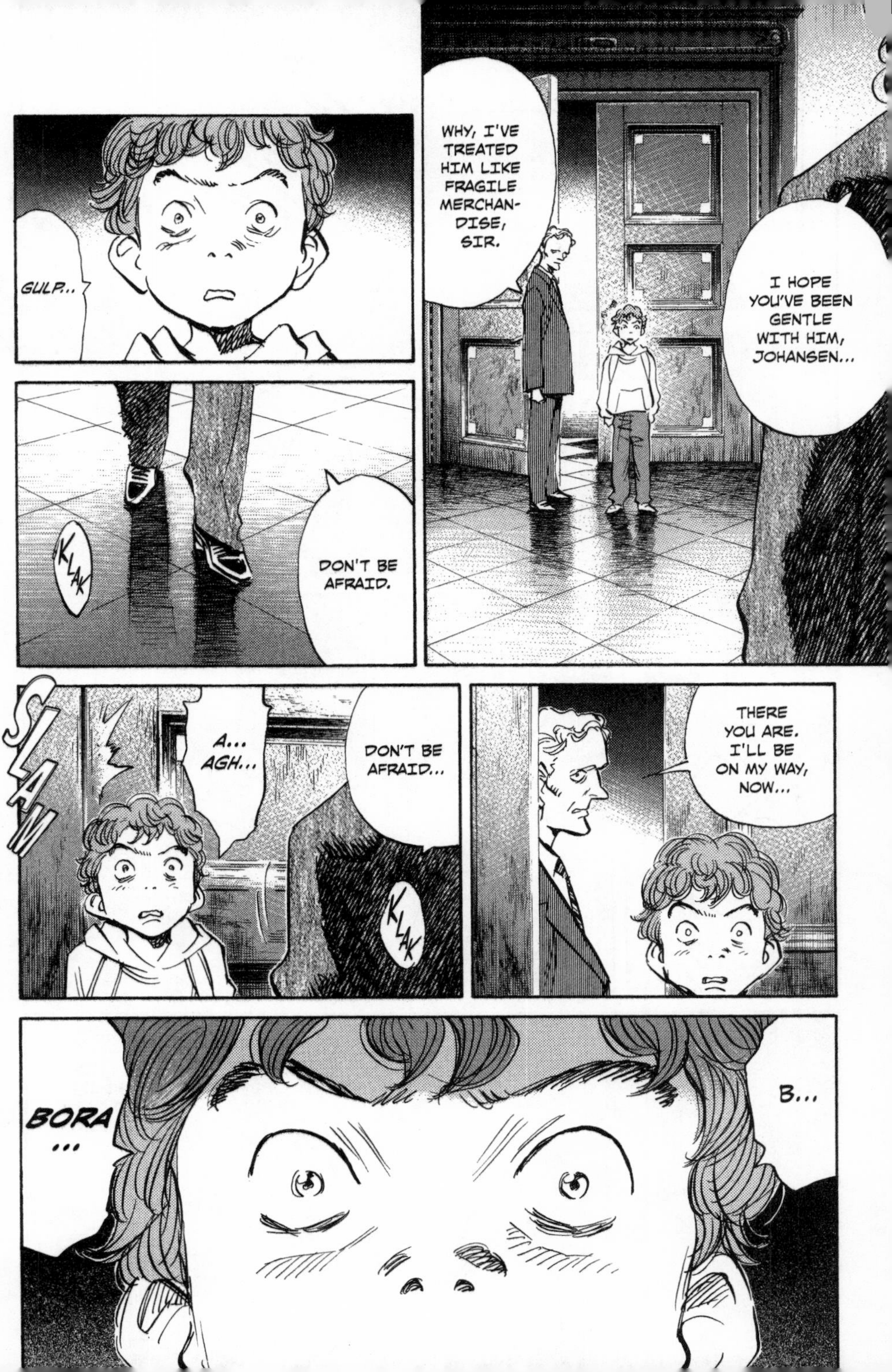
I HOPE YOU'VE BEEN GENTLE WITH HIM, JOHANSEN...
WHY, I'VE TREATED HIM LIKE FRAGILE MERCHANDISE, SIR.
GULP...
DON'T BE AFRAID.
KLAK
THERE YOU ARE. I'LL BE ON MY WAY, NOW...
DON'T BE AFRAID...
A... AGH...
KLAK
SLAM
B...
BORA ...

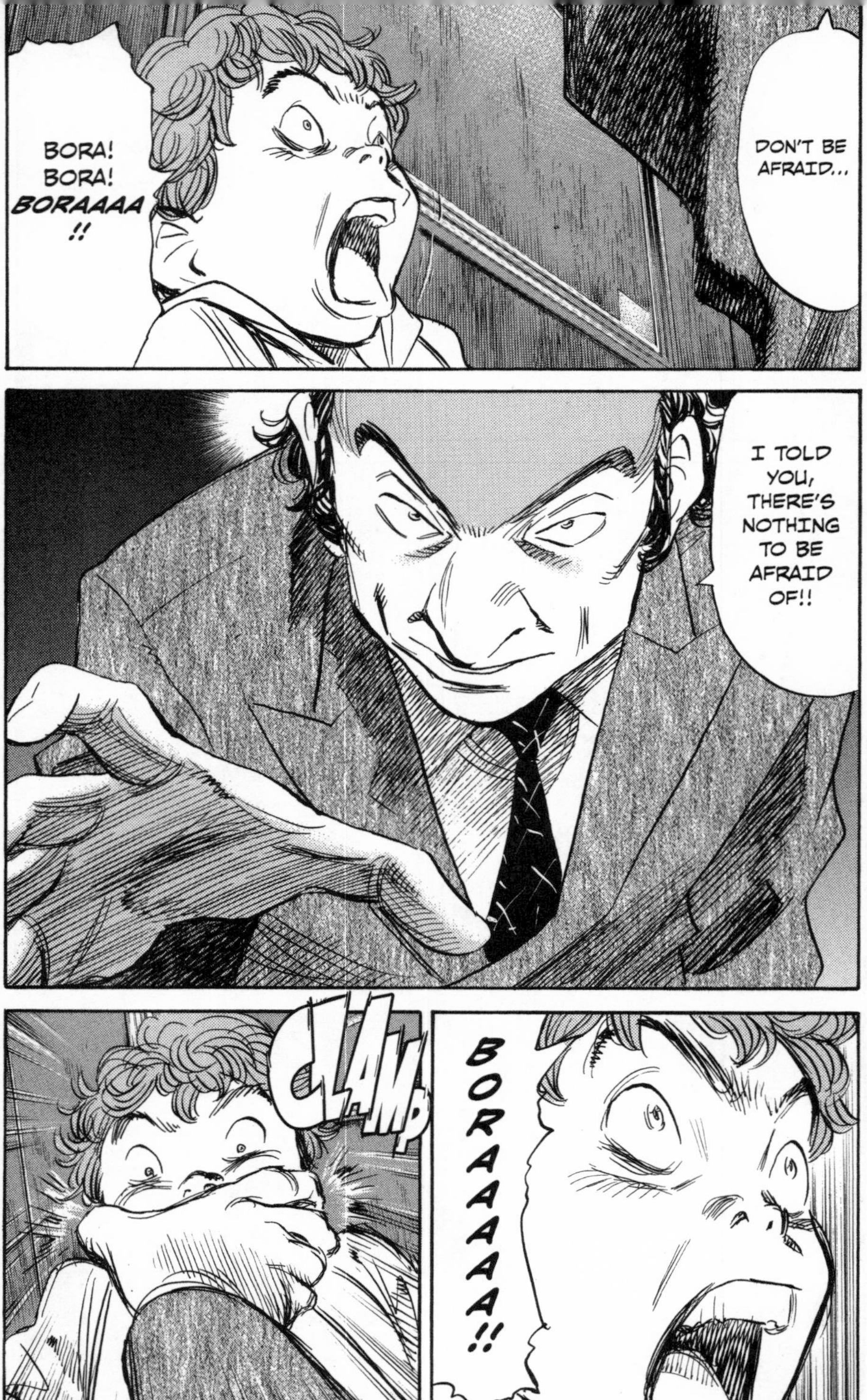
DON'T BE AFRAID...
BORA! BORA! BORAAAA!!
I TOLD YOU, THERE'S NOTHING TO BE AFRAID OF!!
BORAAAAAAA!!
CLAMP

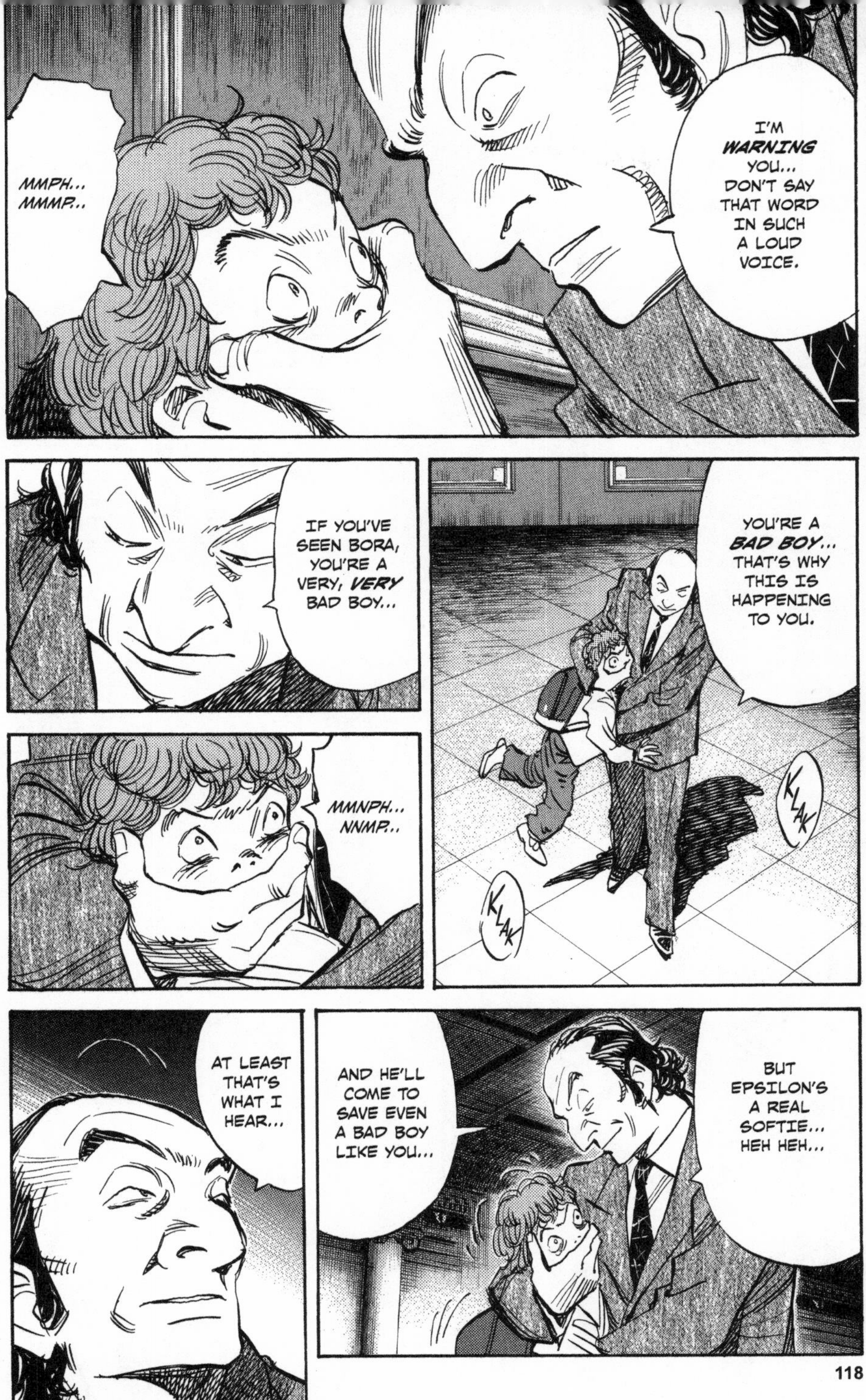
I'M WARNING YOU... DON'T SAY THAT WORD IN SUCH A LOUD VOICE.
MMPH... MMMP...
YOU'RE A BAD BOY... THAT'S WHY THIS IS HAPPENING TO YOU.
KLAK
KLAK
IF YOU'VE SEEN BORA, YOU'RE A VERY, VERY BAD BOY...
MMNPH... NNMP...
BUT EPSILON'S A REAL SOFTIE... HEH HEH...
AND HE'LL COME TO SAVE EVEN A BAD BOY LIKE YOU...
AT LEAST THAT'S WHAT I HEAR...

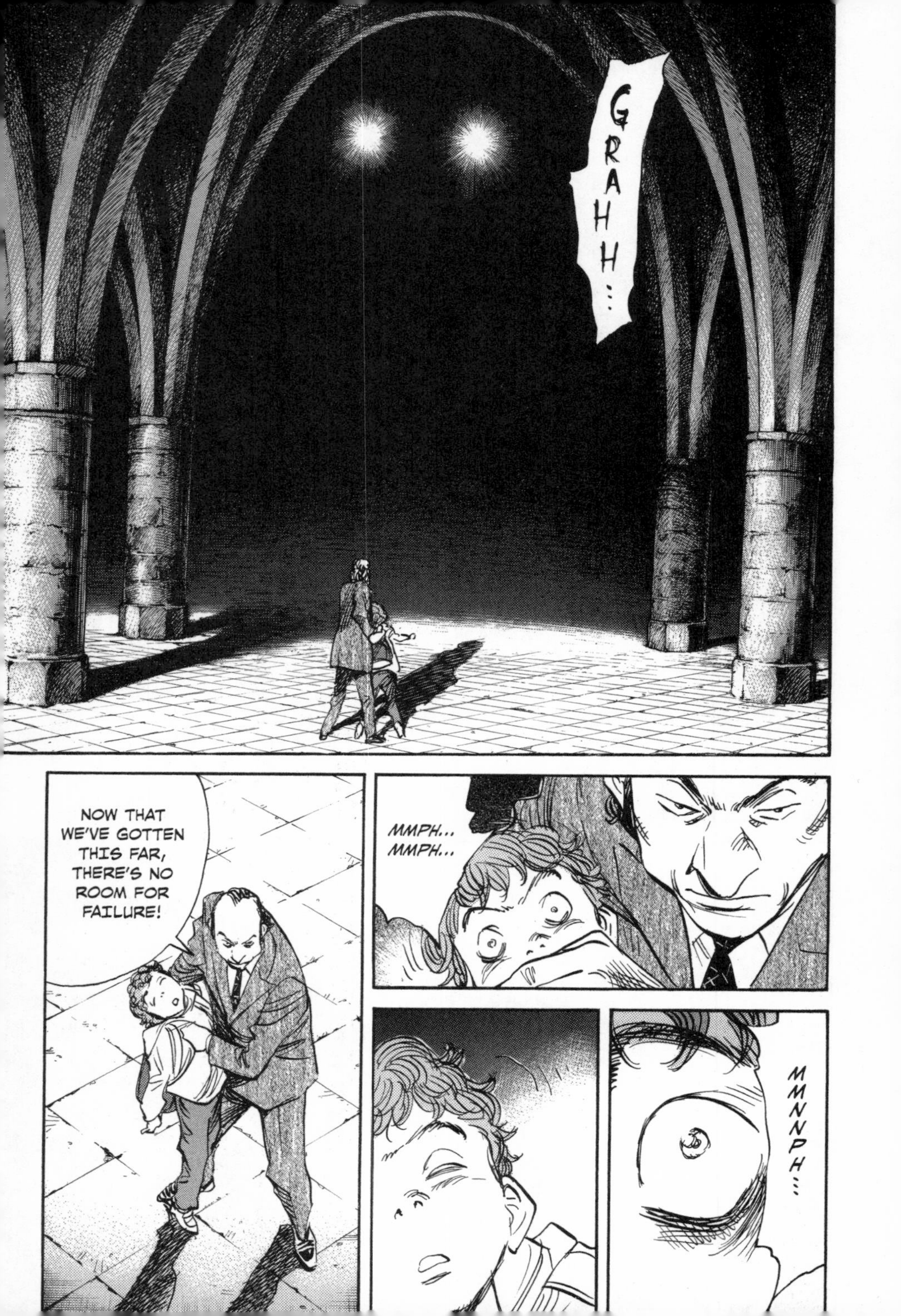
GRAHH...
MMPH... MMPH...
MMNNPH...
NOW THAT WE'VE GOTTEN THIS FAR, THERE'S NO ROOM FOR FAILURE!

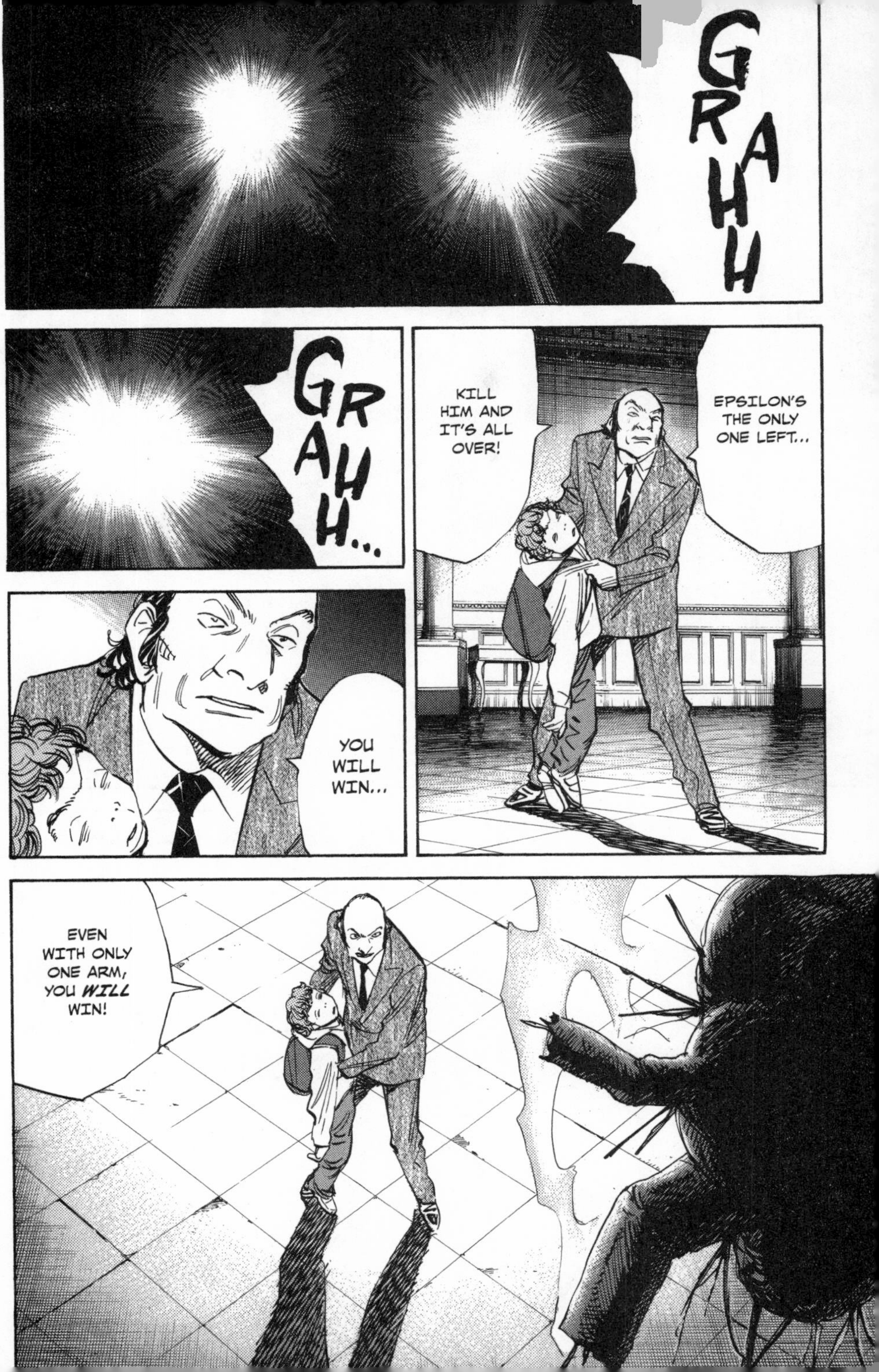
GRAHH
EPSILON'S THE ONLY ONE LEFT...
KILL HIM AND IT'S ALL OVER!
GRAHH...
YOU WILL WIN...
EVEN WITH ONLY ONE ARM, YOU **WILL** WIN!

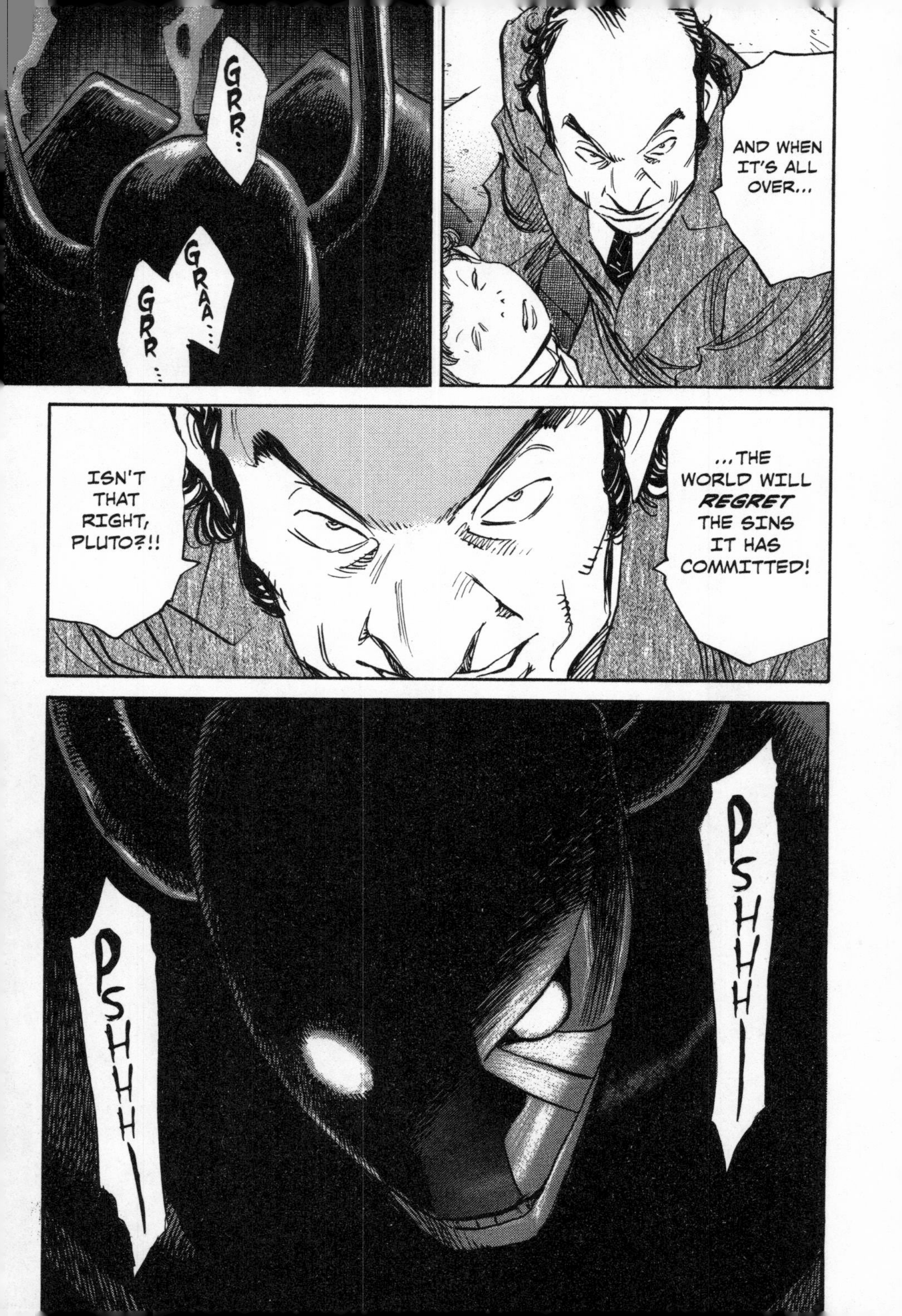
AND WHEN IT'S ALL OVER...
GRR...
GRAA...
GRR...
...THE WORLD WILL *REGRET* THE SINS IT HAS COMMITTED!
ISN'T THAT RIGHT, PLUTO?!!
PSHH—
PSHH—

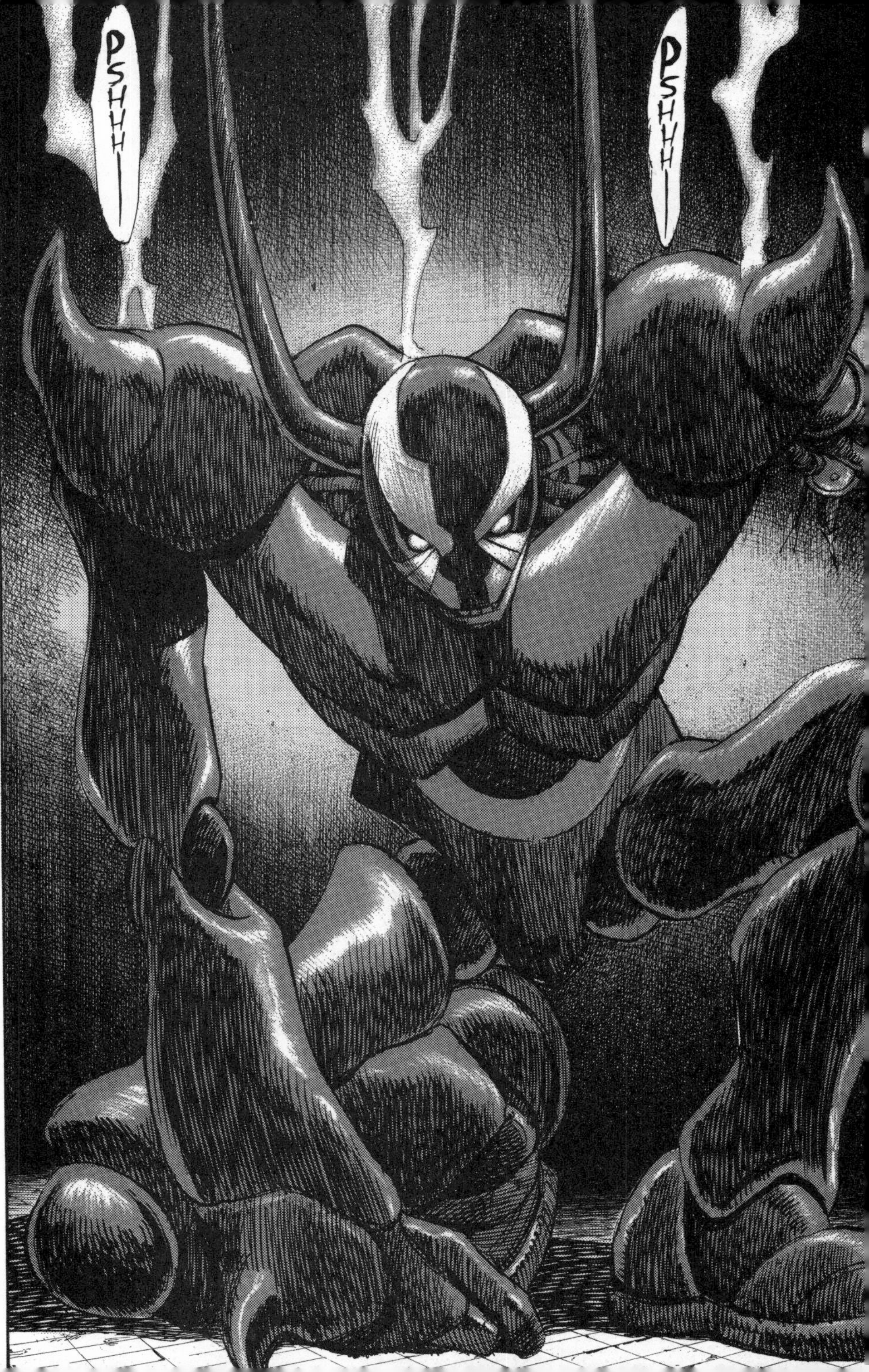
PSHHH
PSHHH

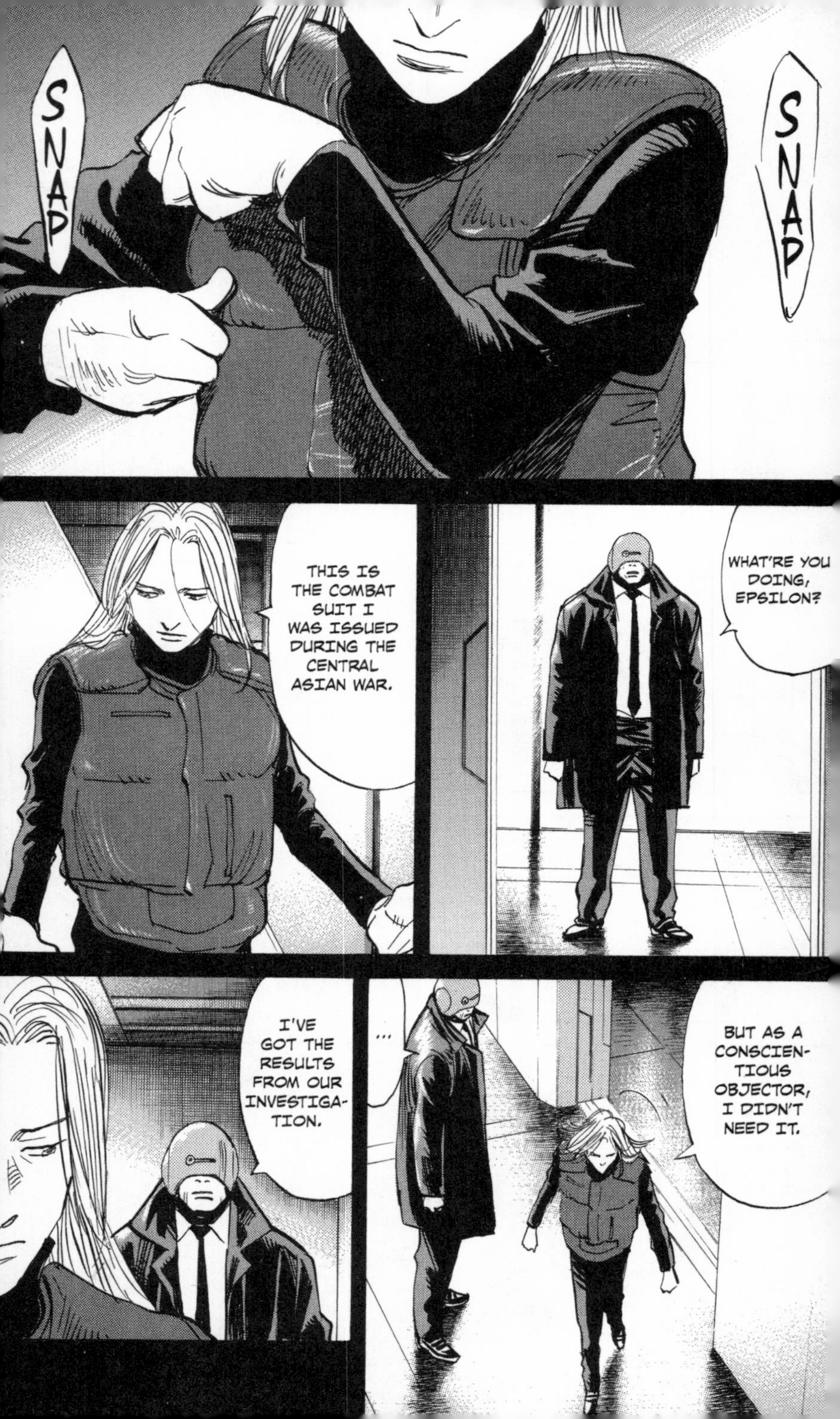
SNAP
SNAP
WHAT'RE YOU DOING, EPSILON?
THIS IS THE COMBAT SUIT I WAS ISSUED DURING THE CENTRAL ASIAN WAR.
BUT AS A CONSCIEN-TIOUS OBJECTOR, I DIDN'T NEED IT.
...
I'VE GOT THE RESULTS FROM OUR INVESTIGA-TION.

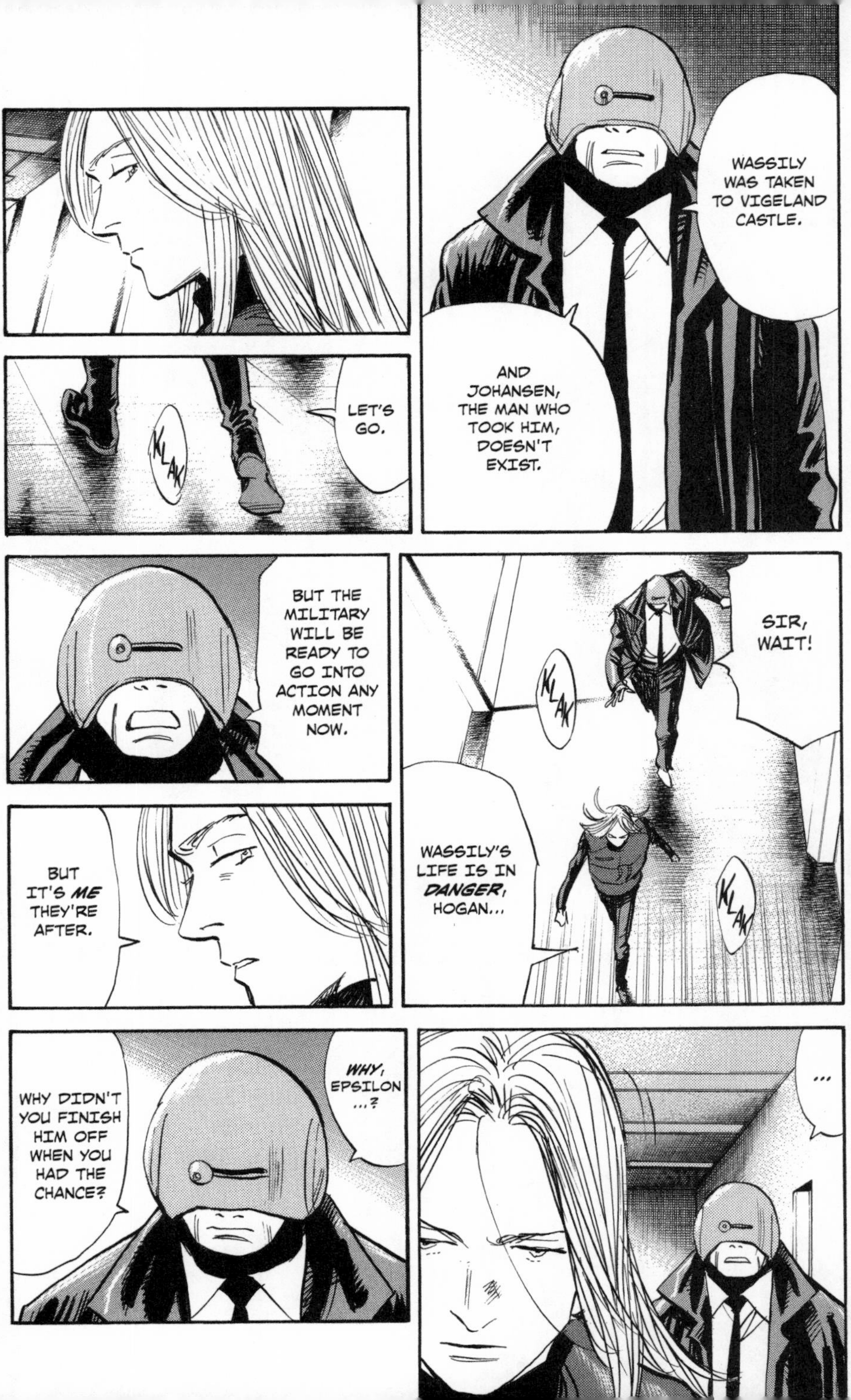
WASSILY WAS TAKEN TO VIGELAND CASTLE.
AND JOHANSEN, THE MAN WHO TOOK HIM, DOESN'T EXIST.
LET'S GO.
KLAK
SIR, WAIT!
KLAK
WASSILY'S LIFE IS IN *DANGER*, HOGAN...
KLAK
BUT THE MILITARY WILL BE READY TO GO INTO ACTION ANY MOMENT NOW.
BUT IT'S *ME* THEY'RE AFTER.
...
WHY, EPSILON ...?
WHY DIDN'T YOU FINISH HIM OFF WHEN YOU HAD THE CHANCE?

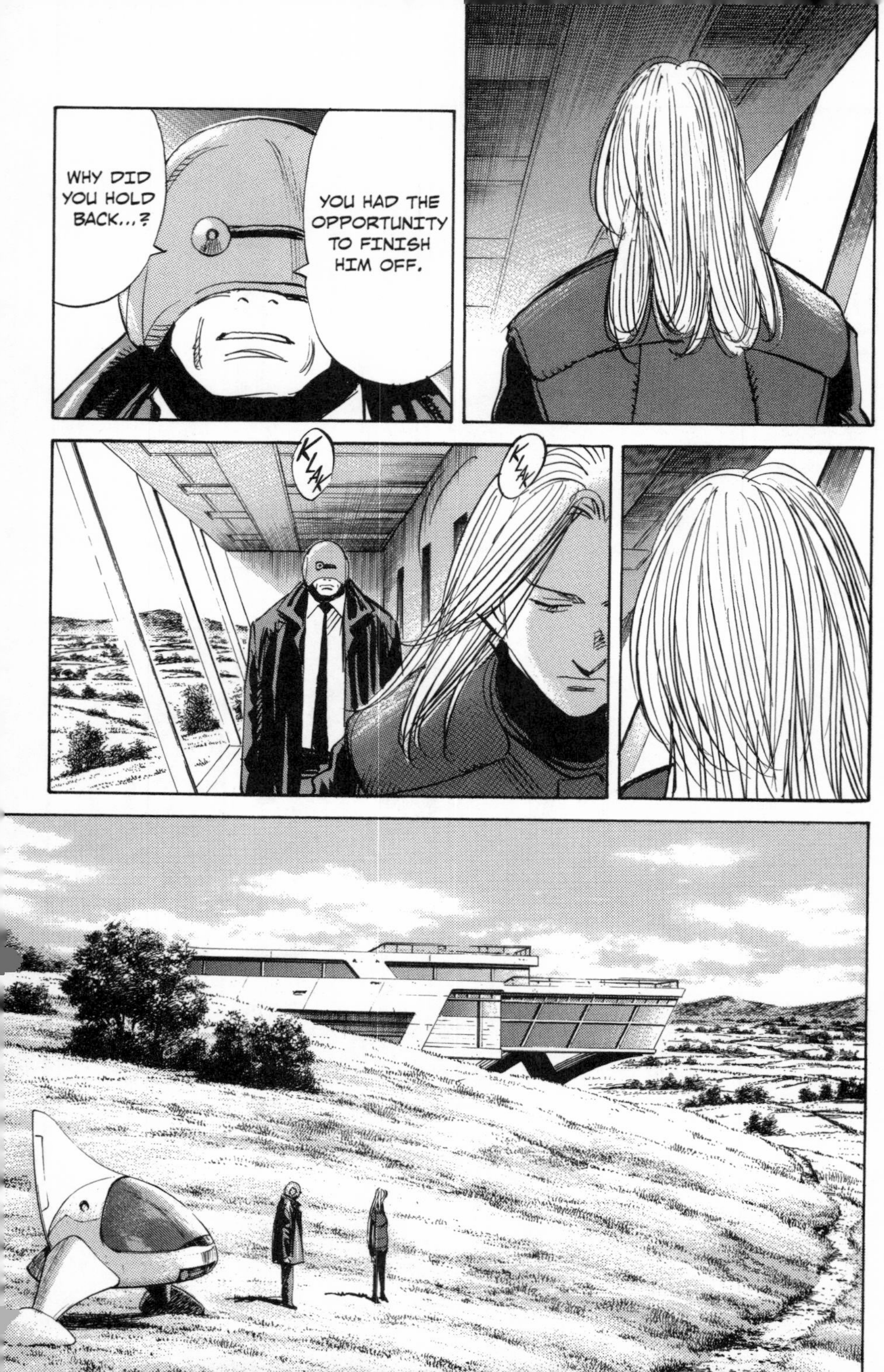
YOU HAD THE OPPORTUNITY TO FINISH HIM OFF.
WHY DID YOU HOLD BACK...?
KLAK
KLAK

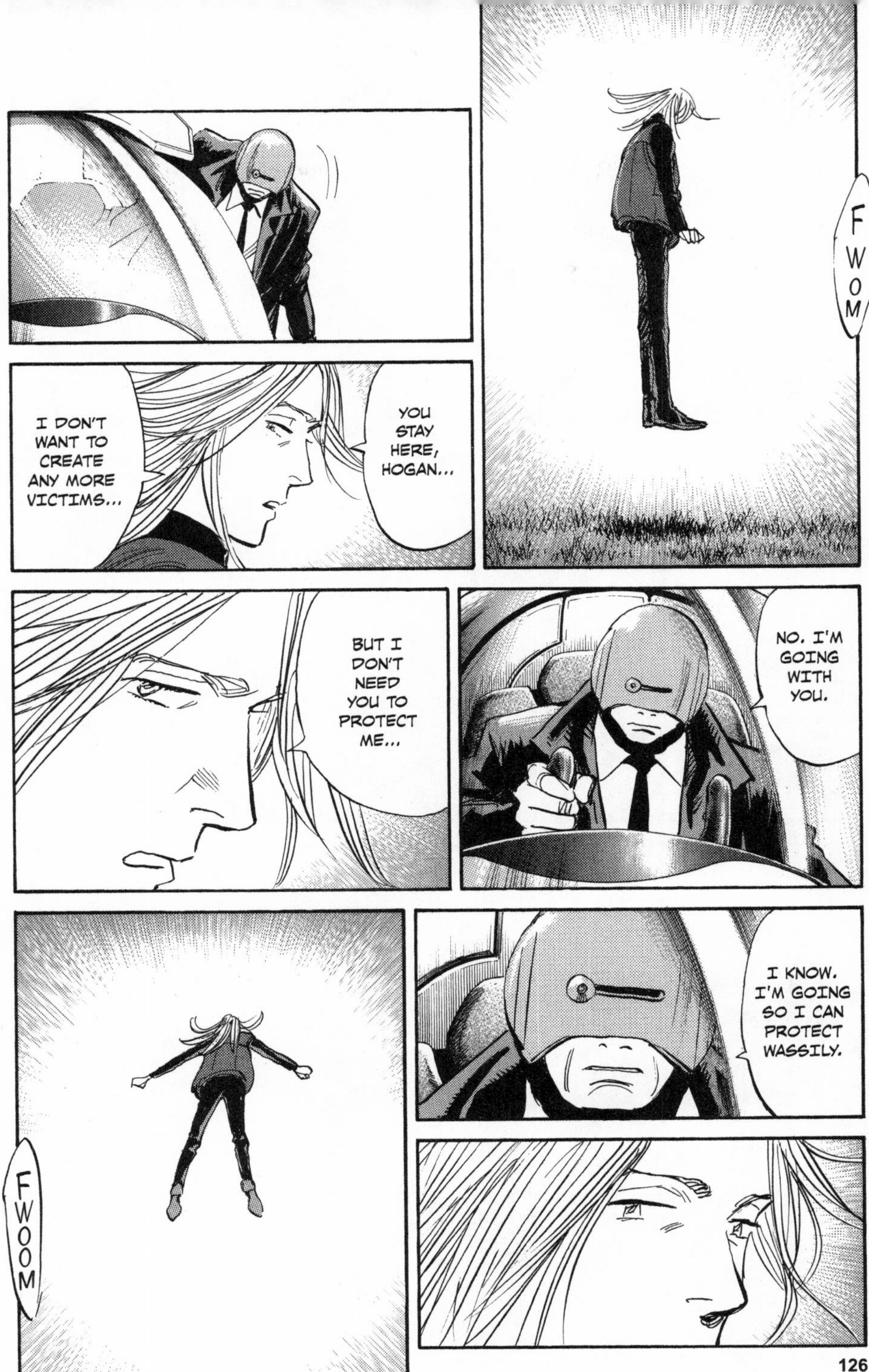
FWOM
YOU STAY HERE, HOGAN...
I DON'T WANT TO CREATE ANY MORE VICTIMS...
NO. I'M GOING WITH YOU.
BUT I DON'T NEED YOU TO PROTECT ME...
I KNOW. I'M GOING SO I CAN PROTECT WASSILY.
FWOOM

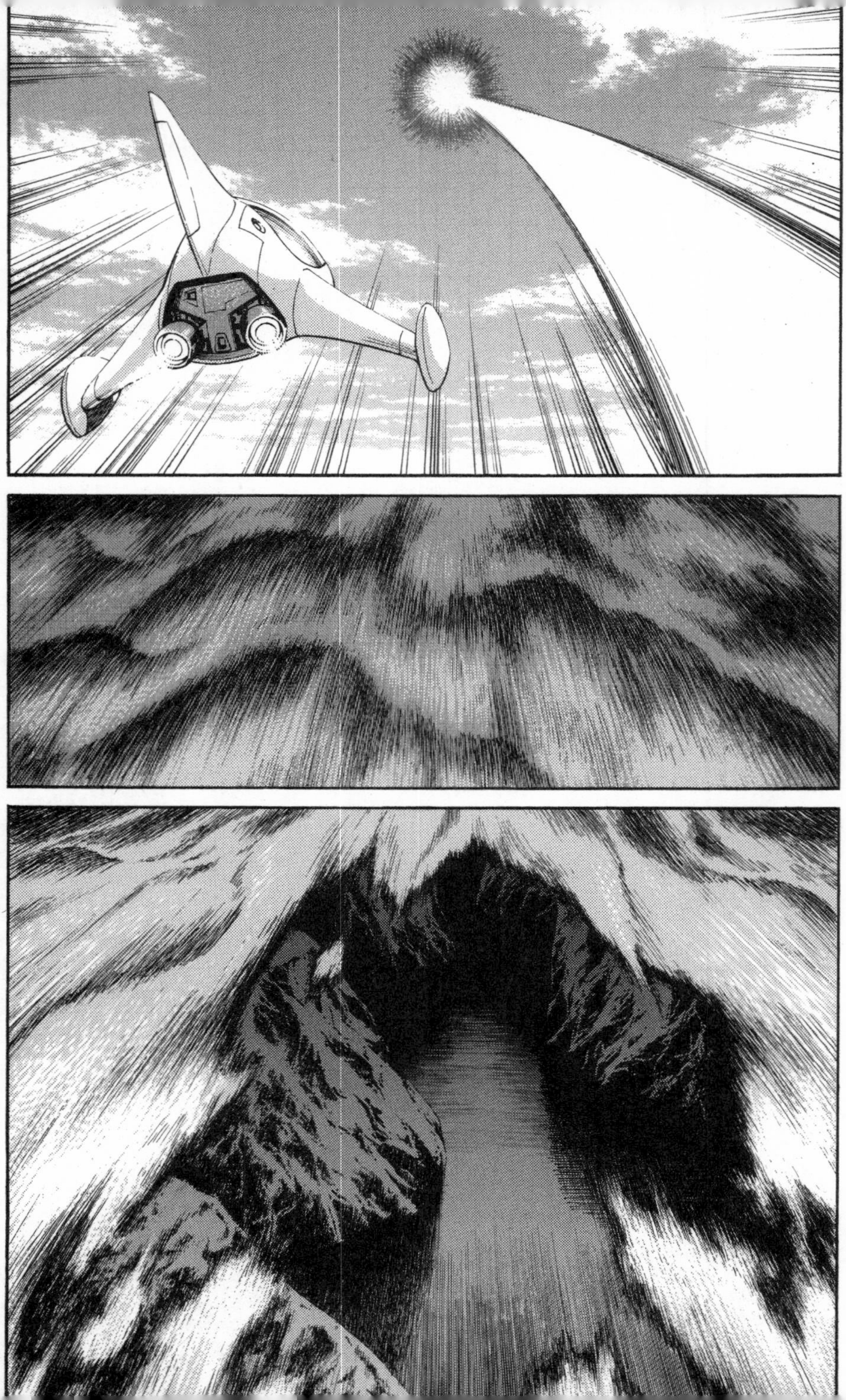

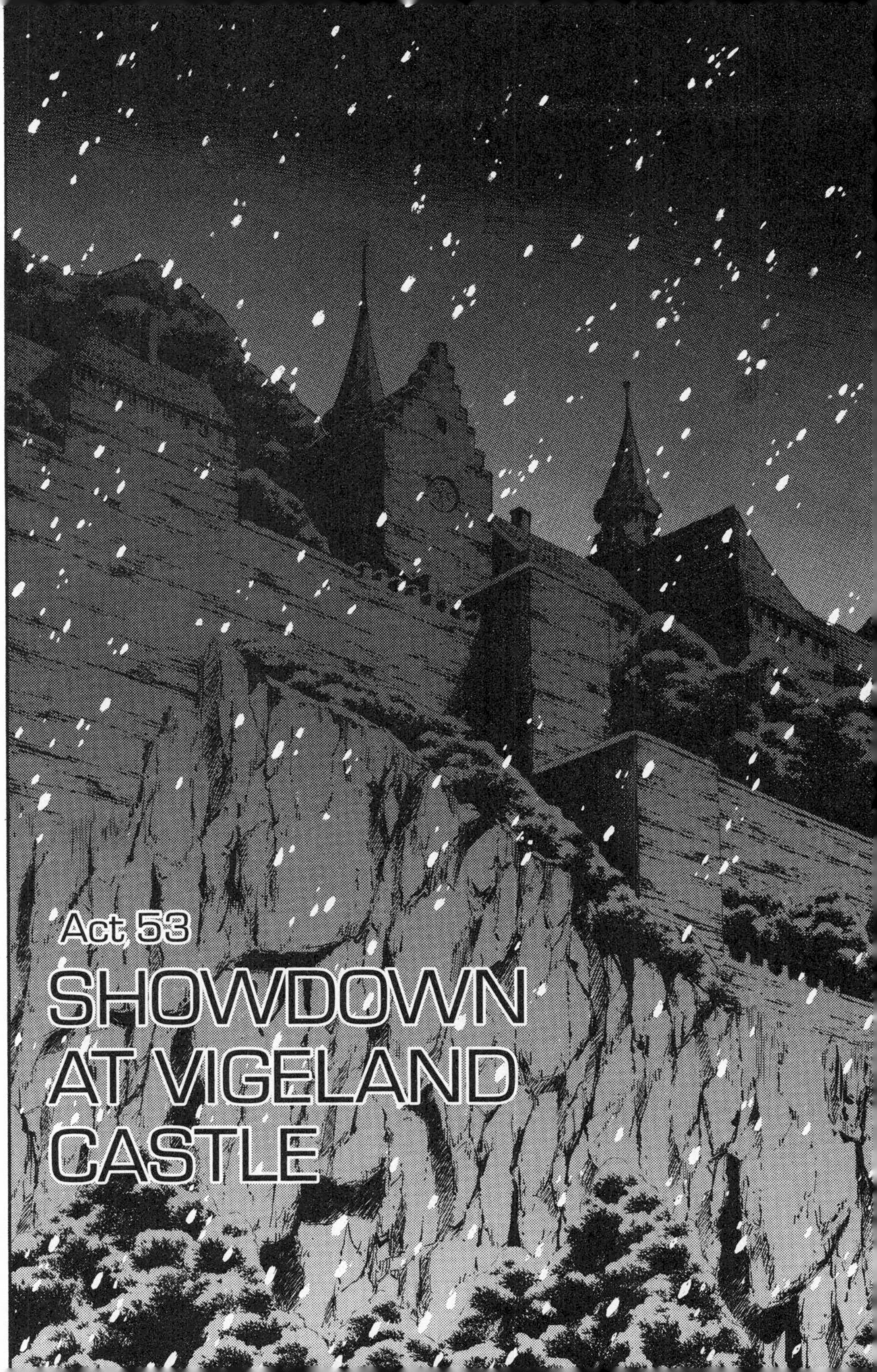
Act 53
SHOWDOWN AT VIGELAND CASTLE

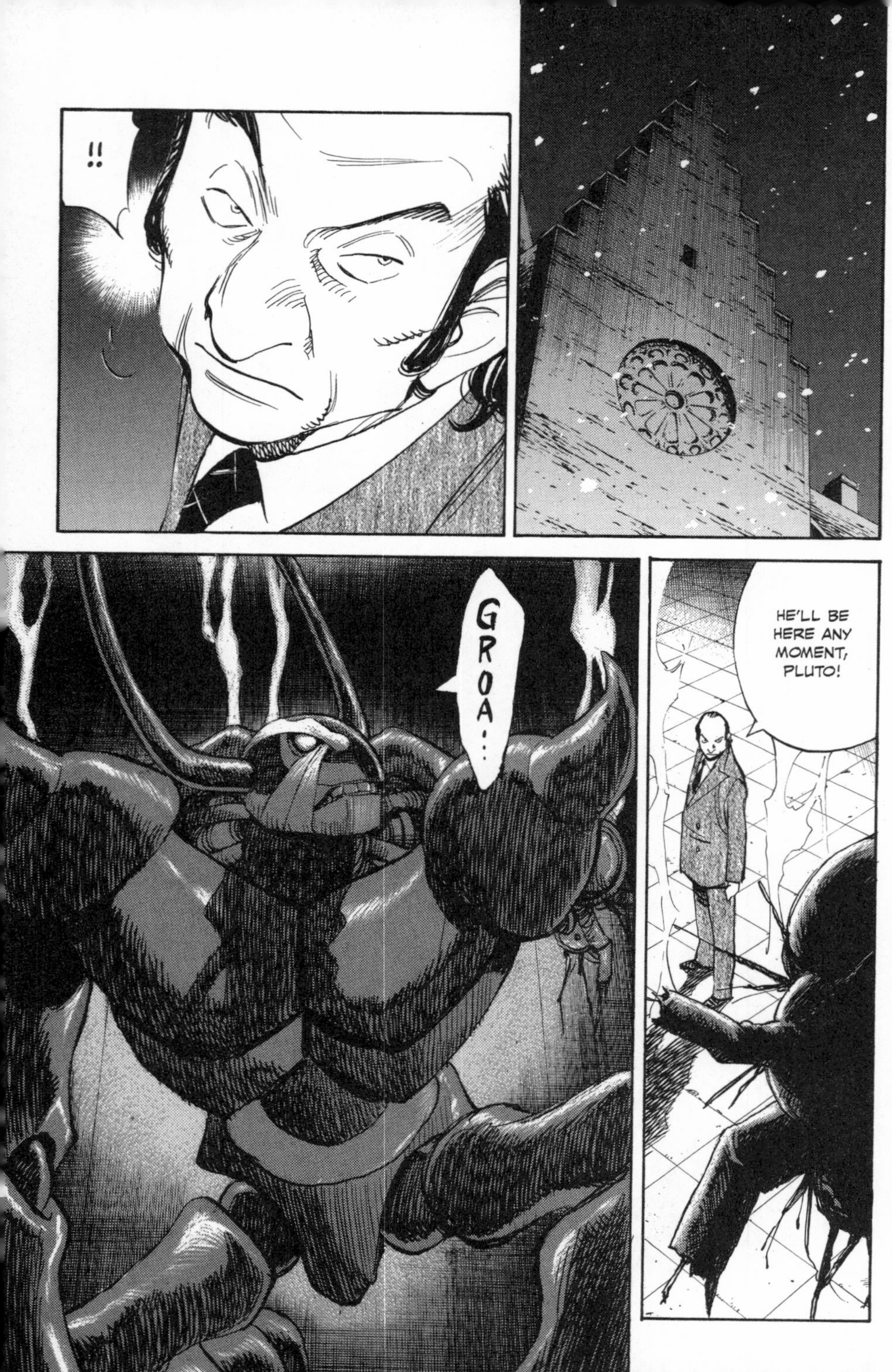
!!
HE'LL BE HERE ANY MOMENT, PLUTO!
GROA...

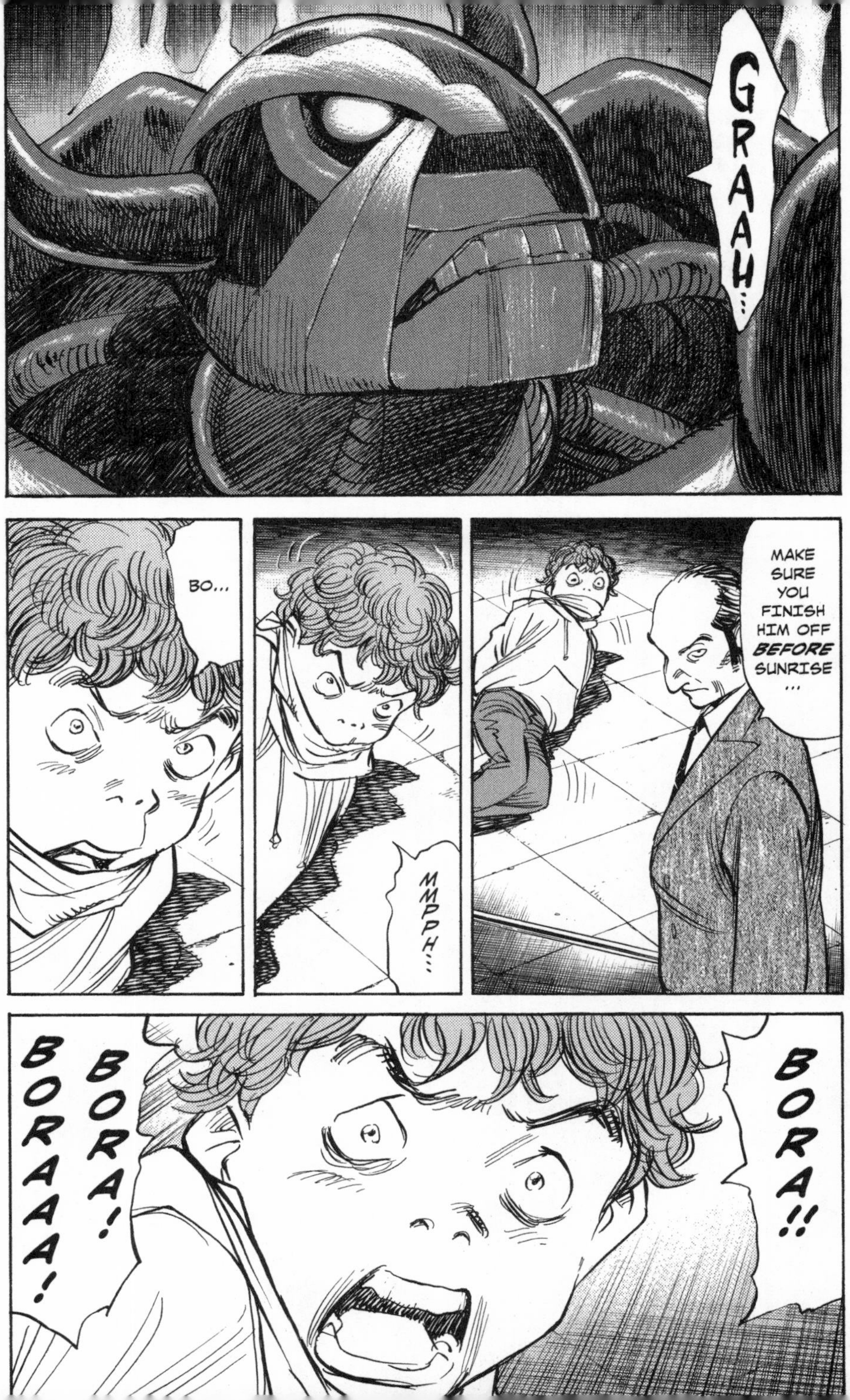
GRAAH...
MAKE SURE YOU FINISH HIM OFF *BEFORE* SUNRISE...
MMPPH...
BO...
BORA!!
BORA!!
BORAAA!!

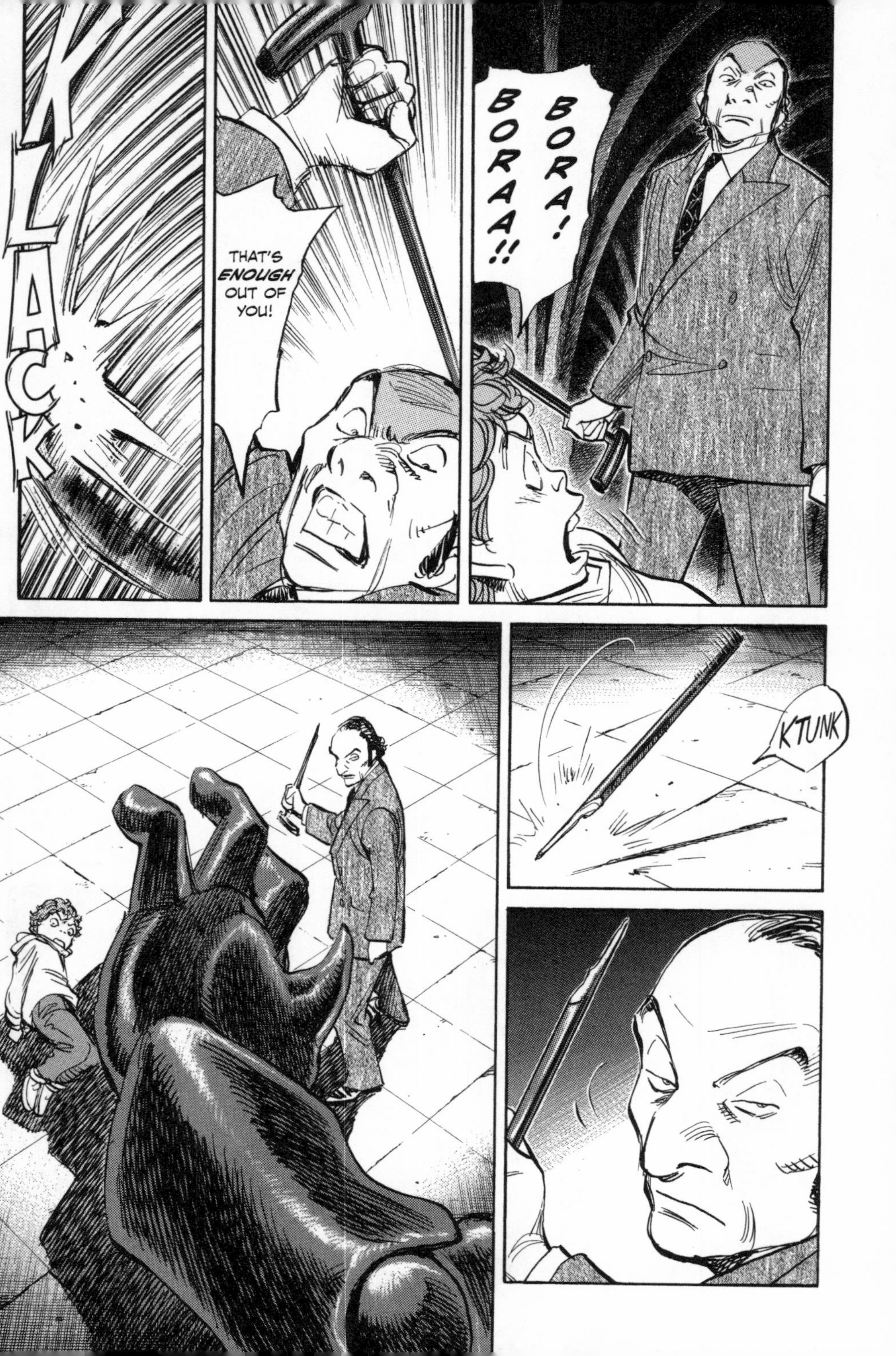
BORA! BORAA!!
THAT'S ENOUGH OUT OF YOU!
KLACK
K'TUNK

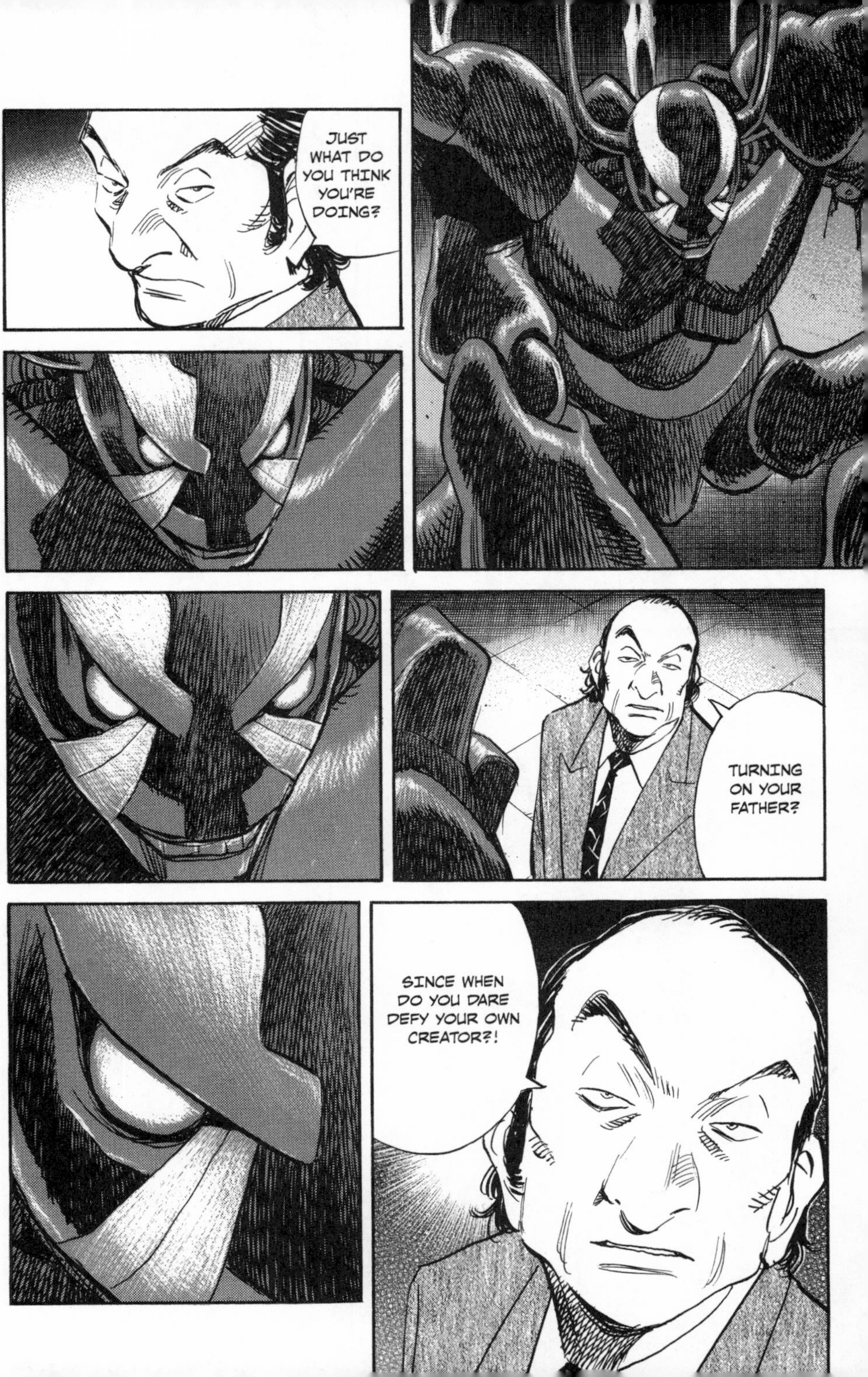
JUST WHAT DO YOU THINK YOU'RE DOING?
TURNING ON YOUR FATHER?
SINCE WHEN DO YOU DARE DEFY YOUR OWN CREATOR?!

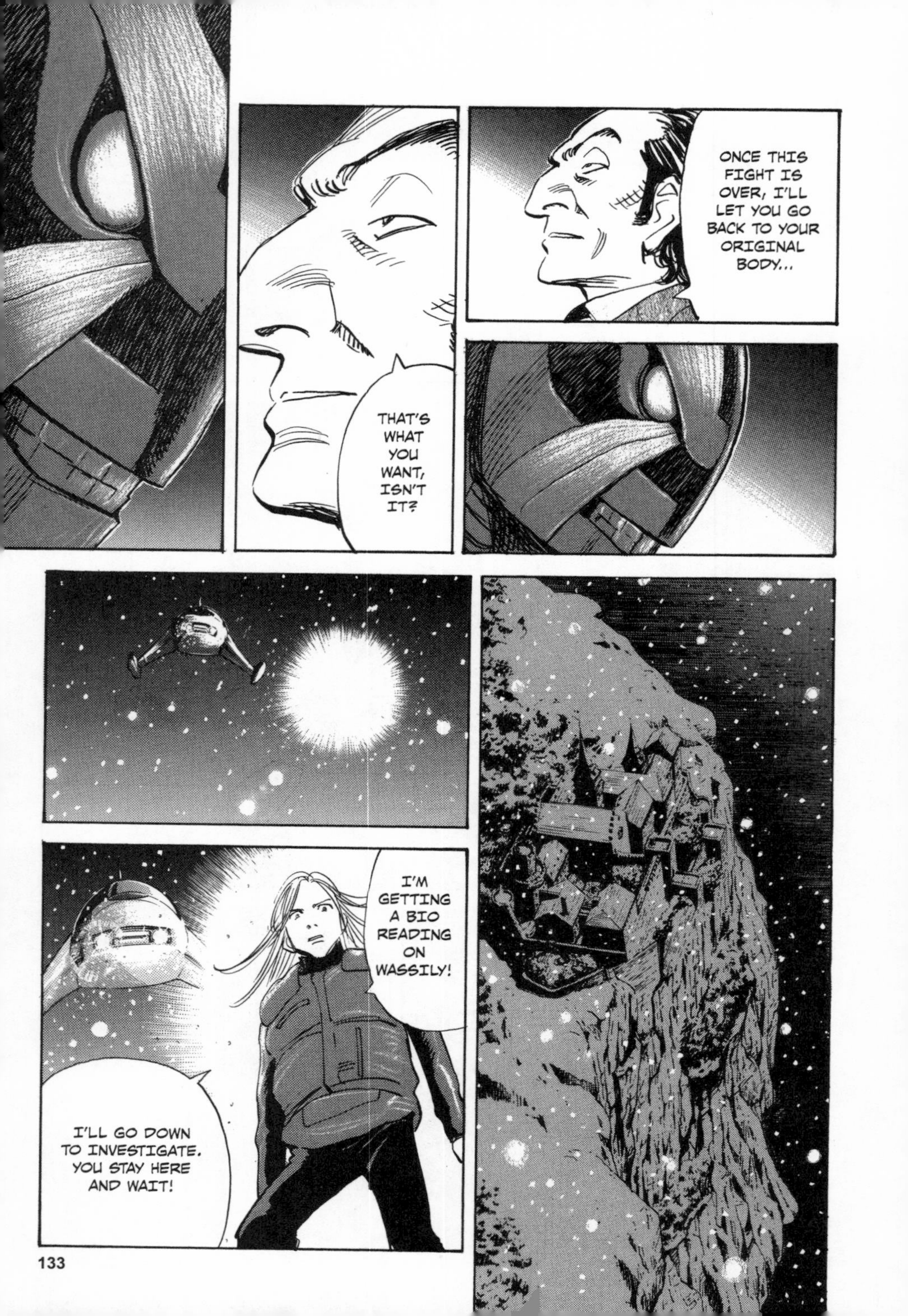
ONCE THIS FIGHT IS OVER, I'LL LET YOU GO BACK TO YOUR ORIGINAL BODY...
THAT'S WHAT YOU WANT, ISN'T IT?
I'M GETTING A BIO READING ON WASSILY!
I'LL GO DOWN TO INVESTIGATE. YOU STAY HERE AND WAIT!

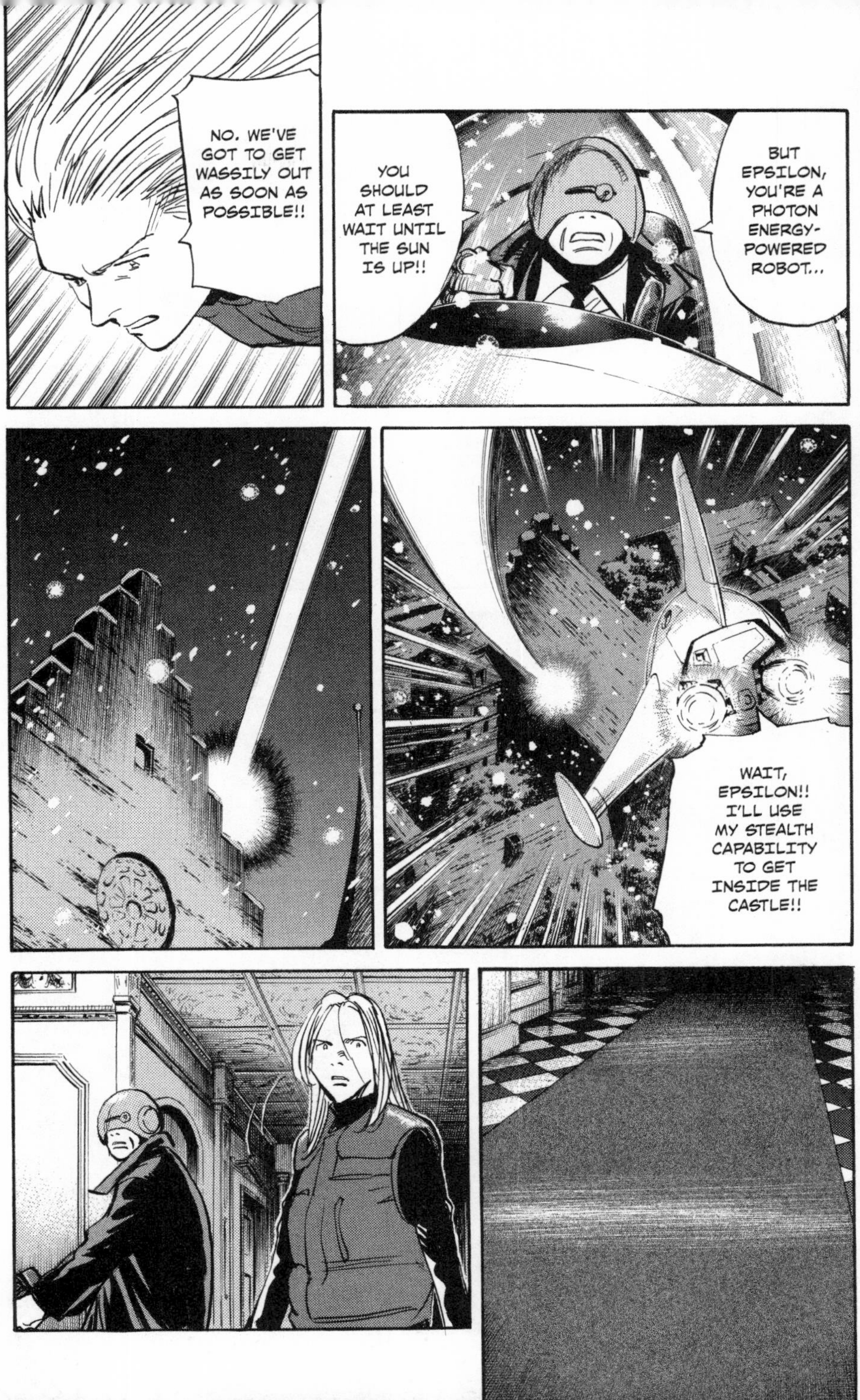
BUT EPSILON, YOU'RE A PHOTON ENERGY-POWERED ROBOT...
YOU SHOULD AT LEAST WAIT UNTIL THE SUN IS UP!!
NO. WE'VE GOT TO GET WASSILY OUT AS SOON AS POSSIBLE!!
WAIT, EPSILON!! I'LL USE MY STEALTH CAPABILITY TO GET INSIDE THE CASTLE!!

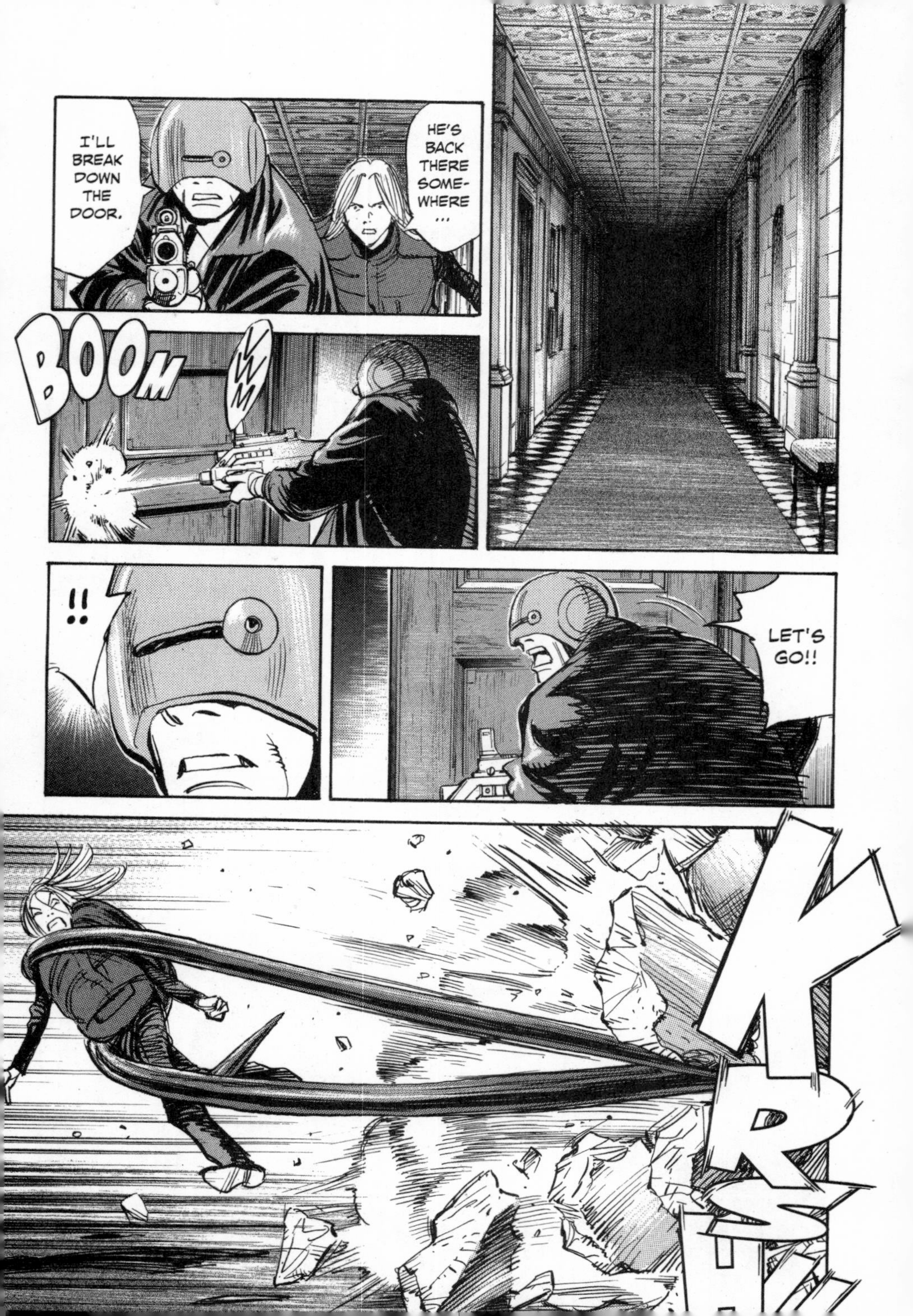
HE'S BACK THERE SOME-WHERE ...
I'LL BREAK DOWN THE DOOR.
BOOM
LET'S GO!!
!!

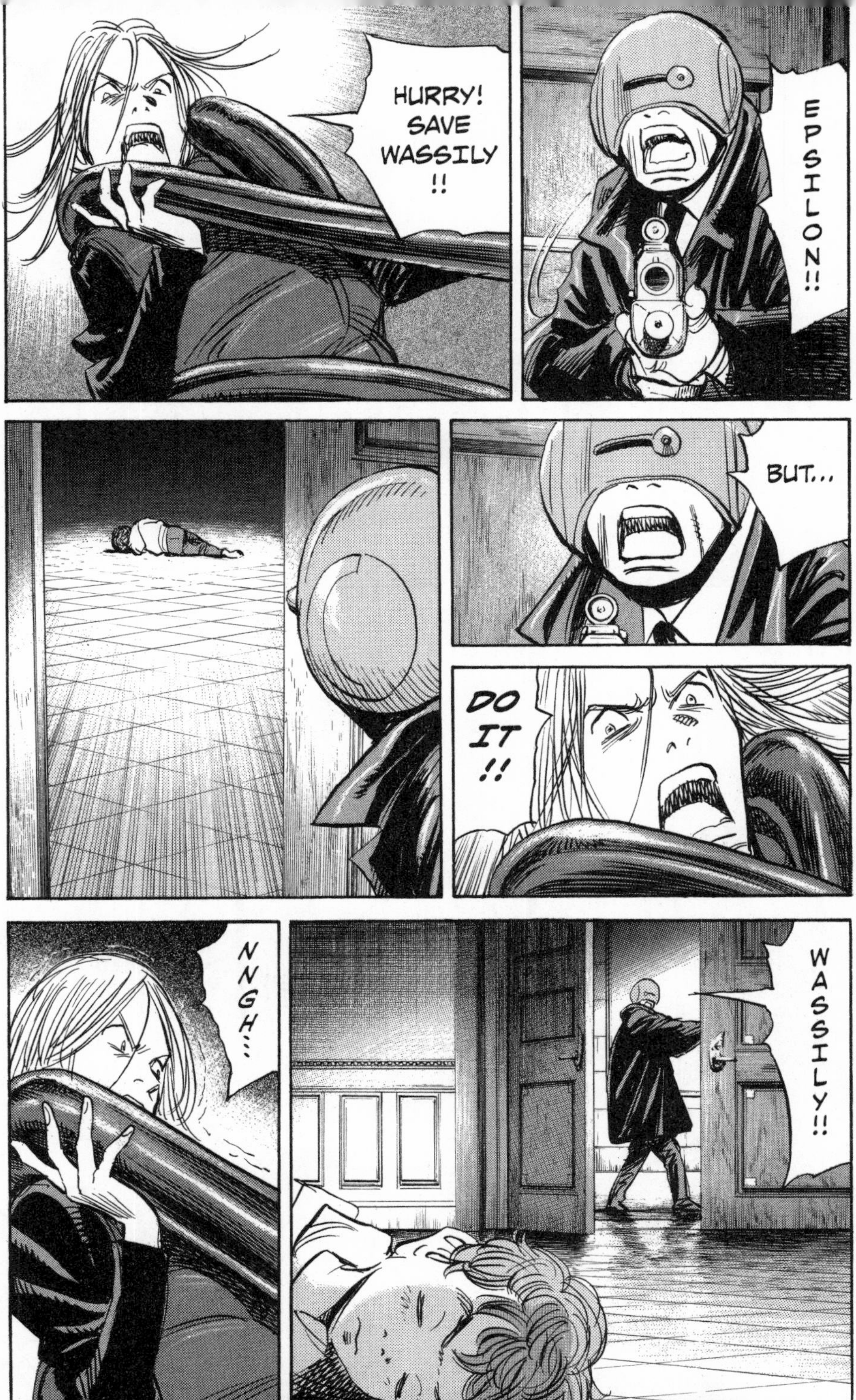
EPSILON!!
HURRY! SAVE WASSILY!!
BUT...
DO IT!!
WASSILY!!
NNGH...

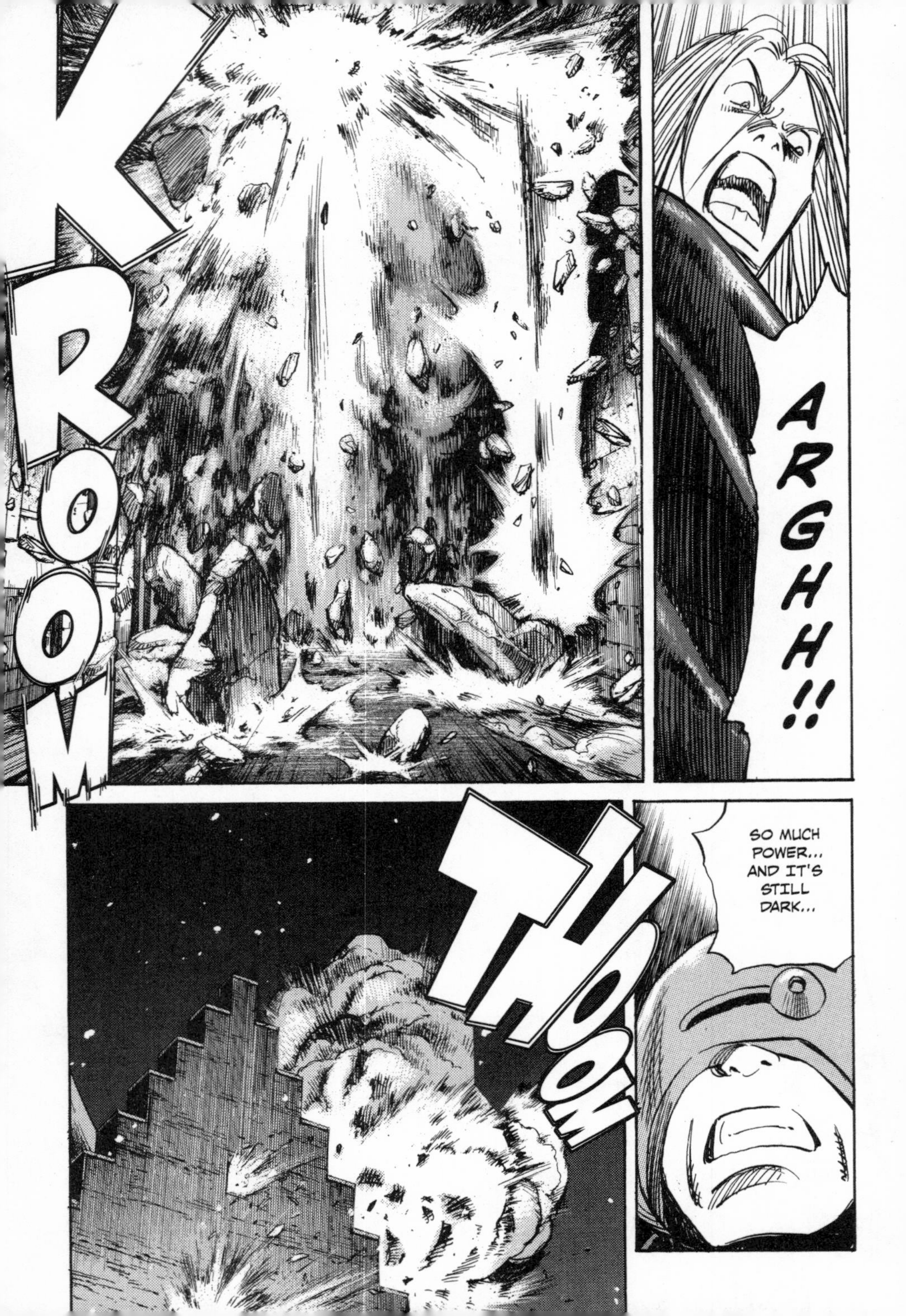
ARGHH!!
KROOM
SO MUCH POWER... AND IT'S STILL DARK...
THOOM

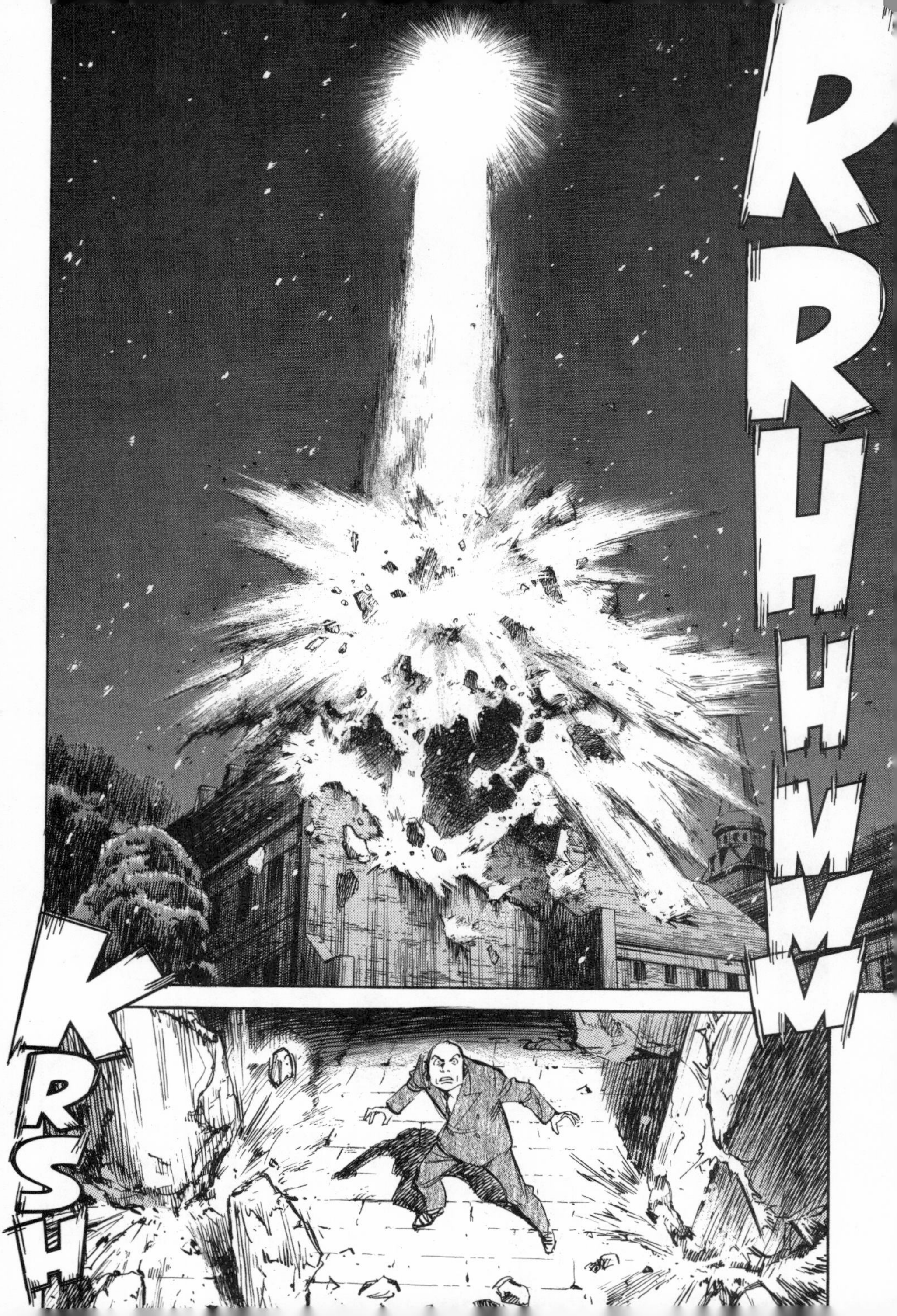
RRHHMMM
KRSH

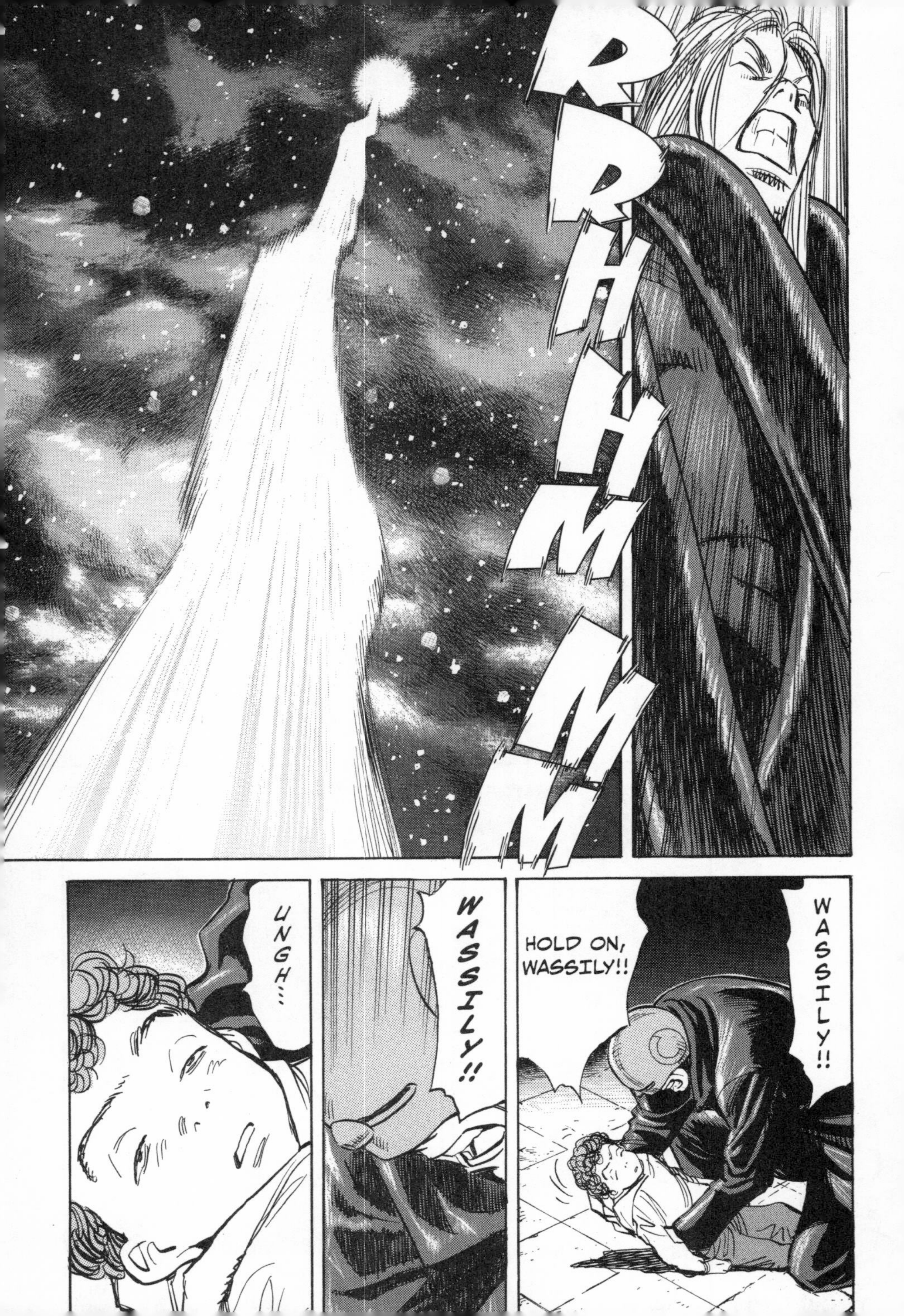
RRHHMMMM
WASSILY!!
HOLD ON, WASSILY!!
WASSILY!!
UNGH...

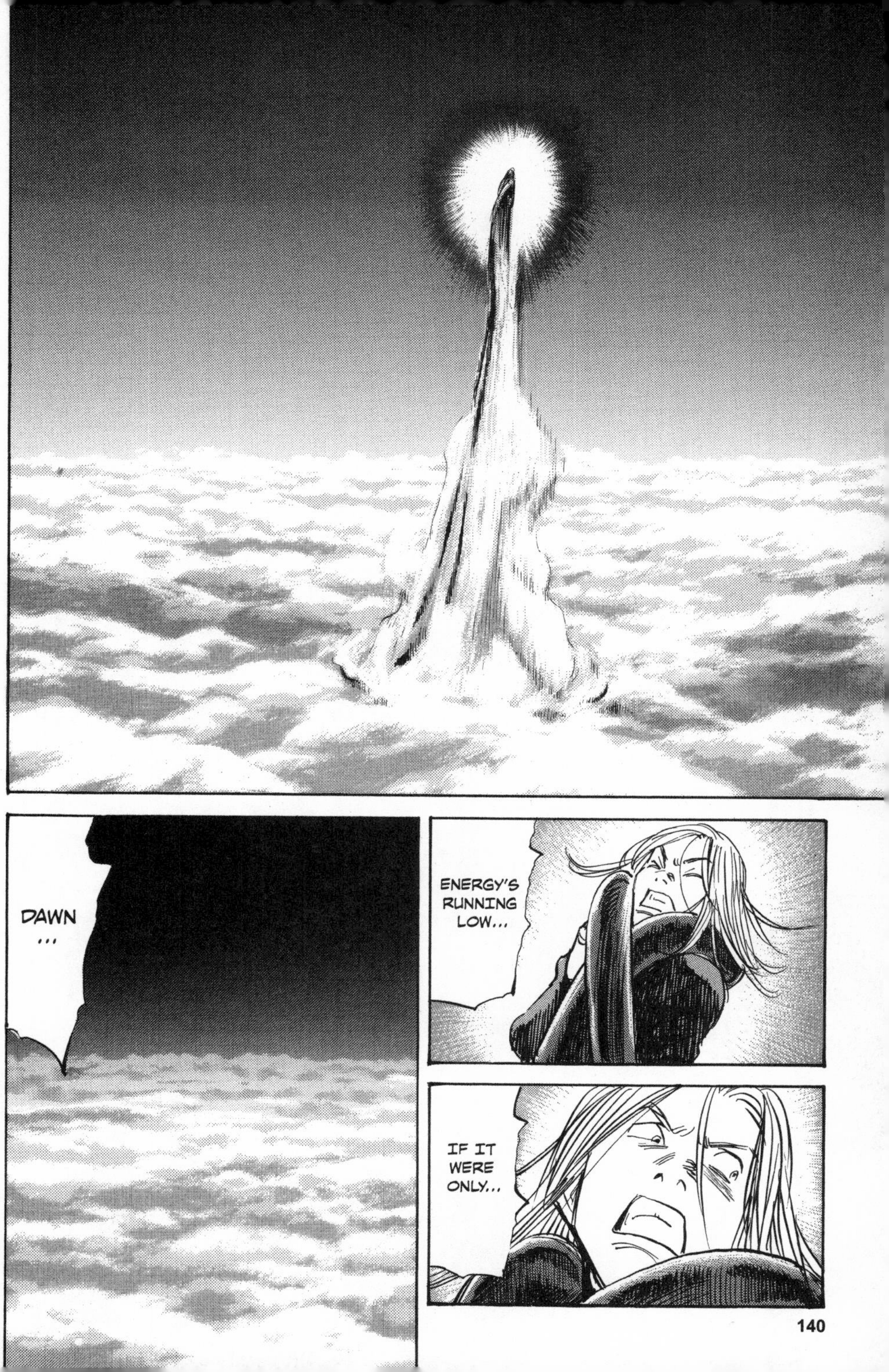
ENERGY'S RUNNING LOW...
IF IT WERE ONLY...
DAWN ...

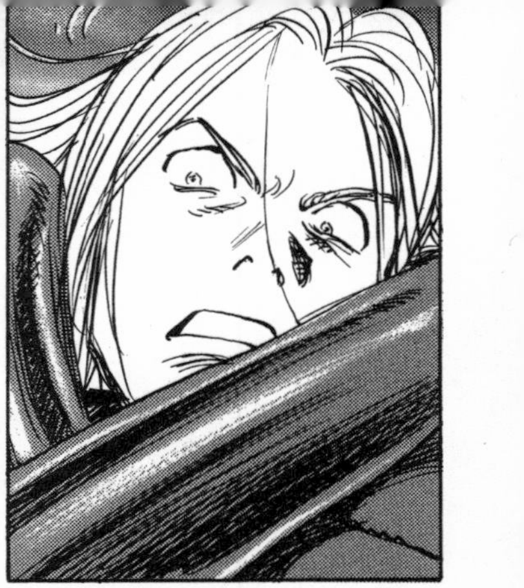

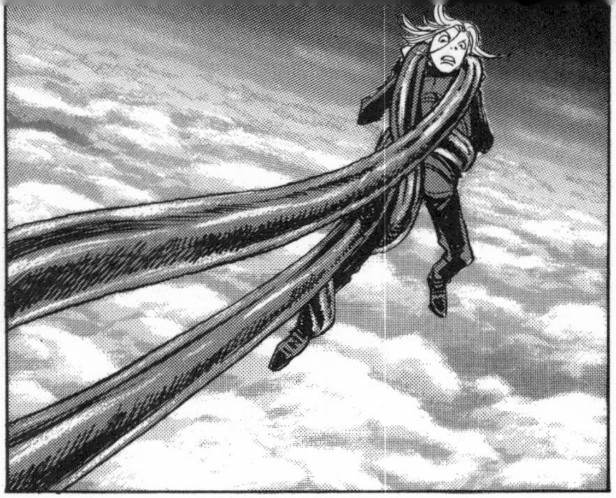

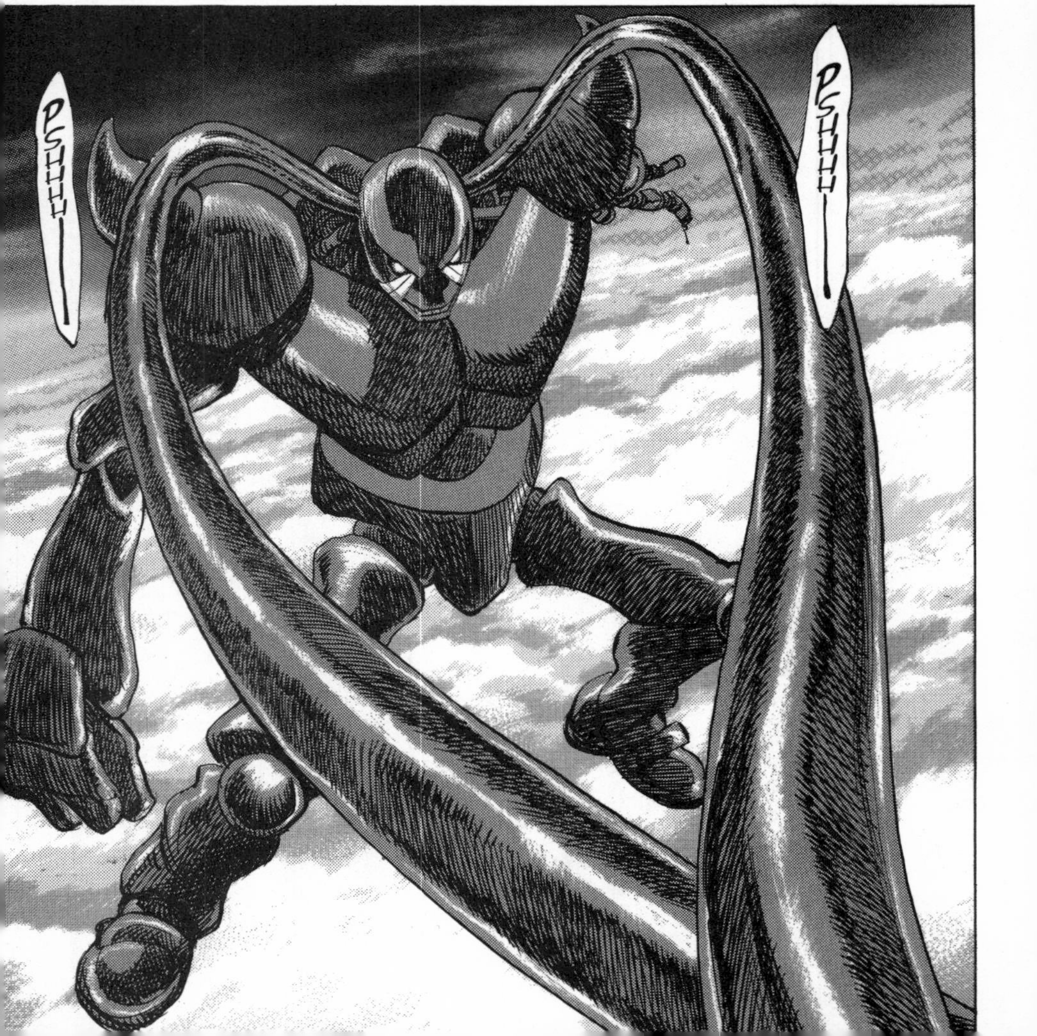
PSHHHH—
PSHHHH—

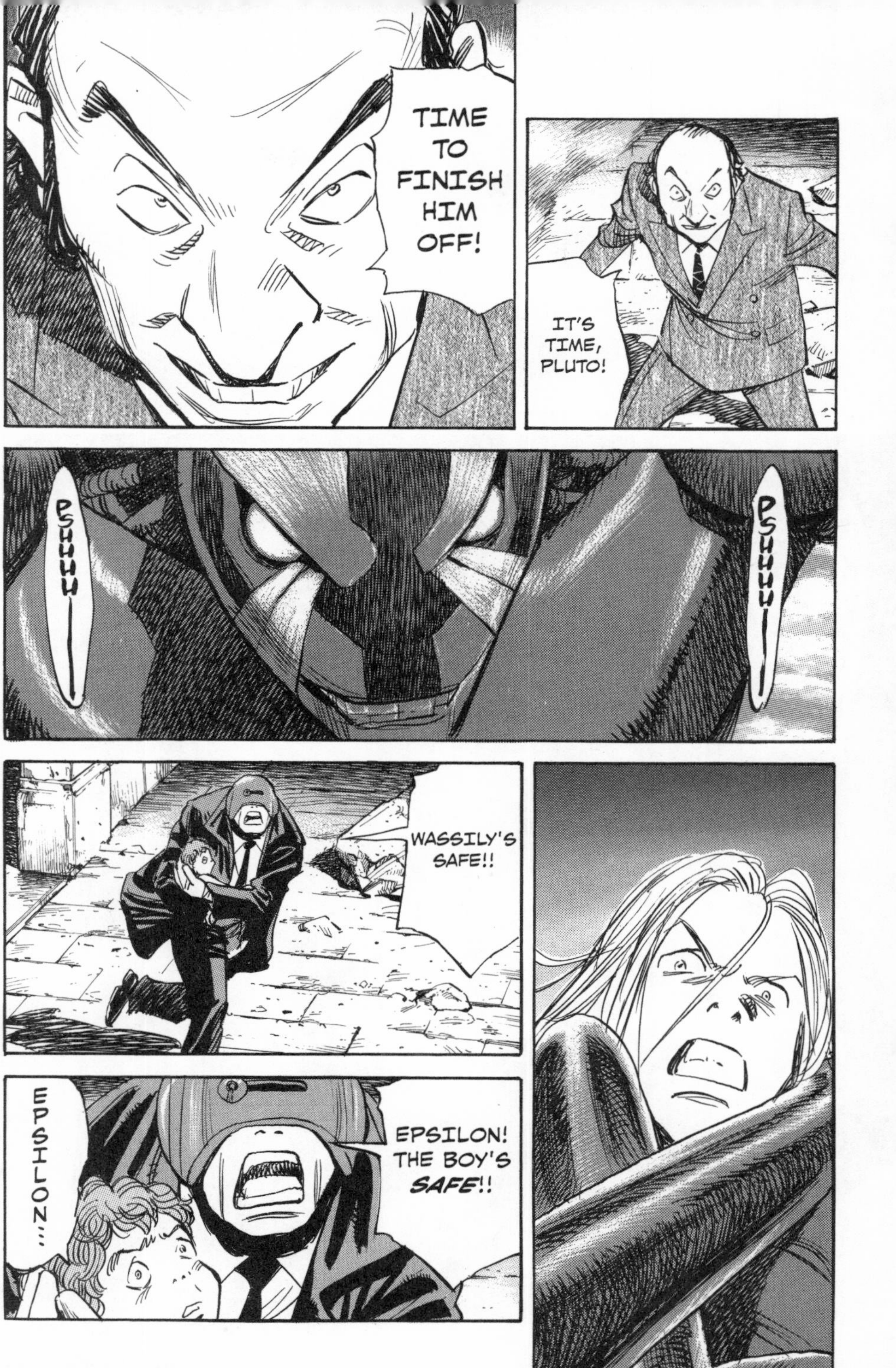
IT'S TIME, PLUTO!
TIME TO FINISH HIM OFF!
PSHHHH
PSHHHH
WASSILY'S SAFE!!
EPSILON! THE BOY'S *SAFE*!!
EPSILON...

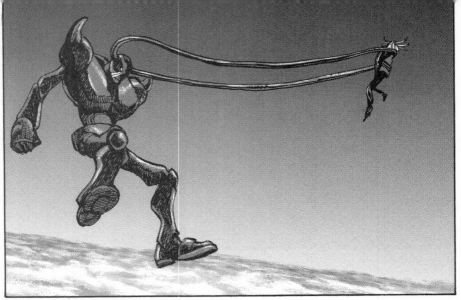

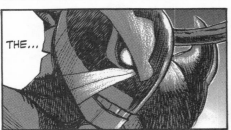

THE...

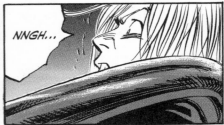

NNGH...

Y-YOU MEAN *WASSILY*?

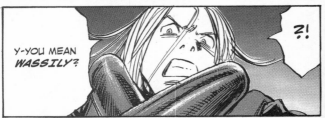

Z?!

THE CHILD...

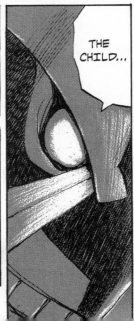

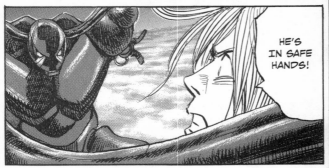

HE'S IN SAFE HANDS!

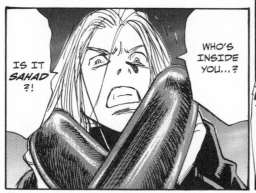

IS IT *SAHAD* ?!

WHO'S INSIDE YOU...?

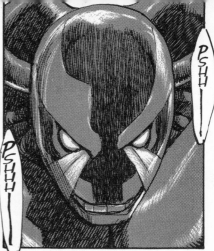

PSHH

PSHH

WHAT HAPPENED TO YOU?

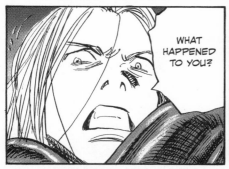

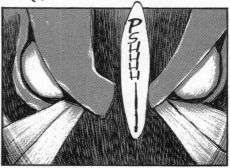

PSHHH

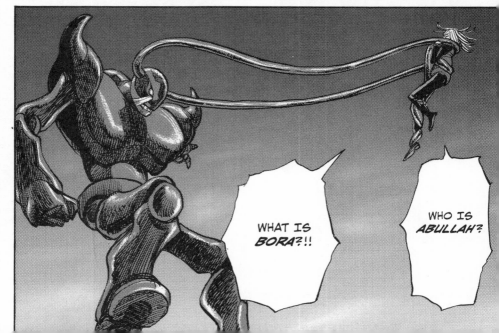

WHAT IS *BORA*?!!

WHO IS *ABULLAH*?

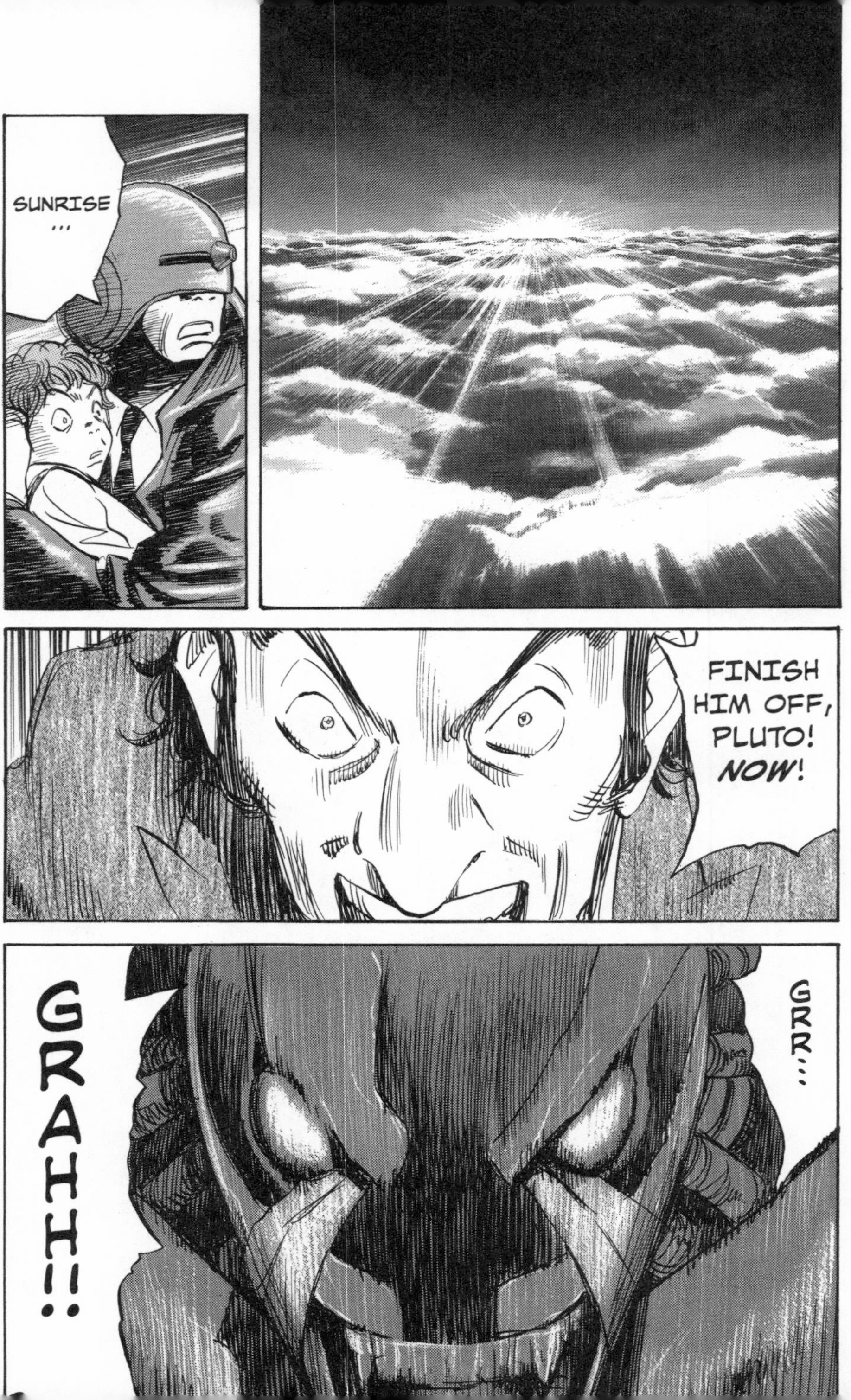
SUNRISE ...
FINISH HIM OFF, PLUTO! *NOW*!
GRR...
GRAHH!!

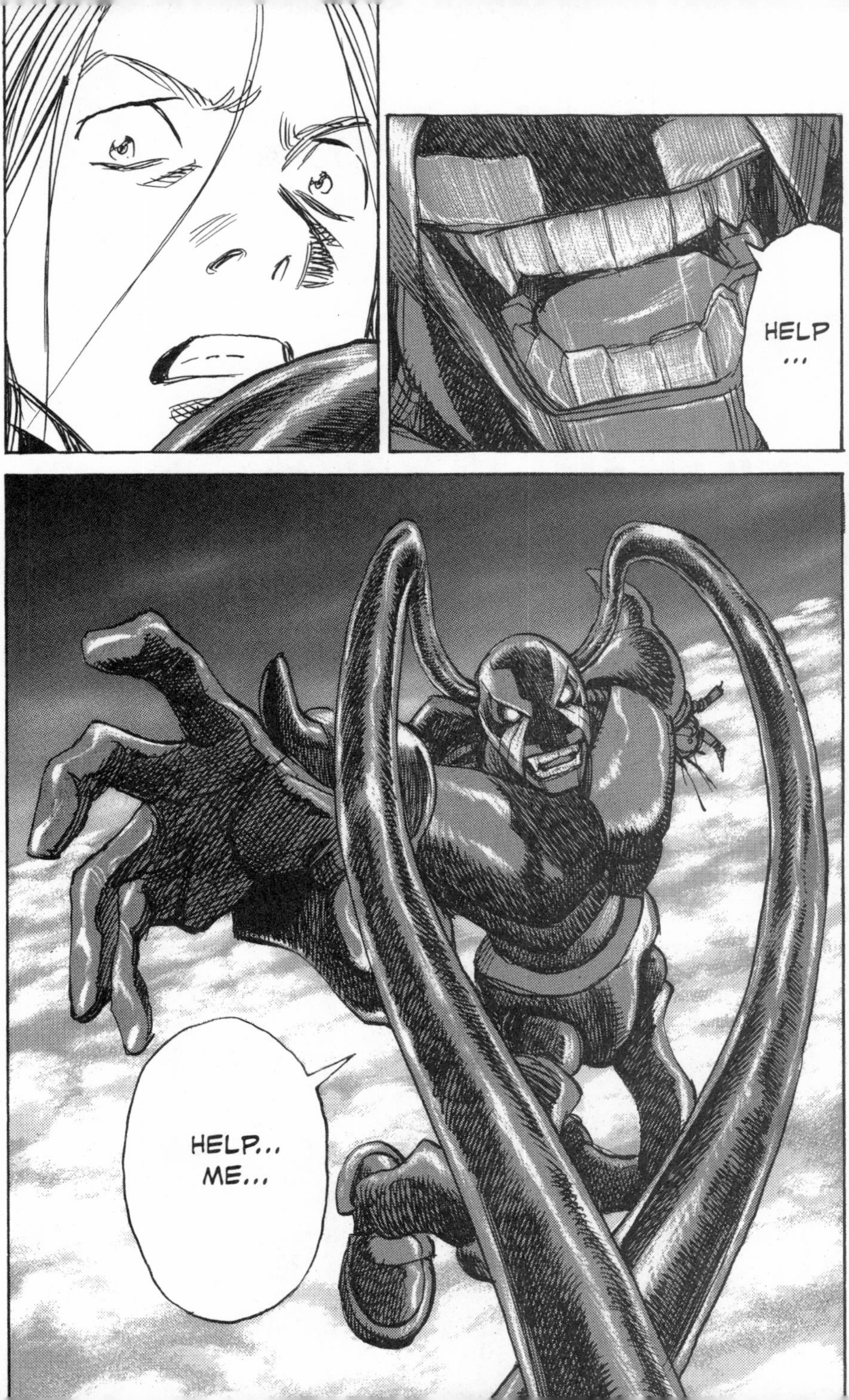
HELP ...
HELP... ME...

Act 54 BURGEONING GRIEF

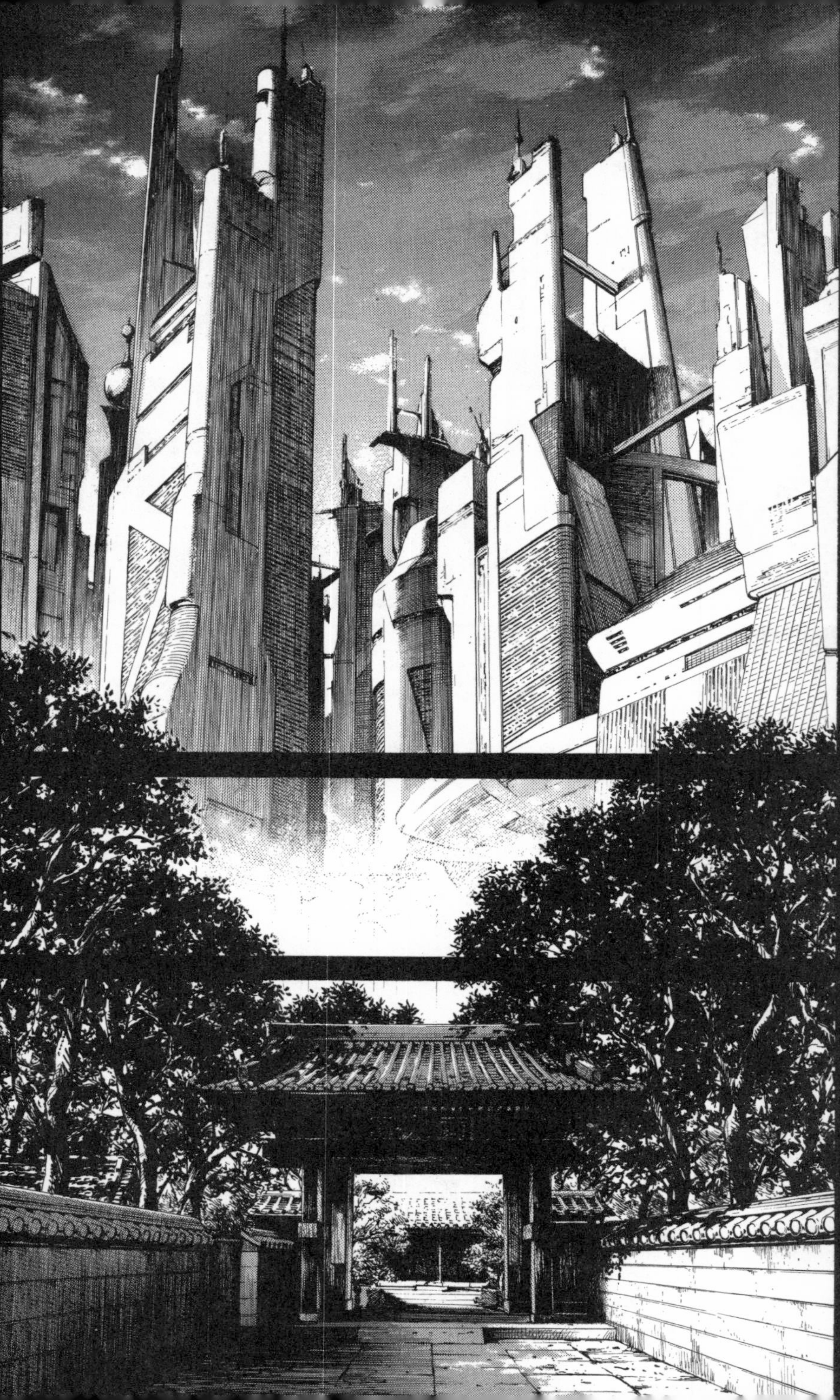

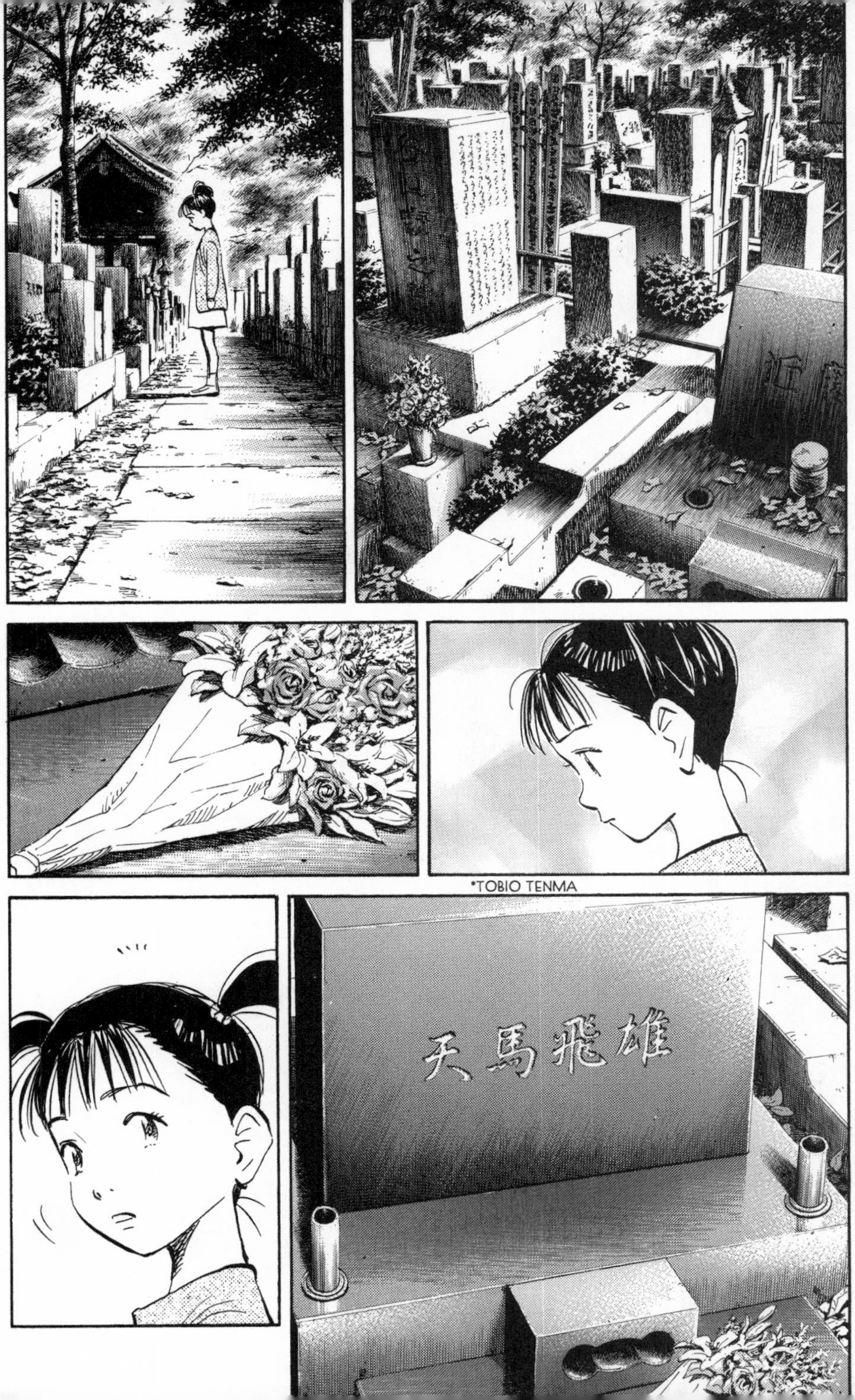
*TOBIO TENMA
天馬飛雄

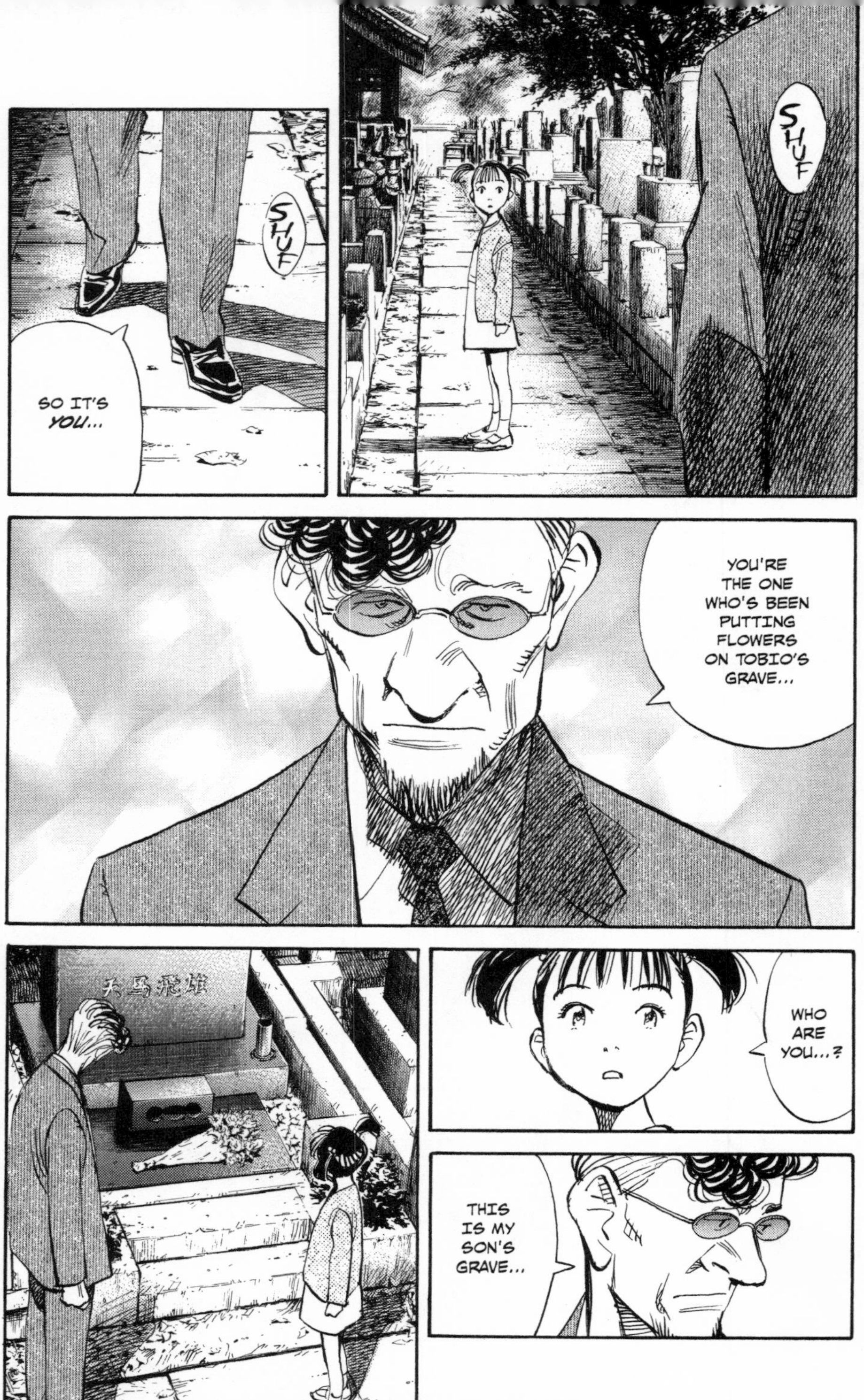
SHUF
SHUF
SO IT'S *YOU*...
YOU'RE THE ONE WHO'S BEEN PUTTING FLOWERS ON TOBIO'S GRAVE...
WHO ARE YOU...?
THIS IS MY SON'S GRAVE...
天馬飛雄

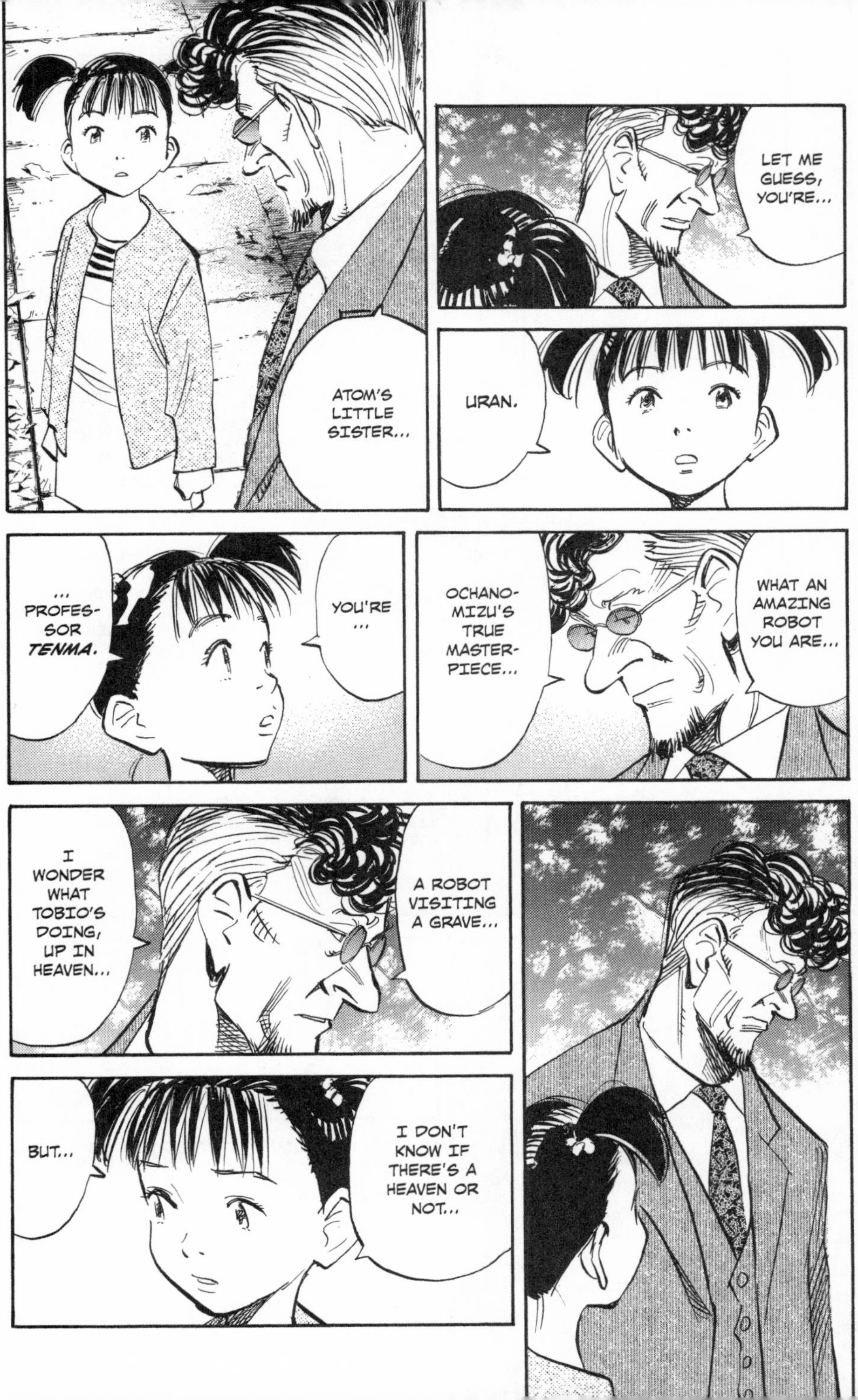
LET ME GUESS, YOU'RE...
URAN.
ATOM'S LITTLE SISTER...
WHAT AN AMAZING ROBOT YOU ARE...
OCHANOMIZU'S TRUE MASTERPIECE...
YOU'RE ...
... PROFESSOR *TENMA.*
A ROBOT VISITING A GRAVE...
I WONDER WHAT TOBIO'S DOING, UP IN HEAVEN...
I DON'T KNOW IF THERE'S A HEAVEN OR NOT...
BUT...

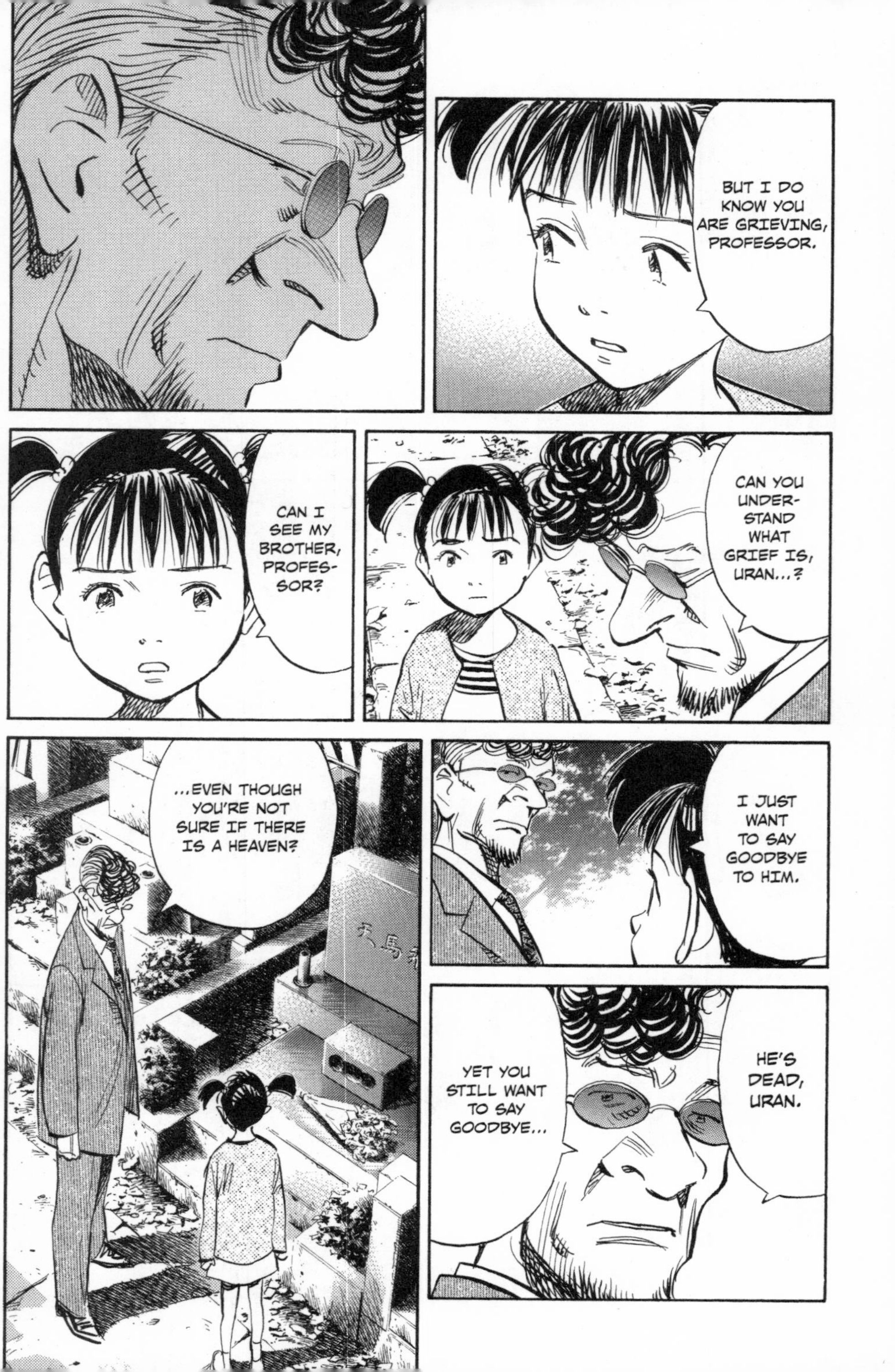
BUT I DO KNOW YOU ARE GRIEVING, PROFESSOR.
CAN YOU UNDER-STAND WHAT GRIEF IS, URAN...?
CAN I SEE MY BROTHER, PROFES-SOR?
I JUST WANT TO SAY GOODBYE TO HIM.
HE'S DEAD, URAN.
YET YOU STILL WANT TO SAY GOODBYE...
...EVEN THOUGH YOU'RE NOT SURE IF THERE IS A HEAVEN?

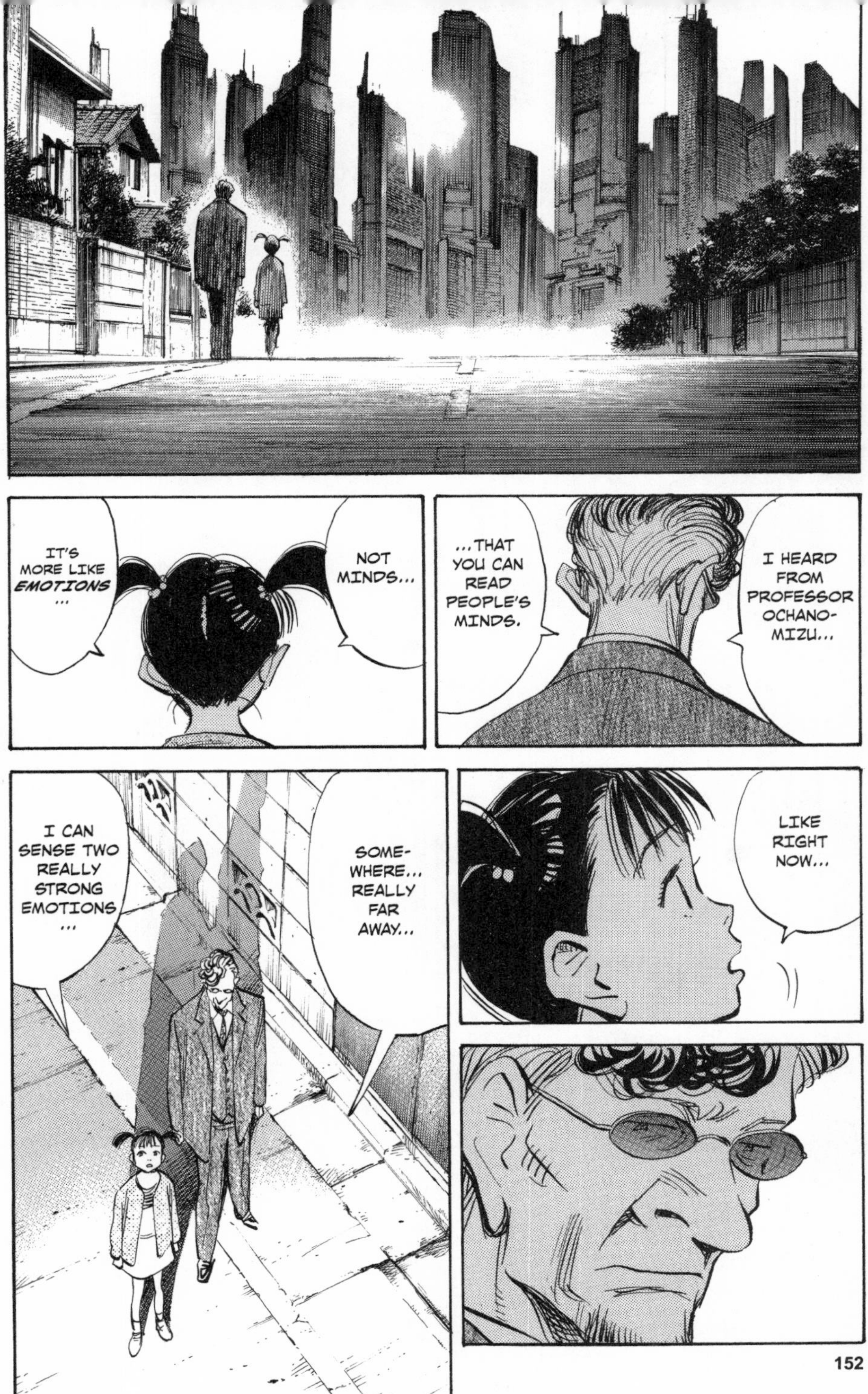
I HEARD FROM PROFESSOR OCHANO-MIZU...
...THAT YOU CAN READ PEOPLE'S MINDS.
NOT MINDS...
IT'S MORE LIKE *EMOTIONS*...
LIKE RIGHT NOW...
SOME-WHERE... REALLY FAR AWAY...
I CAN SENSE TWO REALLY STRONG EMOTIONS...

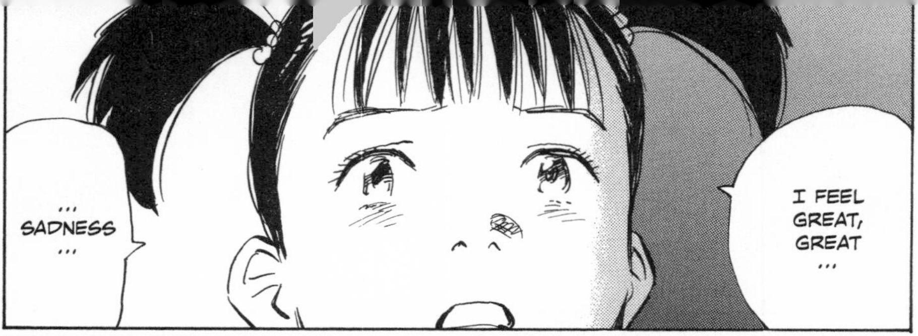
I FEEL GREAT, GREAT ...
... SADNESS ...

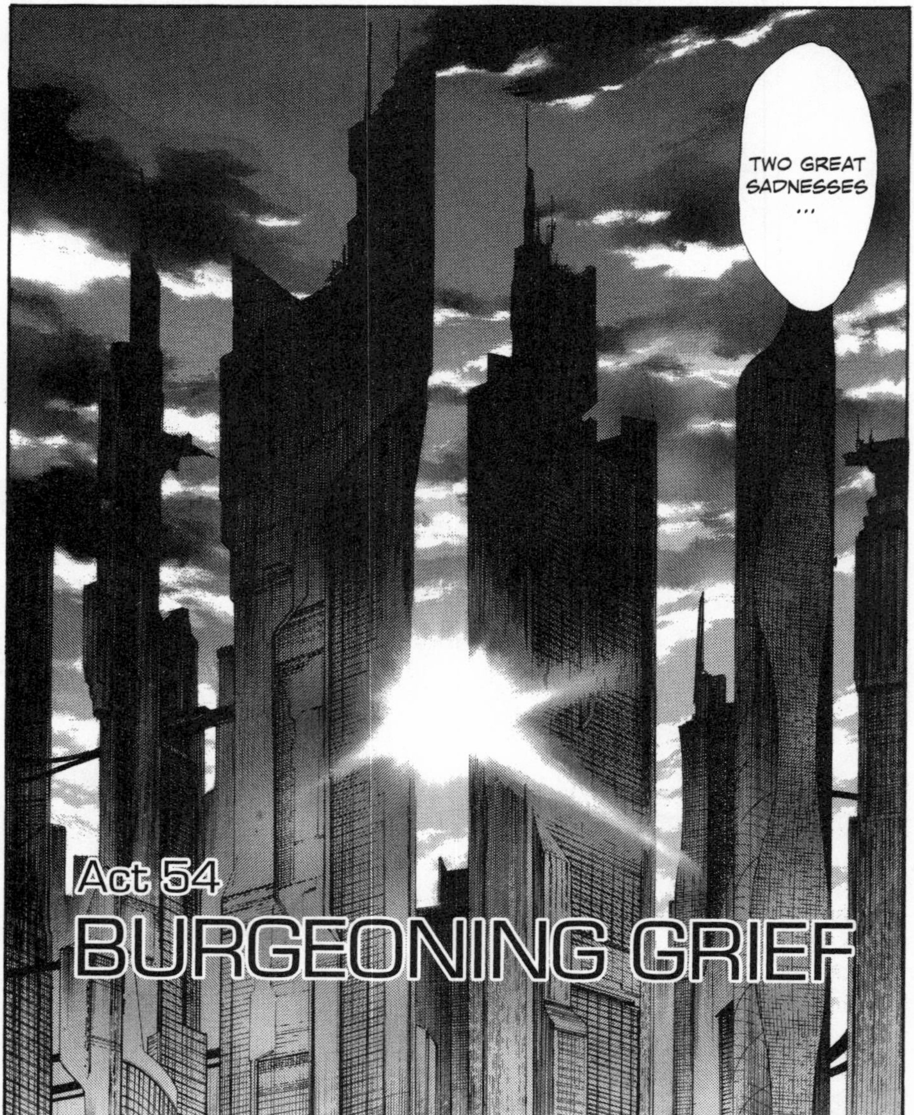
TWO GREAT SADNESSES ...
Act 54
BURGEONING GRIEF

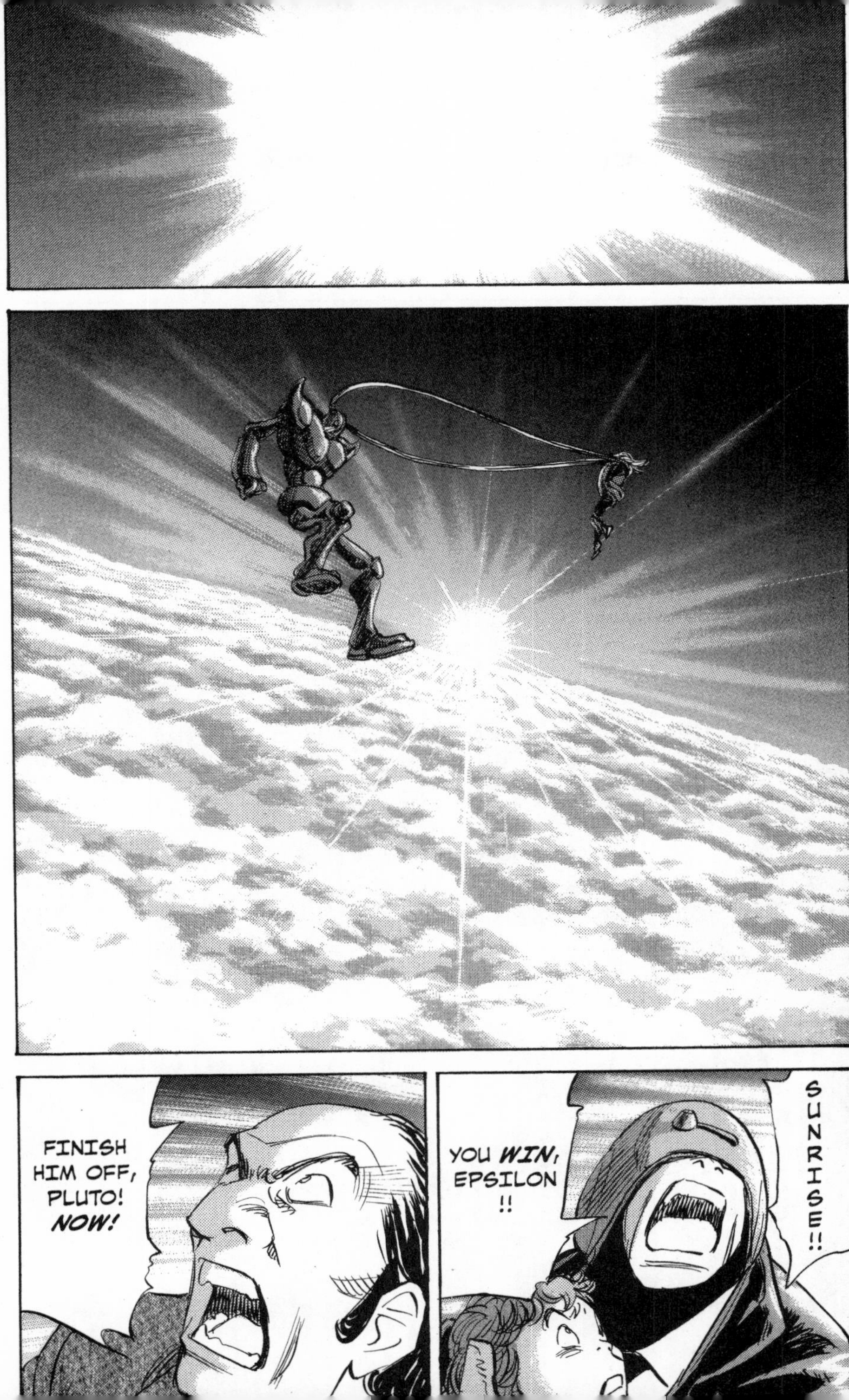
SUNRISE!!
YOU WIN, EPSILON!!
FINISH HIM OFF, PLUTO! NOW!

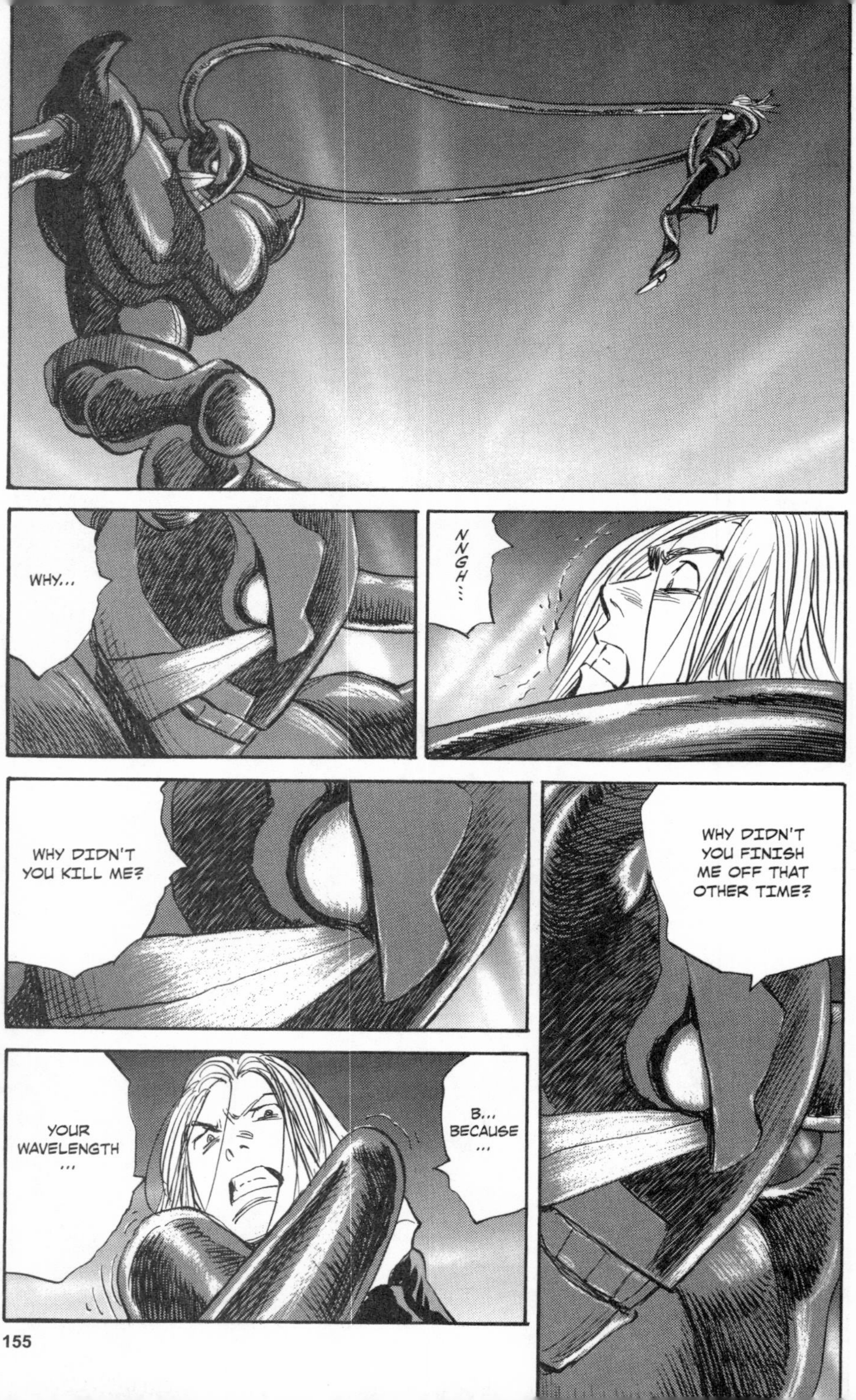
NNGH...
WHY...
WHY DIDN'T YOU FINISH ME OFF THAT OTHER TIME?
WHY DIDN'T YOU KILL ME?
B... BECAUSE ...
YOUR WAVELENGTH ...

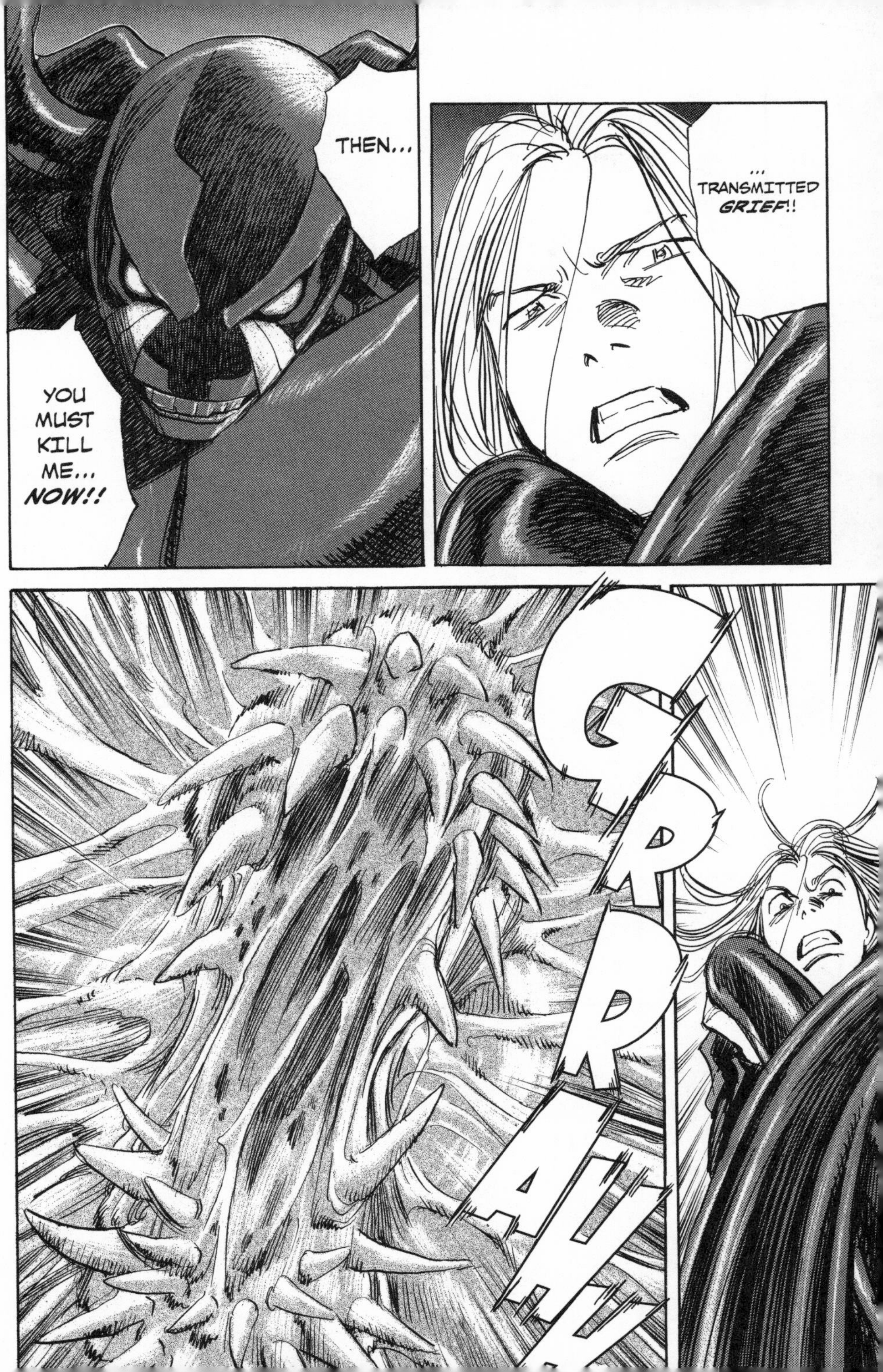
...TRANSMITTED GRIEF!!
THEN...
YOU MUST KILL ME... NOW!!
GRRAH!

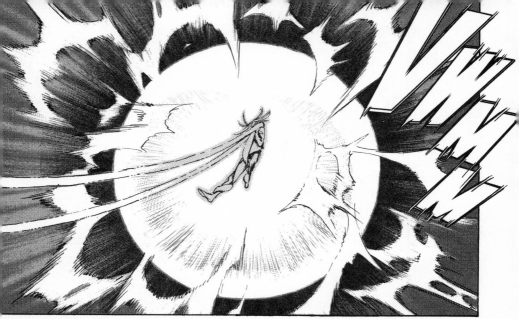

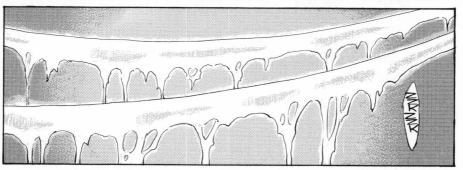

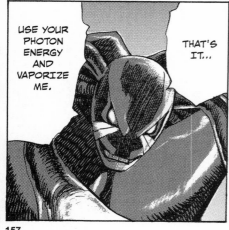

USE YOUR PHOTON ENERGY AND VAPORIZE ME.

THAT'S IT...

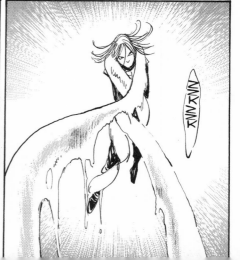

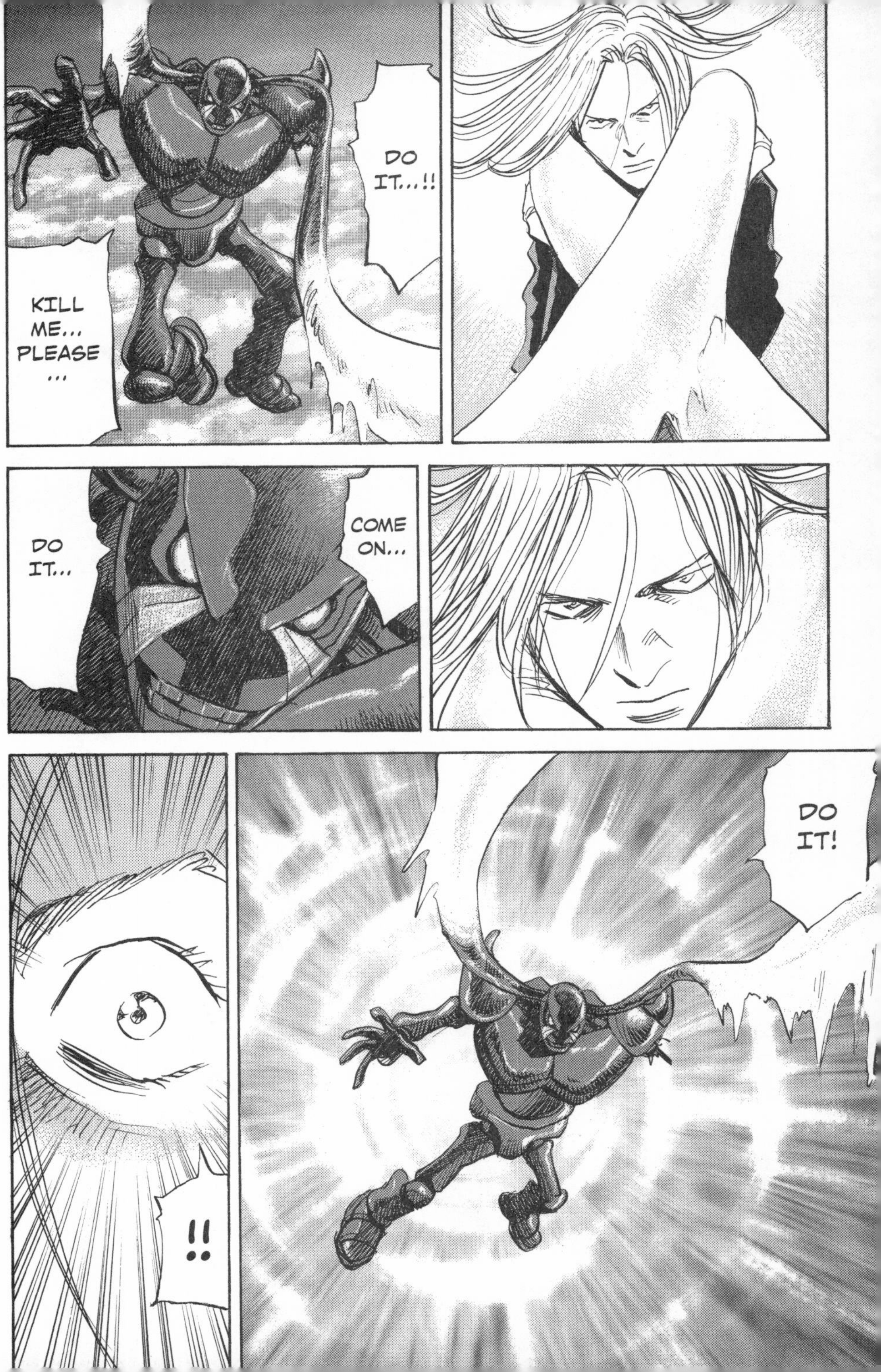
DO IT...!!
KILL ME... PLEASE ...
COME ON...
DO IT...
DO IT!
!!

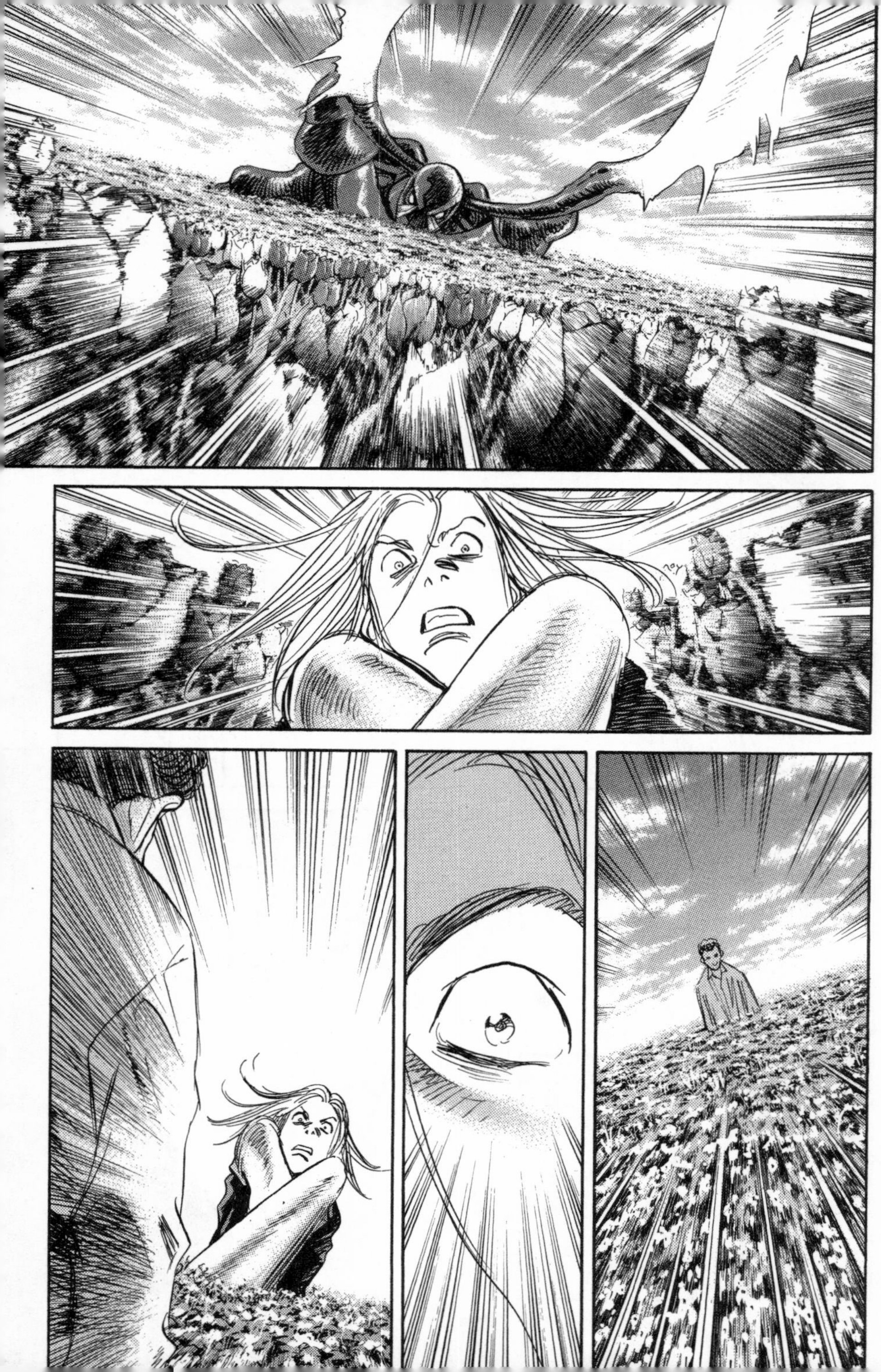

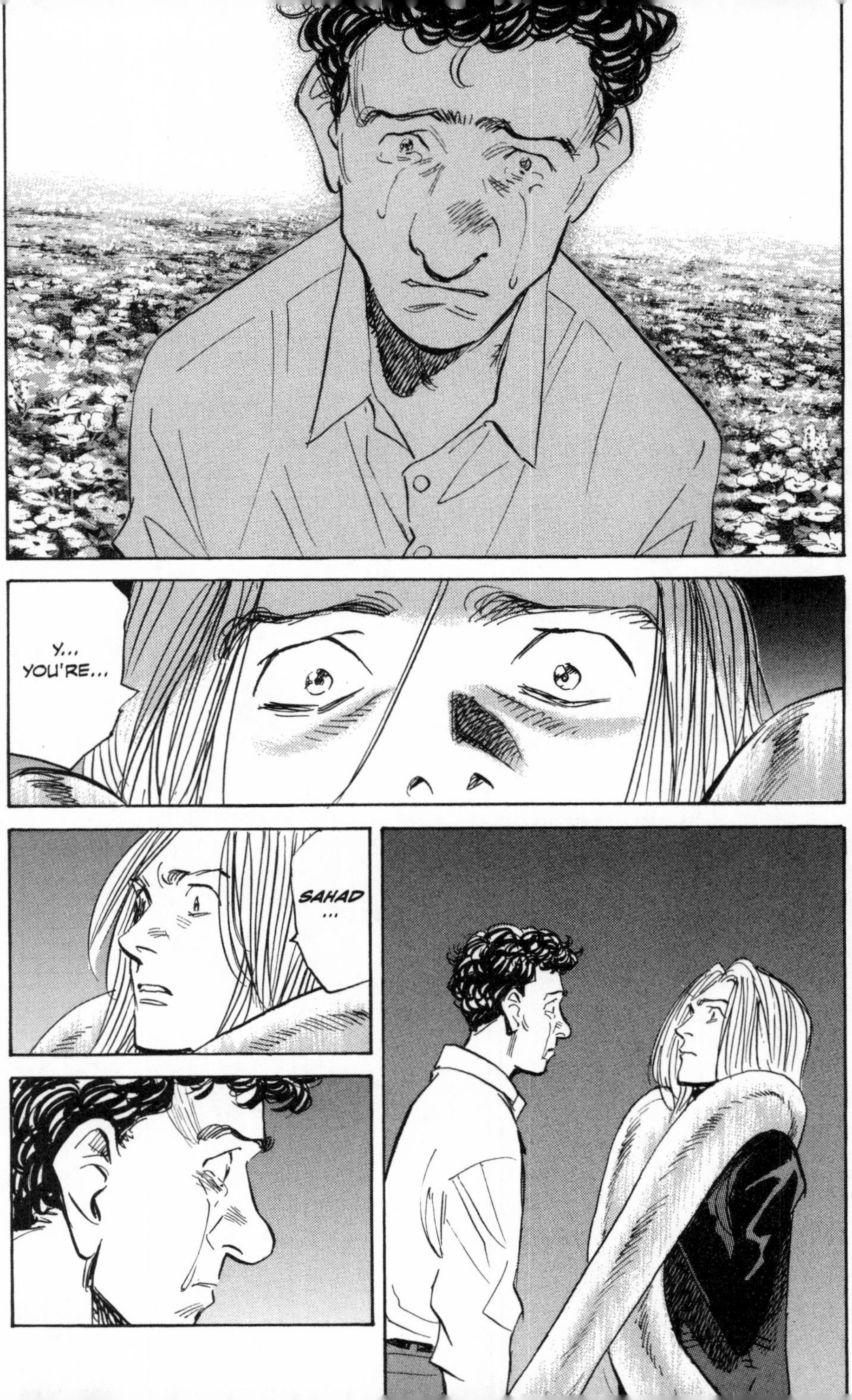
Y... YOU'RE...
SAHAD ...

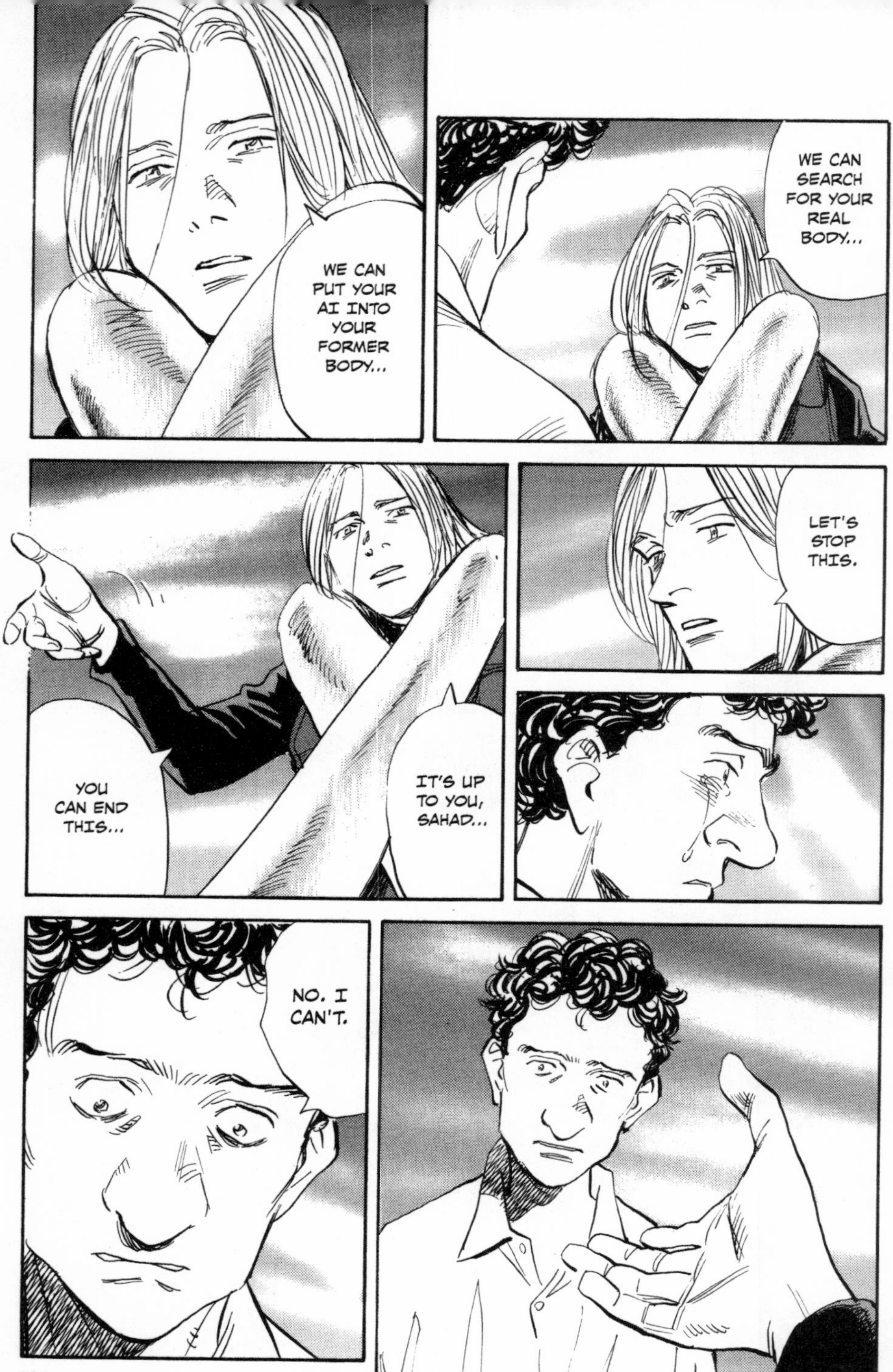
WE CAN SEARCH FOR YOUR REAL BODY...
WE CAN PUT YOUR AI INTO YOUR FORMER BODY...
LET'S STOP THIS.
IT'S UP TO YOU, SAHAD...
YOU CAN END THIS...
NO. I CAN'T.

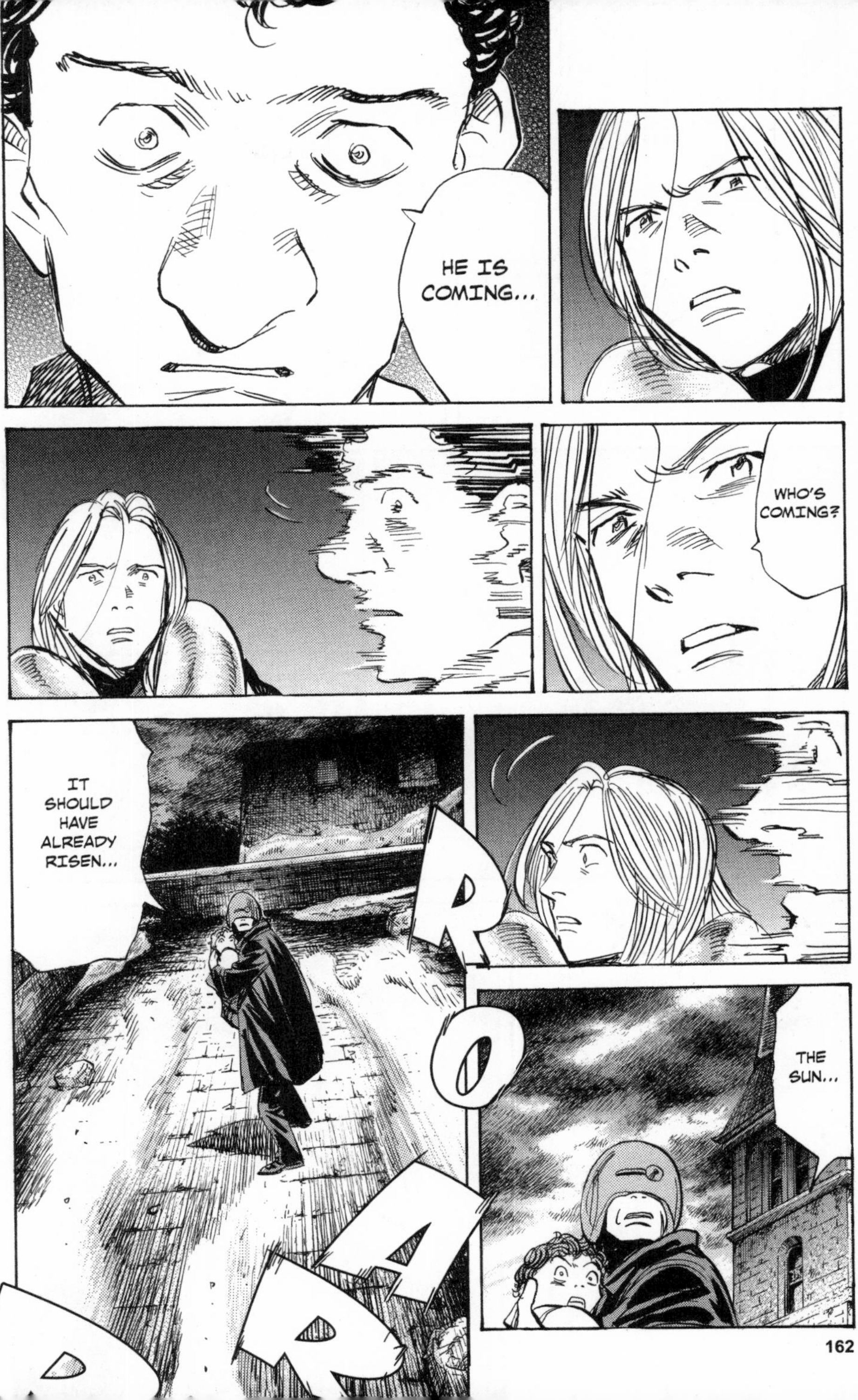
HE IS COMING...
WHO'S COMING?
THE SUN...
IT SHOULD HAVE ALREADY RISEN...

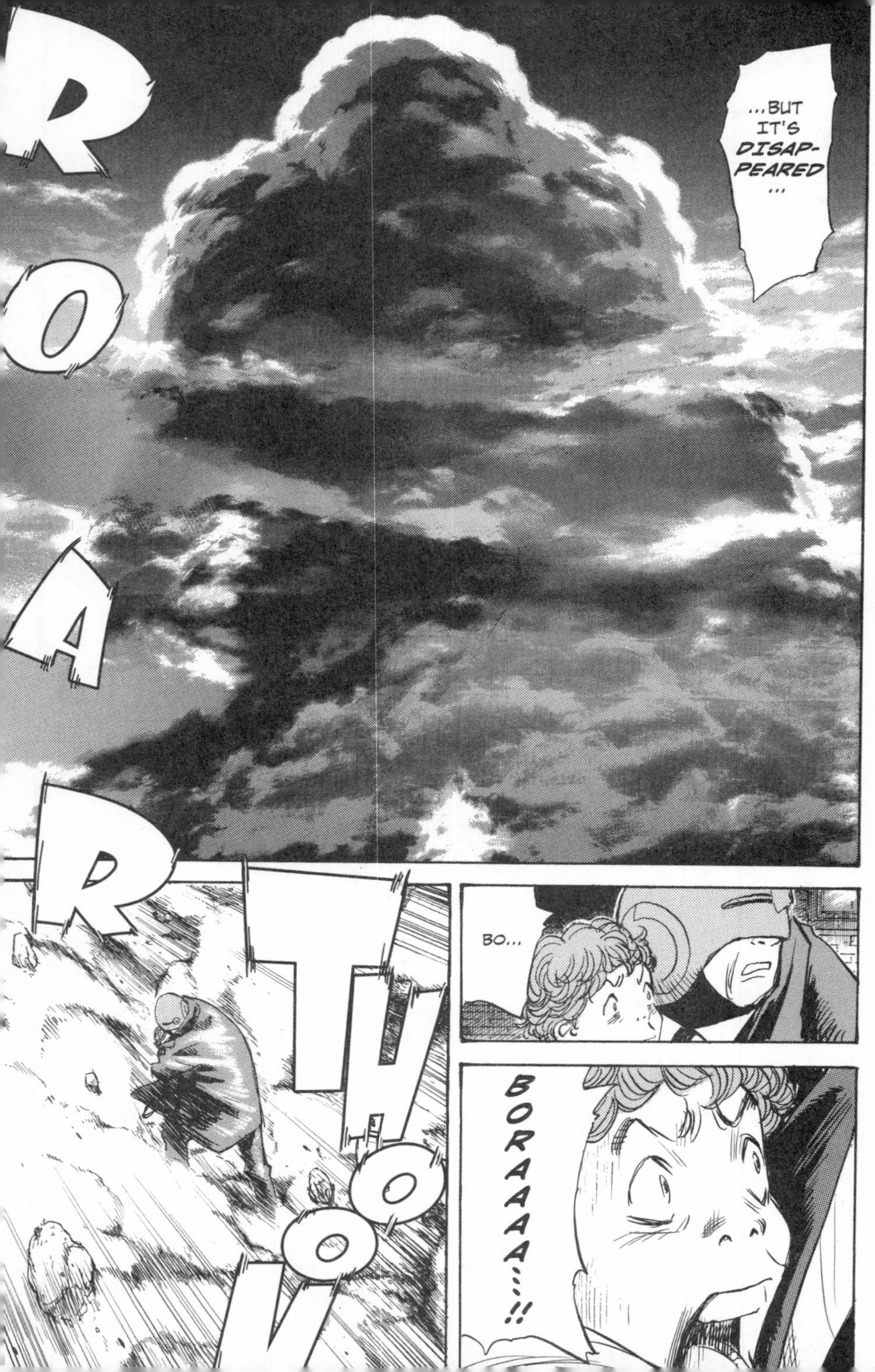
...BUT IT'S DISAPPEARED...
ROAR
BO...
BORAAAAA...!!
THOO

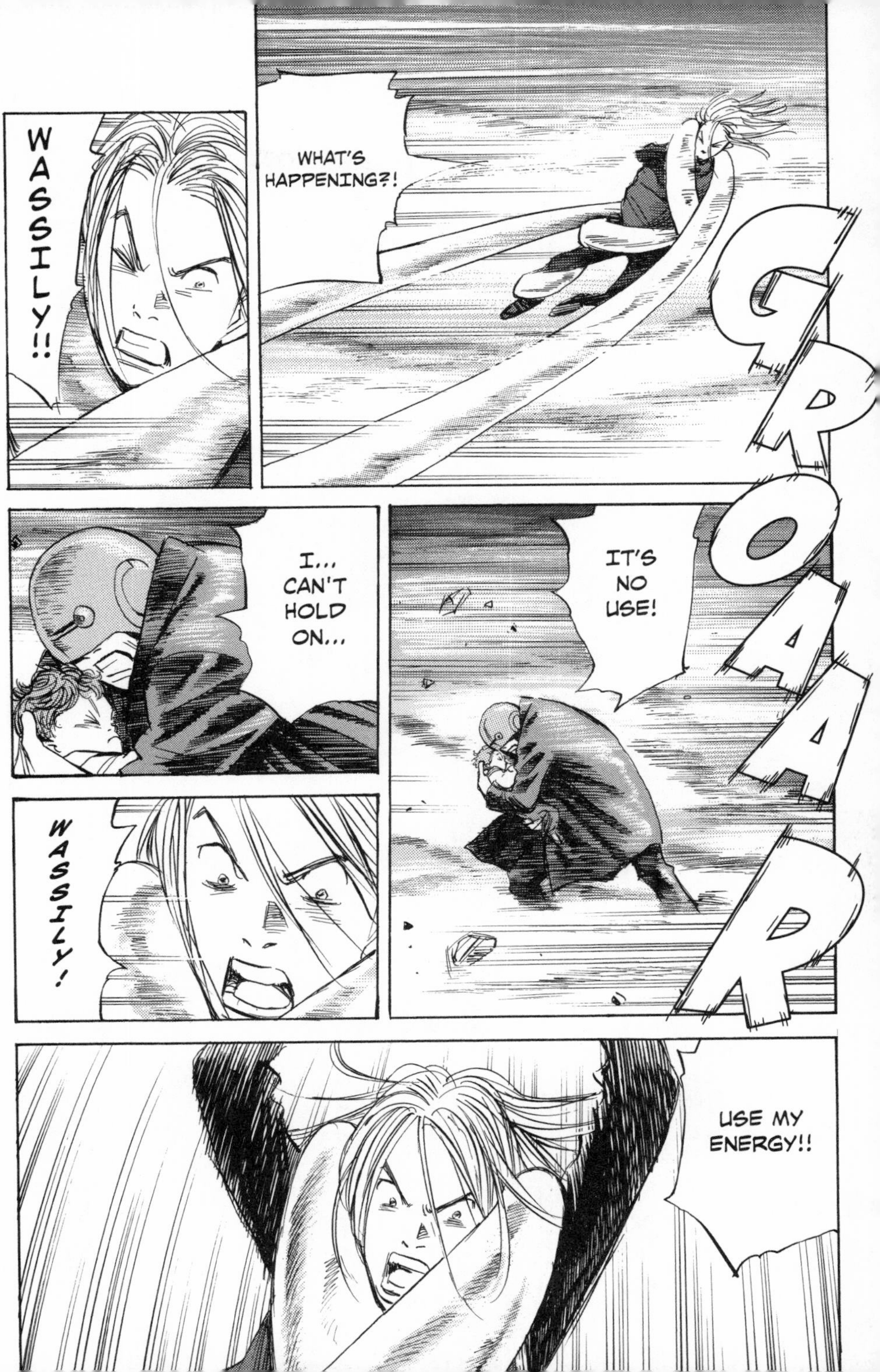
WHAT'S HAPPENING?!
GROOAAR
WASSILY!!
IT'S NO USE!
I... CAN'T HOLD ON...
WASSILY!
USE MY ENERGY!!

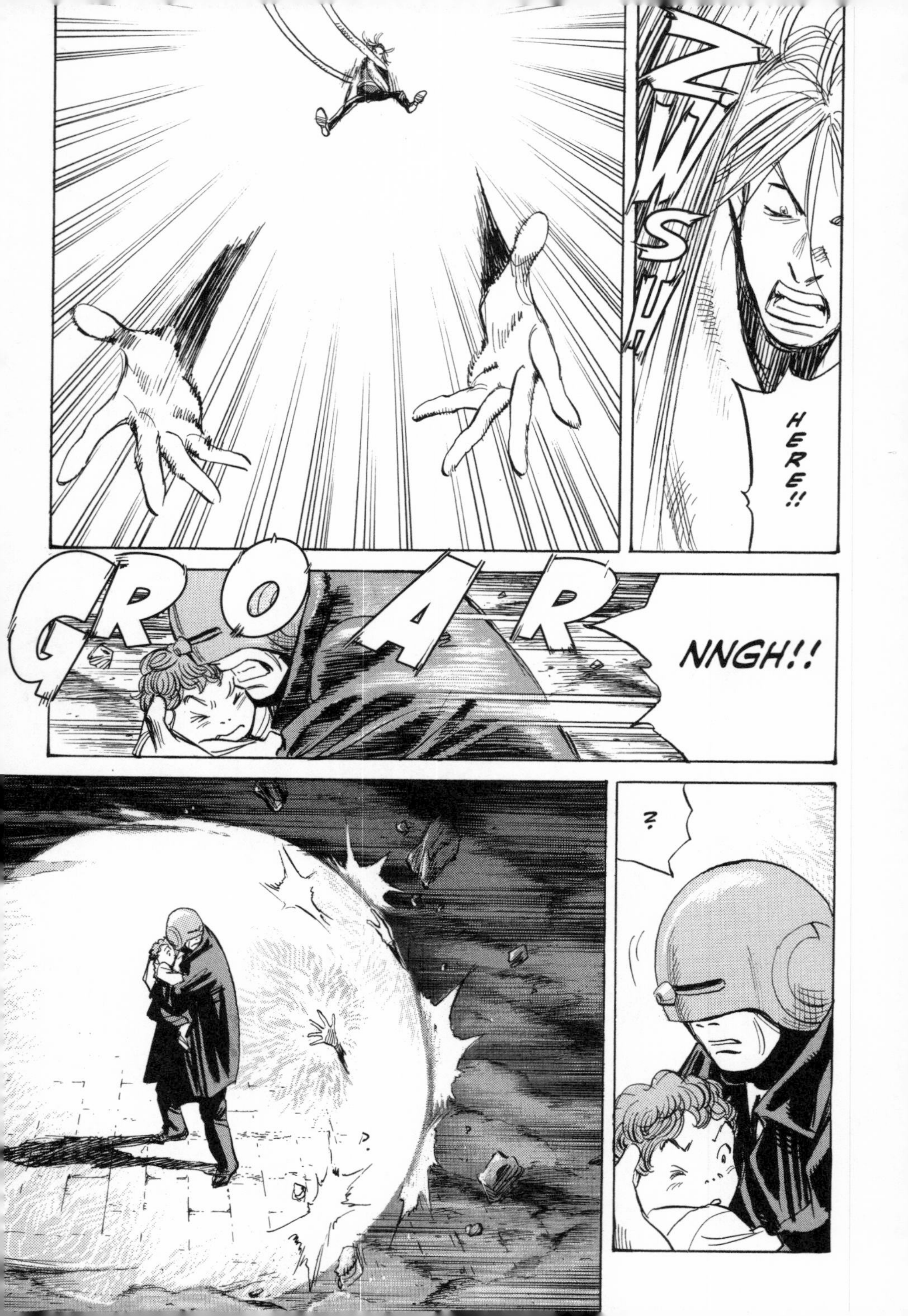
ZWS!!
HERE!!
GROAR
NNGH!!
?
?

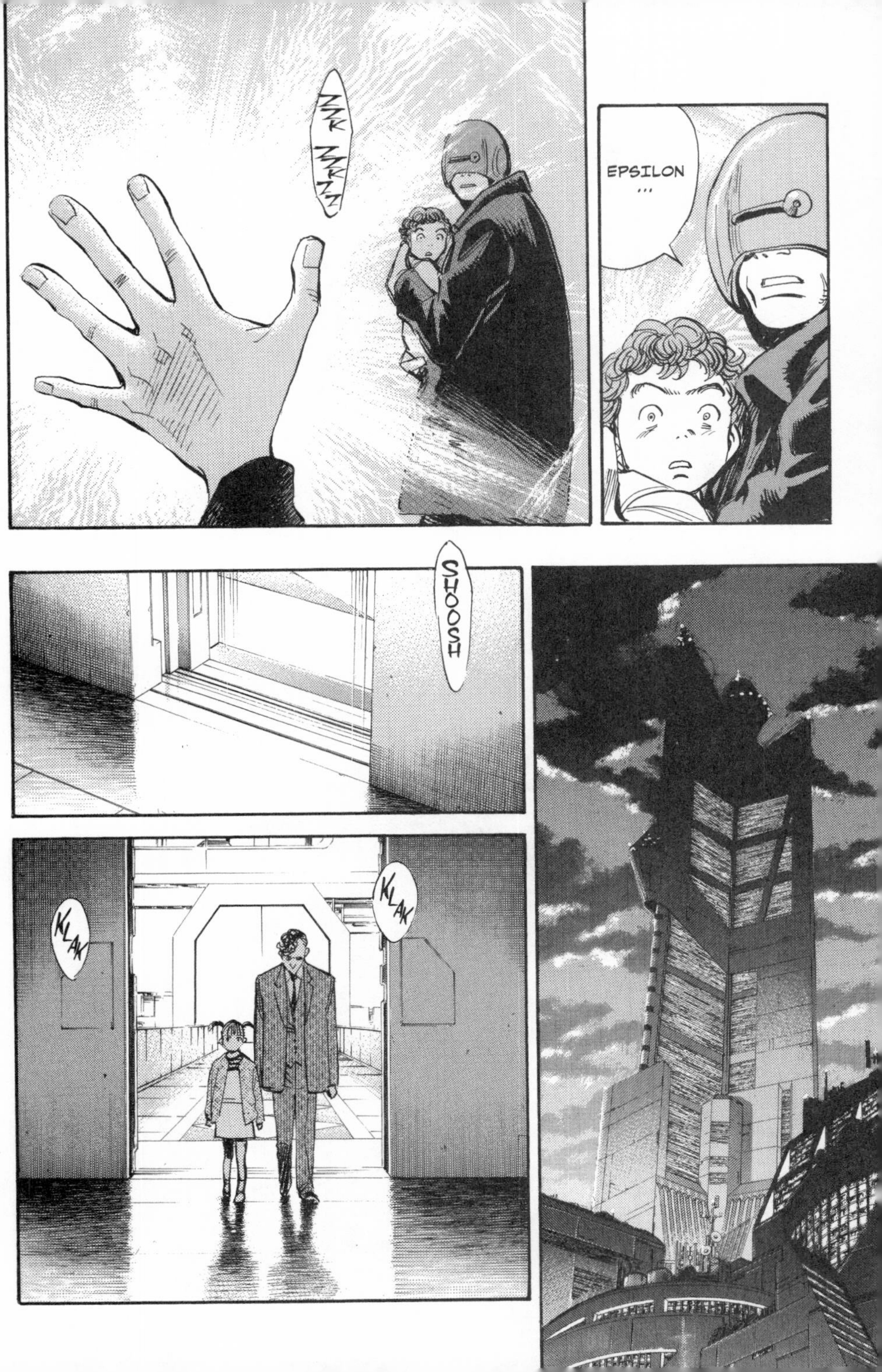

EPSILON ...
ZZK ZZKZZ
SHOOSH
KLAK
KLAK

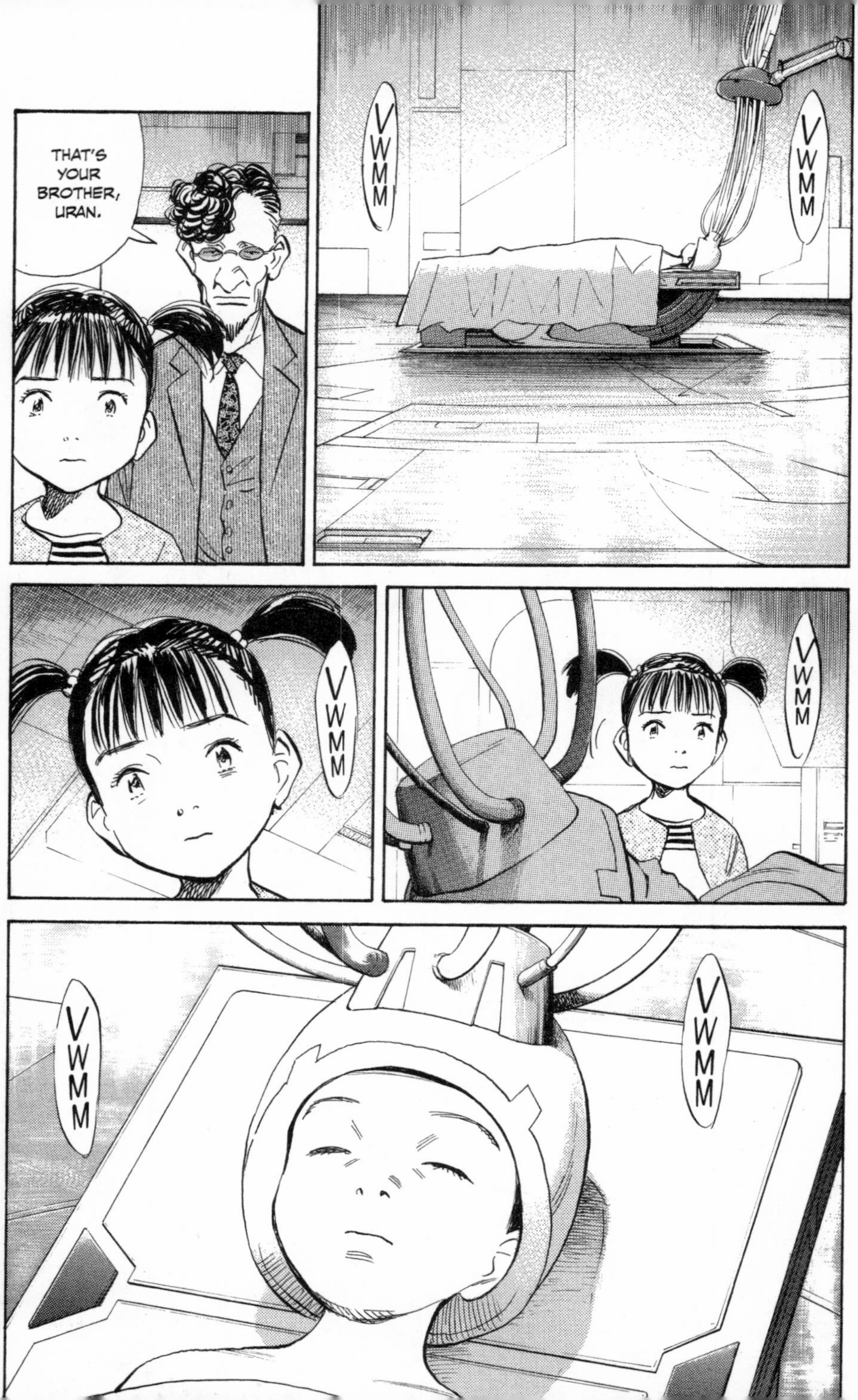
VWMM
VWMM
THAT'S YOUR BROTHER, URAN.
VWMM
VWMM
VWMM
VWMM

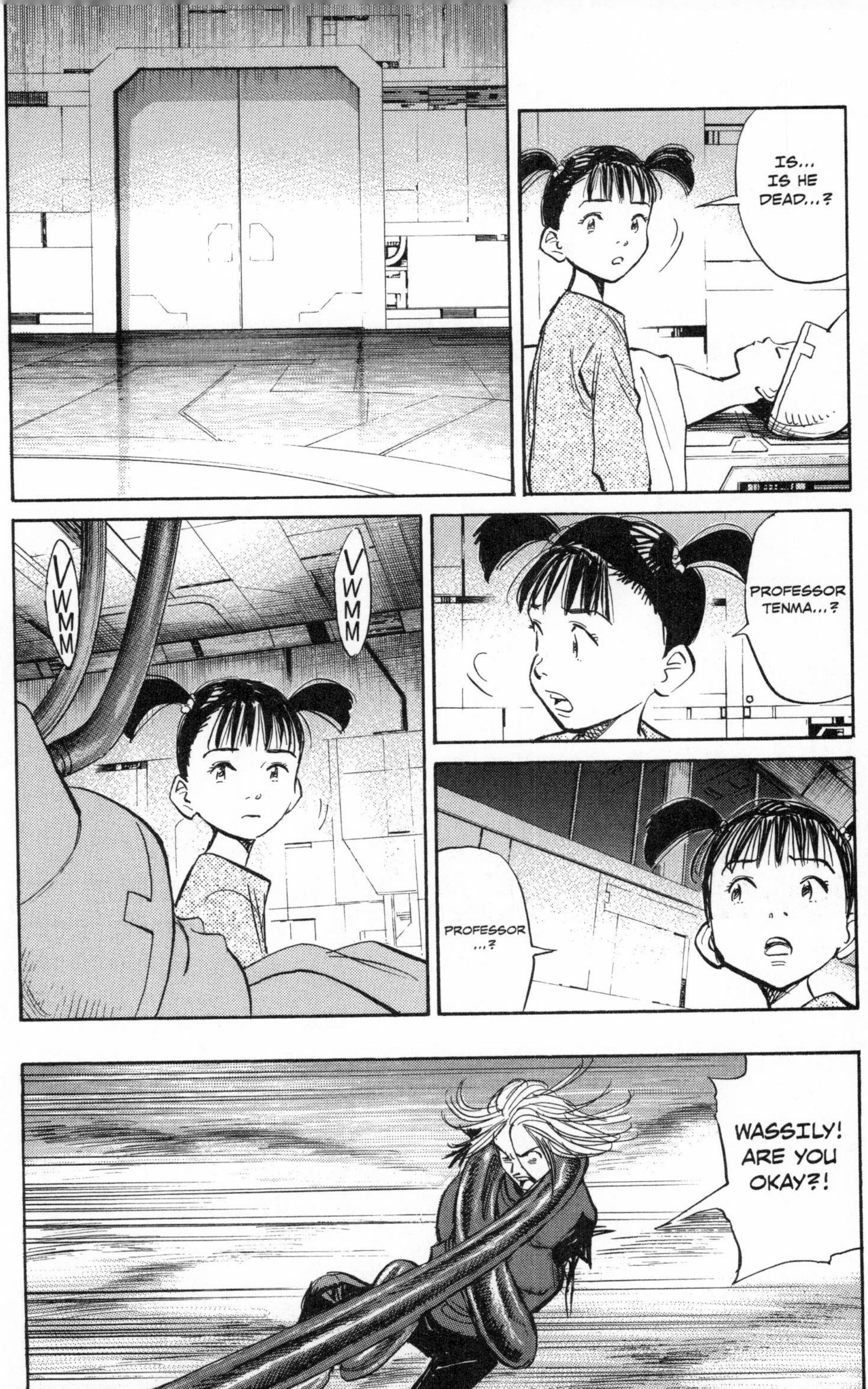
IS... IS HE DEAD...?
PROFESSOR TENMA...?
PROFESSOR ...?
VWMM
VWMM
WASSILY! ARE YOU OKAY?!

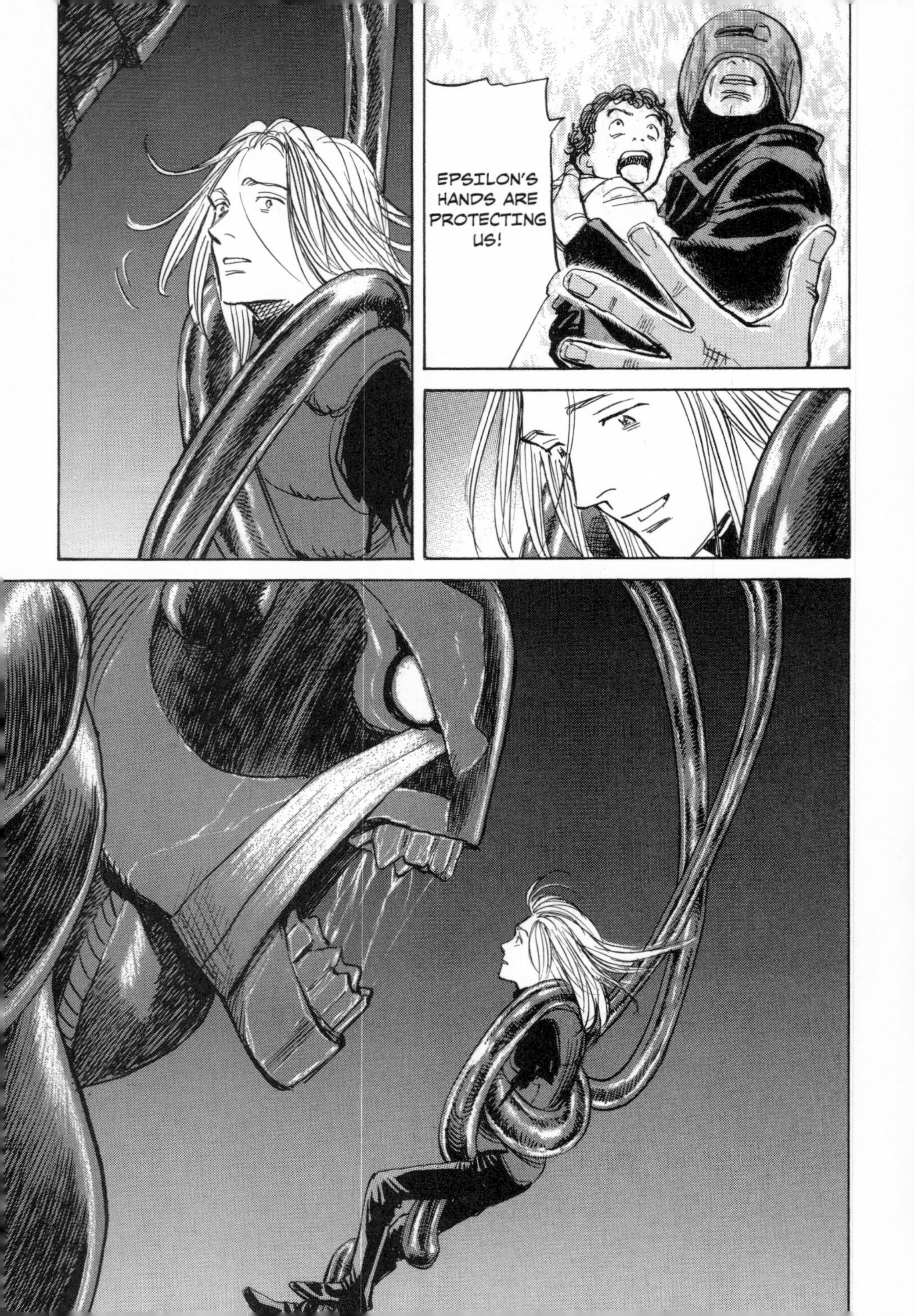
EPSILON'S HANDS ARE PROTECTING US!

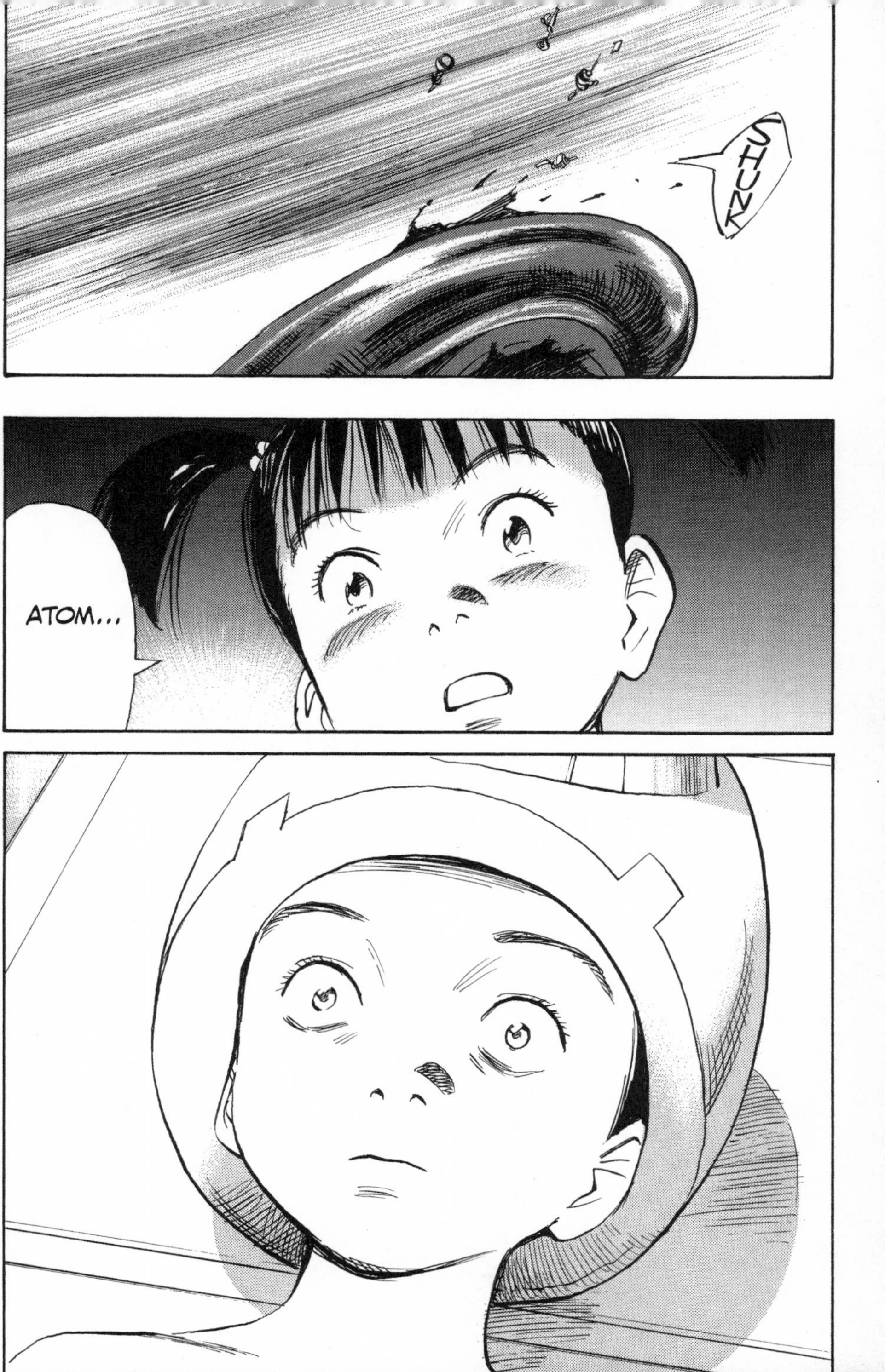
SHUNK
ATOM...

Act 55 THE GREAT AWAKENING

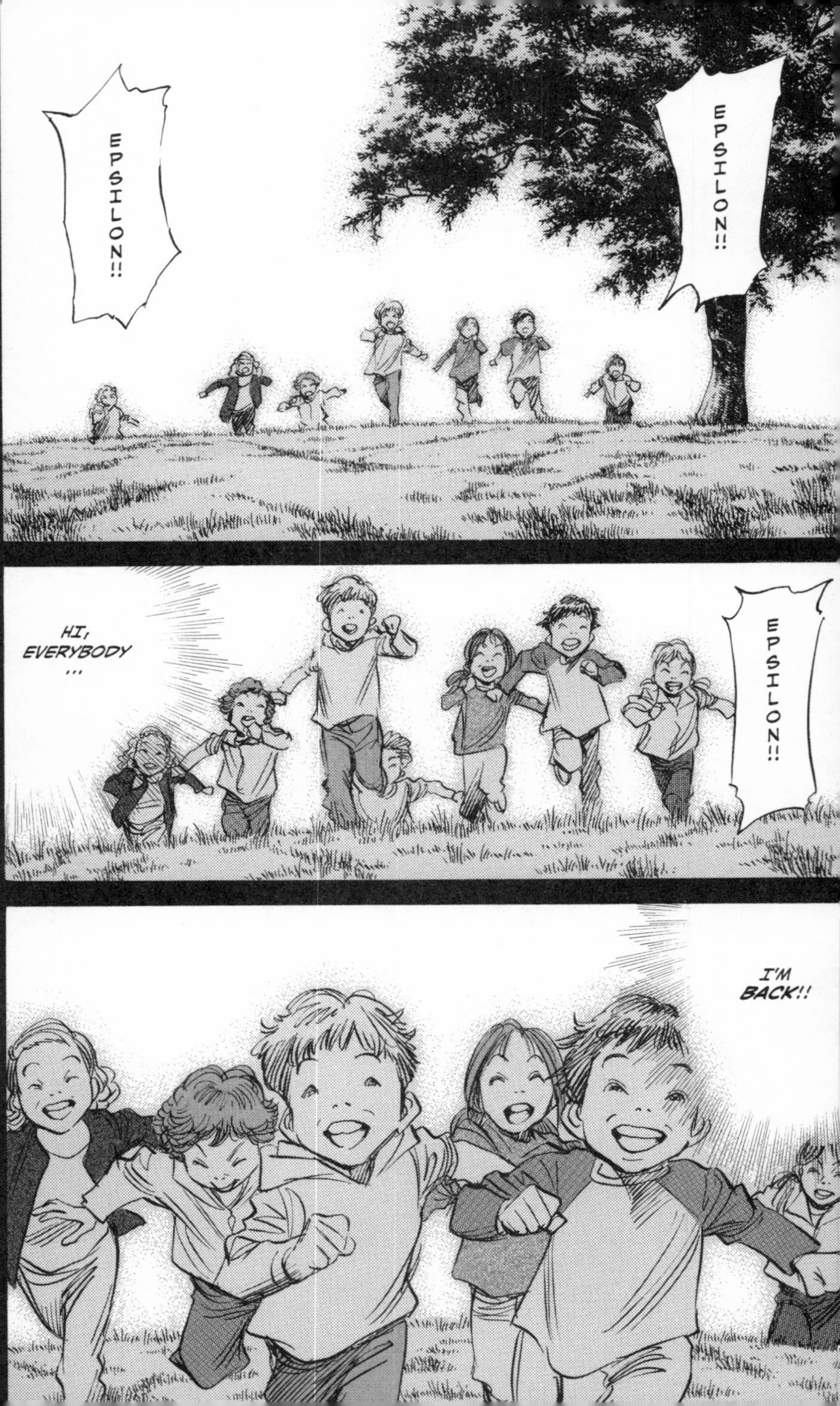
EPSILON!!
EPSILON!!
EPSILON!!
HI, EVERYBODY ...
I'M BACK!!

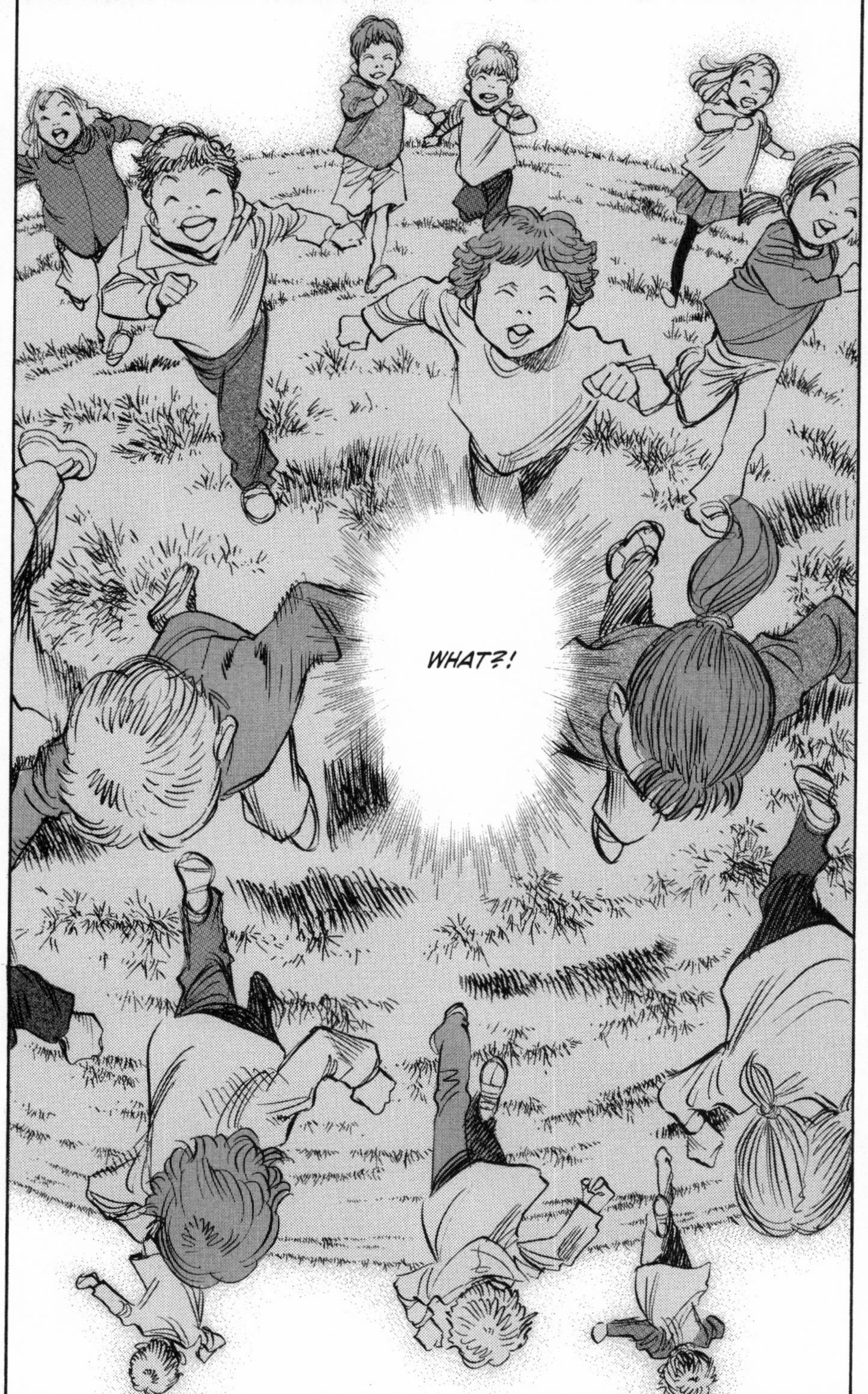
WHAT?!

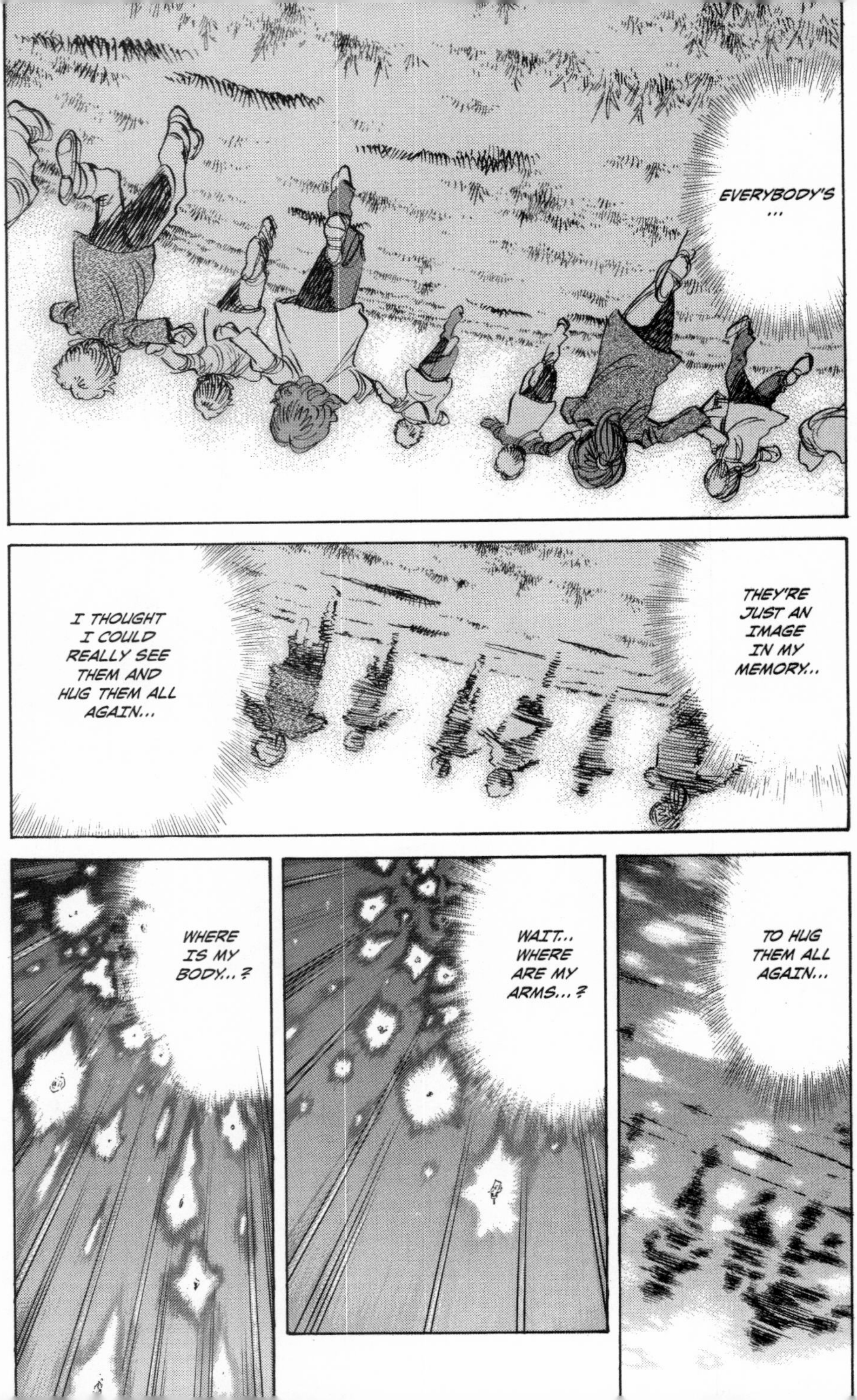
EVERYBODY'S ...
THEY'RE JUST AN IMAGE IN MY MEMORY...
I THOUGHT I COULD REALLY SEE THEM AND HUG THEM ALL AGAIN...
TO HUG THEM ALL AGAIN...
WAIT... WHERE ARE MY ARMS...?
WHERE IS MY BODY...?

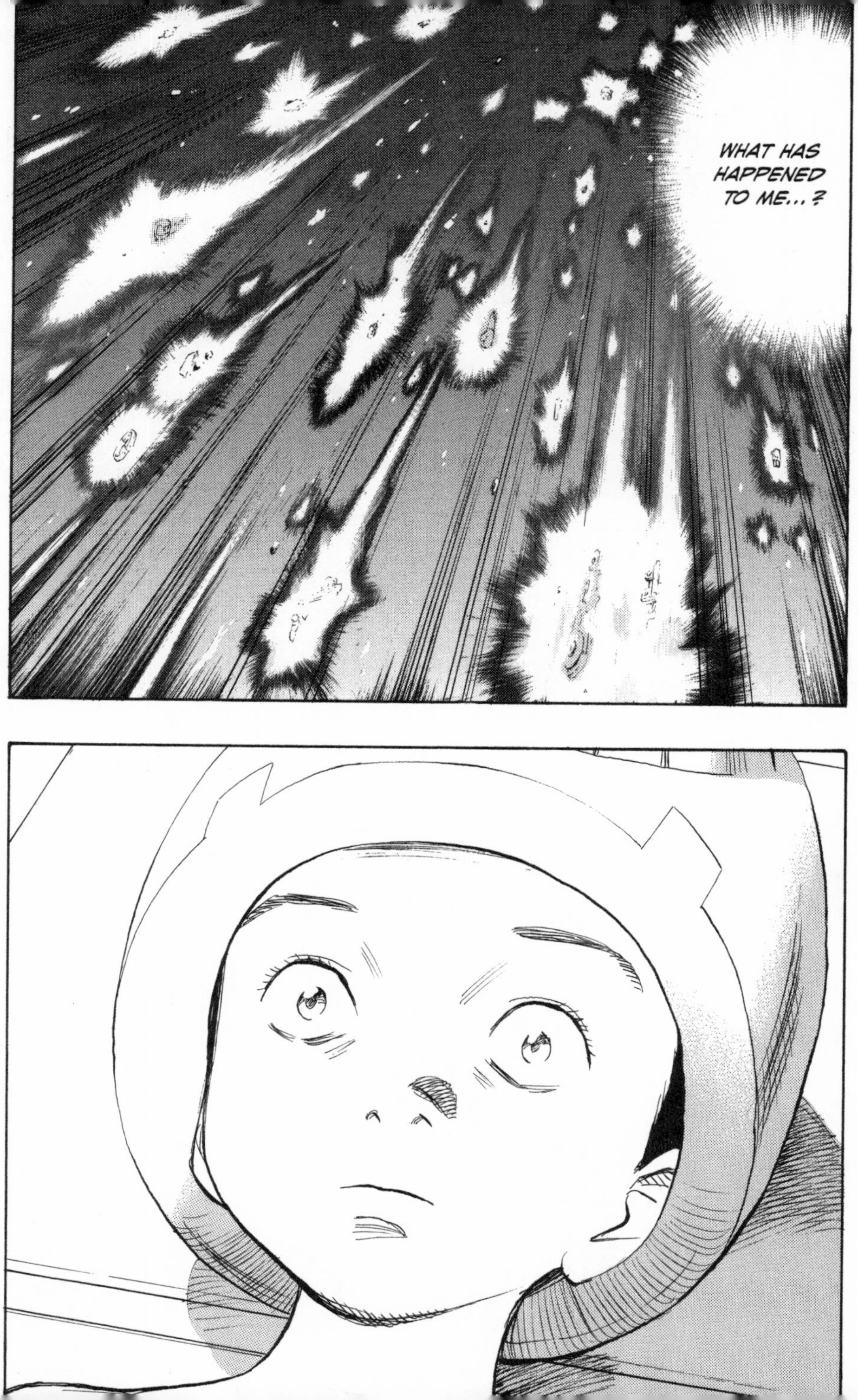
WHAT HAS HAPPENED TO ME...?

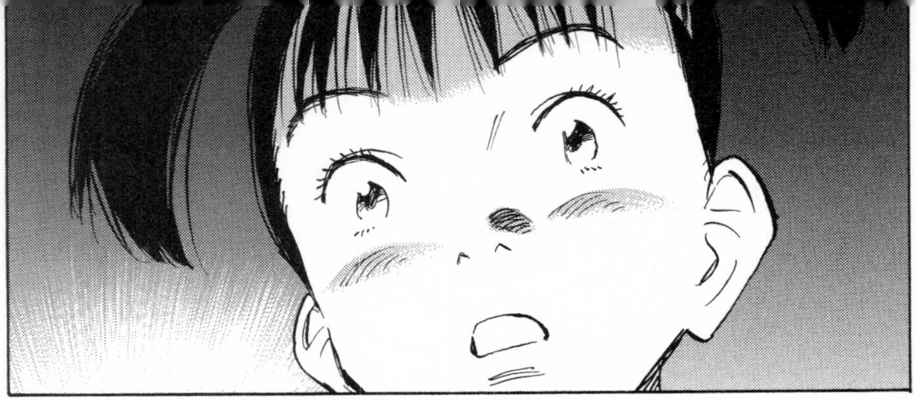

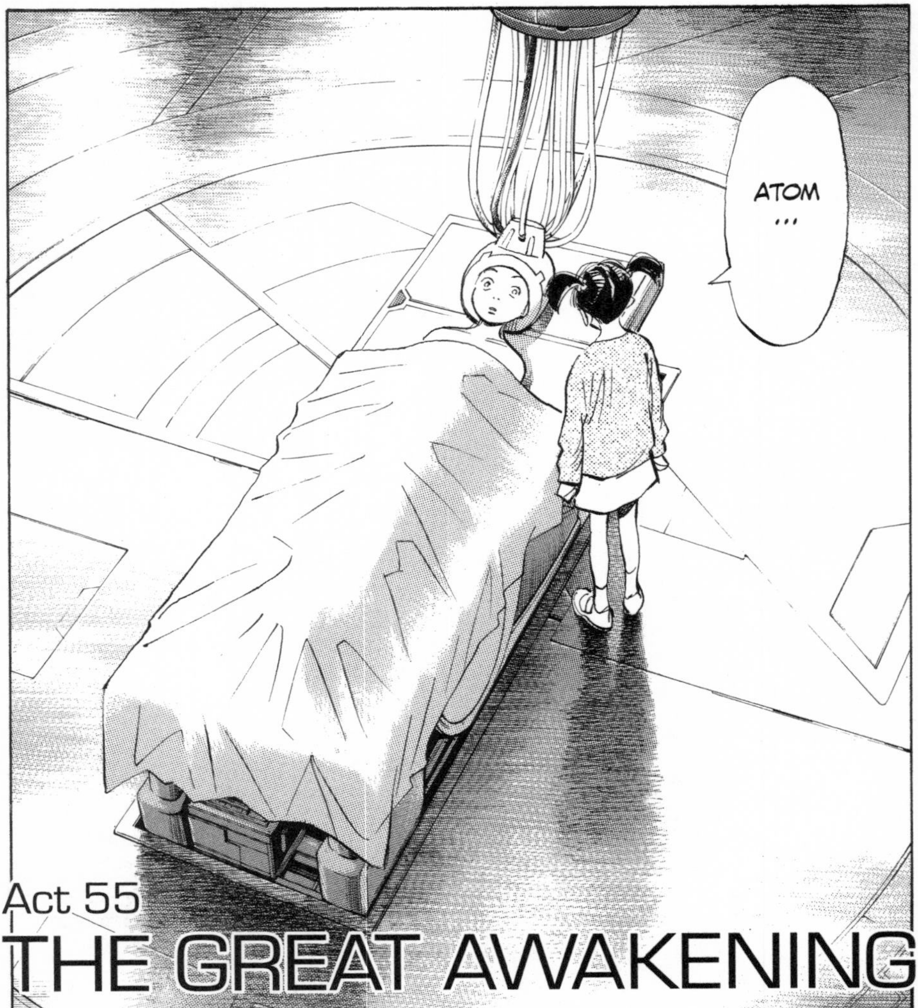
ATOM
...
Act 55
THE GREAT AWAKENING

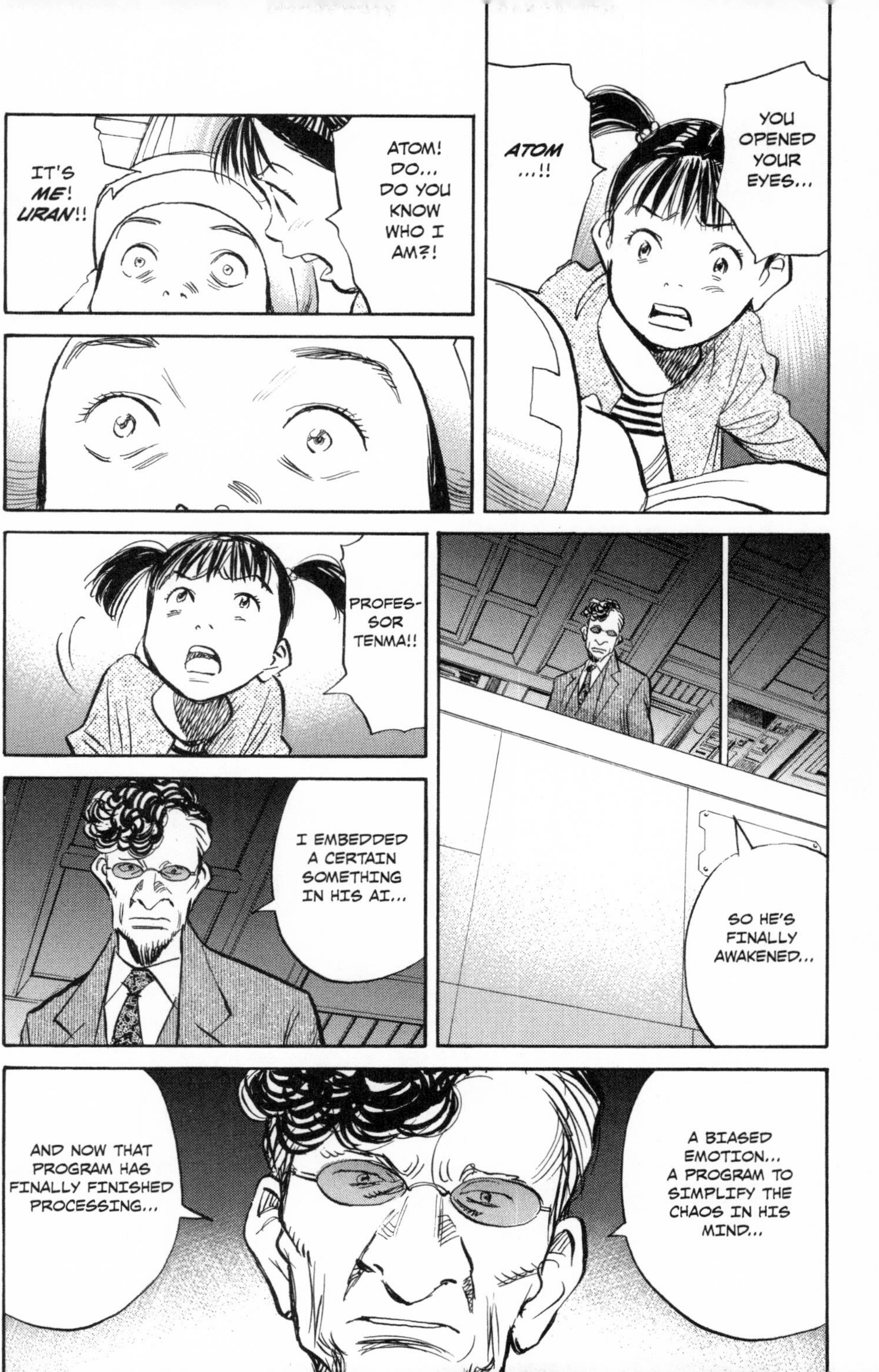
YOU OPENED YOUR EYES...
ATOM ...!!
ATOM! DO... DO YOU KNOW WHO I AM?!
IT'S ME! URAN!!
SO HE'S FINALLY AWAKENED...
PROFES-SOR TENMA!!
I EMBEDDED A CERTAIN SOMETHING IN HIS AI...
A BIASED EMOTION... A PROGRAM TO SIMPLIFY THE CHAOS IN HIS MIND...
AND NOW THAT PROGRAM HAS FINALLY FINISHED PROCESSING...

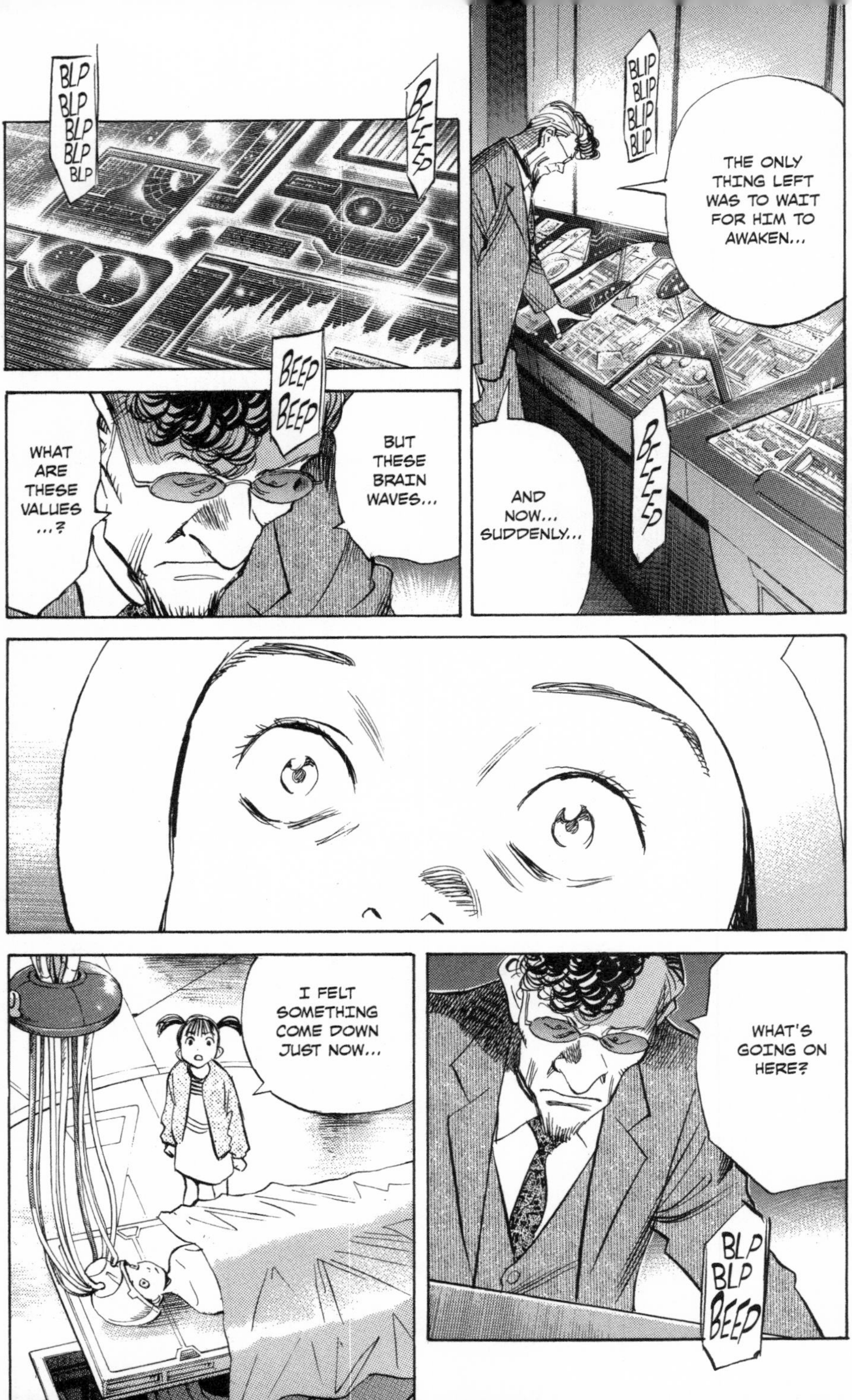
BLIP BLIP BLIP BLIP
THE ONLY THING LEFT WAS TO WAIT FOR HIM TO AWAKEN...
AND NOW... SUDDENLY...
BEEEP
BLP BLP BLP BLP BLP
BEEEP
BEEP BEEP
BUT THESE BRAIN WAVES...
WHAT ARE THESE VALUES...?
WHAT'S GOING ON HERE?
BLP BLP BEEP
I FELT SOMETHING COME DOWN JUST NOW...

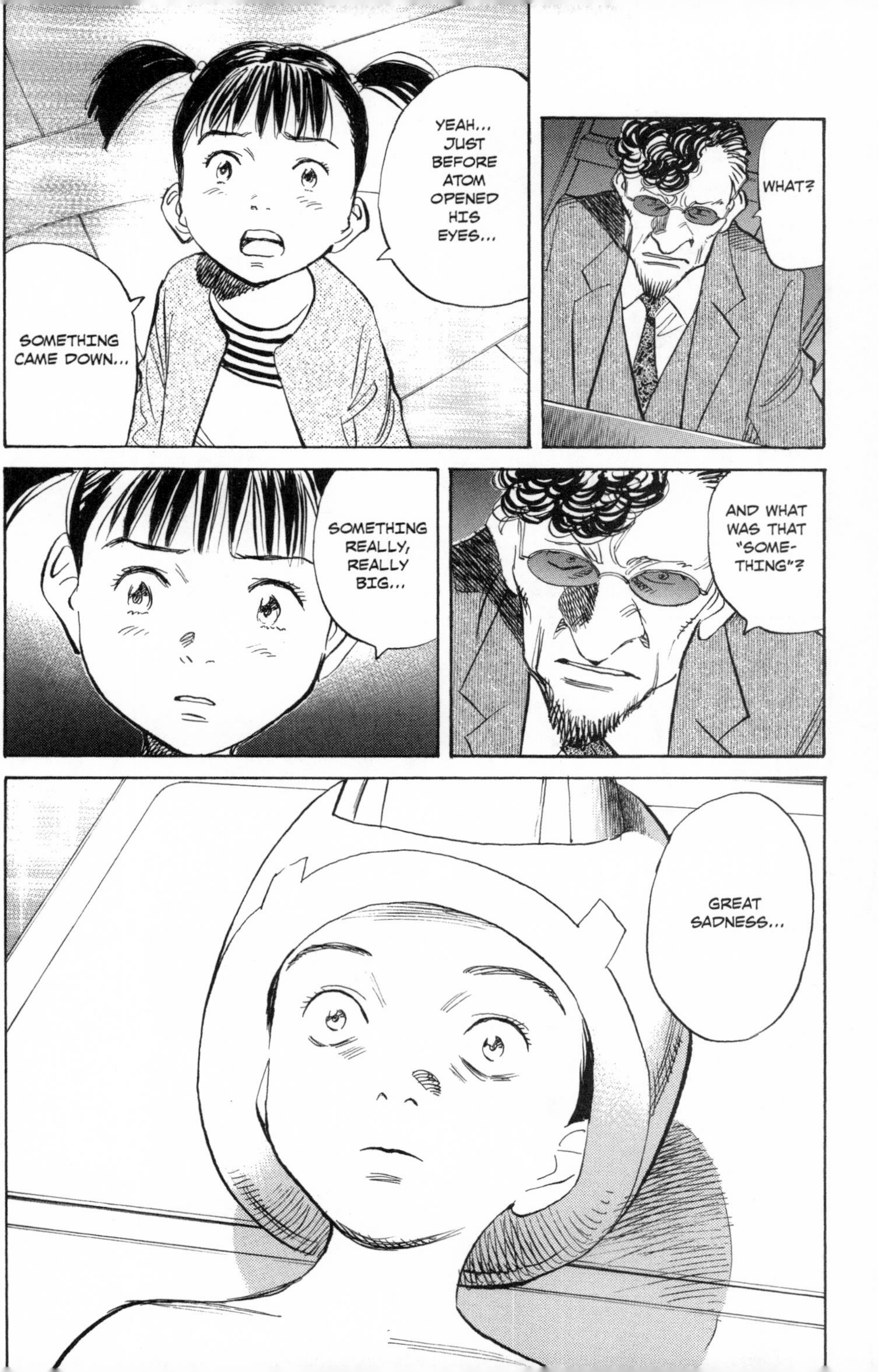
WHAT?
YEAH... JUST BEFORE ATOM OPENED HIS EYES...
SOMETHING CAME DOWN...
AND WHAT WAS THAT "SOME-THING"?
SOMETHING REALLY, REALLY BIG...
GREAT SADNESS...

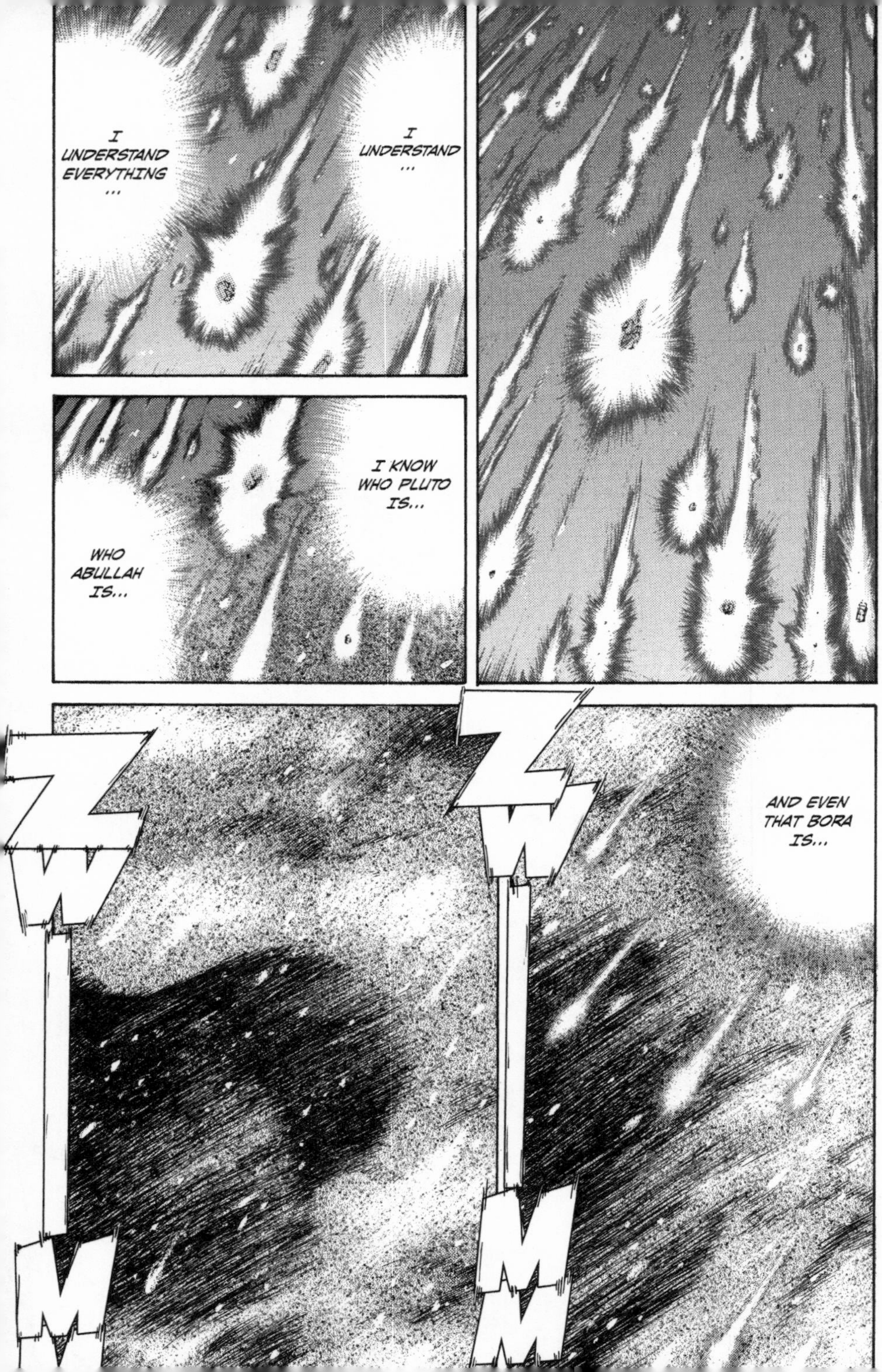
I UNDERSTAND ...
I UNDERSTAND EVERYTHING ...
I KNOW WHO PLUTO IS...
WHO ABULLAH IS...
AND EVEN THAT BORA IS...
ZWMMM
ZWMM

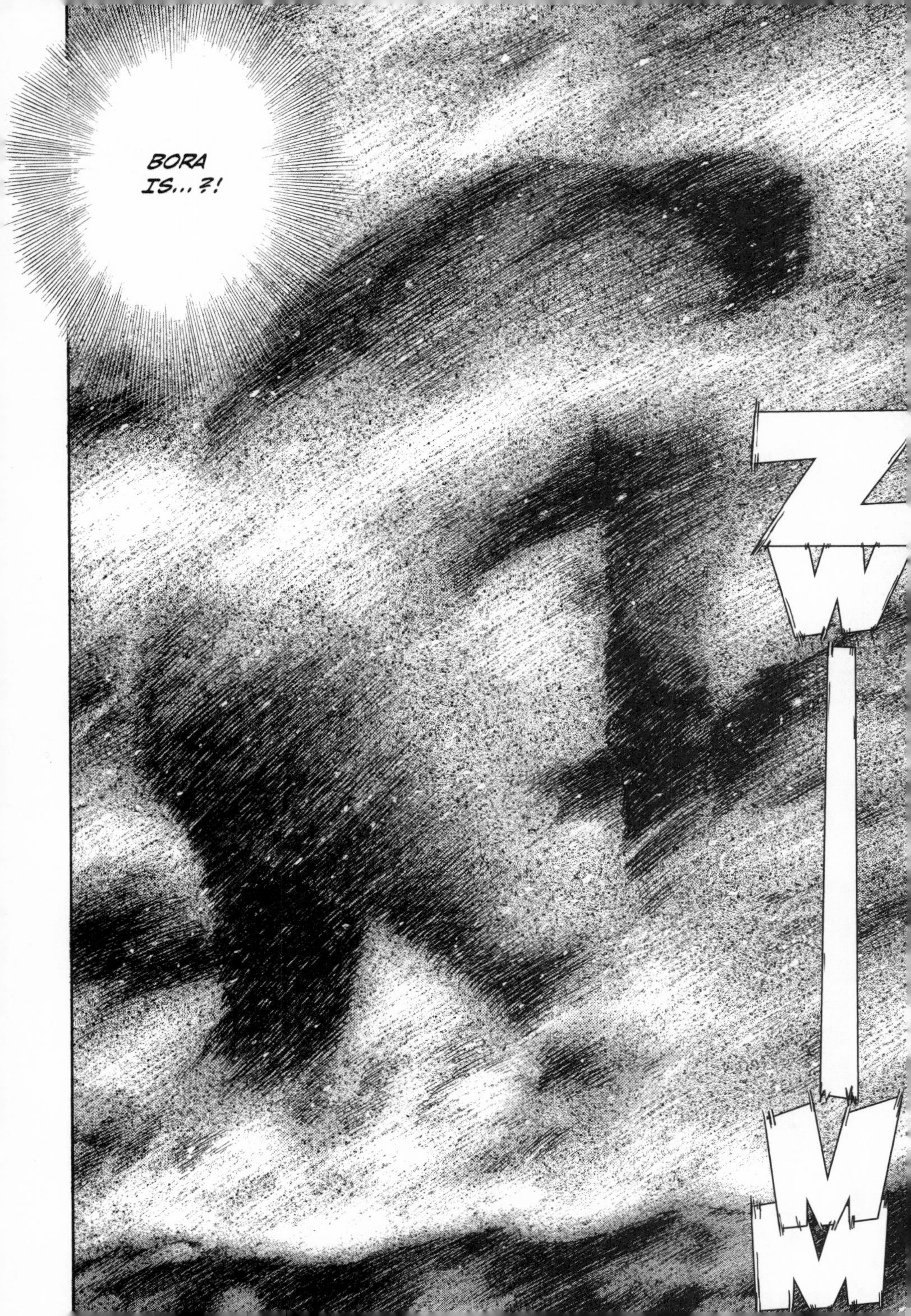
BORA IS...?!
ZWOOOM

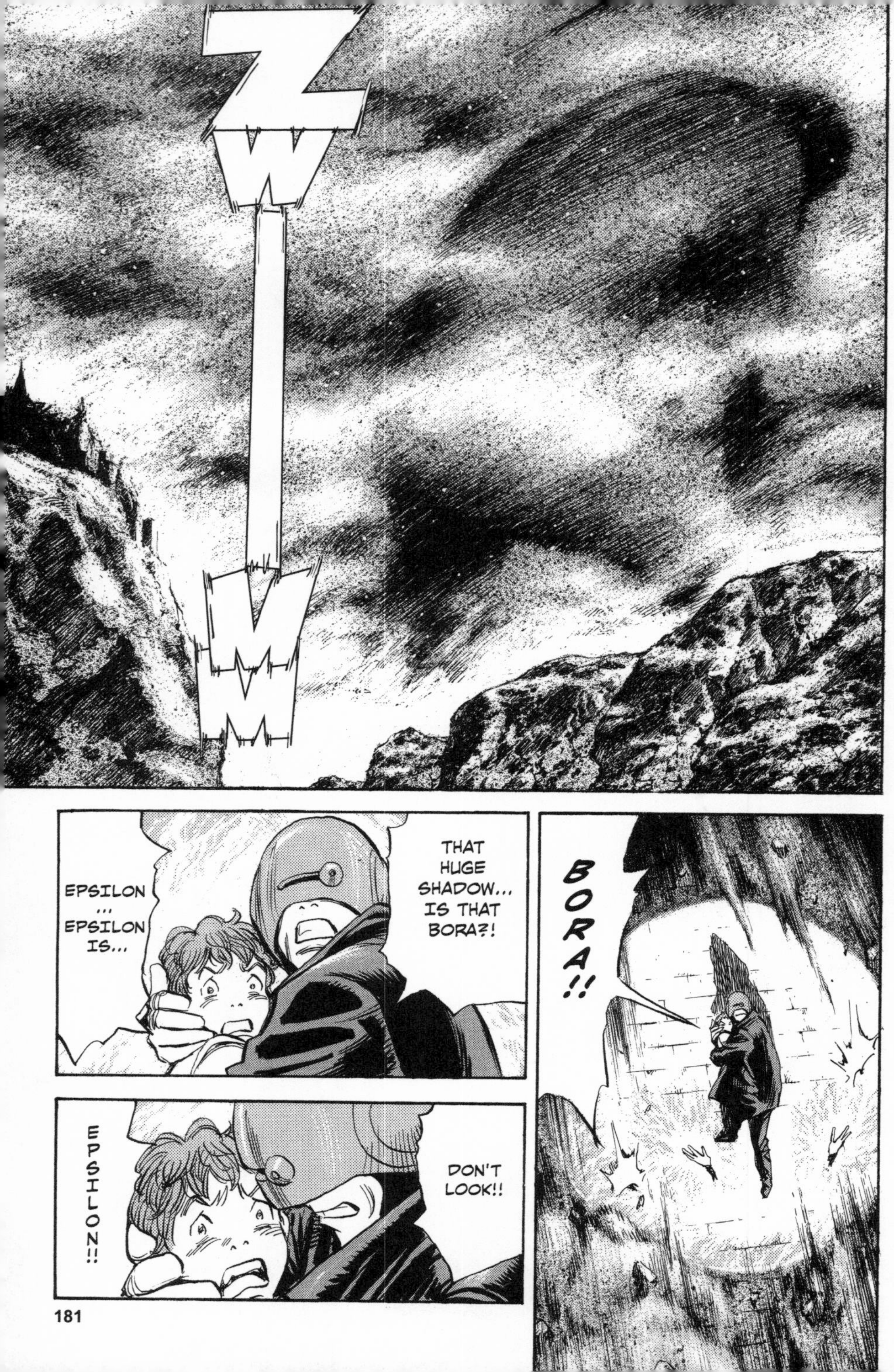
ZWMM
BORA!!
THAT HUGE SHADOW... IS THAT BORA?!
EPSILON... EPSILON IS...
DON'T LOOK!!
EPSILON!!

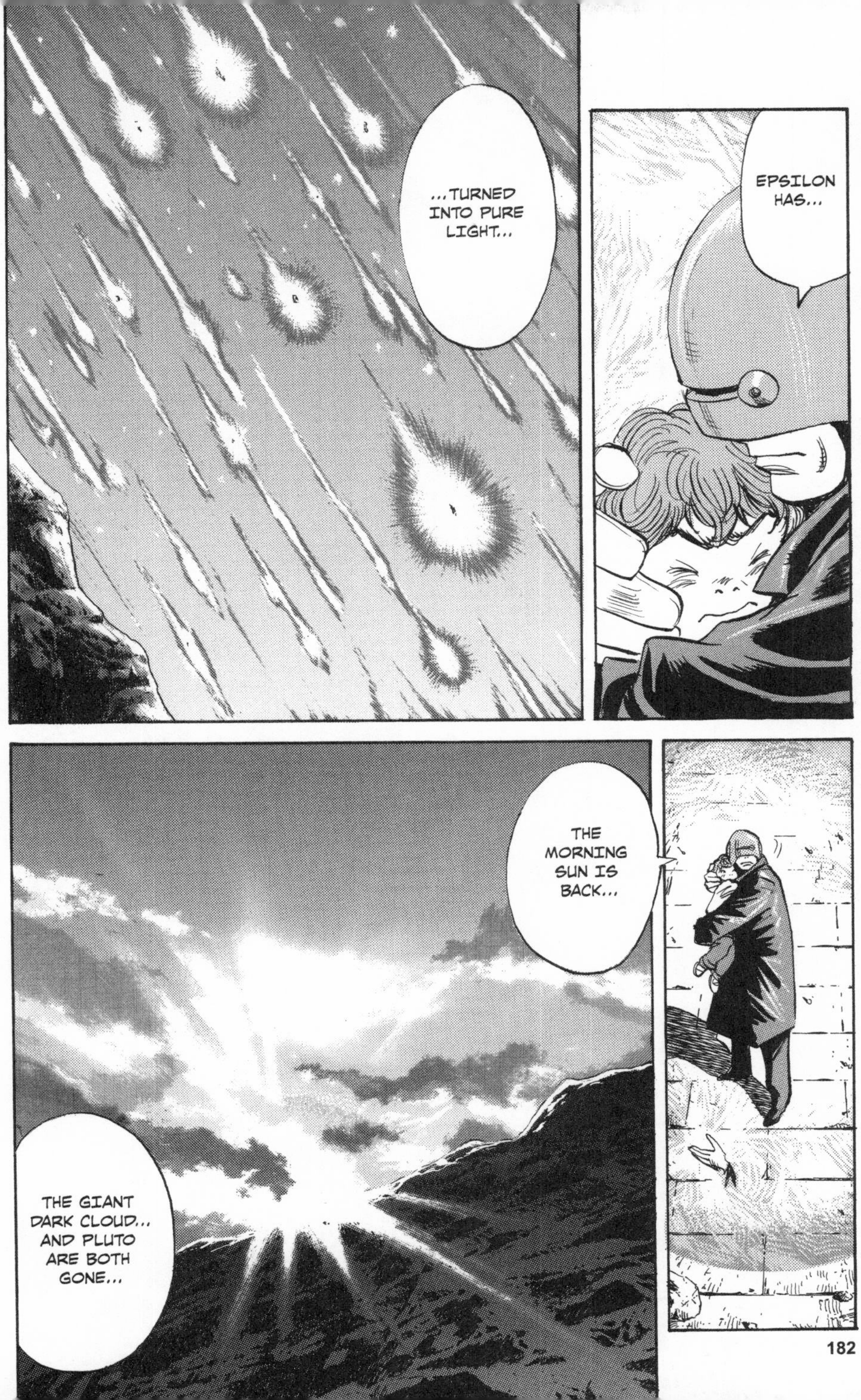
EPSILON HAS...
...TURNED INTO PURE LIGHT...
THE MORNING SUN IS BACK...
THE GIANT DARK CLOUD... AND PLUTO ARE BOTH GONE...

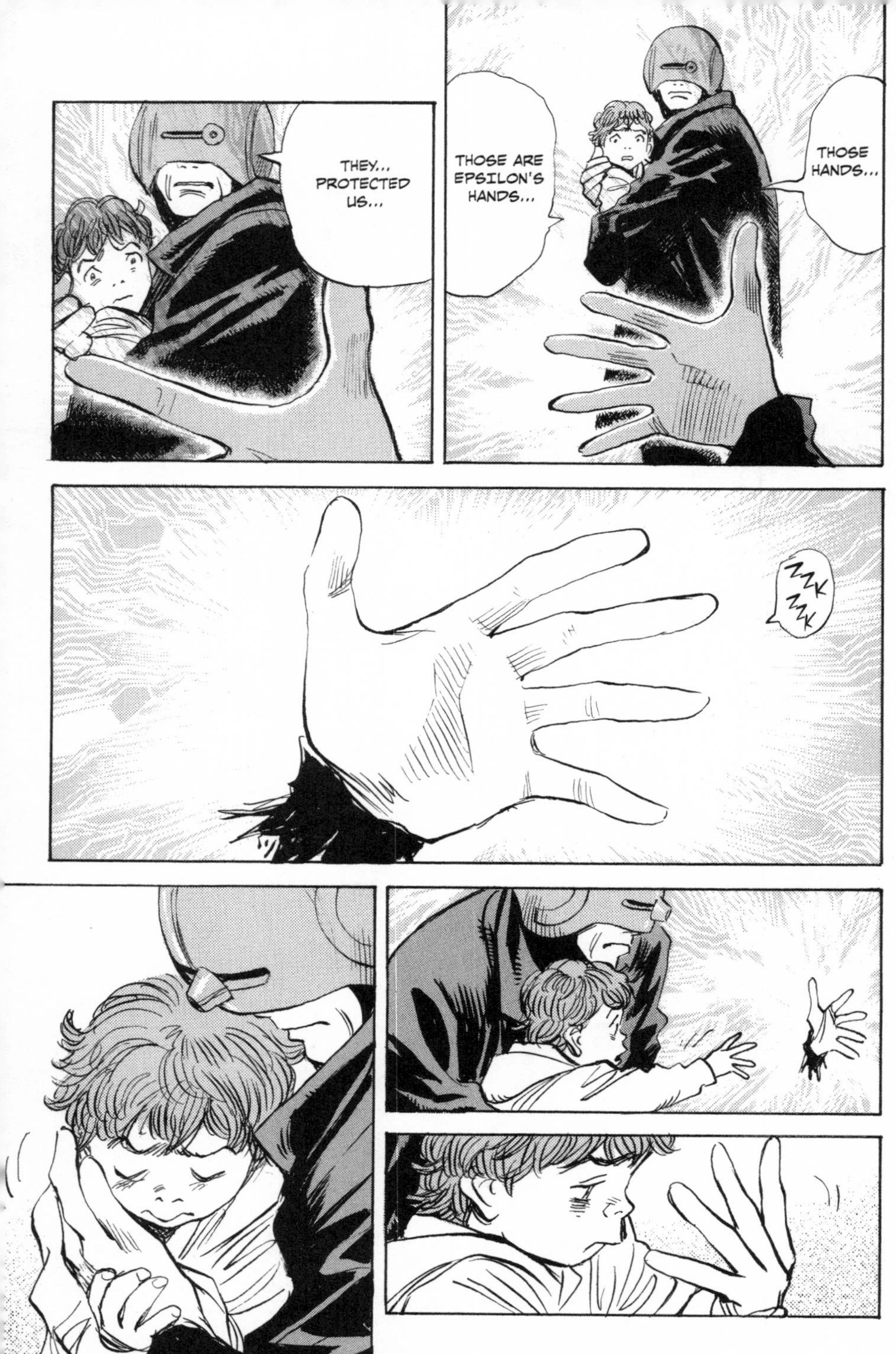
THOSE HANDS...
THOSE ARE EPSILON'S HANDS...
THEY... PROTECTED US...
ZZK ZZK

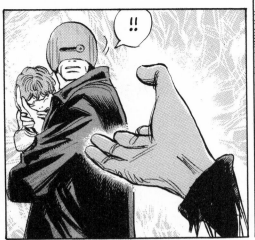

!!

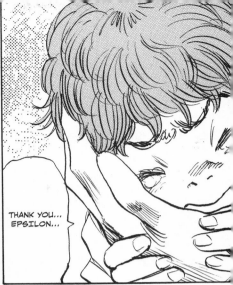

THANK YOU...
EPSILON...

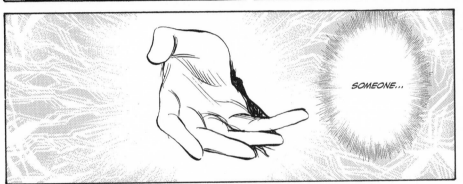

SOMEONE...

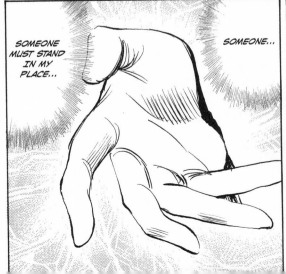

SOMEONE
MUST STAND
IN MY
PLACE...

SOMEONE...

EPSILON
...?

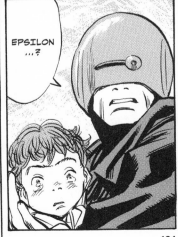

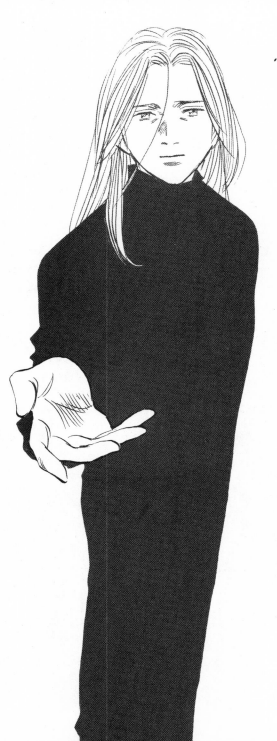

...TO SAVE EARTH...

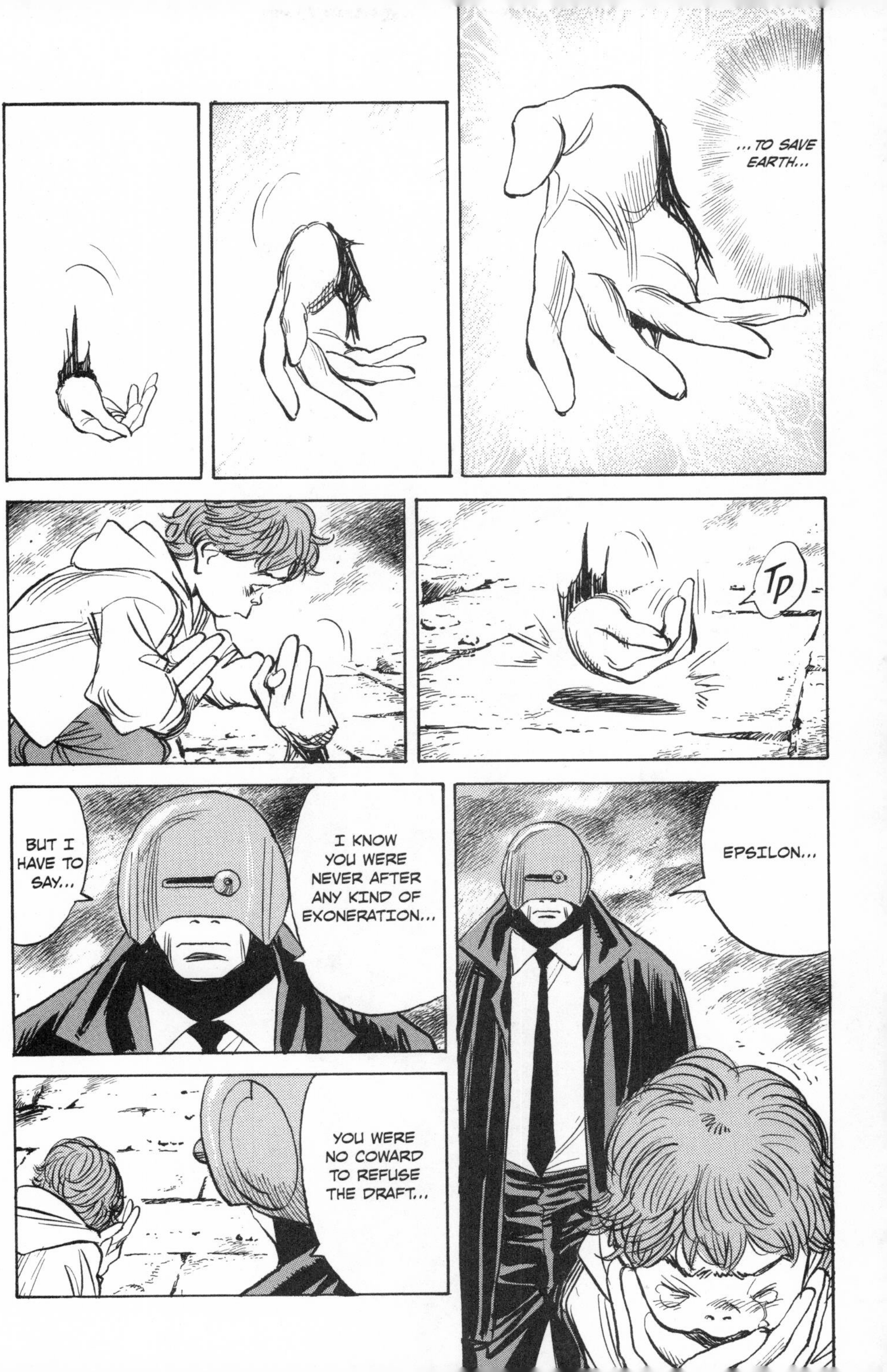
...TO SAVE EARTH...
TP
EPSILON...
I KNOW YOU WERE NEVER AFTER ANY KIND OF EXONERATION...
BUT I HAVE TO SAY...
YOU WERE NO COWARD TO REFUSE THE DRAFT...

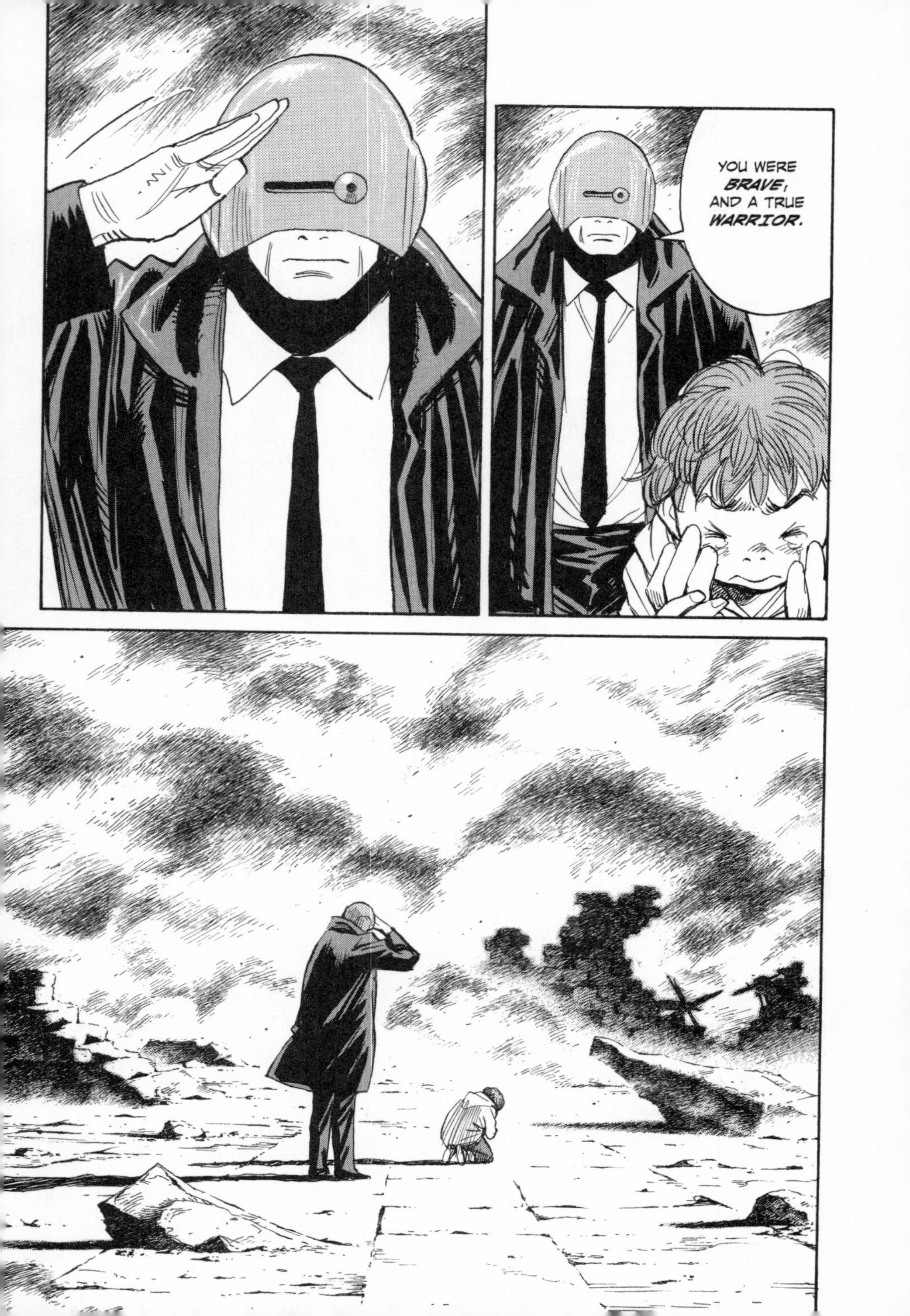
YOU WERE BRAVE, AND A TRUE WARRIOR.

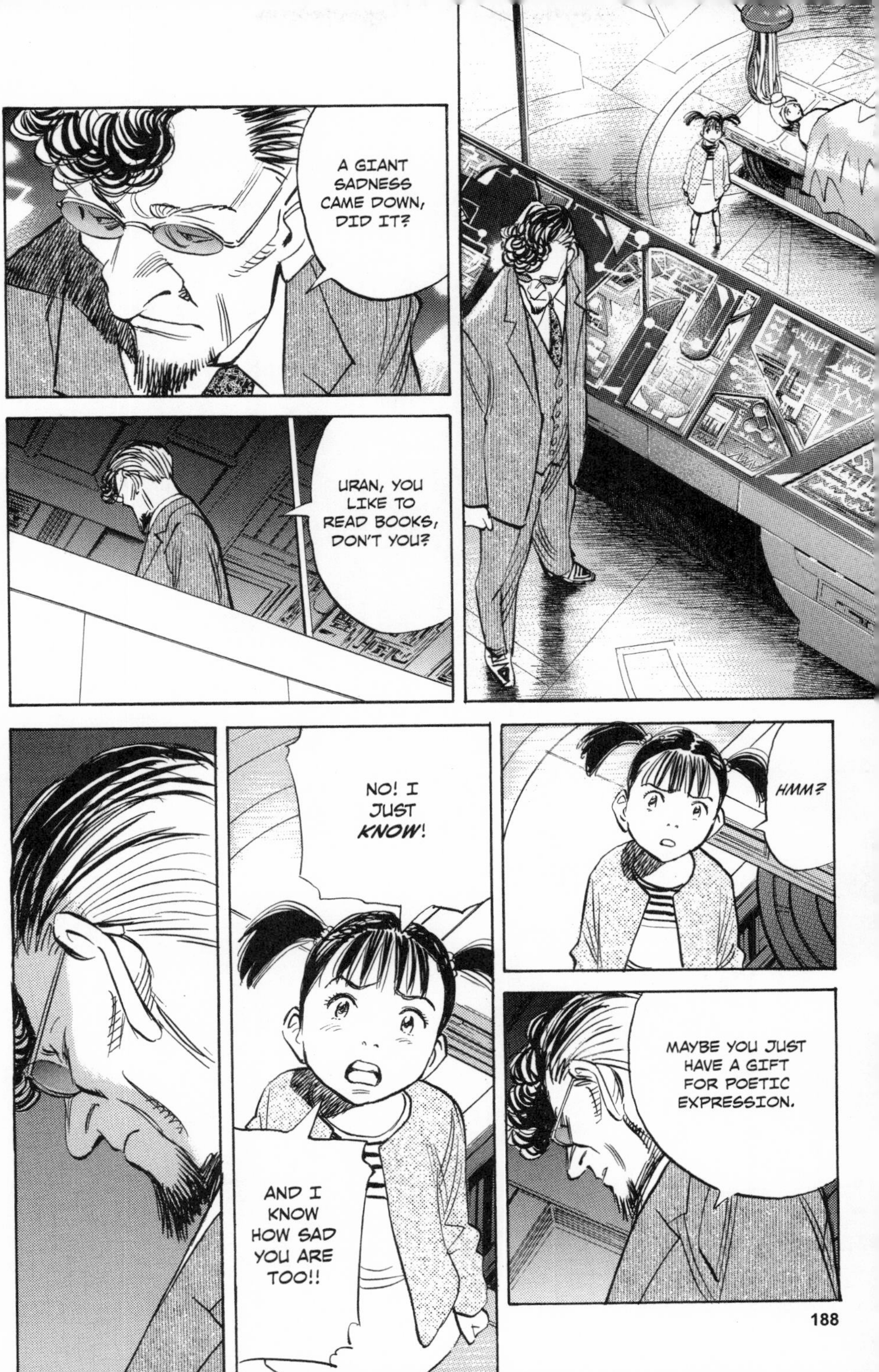
A GIANT SADNESS CAME DOWN, DID IT?
URAN, YOU LIKE TO READ BOOKS, DON'T YOU?
HMM?
MAYBE YOU JUST HAVE A GIFT FOR POETIC EXPRESSION.
NO! I JUST *KNOW*!
AND I KNOW HOW SAD YOU ARE TOO!!

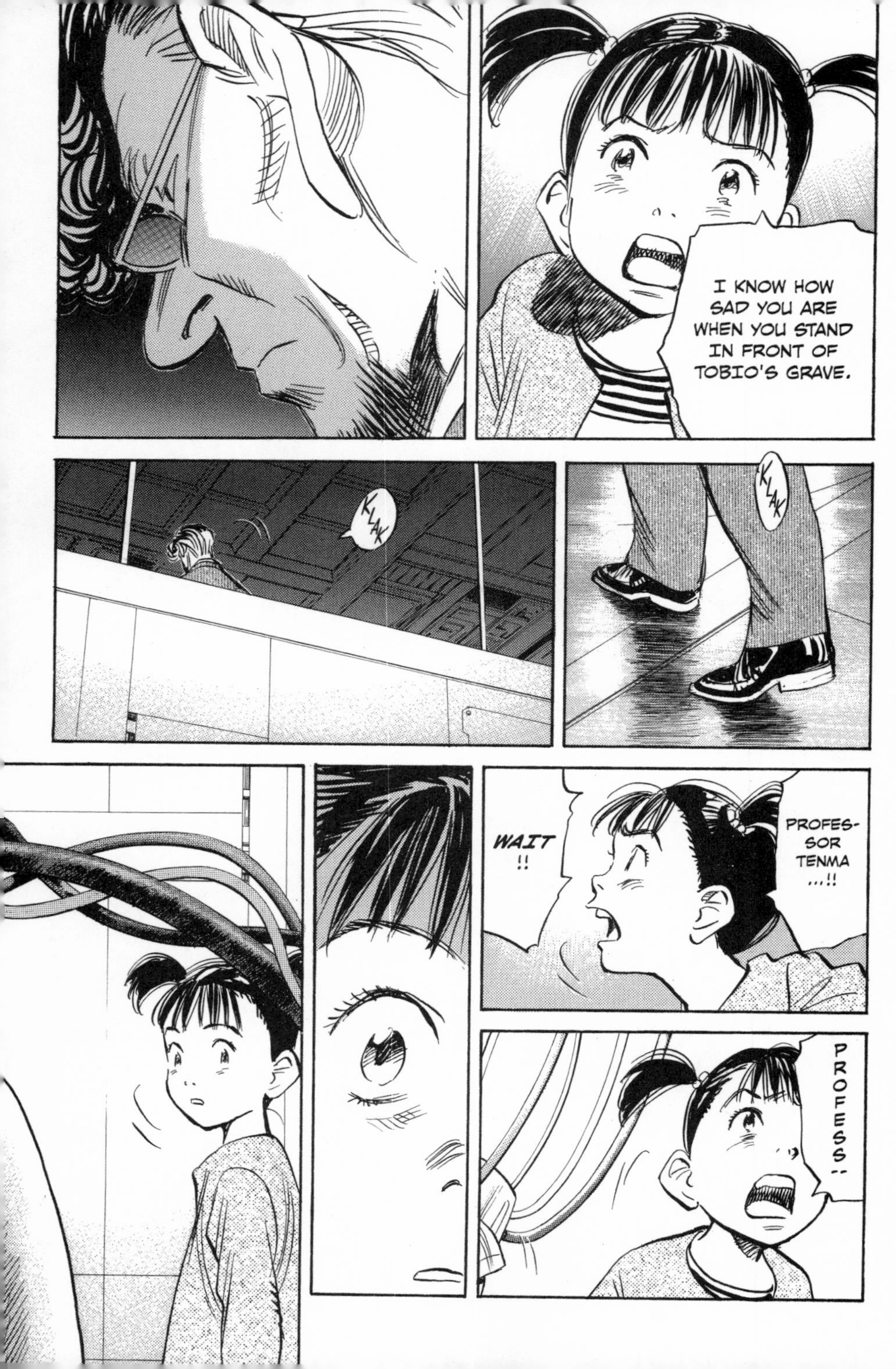
I KNOW HOW SAD YOU ARE WHEN YOU STAND IN FRONT OF TOBIO'S GRAVE.
KLAK
KLAK
PROFES-SOR TENMA ...!!
WAIT !!
PROFESS..

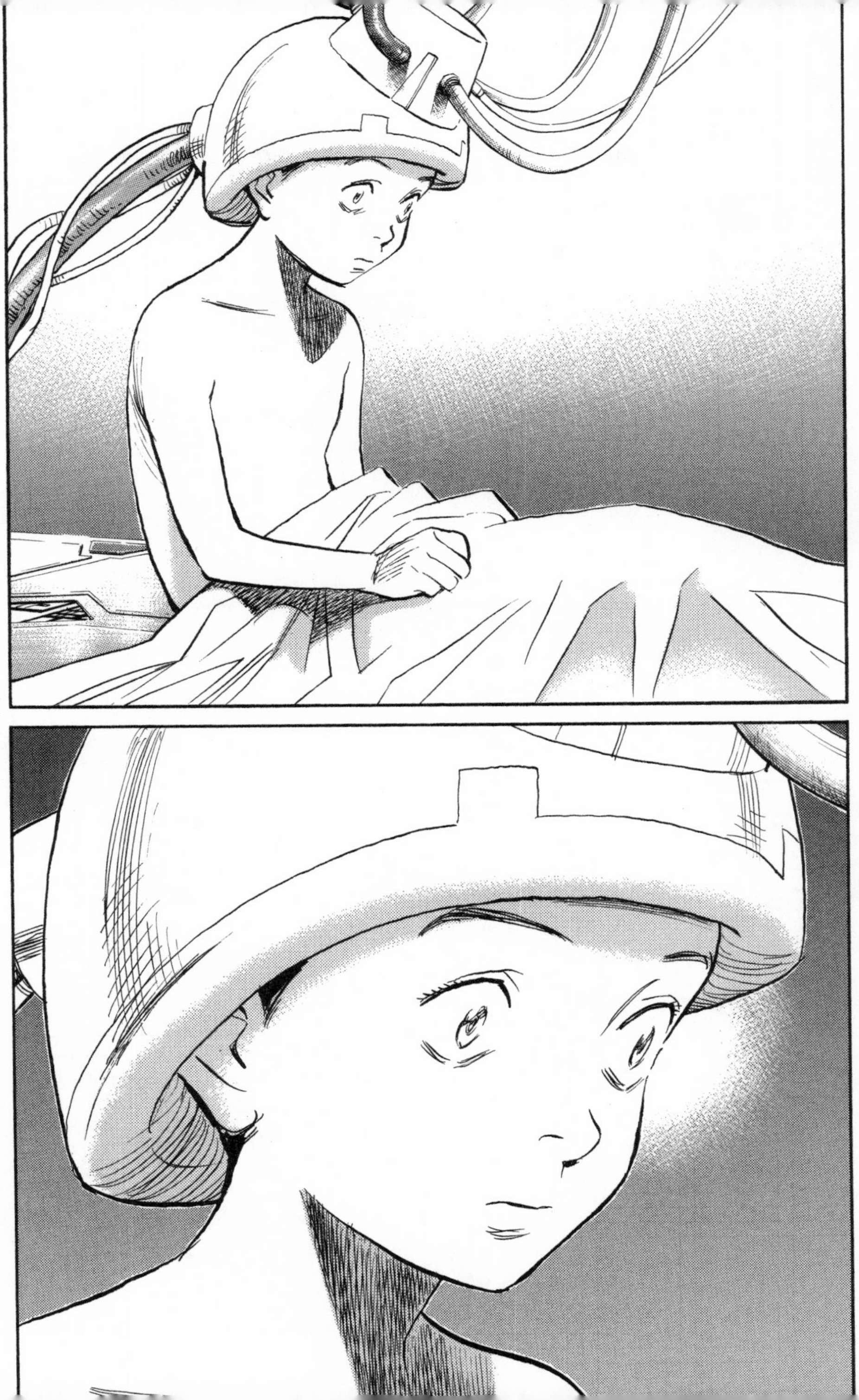

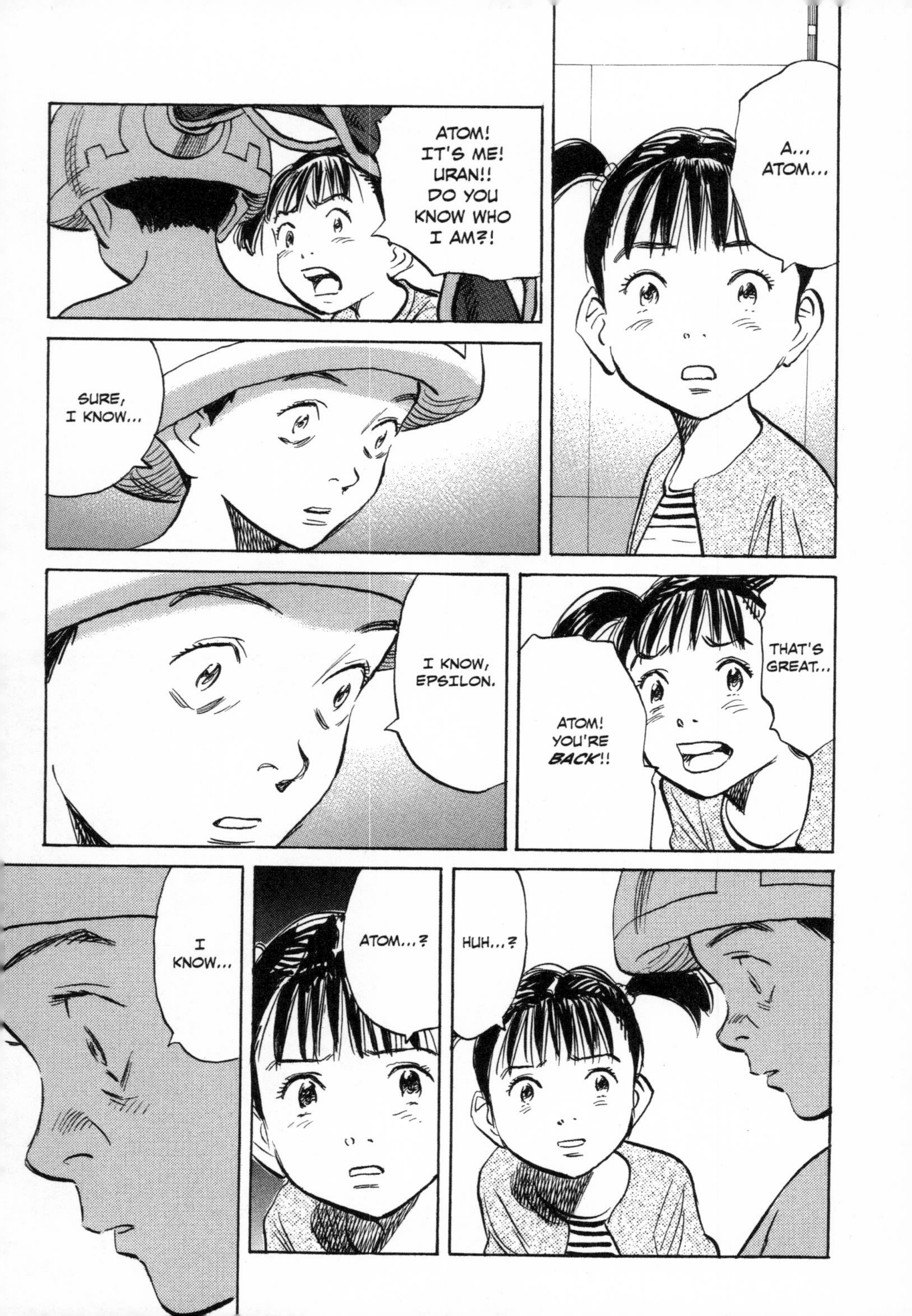
A... ATOM...
ATOM! IT'S ME! URAN!! DO YOU KNOW WHO I AM?!
SURE, I KNOW...
THAT'S GREAT...
ATOM! YOU'RE **BACK**!!
I KNOW, EPSILON.
HUH...?
ATOM...?
I KNOW...

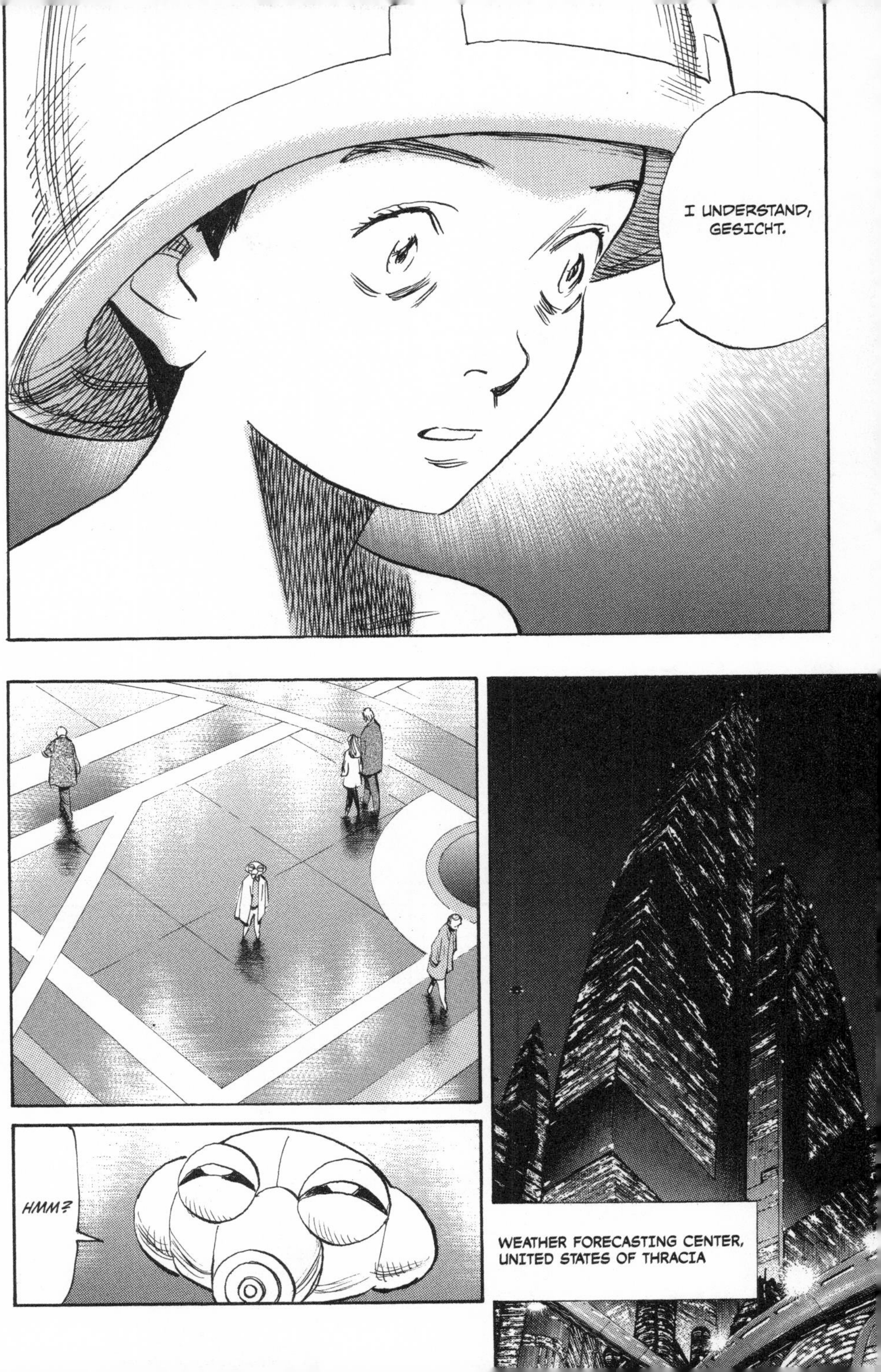
I UNDERSTAND, GESICHT.
WEATHER FORECASTING CENTER, UNITED STATES OF THRACIA
HMM?

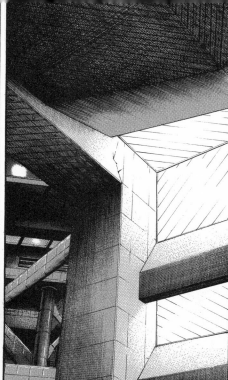

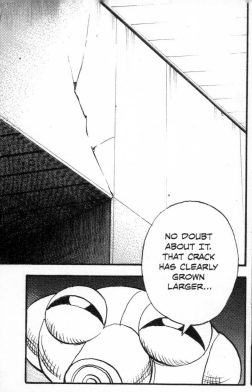

NO DOUBT ABOUT IT. THAT CRACK HAS CLEARLY GROWN LARGER...

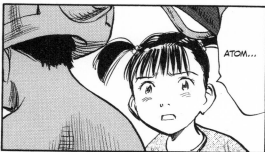

ATOM...

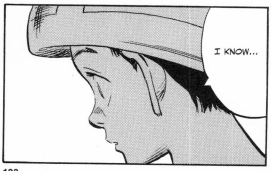

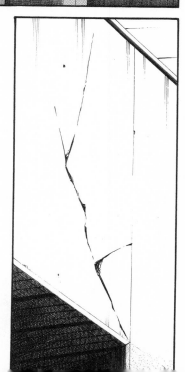

I KNOW...

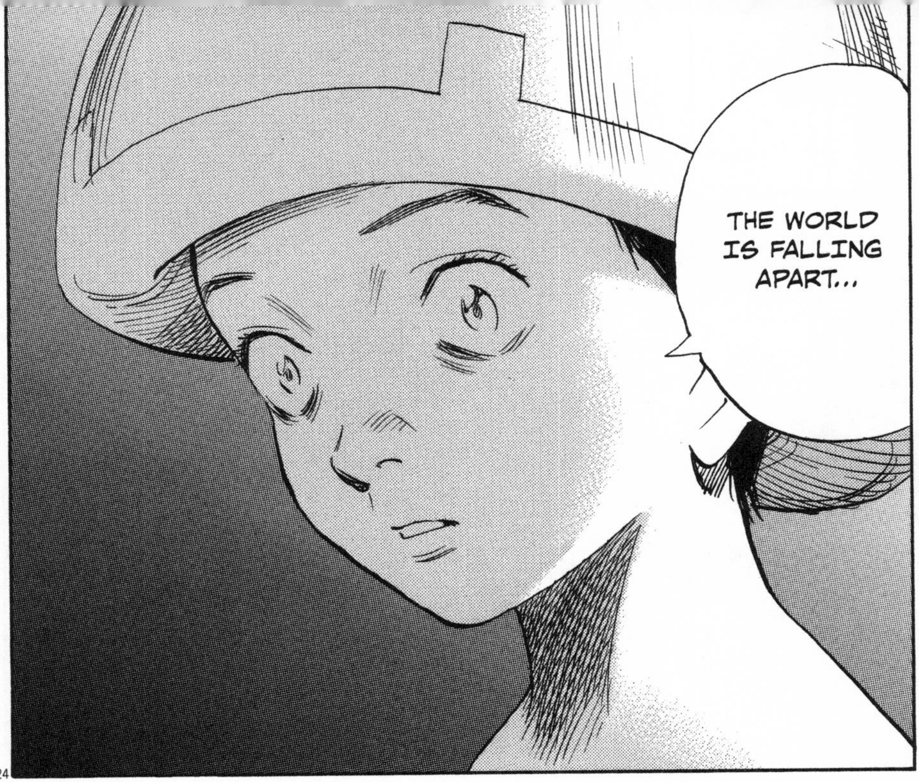
THE WORLD IS FALLING APART...

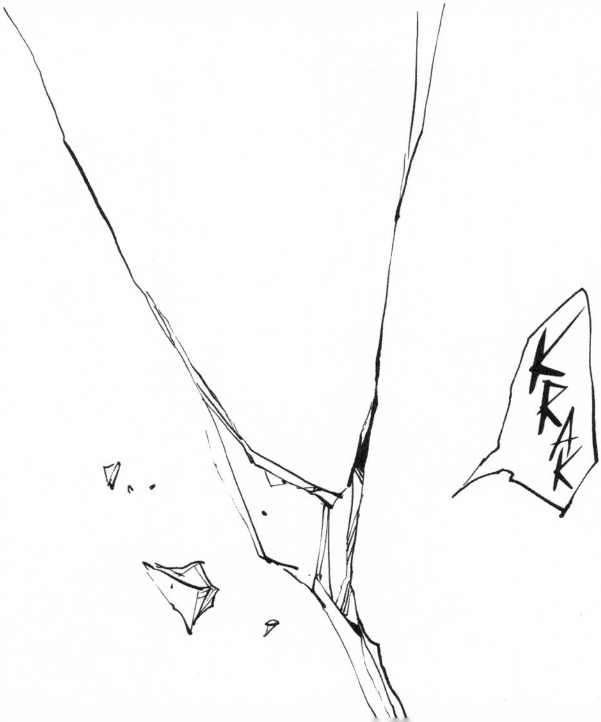
KRAK

POSTSCRIPT

Masao Maruyama, Chief Creative Officer of MAD HOUSE, Ltd.

Come to think of it, when I was a kid, we weren't allowed to bring manga to school. But now it's not uncommon to see middle-aged men reading manga while riding on the trains. How could such a revolutionary change come about in but half a century? I believe there is only one answer. It is all due to the miraculous existence of one person—Osamu Tezuka.

Manga—long banned from schools—eventually became acceptable reading material if they were works like Osamu Tezuka's *Astro Boy* or *Kimba, the White Lion*. Osamu Tezuka's manga took on serious subjects but also had humor, horror and eroticism, and they taught us about such things as philosophy, biology and zoology in ways both interesting and easy to understand. Tezuka went on to foster other manga artists in both his own era and the next and to enthrall readers and elevate manga into a cultural and educational medium. It is, indeed, thanks to Tezuka that manga have become recognized as an important part of our culture and that Japan is the world's only manga superpower.

The anime that Japan now produces is no longer considered to be just "animation" or "cartoons." In fact, as the newly globalized word *anime* indicates, this unique culture has now swept the entire world. And at the foundation of this new cultural phenomenon is Japanese manga, or comics, culture with all its depth. From the start, anime was fated to enjoy an intimate and happy relationship with comics. And we must not forget that when anime was just getting started, we were fortunate enough to have Osamu Tezuka.

Astro Boy first aired on television in 1963. In fact, Osamu Tezuka specifically founded his company Mushi Pro in 1961 in order to produce *Astro Boy* as an animated television series. Today, I often wonder how many people involved in those early days of production imagined that they would continue in this line of work for the rest of their lives. Of course, a superhuman like Osamu Tezuka could see the potential of the medium. But there were probably only a handful of other artists who worked on *Astro Boy* who saw where the future was headed. They included "Gicchan," or Gisaburo Sugii, who had already dabbled in animated theatrical releases at Toei and would become known for directing such features as *Night on the Galactic Railroad* and *Arashi no Yoru ni* (Stormy Night); Rintaro, who later directed such films as *Galaxy Express 999* and *Metropolis*; "Kicchan," Yoshikiri Kishimoto, the first head of what is currently Sunrise, who graduated from Nihon University's Art Department and, if not intending to become an animator, at least aspired to be a movie maker; Yoshiyuki Tomino (who Tezuka, for some reason, always referred to with the more formal "-*shi*," or "Mr." after his name, instead of the diminutive "-*chan*" that he used for all the other artists who once worked for him); and Ryo-chan, Ryosuke Takahashi, who later directed *Armored Trooper VOTOMS* and amazed us all after *Astro Boy* by taking a temporary leave of absence from the animation world, joining the musical group Tokyo Kid Brothers and declaring that he would tour the world. With the exception of the departed Kicchan (Kishimoto), these men are still recognized as major names in the anime world.

What we now call *anime* was conceived during the era when the only animation we could see was limited to Walt Disney films from America, or theatrical releases made by Toei that were only released every few years. It all rose out of what was then considered Tezuka's reckless decision to create Mushi Pro, a company that was created to produce weekly thirty-minute animated shows for TV based on his original *Astro Boy* manga series.

To carry out his seemingly crazy plan to make TV animation, Osamu Tezuka decided to employ (and wound up popularizing) the grossly reduced three-frame animation technique. Instead of the fluid movement achieved in animation with 24 frames per second (used by Disney and later Toei), the three-frame technique

used newly drawn cells only every third frame of the film, relying on the afterimage in the viewer's eye to create a feeling of motion. The effect was similar to drawing progressive images in the corner of a notebook or magazine and then flipping the pages quickly; static images suddenly appear to move because even at the reduced rate of only eight frames per second the viewer still effectively sees "motion." In Tezuka's case, by moving only one animation cell back from the camera in successive shots, he could make Atom look like he was flying through the sky. It was more than a technical innovation; it was almost like magic. Those early days surely required someone as crazed and obsessed as Osamu Tezuka with his sense of innovation and adventure to make what otherwise seemed an impossible endeavor a success.

As for myself, I plunged into this world without really knowing exactly what anime was. Looking back on it, I never thought that I'd remain in the industry for such a long time or have so many wonderful memories. I recall with great fondness the monthly morning assemblies held in the garden of Tezuka's house that abutted the Mushi Pro offices and the little presents given to employees who had birthdays in any given month. When I worked on the backgrounds for *Wonder Three*, I also fondly remember how "Hokufu" Tezuka (Osamu's father) photographed and made prints of them for me, and how when I used to go meet him for meetings or to pick up something I became aroused to the point of a nosebleed when he secretly showed me what were then very rare blue films in the darkroom. I'm also embarrassed to recall how I often happily waited to be rewarded by Tezuka's mother with some sweets wrapped in Japanese *washi* paper as an expression of gratitude "for working so hard," when in fact I was often just hanging around the garden of the house without any particular purpose.

Afterwards, I participated in preparations for the feature-length animated film *A Thousand and One Nights* in the creative department of the main office. But besides that, I mostly worked on various animated projects that didn't have any relation to the main office, including *Goku no Dai Boken* (Goku's Great Adventure) at Studio 5, *Ashita no Joe* (Tomorrow's Joe) at the Toshima-en Studio, and *Kunimatsu-sama no Otoori dai* (Make Way for Kunimatsu) at the Shakujii Studio. Eventually, I left Mushi Pro and formed Mad House with some coworkers, but even while there I still recall thinking of *Ashita no Joe* as a Mushi Pro project. In retrospect, Tezuka had all of us ex-Mushi Pro people in the palm of his hand, but he always allowed us to experiment and express our own kind of selfishness. And even though Mad House contributed only two scenes to *Legend of the Forest*, which became Osamu Tezuka's final animated work, I will always regard it as one of the greatest achievements of my lifetime.

Mad House's subsequent animated film catalogue includes such important works by Urasawa as *Yawara!* (1989), *Master Keaton* (1998), and *Monster* (2004). And now there is *Pluto*. I have had the tremendous good fortune to work with both Osamu Tezuka and Naoki Urasawa in the past, and I am awed by the opportunity to witness the results of their collaboration!

I am moved by the fact that, even though Atom and Uran in *Pluto* are drawn by Urasawa, they are still unmistakably Tezuka's Atom and Uran characters. I am already older than Tezuka was when he passed away and thus more sentimental, and when I look at Urasawa's depiction of Professor Ochanomizu, tears even now well up in my eyes.

Thank you, Urasawa-san and Nagasaki–san, for showing us once again the fierce yet noble way that Osamu Tezuka created a new age for all of us.

The late Osamu Tezuka, a manga artist for whom I have the utmost respect, created the series *Astro Boy*. This timeless classic has been read by countless numbers of fans from when it was first created in the fifties to now. As a child, "The Greatest Robot on Earth" story arc from *Astro Boy* was the first manga I ever read that really moved me and inspired me to become a manga artist. With *Pluto* I've attempted to infuse that story with a fresh new spirit. I hope you enjoy it.

NAOKI URASAWA

Manga wouldn't exist without Osamu Tezuka. He is the Leonardo da Vinci, the Goethe, the Dostoevsky of the manga world. Naoki Urasawa and I have always felt that his achievements and work must not be allowed to fade away. Tezuka wrote that Atom, the main character of his most representative work *Astro Boy*, was born in 2003. This was the same year that we re-made "The Greatest Robot on Earth" story arc from the *Astro Boy* series. Who was Osamu Tezuka and what was his message? For those of you readers who are interested in *Pluto*, I highly recommend you read it alongside Tezuka's original work.

TAKASHI NAGASAKI

PLUTO: URASAWA × TEZUKA
VOLUME 7
VIZ SIGNATURE EDITION

BY Naoki Urasawa & Osamu Tezuka
CO-AUTHORED WITH Takashi Nagasaki
WITH THE COOPERATION OF Tezuka Productions

TRANSLATION Jared Cook & Frederik L. Schodt
TOUCH-UP & LETTERING James Gaubatz
COVER ART DIRECTION Kazuo Umino
LOGO & COVER DESIGN Mikiyo Kobayashi & Bay Bridge Studio
VIZ SIGNATURE EDITION DESIGNER Courtney Utt
EDITOR Andy Nakatani

VP, PRODUCTION Alvin Lu
VP, SALES & PRODUCT MARKETING Gonzalo Ferreyra
VP, CREATIVE Linda Espinosa
PUBLISHER Hyoe Narita

Published by VIZ Media, LLC
P.O. Box 77010
San Francisco, CA 94107

10 9 8 7 6 5 4 3 2 1
First printing, January 2010

www.viz.com

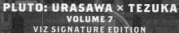

www.vizsignature.com

Osamu Tezuka's iconic *Astro Boy* series was a truly groundbreaking work about a loveable boy robot that would pave the way for all manga and anime to follow. Tezuka created the manga in 1951 and in January of 1963 adapted it to become the first weekly animated TV series ever to be broadcast in Japan. In September of that same year, it became the first animated TV series from Japan to hit the airwaves in the United States. The series and its title character were originally known in Japan as *Tetsuwan Atom*, which translates to "mighty Atom" – or for the more literally minded, "iron-arm Atom" – but was released in the U.S. as *Astro Boy*. Decades later, in 2000, Dark Horse Comics brought the manga for the first time to English readers, also under the title *Astro Boy*.

Within the context of the story for this English edition of *Pluto: Urasawa × Tezuka*, the precocious boy robot will be referred to as "Atom" in the manner in which he has been known and loved in Japan for over fifty years. Elsewhere, such as in the end matter, the series will be referred to as *Astro Boy* as it has been known outside of Japan since 1963.